D0226074

VOICE
AND DICTION
FITNESS

VOICE AND DICTION FITNESS

A COMPREHENSIVE APPROACH

ANN SEIDLER
DORIS BALIN BIANCHI
Montclair State College

1817

HARPER & ROW, PUBLISHERS, New York
Cambridge, Philadelphia, San Francisco, Washington,
London, Mexico City, São Paulo, Singapore, Sydney

ALBRIGHT COLLEGE LIBRARY

Acknowledgments

Page 123. "Resume" by Dorothy Parker.
From *The Portable Dorothy Parker,* copyright © 1926, 1954 by Dorothy Parker. Reprinted by permission of Viking Penguin, Inc.

Page 124. "Miss Rosie" by Lucille Clifton.
From *Good Times* by Lucille Clifton. Copyright © 1969, Random House. Reprinted by permission of the publisher.

Page 126. "Sing a Song of Cities" by Morris Bishop.
Reprinted by permission. Copyright © 1943, 1971, The New Yorker Magazine, Inc.

Sponsoring Editor: Barbara Cinquegrani
Project Editor: Brigitte Pelner
Text Design: Emily Harste
Cover Design: Delgado Design
Text Art: Vantage Art, Inc.
Production Manager: Jeanie Berke
Production Assistant: Beth Maglione
Compositor: TAPSCO
Printer and Binder: R. R. Donnelley & Sons Company
Cover Printer: Phoenix Color Corp.

VOICE AND DICTION FITNESS
A Comprehensive Approach

Copyright © 1988 by Harper & Row, Publishers, Inc.

All rights reserved. Printed in the United States of America. No part of this book may be used or reproduced in any manner whatsoever without written permission, except in the case of brief quotations embodied in critical articles and reviews. For information address Harper & Row, Publishers, Inc., 10 East 53d Street, New York, NY 10022.

Library of Congress Cataloging in Publication Data

Seidler, Ann G.
    Voice and diction fitness.

    Bibliography: p.
    Includes index.
        1. Voice culture.   I. Bianchi, Doris Balin.
II. Title.
PN4162.S38   1988   808.5   87-33360
ISBN 0-06-040665-8

88 89 90 91 9 8 7 6 5 4 3 2 1

808.5
S458v

207914

CONTENTS

22,50

4

SUPPORT OF TONE: RESPIRATION   39*

5

ACHIEVING CLEAR SOUND: PHONATION   57

---

* From here on, exercise material is interspersed throughout and not listed separately. For complete exercise breakdown, see Index: "Exercises."

6

RESONATION: IMPROVING QUALITY 78

7

ACHIEVING AN EXPRESSIVE VOICE: VOCAL VARIETY 105

8

AN INTRODUCTION TO PHONETICS AND THE IPA 128

9

VOWELS AND DIPHTHONGS   140

10

THE CONSONANTS   198

11

A GUIDE FOR THE FOREIGN SPEAKER OF AMERICAN ENGLISH   301

---

* This section may also be helpful to students from Southeast Asia.

PREFACE

This book is intended for the general student enrolled in an introductory course in voice and diction and for the communications, broadcasting, and acting student for whom such a course is essential in the refinement of skills. Students in the communication sciences will find it useful for the wealth of suggestions for correction of vocal and articulatory faults. It can meet the needs of differing groups because it is a comprehensive and practical resource designed to address problems that we and our colleagues have encountered over the years of teaching such classes. We are confident that it will reflect your concerns, too.

HOW IT DIFFERS FROM OTHER TEXTS

The format addresses the diversity of ability within a single classroom. Using an up-to-date fitness program as a metaphor, exercises are presented on three levels of difficulty throughout: Warm-up Exercises, Adding On for Proficiency, and Super Exercises, providing challenging material for students at all levels of proficiency and allowing the instructor to tailor improvement work to individual level and ability.

The text allows either a general or a more intensive study of theory. "Further Explanation" boxes are interspersed throughout the theory chapters to separate the more detailed explanations from the basic chapter text, thus giving the instructor the option of assigning the text only or the text and the extra explanatory material.

The practice drills and exercises reflect the philosophy that the more a student's interest is caught, the more apt he or she will be to actively participate in practice, which is the key to improvement. In addition to the customary practice sentences and literary excerpts for further refinement of skills, there is a wealth of innovative exercises designed to appeal to students growing up in a media-oriented society. Included are "soap opera updates," commercials, newscasts, *Just Incredible!* TV scripts, open-ended dramatic scripts for the class to finish, and "Something's Wrong" stories for discussion and analysis, developed with a sense of humor over the years by trial and error in the classroom.

This text addresses the needs of foreign students, who represent a growing segment of voice and diction course enrollees, and includes easily identifiable material specifically designed for this group. Comments or activities that have particular relevance to the nonnative speaker of American English are marked with a star ☆ in the left-hand margin throughout. Carryover exercises, similarly identified, are constructed out of a more limited vocabulary so that students will not be distracted from their practice of target sounds by unfamiliar words.

One chapter, "A Guide for the Foreign Speaker of American English," contains specific information about stress and intonation as well as phonetic analyses of the predictable errors native speakers of various languages might expect to confront when learning English, cross-referenced to exercises in the text.

In addition, each chapter, with the exception of Chapter 1, starts with a Challenge Exercise to capture the interest of the students, focus attention on what the chapter will contain, and give an idea of what to strive for.

In the chapters on voice, students who need work on specific vocal faults can be directed to self-contained exercises that come after the general improvement work in each chapter. In the chapters on articulation, in addition to general information (sound production, spellings, standard variations, etc.) and an analysis of common regional and foreign errors for each phoneme, self-contained exercises are provided for students who need extra practice. There is also a special section for students who lisp.

Instructors who wish students to have facility with phonetics are given many options. "Phonetic Trivia" exercises, accompanying the discussion of each phoneme, can be formally assigned, and students can be referred to the Phonetic Practice appendix, which contains adages, clichés, and scrambled titles to decipher.

WHAT IT SHARES WITH MANY TEXTS

Chapter 1 addresses the student directly, providing a rationale for a fitness approach to improvement and laying a general groundwork on self-monitoring, evaluating speech, and handling stage fright. Chapters 2 and 3, the theory chapters, establish basic perspectives on voice and speech and the systems that coordinate them. Chapters 4 through 7, practical voice chapters, deal with support and initiation of tone, developing pleasing quality, and vocal variety and expressiveness.

Chapter 8 marks the transition to work on articulation by introducing accents, dialects, and the International Phonetic Alphabet. Chapter 9 considers the vowels and diphthongs and Chapter 10 the consonants. Chapter 11 is directly addressed to foreign students.

Basic improvement techniques appear in appropriate chapters: voice conservation principles, optimum versus modal pitch, working for forward focus and projection, developing agility of the articulators, working for improved nasal resonance, sustaining and blending, and increasing loudness.

The pedagogical devices used in this book are based on sound methodology. Specific goals for each chapter are set early on in all chapters where applicable. The theory chapters end with a summation, and the practical chapters conclude with Checkpoint Exercises in which students demonstrate that they have (or have not) acquired the skills considered in the chapter. A glossary appears in the appendix, and there are clear diagrams of the various organs used for speech in the theory chapters.

ACKNOWLEDGMENTS

A book of this scope is dependent on the advice and help of a great number of people. First, William Seidler deserves a very special and warm acknowledgment for his continuous support, encouragement, and interest from the moment of the book's inception. Special appreciation also goes to Carol Plapinger for her help with the manuscript. John Ehrenburg warrants special mention for his drawings and diagrams, as does Cindy Mills for the comprehensive section on lisping. Our colleagues in the School of Fine and Performing Arts at Montclair State College have provided valuable support and advice. And of course without Ellen Kauffman there would be no book at all.

Countless other people also contributed essential ingredients without which this book would not exist. Thanks are due to the hundreds of undergraduate and graduate students on whom the exercises have been tried. And special thanks go to Katie Sarles, Joe Wohlgemuth, and Karen Rush, who wrote many of the student-written materials in the text.

Finally, to all the many other people who have helped with *Voice and Diction Fitness* and whom space does not permit us to mention by name, a very warm thank you.

Ann Seidler
Doris Balin Bianchi

1
OVERVIEW

Everyone has inside him a piece of good news.
The good news is you don't know how great you
can be! . . . What you can accomplish! And what
your potential is!

ANNE FRANK

Have you ever winced when you heard yourself on tape and said, "But that can't be me"?

Outside the circle of your family and friends, do you ever worry about your speech and the way you may be coming across to others—in a job interview, giving an oral report before a class, or in a group of people in which you feel underqualified?

And what about when you graduate? Does your speaking style match that of a person who is already in the kind of career you are aiming for?

Physical fitness is a way of life today. Exercise formats influence the way many people live, eat, and even dress. The trim, well-exercised body is a goal almost everyone wants to achieve, not only to feel better physically but also to feel more confident about the image that is coming across to other people.

But what about the image you project when you speak? Does your speech convey the impression you want people to have of you? Are you satisfied with the sound of your voice and the way you articulate your thoughts? Can you be expressive in sharing ideas when called upon to do so?

Just as a well-toned body can be within your reach in return for an investment of time and work, so, too, can a more effective way of speaking.

Much about improving voice and diction is similar to a bodybuilding program. Both involve setting goals and knowing what you are aiming for, to be achieved in graded steps, not one giant leap. They include some background theory and some understanding of muscle function. The development of self-monitoring skills is encouraged from early on, so that in the heart of the program, the exercising of the muscles that will attain the ideal body or the expressive speaking style can be done correctly and efficiently. Finally, attention must be given to transferring this new skill into everyday use.

What you are about to embark upon, then, is a voice and diction fitness program. It will include all the areas mentioned above, and like most programs of this nature, the practice materials will include warm-up, development, and proficiency exercises.

PRACTICAL OUTCOMES

Shakespeare wrote:

> All the world's a stage,
> And all the men and women merely players:
> They have their exits and their entrances;
> And one man in his time plays many parts . . .

So it is that each one of us plays many parts in our daily lives.

At the moment you are playing the role of a student, but you also play son or daughter, aunt or uncle, sister or brother, employee, friend. You may also be an officer of an organization, the member of a team, or a performer.

Each role determines different behavior and ways of speaking. For example, would you talk the same way to a professor as you would to your kid brother? Is your style the same when you speak with a close friend as it was when you were interviewed for college acceptance?

The point is that we all have many speaking styles that we slip into and out of to suit the occasion, the role that we are playing. The goal of a course like this is not to try to make everyone sound the same. Rather, its aim is to put you in control of how you want to sound in any given situation.

Also, if one accepts the premise that the goal of a college education is to open doorways to broader personal interests and professional prospects, what kind of speaking styles will be appropriate for these new roles you will be assuming once you graduate? Can you imagine slipping into these speaking styles as easily as you do the ones you use now?

In the most practical sense, think of a program like this as one that gives you options, not only for the present but for the years ahead as well.

WHAT IS GOOD SPEECH?

Good speech has three interacting aspects: It is appropriate, it is easily understood, and it is unobtrusive. For instance, good speech should be *appropriate* to the occasion, the speaker, and the audience. The language style that is appropriate for your friend in the coffee shop may not be right for your talk with a college professor and would almost certainly not be suitable for a job interview. You might find, too, that the rather formal style your professor uses in lectures is not at all evident when he or she is off campus. But each style is appropriate in its particular environment.

Since the whole point of speaking is to convey ideas to other people, it is almost a truism to say that the content should be *easily understood*—that it be clear and loud enough to be heard and that the central ideas be differentiated, highlighted, and phrased for ready understanding.

Good speech is *unobtrusive*. The listener should not be distracted by mannerisms punctuating the speaker's delivery, leading the listener to the extraneous thought: "Where was *he* educated?" "How grating her voice is!" "Is that a lisp?" "I wish she'd stop putting on airs."

There will be more about Standard American English as compared to regional dialects in the chapter on phonetics, but the point of learning Standard American is that it transcends geographic boundaries and is unobtrusive anywhere. Conversely, outside the confines of the area in which you live, the regional pattern that seems the norm might label you. People will immediately recognize that you come from elsewhere by your accent.

Some students resist using the more precise articulation patterns of Standard at first. "I can't go around talking like that! My friends would call me a phony!" Our answer to this is that we are not asking you to discard old communication patterns that suit you in present roles. What we are asking is that you widen your options by adding an additional style that you can comfortably adopt when needed.

Martin Luther King was an excellent example of this. When he was addressing a Southern black audience he was enormously persuasive because he slipped right into that dialect. But when he was speaking at a Harvard commencement ceremony, he might have been thought of as a speech professor.

MONITORING SKILLS

As in any program of this nature, you will need to build special awareness so that you can begin to monitor yourself when you practice the exercises.

You need to get a sense of how the muscles used in speaking *feel* (kinesthesia) when they are performing efficiently as opposed to when they are not.

In some cases, *sight* will help you. You can see alignment and positioning in others and then compare yourself in a mirror or on videotape.

Most important, you will have to refine a skill that is critical to this kind of fitness program—*listening,* especially self-listening.

Listening is a very active process, difficult to sustain at best. That one *hears* does not mean that one *listens.* Listening involves the fastening of attention, processing, remembering, and responding to what is heard. Because it involves such a selective focus, one's tendency is to drift in and out rather than to sustain attention.

Here is how one student describes his general listening abilities:

Being a full-time student and a part-time grocery clerk, one would think my listening skills were perfected. Unfortunately, the skill I have perfected is "tuning out." Fifteen minutes into my oceanography class I find myself floating on a raft, drinking a piña colada in the Gulf of Mexico. About an hour into my part-time job I find myself answering "yes" to questions I didn't even hear. For all I know I could have agreed to sell my mother into slavery.

I find myself not listening not only in my professional life but also at my leisure. I find it very difficult to sit in a movie theater and listen to all the words spoken on the screen. This is frustrating because instead of paying five dollars, I could stay home and not listen to my mother for free.

Research shows that listening ability can be improved.[1] One of the key avenues to better listening is to develop awareness of your own listening behaviors. The

---

[1] Many studies have been conducted. One that researched the effects of a relatively short period of time is Ann Seidler and Linda Tamesian, "The Effects of Five Hours of Direct Instruction in Listening on the Listening Comprehension of College Students," *Florida Communication Journal* (Summer 1984).

student just quoted was doing that. So was the next, who was analyzing her self-listening abilities and her gradual improvement in them.

> When I first heard myself on tape it sounded so awful I just rejected it. And lost in the blur was my teacher's criticism that I should listen for my vowels, which were nasal and tense; I didn't know what she was talking about. Besides, nobody ever told me there was anything wrong with my speech before—everybody I know talks like me.
>
> I don't know when it first happened, but I began to listen to other people, and some of them had *awful* vowel sounds that I had never noticed before. (I tried to tell my mother how bad hers sounded but she just got angry.) One day I heard this same sound, only it was coming from me! Then I began to listen to myself, really *listen,* because I sure didn't want to sound like that. How had I never noticed?

It is much easier and more natural to speak without thought to the *how* of your speaking; you want to concentrate solely on *what* you are saying. But with conscious self-awareness and effort you will discover that such listening too can be pulled and stretched to fuller efficiency.

SOME THOUGHTS ABOUT STAGE FRIGHT

In the Wallace family's *Book of Lists,* people were asked their greatest fear. The top of the list was not fear of dying or of being in an accident but the fear of speaking in public!

So when you get knots in the stomach, quivers in the knees, sweaty palms, a buzzing head, and the fervent desire to have the floor open up and drop you out of sight of that bank of eyes staring up at you alone, you can take heart that at least you are in good company! Most of your classmates feel exactly the same way, and there may be some comfort in that thought, since, as the old saying goes, "Misery loves company."

Stage fright will probably never leave you entirely. Seasoned performers and top stars talk of recurrent bouts of the sweats on opening nights. The difference between them and you is that they understand what it is and try to make it work for them.

Stage fright is the body's undifferentiated response to being in a stressful situation. Adrenaline pumps into the bloodstream to prepare the body to cope in a heightened way with a sudden extra flow of energy. But as this happens, one is often only aware of the unpleasant symptoms that accompany it.

Concentrate on that extra flow of energy. Like it or not, it is there to help you, to heighten your awareness, to give you a sudden extra reserve of strength. That is the first thing to know in understanding it and using it to your advantage.

You will notice, too, that once you've actually started to speak, the symptoms begin to subside, and speaking seems easier. Translate this into the technique of knowing the first line or two of what you are going to say so thoroughly that you can be confident you can get through the hardest part, the beginning. Focus on transferring all the extra tension into the muscles of your stomach, where it rightly belongs for good support of tone.

Finally, even if the unpleasant sensations of stage fright never leave you entirely, desensitization does help. With successive performances in front of a group you will find that each one becomes a bit less upsetting.

THE FIRST STEP: EVALUATING PRESENT PATTERNS

To know what particular areas of speech you need to concentrate on and where your strengths and weaknesses lie so that you can set specific goals—a necessity for any fitness program—your instructor will make an evaluation of you on a form like the one that follows. Examine this form to get an idea of the various ways in which you are judged when you speak.

The evaluation will take place in three parts and should be tape-recorded.

1. Read aloud the soap opera synopsis at the top of the form.
2. Next, your instructor will give you a short passage to read aloud.
3. Your instructor will ask you to speak for about a minute on a topic provided.[2]

The voice and diction terms used in this initial evaluation are defined for you in the following list. Each will be treated in more depth in the text itself, but this listing provides you with a set of capsule definitions for ready reference.

Voice and diction terms used in the initial evaluation

VOICE

A. Overall impression
   1. *Vocal variety* refers to the appropriate blending of pitch, volume (loudness), rate and sometimes quality in order to be expressive in getting meanings across.
B. Volume (loudness)
   1. *Appropriate* means that the speaker is using the right projection to be heard comfortably by the listeners in a particular space.
   2. *Fading* refers to a decline in the loudness level, most often at the ends of phrases, although this could occur at any point of a phrase. It sounds rather like losing a particular radio station on your car radio as you travel from town to town.
   3. *Too soft* means that the speaker is speaking too quietly to be heard or to command attention from the listeners.
   4. *Too loud* means that the speaker's volume is excessive for the particular circumstance or the space involved.
C. Pitch
   1. *Good variety* means that the pitch or inflection used by the speaker enhances meaning and that the voice has color.
   2. *Monotonous* means there is very little variety in the notes up or down the scale used in the speaker's delivery, which makes it sound dull or boring.

---

[2] To the instructor: Since portions 2 and 3 should be unrehearsed, we suggest that you provide your own passages and topics on the spot or use the ones provided in the instructor's manual. Note that the passage at the top of the sample form has purposely been loaded with difficult sound combinations.

INITIAL EVALUATION FORM

Name: _____

Read aloud:

In our last episode of *The First Blackened Night,* a major power failure has caused a dark, starless night to descend upon the citizens of Mansfield, Connecticut. Betty Martin learns that the last act of *Who Asked You?*, the new comedy at the Next Act Theater, has to be abruptly ended. Amidst the nighttime confusion, Dr. Ernest Post is told that Annabelle Wright has escaped from the lunatic asylum and that the matron didn't set off the emergency alarm. . . .

(Write the appropriate number in the boxes.)

	Reading	*Conversational speech*
Voice Overall impression: 1. good vocal variety 2. lacks vocal variety		
Volume: 1. appropriate 3. too soft 2. fading 4. too loud		
Pitch: 1. good variety 4. too low 2. monotonous 5. patterned 3. too high		
Rate: 1. appropriate 4. patterned 2. too fast 5. choppy 3. too slow		
Quality: 1. breathy 7. strident 2. thin 8. tense, harsh 3. nasal 9. denasal 4. flat 10. hoarse, husky 5. throaty 11. tremulous 6. glottal fry		
Diction Overall impression: 1. clear 5. omissions: 2. slack 6. additions: 3. weak endings 7. distortions: 4. substitutions:		
Eye contact 1. appropriate 2. poor		
Visible impression 1. poised 3. energetic 2. nervous 4. lacks energy		

Comments

3. *Too high* means that the speaker's overall pitch sounds too high for that person's vocal structure. The effect may cause the speaker to sound weak, shrill, or immature.

4. *Too low* means that the speaker's overall pitch sounds too low for that person's vocal structure. The effect may cause the speaker to go into glottal fry on downward inflections or to sound harsh.

5. *Patterned* means that the pitch pattern tends to sound singsongy. The predictable patterns become monotonous and are not related to meaning.

D. Rate

1. *Appropriate* means that the speaker speaks at a speed that enhances meaning and communicates intention and that the speaker pauses to separate thoughts.

2. *Too fast* means that the speaker's rate is too rapid to enhance meaning or possibly to be understood.

3. *Too slow* means that the speaker's rate is too slow to retain the listener's focus, due either to prolonging syllables or pausing too long in between words.

4. *Patterned* means that the speaker is using a measured rate that sounds slightly robotic. The monotonously repeated patterns are predictable and do not reinforce meanings.

5. *Choppy* means that the speaker's delivery is jerky or stop-and-start, unrelated to phrasing for thoughts.

E. Quality (tone, timbre)

1. A *breathy* quality causes the speaker to sound as if a lot of air is escaping along with the voice. It is sometimes thought of as the stereotypical "sexy" voice, but it is inefficient and wastes air and energy.

2. A *thin* quality lacks the richness of a resonant voice. It may make the speaker sound weak or childlike.

3. A *nasal* quality has the whining sound usually associated with the stereotypical voice of the chronic complainer. This quality may be prevalent over the speaker's entire voice but is probably more obvious on vowel sounds. Sometimes nasality may be apparent only on individual vowel sounds or vowel sounds that precede or follow *m, n,* and *ng.*

4. A *flat* quality makes the speaker's voice sound "tinny" and "twangy," lacking in depth and richness of tone.

5. A *throaty* voice quality sounds like a cartoon character whose voice comes from a cave. It gives the impression of having been swallowed.

6. *Glottal fry* makes the voice sound as if it is crackling. It most often occurs at the ends of phrases or if a person's voice is pitched too low. It makes the voice sound like a motor that needs revving up.

7. A *strident* voice sounds like it can shatter glass. It sounds strained, screechy, and overaggressive.

8. A *tense* or *harsh* quality sounds tight and constrained, as if clamps had been put around the speaker's throat.

9. A *denasal* quality means that there is a lack of nasal resonance on *m, n,* and *ng* sounds. An advanced case will give a speaker the stereotypical sound of a punch-drunk fighter.

10. A *hoarse* or *husky* quality makes the speaker sound as if he has laryngitis. The voice sounds strained, usually with some noise component of air escaping.
11. A *tremulous* quality makes the speaker sound as if he or she were shaking. The voice trembles, and the speaker sounds scared.

DICTION

A. Overall impression
   1. *Clear* diction means that the speaker can be easily understood and communicates the intended content with no distracting misarticulations.
   2. *Slack* diction means that the speaker omits or assimilates a great many sounds (phonemes), usually consonant sounds, giving the impression of an imprecise speech pattern: "Wha' cha doin'?" " 'Samatta wi' choo?" and the like.
   3. *Weak endings* means that the speaker often doesn't articulate the final consonant sounds, particularly *t* and *d. First* becomes "firs' " and *last,* "las'."
   4. *Substitutions* refer to the replacement of one sound for another, such as "dat" for *that,* with *d* substituted for the *th* sound, or "'pwetty" for *pretty,* with *w* substituted for *r.*
   5. *Omissions* refer specifically to the leaving off of a sound that should be articulated. For example, a speaker who says "fi daz" instead of *five dollars* has omitted the *v* sound in *five* and the *lar* sounds in *dollars.*
   6. *Additions* refer to the adding on of extra sounds where they should not be. Thus a speaker may ask for a "soder" instead of a *soda,* hoping you'll get the "idear" despite the addition of the extra *r.*
   7. *Distortions* refer to the articulation of a phoneme that is recognizable as representing the sound intended, but something in the pronunciation of the sound calls attention. A nasal twang on the *a* in *man* or *candy* is a good example of a distortion, as is too much of a whistle on every *s* sound.

FIRST CHALLENGE EXERCISE

Most chapters will start with a Challenge Exercise to give you something to stretch toward in your fitness program or in some cases just to pique your interest. As a way of familiarizing you with these, this chapter ends with one:

Challenge exercise   Read the following passage out loud.

To be or not to be? To continue with manned space exploration or to abandon it to future generations?

Ever since the first caveman stepped farther back into the black, unexplored cave to find a better sleeping ledge, to discover a fresh supply of water, or just to know what was there, man has explored: Man has dared the unknown.

So why ponder the dangers or the costs of continued exploration in space? Man knows that it is there, and the basic nature of man cannot be denied.

Were you reading the ideas, or were you primarily concerned with just getting through the passage?

It has been our experience that most people, until they have had a course like this, do the latter.

Try reading it aloud again, as if it were written down like this:

> To *be* . . . or *not* to be?
>
> To *continue* with manned space exploration . . . or to *abandon* it to future generations?
>
> Ever since the *first caveman* stepped farther back into the black, *unexplored* cave . . . to find a better sleeping ledge, . . . to discover a fresh supply of water, . . . *or* . . . *just to know what was there,* . . . man has explored: *Man* . . . has *dared* the *unknown.*
>
> So why ponder the costs of continued exploration in space?
>
> Man *knows* that *it is there.*
>
> And the *basic nature* of *MAN* . . .
>
> *CANNOT* . . . be *denied.*

Your voice, timing, pausing, inflecting, and emphasis bring ideas alive. Words, after all, have meaning only as they illuminate the ideas they are trying to convey.

So keep this first challenge exercise in mind as an overall framework for the workouts that follow.

2

HOW IT ALL WORKS: VOICE AND SPEECH PRODUCTION

Speech is so familiar a feature of daily life that we
rarely pause to define it. It seems as natural to
man as walking, and only less than breathing.

EDWARD SAPIR

Challenge exercise   Which are longer, men's vocal folds or women's? Do you
know how elephants communicate with each other? Who Donald Duck really
was? Why violins aren't made of plastic? What voice problems transsexuals face?

For answers, read on. . . .

TWO IMPORTANT UNDERLYING PERSPECTIVES

The story is told of two women sitting in a Greek diner sipping a cup of coffee.
The owner's two little children were playing house in a corner, chatting away,
lost in their game. "Isn't it amazing," marveled one of the women, "how well
those little children have learned to speak a difficult language like Greek!"

Modern linguistic theory suggests that man has an innate ability to produce
language, the intricate, mutually agreed-on symbol system used for communication. Actual production of *speech* is learned in the early environment in which
a child is born or brought up.[1] And for every American marveling at how smart

---

[1] A further clarification of the difference between language and speech may be helpful here. In *Language
and Languages* (San Francisco: Chandler, 1972) George L. Trager defines language as

the learned system of arbitrary vocal symbols by means of which human beings, as members of
society, interact and communicate in terms of their culture. . . . The symbols of which language
consists are vocal. Thus, when a person talks, his vocal activity may be termed speech. (p. 7)

Noam Chomsky uses the term *competence* to refer to a person's knowledge of his language and
performance (speaking) for the actual use he makes of that knowledge in concrete situations.

Perhaps the difference is best summarized thus: Ferdinand de Saussure . . . once remarked that
there was an important difference between a symphony and any particular performance of the symphony; the mistakes that musicians make in playing the symphony do not affect what the symphony
actually is. Saussure was of course thinking of the distinction between language and speech. (Frank
Smith and George H. Miller, eds., *The Genesis of Language: A Psychoanalytic Report,* Cambridge,
Mass.: M.I.T. Press, 1966, p. 11)

children are to learn Greek, there are undoubtedly any number of Greeks in awe of the American children who learn an impossible language like English.

This is an important perspective for you to keep in mind, because for most of you, your present speaking style represents learning that went on when you were very young and little aware of it. It was patterned from models—your parents, your close family—representing, in turn, the patterns spoken in that particular part of the country, or patterns your parents themselves learned in the same way. Very quickly, certainly by the age of 6 or so, your speaking went on automatic pilot, as it were, and in the intervening years has become a deeply embedded habit pattern.

The second general perspective has to do with a rather supreme irony. If you were challenged to name the most important skill man possesses, after some thought you would have to agree that it is the ability to speak, to produce an oral language.

After all, dogs bark, birds sing, and firecrackers pop, but man can create vocal sound that can pass information from one person to the next, one generation to the next; through it he is able to reveal his innermost thoughts; using it he can sometimes sway people or whole nations: "We declare these truths to be self-evident"; "Go west, young man"; "I have a dream." Thanks to its written form, all learning and civilization itself have been made possible: We have a Bible, a *Hamlet,* a *Pilgrim's Progress.*

On a practical level, speech is inextricably woven into our daily lives. We rely on it for social interchange and the myriad communications we have with others throughout the day. In fact, how much we use it, and how much we take it for granted, often dawns on us only when we suddenly find ourselves without it. Do you remember how you felt when you had acute laryngitis and suddenly couldn't talk?

Yet not only was your prime training in this, your most important skill, done in the years before you were conscious of the need to do anything but express yourself, but it was done by people who in most cases were probably little trained for the job. That is why people say, "Speech is caught, not taught."

Also, what familiarity were you given with the instrument itself, the various organs and muscles you use with split-second synchronization to produce speech? For most of you this most critical skill was simply a matter of trial and error, and for a lifetime of use it has just been taken for granted—until now.

Any of you who have worked to perfect a skill, be it a sport, a musical instrument, or an intellectual pursuit, know that an important first step is to understand what you are dealing with. That is what this chapter is about.

GOALS FOR READING THIS CHAPTER

As the basis of your voice and diction fitness program, you will need the following information:

1. To know what speech is, what voice is, and what sound is
2. To understand that to create sound, a power source, a vibrating source, and a resonating source are needed and to locate the systems that provide these in yourself and know how they work

3. To differentiate the four properties of sound and to know where and how volume, pitch, quality, and duration are generated and regulated.

A CLOSER LOOK AT SPEECH

Speech is simply sound, as is the bark of the dog, the rustle of someone's clothing, the plop of water dripping in the sink, the honk of the horn out in the street. But voice, the vibrated tone produced by the vocal mechanism, is sound that goes through one additional and key process: It is stopped or hindered or formed as it leaves our mouths by the lips, teeth, tongue, and other structures. It is *articulated* into 42 distinct speech sounds (*phonemes*) in Standard American English that in turn group into agreed-on patterns of symbols within a prefixed rule system.[2]

Dot dot dot, dash dash dash, dot dot dot.

"Help!" That is about the only meaning most of us can get from the Morse code, but it, too, is a system that signals meaning through sounds. It uses only two of them and is by no means as intricately and elaborately structured as speech, but it seems like a bunch of noises to us unless we have learned the agreed-on code patterns that stand for the meanings.

That is what we have learned from our early environment—the flowing pattern of a set number of particular phonemes used to signal meanings in a particular language or dialect. That too, is why a language we do not know seems like a collection of strange sounds to us: We haven't familiarized ourselves with the particular pattern of phonemes that make up that code.

☆   *Note to nonnative speakers*   Every language uses a set number of phonemes to build meaning patterns. In learning American English, you are transferring to a different group from the ones that are already deeply embedded from your original language. Many of the ones we use will be the same as the ones you have been using, and they will give you no difficulty. However, American English has some phonemes that appear in few other languages, and others that vary slightly in their production from language to language, and these may give you difficulty. You may be substituting sounds in your native language for unfamiliar American sounds, as they sound much the same to you, or, for the same reason, you may be distorting the sound of some others. It's like transferring the parts of one motor to another one: Some fit perfectly, but others that seem the same just don't quite go in place. The new motor works, but with odd, recurring hums.

For you, in the section of this book in which the production of the 42 phonemes in American English are analyzed in depth, the phonemes that either do not exist in many other languages or exist in a slightly different form have been marked with a star to alert you to potential troublesome

---

[2] Phoneticians vary in their calculation of the exact number of phonemes in standard American English, depending on whether they differentiate between stressed and unstressed sounds and how broadly they define diphthongs.

sounds. You can determine the ones you need to work on. Also, you will want to check Chapter 11, "A Guide for the Foreign Speaker of American English," to see if the differences between your specific language and American English have been listed for you.

HOW YOUR VOICE REVEALS YOU

You've certainly had this experience: The telephone rings and the caller says no more than "Hello" for you to exclaim, "Mary, what's the *matter?* What's happened?"

If the person is a friend, you recognize the voice instantly because each one is unique. This is due to many factors. Heredity and sex may determine whether you have an alto voice like your mother or a deep bass like your father. The way people in your immediate environment spoke as you were learning has a good deal to do with it, as does the formation of your own physical voice structures. The culture you represent will also play a role: If you come from one that prizes a well-modulated, soft voice, that is what you will undoubtedly produce. Age is another factor; voices take on differences with age.

Also, you were able to tell that something was wrong with your friend just by her tone of voice. Emotional state and physical state are reflected in a person's voice. When someone is sick or depressed, or elated or excited, it takes supreme acting ability to override what the voice reveals. Gross personality traits, too, may show up in the voice. A person who is dull and uninteresting may sound that way; so may someone who is dynamic or frenetic. The phrase "Speech is the mirror of one's soul" has been overworked, but that is because it is so true. Voice is not just a mechanical activity but rather the product of a delicate and complex process that is inextricably bound up in a person's physical, mental, and emotional states.

PRODUCING SOUND

Sound is generally thought of as the sensation perceived through the ear and assigned meaning by the brain. To create sound of any sort, there has to be a power source that meets some sort of resistance, which in turn sets up vibrations. Think of the wind as a power source. When do you actually *hear* the wind? Only as it meets the resistance of some object—a tree, a building, a telephone wire—and vibrations are produced; this sets up a *sound wave,* consisting of alterations in air pressure moving in all directions from the vibrating source. A sound wave is invisible, but picture it as the circles moving outward when a pebble is dropped into a pool of water. Our ear picks up these pressure patterns, transmits them to the brain, and permits us to say we *hear* the wind. (See Figure 2.1 for a diagram of the ear.)

Further explanation   The ear is a very complex instrument, and the acoustic signals go through several changes before they are relayed to the brain. Basically, airborne sound waves are collected in the outer ear and

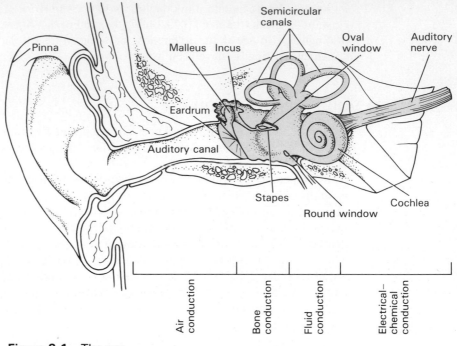

Figure 2.1   The ear

From Peter H. Linday and Donald A. Norman, *Human Information Processing: Introduction to Psychology,* Second Edition. Copyright © 1977 by Harcourt Brace Jovanovich, Inc. Reproduced by permission of the publisher.

pass through the auditory canal. As they strike the eardrum, a very elastic membrane that separates the outer ear from the middle ear, it begins to vibrate, in turn transmitting the vibrations from one to the next of the small bones contained in the middle ear, the *malleus,* the *incus,* and the *stapes.* The vibrations thus conducted reach the *oval window,* which separates the middle ear from the inner ear, the *cochlea,* agitating the fluid contained therein and activating the hairlike nerve endings, *cilia,* of the auditory nerve. Transmission to the brain along the nerve fibers of this sensory nerve is accomplished electrochemically.

Let's take this one step further, to the sound of a guitar. A hand moving through the air is the power source. Resistance is met when one of the fingers comes into contact with a string, setting up the initial vibrations. But something else occurs as well. The guitar body reinforces and modifies the basic sound wave pattern. The quality of a sound depends not merely on the action of the vibrator but also on its ability to transfer its vibratory action selectively to another sonorous body that amplifies the sound and gives it its distinctive *tone* or *quality.* Such a body is called a *resonator,* and the power of selective reinforcement is called *resonance.*

Our human sound, our *voice,* is created in much the same way. The power source is the air being exhaled from the lungs. Most of the time we create no sound, because resistance is not met. But once we begin to speak, at a signal from the brain, the vocal folds within our *larynx,* commonly known as the "voice box," are brought together, getting in the way of the airstream, and vibrations are thus set up. By the way, our use of the phrase "most of the time" was deliberate, for the voice sound is by no means the only sound we can make when our airstream meets resistance; we burp, we whistle, we snore.

The basic sound wave pattern for speech, initiated at the vocal folds, is then amplified and given its distinctive quality; it is *resonated* due in some small part to the covibrations occurring in the bones of the chest and the head and for the larger part to the covibrations of our resonating chambers through which the sound must pass on its way out of the mouth. The guitar has but one chamber (box), and its size and the texture of its walls do not change. By contrast, if we count the larynx as a resonance chamber or cavity, the human system has four. The throat, mouth, and nose are organs we have control over; not only can we alter the size of the throat and mouth at will, but we can also change the texture of their walls by increasing or decreasing muscle tension. As you will see later, what you do in terms of the size, texture, shape, and openings of those resonators is critical in determining how your voice actually sounds to others—the quality of your voice.

To sum up in technical terms, *respiration* provides the power; *phonation* occurs as the vocal folds are drawn together; *resonation* takes place from the chest up, but primarily in the cavities of the throat, mouth, and nose; and the uniquely human act of *articulation,* the shaping of sound into speech, happens primarily within the oral cavity, the mouth. Figure 2.2 gives you a good idea of where each process takes place.

PROPERTIES OF SOUND

Sound of any sort has four properties: volume, pitch, quality, and duration. If you were asked to differentiate among the hum of an electric clock, the screech of chalk on a blackboard, and water dripping into a sink, these are the characteristics you would mention. The same would be true if you were describing differences in the voices of people you know.

To understand how these occur, a brief explanation of the physical properties of sound is in order. Although the human eye cannot see sound waves, a machine called an oscilloscope translates them into visible form on a screen. On this it can be seen that every wave set up will have a certain measurable size, or *amplitude,* that helps determine the volume. At the same time, the vibrations occur at a certain rate, or *frequency,* and this largely determines the perceived pitch.

Finally, although a fundamental frequency of vibration occurs when sound is produced, covibrations called *partials* or *overtones* are also generated, so what actually results is a *complex tone* consisting of many frequencies.

Further explanation   Certain of the partials are termed *harmonic* partials because they are multiples of the fundamental frequency of vibration. For

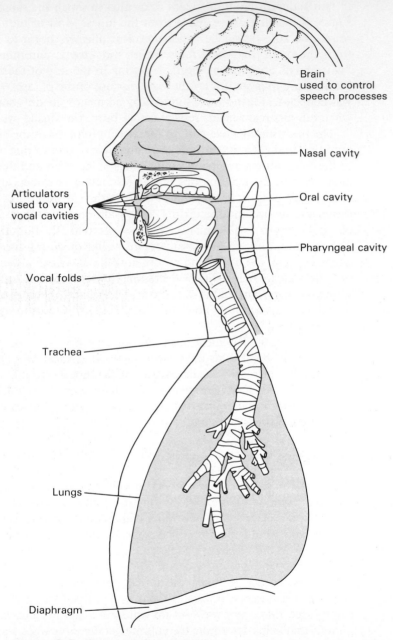

Brain
used to control
speech processes

Nasal cavity

Articulators
used to vary
vocal cavities

Oral cavity

Pharyngeal cavity

Vocal folds

Trachea

Lungs

Diaphragm

Figure 2.2 The speech systems

Reprinted by permission of Voice Indentification, Inc., "Voice Print Indentification Manual." From Ralph K. Potter, George A. Kopp, and Harriet Green, *Visible Speech,* copyright © 1947, D. Van Nostrand Inc., and 1966 by Dover Publications. Reprinted by permission of Dover Publications.

example, if the fundamental frequency were 100 cycles per second (cps), the first harmonic partial would be 2×100, with a frequency of 200 cps, the next 3×100, 300 cps, and so on. Other partials are *inharmonic,* not in exact multiples, and can have components at any frequency.

The quality of a sound is dependent on which of these partials is reinforced selectively by a cavity resonator, for such a resonating chamber is tuned to respond better to certain specific frequencies, which it will amplify, while the others will be cancelled out. Think of it this way: You scatter seeds on a plot of land, but the particular soil conditions, light, and drainage determine which seeds come up to form your garden and which die out.

Volume

Why is it that a tiny baby can be heard crying a block away as anguished parents and neighbors so often attest, yet some fully grown adults are difficult to hear even in the same room?

The volume or intensity or loudness of a sound is due to the strength of the power source, the amount of energy with which the vibrations are set into motion, which in turn determines the size of the wave. Also, volume is due to the degree of reinforcement it is given by a resonating body.

The baby expends every ounce of energy on that wail, as clenched fists, bowed back, and scarlet face so plainly show. Yet many adults, for a variety of reasons, use too little energy when they speak.

To return to the guitar, if a guitar string is detached from its box, stretched between two fixed points, and lightly plucked, its oscillations will set into motion correspondingly small waves of air, thus producing a very soft sound. The more vigorously the string is plucked, the larger the swings and the greater the volume. If that same string is reattached to the guitar box and plucked with the same force, the vibratory motion of the wave will be conveyed to the body of the guitar. The box and the air within covibrate along with the original wave, and the effect they produce on the ear will be greatly intensified.

Thus the volume of your voice is dependent on the strength of the air being exhaled from your lungs, which is controlled by an increase or decrease in the energy with which you initiate it. It is augmented by the throat, nose, and mouth as they covibrate with the original wave.

Pitch

A neighbor had a problem. Every night around 11 o'clock he would incur the wrath of the block by standing on his stoop and shouting and whistling for his roving dog, Eric—until modern technology solved his problem. He bought a special whistle to blow for Eric, and once Eric was trained to respond to it, he would come obediently home. The beauty of it was that the neighbors slept blissfully ever after, for Eric could hear the whistle many blocks away, but even the lightest sleeper never heard a thing.

As has been stated, sounds vibrate at different frequencies, which determine the pitch of the sound perceived. We can normally hear sound waves of frequencies between 20 and 20,000 cycles per second (cps). But some animals can hear sounds of a higher frequency, and that is the principle of the dog whistle. Conversely, naturalists have recently discovered that elephants seem to communicate with each other by emitting, through holes in their trunks, sounds below the frequency level of 20 cps that the human ear can perceive.

Most of you know that the thinner and tighter a guitar string being plucked is drawn, the higher the pitch because the frequency of vibration is greater, and, conversely, the looser and thicker the string, the lower the sound because the rate of vibration is less. Translating this to the pitch of the human voice sound, we note that the rate of vibration of the sound wave set up at the vocal folds depends on three factors: their *tension, length,* and *thickness.* The human voice has a wide range of pitch changes because the two vocal folds are capable of so many adjustments in these respects. However, tension is the most important determinant, because tension affects the other two factors within the physical limitations set by the size of the larynx and the vocal folds housed within.

Think of it this way: A man's voice is usually a good deal lower than a woman's because one of the secondary sexual changes that occur at puberty in the man is an enlargement in the size of the larynx and a consequent lengthening and thickening of the vocal folds. Tension in the folds can make the edges thin out and the pitch rise, but there are limits. How many male sopranos do you know? How many female bassos? One of the very difficult adjustments for the male-to-female transsexual to make is to the sound of his old voice in her new body. Many spend fortunes on largely unsuccessful voice lessons, and some even resort to a risky operation to have the folds shortened and tightened.

Quality

Trivia questions: How do you tell a saxophone, a violin, and a clarinet apart? How did Clarence Nash, a man with a very pleasing baritone voice, make a fortune by doing everything wrong with it?

The answer to both is resonance. The instruments have differing resonance boxes, and in the case of Clarence Nash, his instantly recognizable Donald Duck voice was the product of altering the cavities of the throat, mouth, and nose in what might be termed a negative-resonance way to produce a very positive cash flow.

Since the sound initiated at the vocal bands is actually composed of a range of frequencies and since it is a principle of resonance that the size, texture, and length and shape of the openings of the resonating cavity determine which of these will be selectively reinforced, it is obvious that our goal is to create conditions with our resonators that will amplify the pleasing overtones and cancel out the unpleasant ones. Unless, of course, we are a Clarence Nash.

The *throat,* the *mouth,* and the *nose* are our powerful resonators, and the first two of these can simultaneously change in all the ways that affect resonance: for the worse, held constricted and thus small with denser-textured walls because of muscle tension that will enhance higher, unpleasant-sounding partials, or for the better, being kept easily open and large, which will reinforce the lower, richer-sounding tones.

Just how potent even one of these variables is in determining the tone that is reinforced may be made clearer with a few examples. If you had your choice, would you select a violin made of plastic or one made of wood? Unless you are tone-deaf, your answer would be wood. Why? Because the *texture* of the plastic walls creates the condition of amplifying the high inharmonic partials, whereas the wood reinforces the more pleasing ones. But any accomplished violinist would not settle for just any wooden violin, and if money were no object and he wanted the very best, he would try to possess a Stradivarius.

This brings up a resonance problem that violin makers have been grappling with for generations: Why are they unable to reproduce an instrument that has the same richness and beauty of tone as those made by Stradivarius himself some 200 years ago? It seems easy—the size, shape, and opening of the box can be reproduced to the millimeter. The texture of the walls could be replicated if 200-year-old wood rather than modern wood were used to fashion the box. But still the tone would not be the same, and experts now feel that a perfect reproduction can probably never be achieved. The varnish traces and the hairline of glue that holds the top and bottom of the box together are the problem; their molecular structure has altered slightly over the centuries, and even this minute change in texture, which cannot be reproduced by modern means, affects the reasonance.

It has been said that the human voice (well played!) is far superior to any musical instrument. Whereas the latter tend to be fixed in terms of the variables that determine the partials amplified, your throat and mouth are capable of any number of simultaneous changes. Once you understand how your resonators work to effect these changes, you can set about using them to fullest advantage.

Duration

Obviously, sounds vary a great deal with respect to the period of time they last, and so does speech, in a number of ways. There is the overall rate a speaker uses (on the average between 150 and 180 words a minute), which is adjusted to the demands of a particular thought, mood, or audience. It also varies from one speaker to another. You can certainly think of individuals who remind you of rapid-fire machine guns and others whose "molasses mouths" make you want to prod, "Get on with it!"

Rate in speech changes in a variety of other critical ways. If one person reports that he feels *cold* while another says he is *c-o-o-o-l-d*, you know the temperature dropped dramatically for the latter, just because of the prolongation of the phoneme *o*.

Individual syllables in American English vary in length, with the accented syllable held longer than the unaccented.[3] An expensive car gives you a *smoo-oo-ooth* ride, while what most of us drive is just occasionally *smooth;* if a horror movie was *sca-a-a-a-ry,* you really got your money's worth.

Part of the overall component of our speech is silence, or pauses. We do not

---

[3] In some foreign languages, syllables have equal stress and length. If English is not your native tongue, this may be a problem; you may sound "foreign" because of this and will need to work on English stress and syllable length. (A short discussion of this appears in Chapter 11.)

indicate the completion of a thought by saying "period"; we pause to mark the break between one thought and another. Pauses have been called the punctuation marks of speech, and some of them are held longer than others, depending on what is being said. A speaker will use more pauses if the material is thought-provoking or difficult. Sometimes pauses are employed for emphasis, and sometimes simply to allow the speaker time to catch a breath. For whatever reasons they are used, pauses contribute to the overall speech rate.

SUMMARY

This chapter has attempted to give you some insights into what is involved in speaking. It has also tried to give you some understanding of the properties of sound and their determinants, as a foundation for examining the systems that produce human speech.

To highlight: Speech, the most important human skill, is patterned after early speech models, and few people are given training in how to do this to advantage. Speech consists of recognized sounds that are stopped, hindered, or formed by the articulators. A person's voice is the product of heredity, age, sex, culture, personality, and mental and physical health.

Sound is the sensation perceived through the ear and assigned meaning in the brain. All sound has four properties: volume, pitch, quality, and duration. Volume depends on the amplitude of a sound wave, pitch on its frequency of vibration, and quality on the selective amplification of overtones by a resonator. To create human sound, the power source is the exhaling air from the lungs meeting resistance at the vocal folds, which are drawn together and set up vibrations with a fundamental frequency and overtones. The resonators of the throat, mouth, and nose amplify certain of the overtones very selectively to impart quality. The duration or rate of speech varies in a number of ways.

3

THE MECHANISMS
THAT PRODUCE
SPEECH

I consider it a very graceful thing, and a most
proper, for every human creature to know what
the implement which he uses in communicating
his thoughts is, and how to make the very utmost
out of it.

THOMAS CARLYLE

Challenge exercise   The human body has been described as a highly efficient
piece of technology with parts finely tuned for various functions.

Think carefully about this question: We have been given eyes to see with and
ears to hear with. What have we been given to speak with? What is our speech
organ?

Some of you may have answered a tongue, the voice box, the lips, the diaphragm,
the lungs, the palate, the teeth, the mouth. Others may have pointed out that
there is no speech without the brain. All these responses are right; all these parts
and others are used to produce speech. But they did not answer the question:
What is the speech organ?

The correct answer is that there is none solely designed for this. Although
language and speech may be a primary function of man, every organ and muscle
used in speaking also serves an essential biological function in life sustainment
(breathing, eating, drinking).[1] Viewed in this light,

> the act of speech becomes truly extraordinary. All of these many complex
> parts to your speech instrument are essentially borrowed from a primary
> function, yet all work in synchronous fashion with split-second timing to

---

[1] Although Edward Sapir, the eminent linguist, stated unequivocally in 1921 that language was a
cultural, not a biologically inherited, function (*Language: An Introduction to the Study of Speech*,
Orlando, Fla.: Harcourt Brace Jovanovich), more recent theorists suggest the converse. See, for
instance, Kenneth Burke, *Language as Symbolic Action: Essays on Life, Literature, and Method*
(Berkeley: University of California Press, 1966).

produce a voice, articulated into sounds, within a set rhythm pattern. It's on a par with the feat of learning to propel a giant ocean liner across the Atlantic, using the burners from your stove![2]

GOALS FOR READING THIS CHAPTER

Any exercise format is based on a knowledge of the equipment and its use. You will want to understand how each of the systems works and how all work together to produce speech so that your practice sessions will be grounded in an understanding of the organs and muscles involved and how they can best function to help you. You will need to understand the following phenomena:

1. How the brain (*cerebrum*) coordinates all the systems used in speech
2. How *respiration* provides the power; how the muscle control differs for life sustainment and for speech and what muscles will give you optimum control in supporting a tone as you speak
3. How *phonation* actually occurs in the larynx and how to control the muscles as you speak so as to produce a clear tone
4. How *resonation* takes place primarily in the throat, mouth, and nose and how to apply the principles of cavity resonance to impart a pleasing quality to your voice
5. Where and how *articulation* occurs and the kinds of muscle control needed for clear, precise production of sounds

THE BRAIN

Obviously, any discussion of the systems that produce speech begins with the brain, more specifically the *cerebrum* (Figure 3.1), the center for voluntary control and the coordinating station for the central nervous system (CNS). This roughly 3-pound, wrinkled, convoluted mass with the consistency of gelatin and the general appearance of day-old slush works electrochemically. With over 10 billion neurons in ceaseless activity it enables us to sing, run, laugh, remember, dream, hate, think, love, learn, appreciate—to make each one of us the unique human beings that we are. Critical for the discussion at hand, it is the cerebrum that does the highly intricate job of coordinating the act of speech.

Further explanation   The concentrations of neurons in the folded surface layer of the brain known as the cerebral cortex, plus the neurons in some of the lower structures, make up the brain's "gray matter."

The cerebrum is the largest in what might be termed a brain complex. The *cerebellum,* the small brain at the lower rear, coordinates movements and balance, and the *pons* and the *medulla,* small inner brains that are extensions of the spinal cord, monitor vital processes.

---

[2] Doris Balin Bianchi, Wayne Bond, Gerald Kandel, and Ann Seidler, *Easily Understood,* 2d ed. (Wayne, N.J.: Avery Publishing, 1983), p. 88.

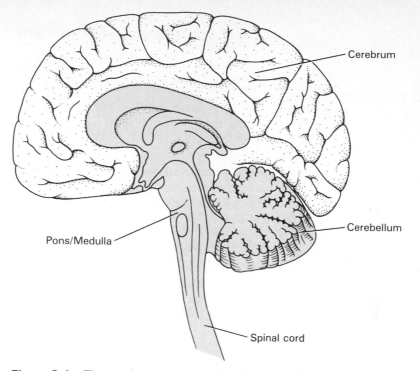

Figure 3.1   The cerebrum, also showing the cerebellum, pons, and medulla

The cerebrum coordinates the speech act because it is the integrating system for the CNS. When someone speaks to you, your sensory nerves send the acoustic stimuli electrochemically to a part of the cerebrum where the impulses are filtered, sorted, and selected. This portion of the brain then fastens on certain of these impulses and decodes them into symbols to which you attach a meaning. *You understand.*

When it is your turn to speak, symbols are formulated in a different part of the cerebrum, and the motor nerves are then activated to send signals to the muscles having to do with speech. These muscles contract and relax in microsecond patterns in order to produce the stoppages and hindrances that others will interpret as meaningful signals. *You speak.*

Further explanation   Speech involves simultaneous action in many parts of the brain. The brain consists of two hemispheres connected by a band of fibers called the *corpus callosum.* The simplified diagram in Figure 3.2 shows the left hemisphere of the cerebrum, which for most people is the hemisphere that coordinates speech. Different areas handle speech understanding (*Wernicke's area*), speech formulation (*Broca's area*), and motor control for speech.

ALBRIGHT COLLEGE LIBRARY   207914

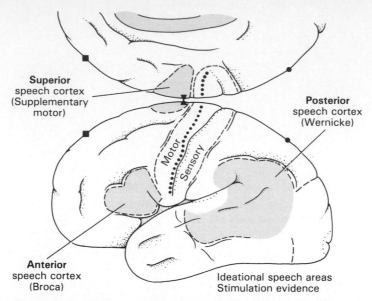

Figure 3.2 Summary map of the areas of the left cerebral hemisphere found by Penfield to be important for speech. The lower drawing shows the lateral surface, while the upper drawing shows the continuation of the areas on the medial cortical surface.

Reproduced through courtesy of Penfield, Wilder, and Lamar Roberts, *Speech and Brain Mechanisms.* Copyright © 1959 by Princeton University Press and the literary executors of the Penfield papers.

Think of the speech act as being coordinated by a compact but seemingly miraculous computer, more complex than any even dreamed of to date. It has its input and its output and its vast complexes of stored information. It programs the trivial ("There's a terrific sale on records and tapes today!") and the momentous ("For the first time in human history Halley's Comet has been seen from only 600 miles away") and everything in between, and the additional wonder of it is that it is doing it using muscles and organs designed to perform critical functions other than speech.

RESPIRATION

Why don't people quit while they're ahead? The fact of the matter is that the more people depend on their voices for a living, such as actors or singers, the more they continue taking voice lessons. Conversely, many less disciplined performers eventually lose their voices because they do not continue to train.

A key aspect of this ongoing training is to gain ever firmer control of the power source—the breath supply. To gain increased control, concentration is on the muscles of the stomach, not on those of the chest area in which the lungs are housed. Why is this so? To answer this and to give you some idea of why you, too, will be focusing on your abdominal muscles to achieve ever firmer support, some understanding of how the respiratory system functions is needed.

Figure 3.3 will give you an idea of the respiratory system and the passages through which the air travels on its way in and out of the lungs.

Further explanation   Air leaving the lungs passes up through the windpipe, or *trachea,* through its enlarged upper end, the *larynx,* which houses the vocal folds, up through the throat, or *pharynx,* and out through the nose, or *nasal cavity,* or the mouth, or *oral cavity.* The lungs themselves contain air sacs and small capillaries, where the exchange of gases occurs.

Two types of breathing

Breathing is essential for life. It renews the body's supply of oxygen, which needs replenishment more than any other substance. A few minutes without a fresh supply, and body tissue begins to break down, brain tissue being the first to suffer.

There are two types of breathing. There is the involuntary breathing that occurs 24 hours a day, asleep or awake, monitored by an inner-brain center that coordinates it. In this kind of breathing, the rate of inhalation and exhalation are fairly equal. The other kind of breathing is breathing for speech, in which, without necessarily being aware of it, certain controls are exercised over the

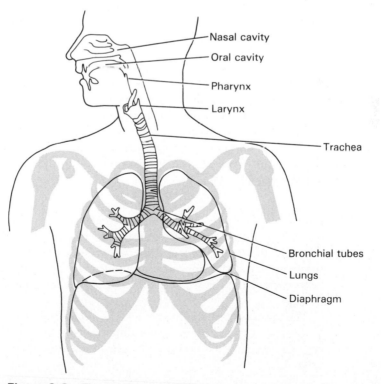

Figure 3.3   The respiratory tract

involuntary breathing pattern. Foremost among these is the fact that since speaking is entirely dependent on outgoing air, inhalation becomes much more rapid, and exhalation becomes more prolonged, with more energy behind it.

Thus the rhythm of breathing changes when you speak. You get an idea and give voice to it on the exhaled breath. You do not talk in individual words but rather in thought groups—phrases, sentences—taking another quick breath between thoughts as you need to. You do . . . not talk . . . like this . . . on your . . . involuntary . . . breathing. Rather, you talk like this . . . because your exhalation is much longer than your inhalation.

The lungs and the cavities in which they are housed

The chest, or *thorax,* is bounded on the sides by the ribs, which are in turn connected above to the collarbone. The lungs housed within are two spongy, highly elastic baglike structures, conical in shape, that nearly fill the thoracic cavity. They rest on the *diaphragm,* a large, tent-shaped muscle sheath that forms the floor of the thoracic cavity (chest cavity) and separates it from the abdominal cavity.

The outside boundaries of the thoracic cavity are important to keep in mind, because the lungs themselves contain no muscle fibers and must be acted on wholly by forces outside the lungs through the principle of equalization of air pressure. Basically, the pressure of contained air lessens as a cavity becomes larger, so to maintain a constant balance of pressure, air flows into a space to equalize pressure with the outside air.

The chest walls are capable of movement to increase or decrease the volume size of the chest cavity. As the diaphragm moves downward through contraction of its muscle fibers, the chest cavity becomes elongated below, and simultaneously muscle attachments within the ribs move them upward and outward, particularly in the lower chest region, increasing the dimension of the cavity side to side and back to back. As this happens, air flows in, and *inhalation* takes place.

The same contracted muscles then relax, and the thoracic cavity becomes smaller. As this happens, the air pressure within increases, and air flows out; *exhalation* occurs.

Further explanation   The ribs, or costals, have muscle attachments between them that allow the expansion of the thoracic cavity. Principal among these are the *intercostals* and the *levatores costarum* muscles, which respectively move the ribs outward and slightly upward, particularly in the lower region, and the *scalenes,* which help lift the upper ribs and the whole rib cage.

The lower abdominal muscles and the *gluteal* muscles, the fleshy muscles at the back of the hips, are very important in speech. Held in a state of easy tonicity, they aid upward controlled pressure on the diaphragm during exhalation.

Optimal breathing for speech

Breathing for speech is best accomplished in the lower chest area in connection with the action of the diaphragm. To feel this lower-chest breathing, place a hand on your lower rib cage as you slowly inhale, and feel the ribs moving outward and slightly upward. Next, critical for speech, think of the diaphragm not as the floor of the chest cavity but as the ceiling of the abdominal cavity, which it also is. Place your hand on your upper abdomen, and as you inhale, feel the hand move slightly outward. The fact that all the tightly packed abdominal viscera have to be displaced somewhere as the ceiling descends on them and there is no other direction in which they can go accounts for this movement.

Thus breathing for speech takes place primarily in the midsection of your body: from the lower rib cage down into the abdomen itself. It is variously called *central, medial, diaphragmatic,* or *abdominal breathing.*

In breathing for life sustainment, once the contraction of muscles governing inhalation has been completed, they relax, returning the thorax to its original size, with the consequent flow of air back outward. In breathing for speech, the lower rib cage does not collapse back into place but is held easily upward and outward to maintain extra space and thus air. Simultaneously, the diaphragm relaxes—not all at once but slowly and gradually by pressure exerted from the misplaced abdominal viscera below. The viscera force the ceiling (the diaphragm) up by means of a gradual contraction of the stomach muscles, pushing inward and thus moving the diaphragm upward to support the controlled outward flow of air. Figure 3.4 shows the change in abdominal size and diaphragmatic position when breathing correctly for speech.

Now you understand why we concentrate on the muscles of the stomach for good breath support rather than on those in the chest where the lungs are housed. Control comes from the abdomen. The more extended the exhaled air needs to be, the tighter the stomach muscles can be gradually drawn, to push ever harder on the movable ceiling.

A visual image of the working of the power source might be that of a spring of water welling up freely out of the ground, with the pressures that propel the flow deep underneath.

A breathing technique to be avoided for speech

It is possible to gain increased volume in the thoracic cavity in another way: The ribs can be pulled up toward the collarbones, or *clavicles,* by hunching the shoulders and pulling up the entire rib cage, thus elongating the cavity in the upper chest region. This is called *clavicular breathing,* and though it may be valuable for gross physical exertions where maximum oxygen needs to be drawn into the lungs at one time, it is not for speaking or singing. In fact, such upper-chest breathing is to be avoided at all costs.

A critical reason for not using clavicular breathing is that a great deal of tension is involved in the upper chest area to lift the weight of the rib cage counter to the force of gravity. An overriding principle in all voice work is that

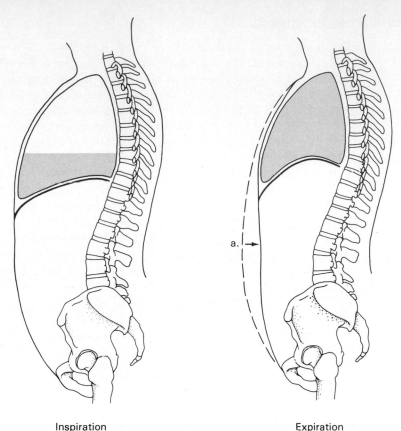

Inspiration   Expiration

Figure 3.4   Diagram of inspiration and expiration

muscle tension radiates, because it is difficult to contract one set of muscles strongly without contracting adjacent muscles too. The unwanted tension involved in this kind of breathing usually transfers up into the neck and throat area as well, where it may prevent the production of a pleasing tone.

In sum, the lungs can work by expanding and contracting in a number of ways, but for speech expansion should take place in the lower chest and downward into the stomach, with exhalation controlled by the gradual tightening of the abdominal muscles.

Next comes practice, which you will find in Chapter 4.

PHONATION

Why is the stereotypical longshoreman or weight lifter gravelly voiced? And why do some wrestlers emit a wheezy "Hhhhhhhhhuhhhhh" each time they put a new hold on an opponent?

Phonation is the setting up of the initial vibrations that produce sound. To help you understand how your sound-generating system works so that you can control it better and, incidentally, to find answers to the two questions just asked, let's take a look at the *larynx,* or voice box.

Air passes in and out of the lungs relatively silently most of the time because it meets no obstruction. The main air tube is the *trachea,* 3 to 4 inches in length and composed primarily of rings of cartilage to keep the air tube open at all times. At its top, the rings that form its main structure are enlarged slightly and modified; this upper section is the larynx.

Most of the time the larynx serves as an open extension of the tube below, but housed within it, and running along the sides, are two folds of elastic connective tissue. Because of the modified cartilages and their muscle attachments, these folds, positioned like shelves, are capable of drawing together, interfering with the airstream and thus producing vibration (more technically, a flutter type of vibration).

The folds are variously called *vocal bands, vocal cords,* and *vocal folds.* Phonation occurs because of the *adduction,* or coming together, of the folds, initiating the basic sound wave pattern with its many frequencies. When a person is not speaking, the folds are *abducted,* back out of the way. Figure 3.5 gives a good idea of the site of the vocal folds and the larynx.

Most people assume that the vocal folds exist specifically for the purpose of speech, as evidenced by the popular name for the larynx, the "voice box," but this is not true. Using sound initiated by the vocal folds as a means of communication probably developed later in the history of man. The folds have several primary biological functions, including serving as a closure mechanism to prevent foreign matter from entering the lungs and to provide an airtight valve for holding air momentarily in the lungs when lifting heavy objects or initiating strenuous physical activity. You can "feel" the closure of your vocal folds if you grasp the sides of a chair in which you are sitting and apply a sudden force to try to push the legs of the chair down against the floor.

Directly behind the larynx and the trachea lies another tube called the esophagus, which passes swallowed food from the throat to the stomach. Because of the proximity of these two tubes and their sharing of the pharynx, an individual occasionally swallows "the wrong way" and may begin to choke as the food gets caught at the opening of the larynx. A cough immediately follows, using air pressure to get rid of the foreign body. If this does not dislodge the offending material, the breathless person will need someone to apply the Heimlich maneuver to keep from choking.

The Heimlich maneuver, by the way, works on a principle that should be clear to you now from the discussion of abdominal breathing. Direct sudden pressure applied to the abdomen forces the diaphragm instantly upward, releasing such a forceful burst of air that it dislodges whatever is in its path.

An occupational hazard of the longshoreman or the weight lifter is occasional damage to the edges of the vocal folds, which shows up as a gravelly voice. Over and over again in the strenuous exertions of lifting heavy objects, the folds are forcefully slammed together. Although they are covered with protective mucous membrane, such constant abuse can do harm to the edges of the folds. The wrestler, by contrast, is applying a learned technique to counter this very thing with his loudly aspirated "Hhhhhhhhhuhhhhh."

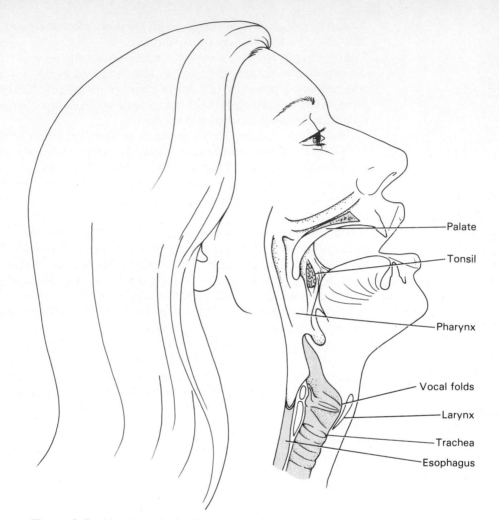

Figure 3.5 Vocal tract, the larynx

Anyone's misuse of the vocal folds in speaking or singing can lead to inefficient performance at best and sometimes to actual damage. We will come back to this point in later chapters.

A closer look at the larynx

The larynx is broad and triangular at the top where it opens into the throat and narrow and cylindrical where it connects with the trachea proper.

Its main structure is the *thyroid* cartilage, which resembles a shield, its two sides wide apart in the back and coming together to a sharp-angled notch in the front. A man's "Adam's apple" is actually the thyroid notch made more visible than in a woman because of enlargement and outward displacement of the larynx during puberty.

Because of interconnecting muscles among the cartilages that form the larynx, the vocal folds can be brought together to produce sound or drawn back out of the way for the free passage of air. These *intrinsic* (inner) muscles, wholly contained within the organ, can also create tension, raising or lowering the pitch, as the edges thin out or thicken. The folds are enormously flexible in terms of the constant inflectional (pitch) changes that occur when we speak.

Figure 3.6 gives you a closer look at the larynx.

Further explanation   The larynx rests below the base of the tongue and is suspended from the only free-hanging bone in the body, the horseshoe-shaped *hyoid* bone. It also has muscle attachments to other parts of the body through its extrinsic muscles.

The structural base of the larynx is the *cricoid* cartilage, shaped like a signet ring, narrow in the front and wide at the back. Critical for speech are the pair of pyramid-shaped small cartilages resting on the cricoid in the back, called *arytenoids.* Because of muscle attachments, the arytenoids are capable of swiveling back and forth and side to side, causing the folds to adduct for speech and abduct for quiet breathing. You will also note the *epiglottis,* a leaf-shaped cartilage situated just above the upper opening of the larynx. Its function has more to do with swallowing and preventing food from entering during eating than with vocalization.

The main intrinsic muscles are the *posterior cricoarytenoids,* which abduct the folds; the *lateral cricoarytenoids,* which adduct the folds; the *cricothyroids* which tense or loosen the folds, altering the pitch; and the *thyroarytenoids,* contained within the vocal folds themselves. It should also be noted that there is another pair of folds of connective tissue above the vocal folds called the *false vocal folds,* important in swallowing and coughing. Some people use them to produce speech, which results in an extremely heavy, strained sound.

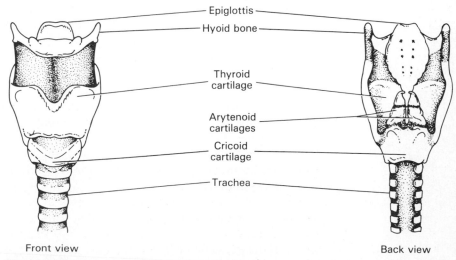

Epiglottis
Hyoid bone
Thyroid cartilage
Arytenoid cartilages
Cricoid cartilage
Trachea

Front view   Back view

Figure 3.6   Front and back views of larynx

The vocal folds and producing voice

The folds run from front to back from a point near the center of the thyroid cartilage to the corners of cartilages in the back. They range in length from under $\frac{1}{2}$ inch to under 1 inch in a woman and from $\frac{3}{4}$ to $1\frac{1}{4}$ inches in a man.

A colleague once told about being invited by a medical student to view an actual larynx and vocal folds in a cadaver. "The shock of the experience is still vivid in my mind," she said. "Not so much because of the cadaver itself or the sickening reek of formaldehyde but because of the sheer insignificance of the folds. They seemed more like two short strands of thread that would be brushed off a sleeve than like something that can create a Bruce Springsteen, a Pavarotti, or an Elvis Presley."

When the folds are drawn apart as in normal breathing, they form a V shape if we were to look down at them from above. The space between them is called the *glottis.* When speech is initiated, they come together to meet at midline, interfering with the airstream so that vibration is produced, and the glottis now takes the form of a mere slit.

Figure 3.7 presents a diagram of their positions in breathing and speaking.

Further explanation Vocal fold vibration is actually more in the nature of a flutter at the edges of the folds as puffs of air come through. Air pressure builds behind the barrier of the vocal folds and is relieved by their blowing apart. Once the pressure is released, the folds, because of their elasticity, return to the closed position, only to have the cycle repeated. Blowing air through your lightly closed lips gives you a good idea of the flutter action.

Controlling the muscles of the larynx

The intrinsic muscles of the larynx make voice possible. They also change the pitch. These muscles are controlled through the brain and the ear. You do not say or even think that you are going to adduct the folds; you begin to talk, and they adduct automatically. Nor do you say that you are going to tense the folds; you raise the pitch, the folds lengthen, and the edges thin out. Lowering the pitch reduces tension within the folds. This may prove a valuable tip for reducing undue vocal tension, as you will see in later chapters.

The extrinsic muscles, which have a point of insertion outside the larynx, position the larynx, raising and lowering it and tilting it out of the way when you are swallowing. To feel how the extrinsic muscles of the larynx work, try this: Place your hand lightly over your larynx and sing, note by note, up a scale and back down again. Did you feel the larynx moving higher as the notes went higher and lower as the notes got lower?

The extrinsic muscles can be under your conscious control, and your fitness program will include many exercises for gaining conscious relaxation of them. The reason you need to learn to keep tension out of them is that they may interfere with the free action of the vocal folds. Every time you tense them you are raising the larynx up into the throat area and making that cavity smaller, which in turn, as in the domino effect, then alters resonance for the worse.

Front view

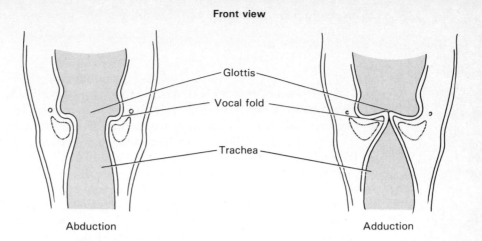

Seen from above

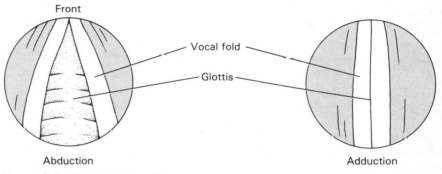

Figure 3.7   Vocal fold positions

From Oliver Bloodstein, *Speech Pathology: An Introduction.* Copyright © 1979 by Houghton Mifflin. Reprinted by permission of the publisher.

Developing clear initiation of tone

Voice work will not alter the structure of the larynx; it simply *is*. As an eminent surgeon once stated, "You cannot tell by any anatomical means the larynx of a prima donna from that of a woman who has the voice of a raven."[3]

But you can do a good deal about using it to its best advantage. This section has given you a knowledge of the structures and muscles. Remember that no power is generated in the larynx, so think of the air flow as moving up and through, unconstricted by tension in the neck and throat area, powered by tension in the abdominal muscles, which energize the entire outward-flowing airstream. With this understanding as the base for your fitness program, you will find ex-

---

[3] V. E. Negus, cited in Virgil Anderson, *Training the Speaking Voice* (New York: Oxford University Press, 1942).

ercises to help control the extrinsic muscles and initiate a clear, easy tone in Chapter 5.

RESONATION

Experts speculate that the sound originating at the vocal folds, without benefit of resonation, is weak and dull. Of course, one can only conjecture, because that outward-flowing air passes immediately from the glottis into the upper part of the larynx, up through the pharyngeal cavity, a resonator, and then out through the oral and nasal cavities, which are also resonators.

Discussion in this section will focus on the three resonating cavities of the throat, mouth, and nose, although, as has been stated, the larynx proper may also serve in this capacity, and certain broad resonance is achieved by the bones of the chest and the bones and sinuses of the head. Singers talk a good deal about "chest resonance," in which the vibrations of the lower notes can actually be felt in the thoracic cavity, and "head resonance" on the higher ones.

The three on which we will focus are the most powerful ones for speech, and the pharynx and the mouth are the ones over which you have (or will soon have!) a great deal of control. Some people say, "You are what you eat"; others say, "You are who your friends are"; we say, "Your voice is what you do with your resonators."

Actors on radio know this; in fact, they, like Clarence Nash, are able to cash in on negative resonance features in any number of ways. The same person may provide the high-pitched voice of a child in one commercial and that of a crusty old codger, a breathy sex symbol, or a complaining whiner in another.

It also must be appreciated that the three resonators do not all work equally at the same time. For most sounds the vocal tract consists of a long tube formed by the pharynx and the mouth coupled together in various fashions by the action of the tongue. The nasal passages are bypassed. On certain phonemes, however— the *m,* the *n,* and the *ng* as in *sing*—the pharynx and the nasal passages are connected, and the oral passage is blocked off by the lips or the tongue. This switching of air passages is made possible through the action of the *soft palate,* a movable fold of strong muscle fibers at the rear of the hard palate that through contraction of its own muscle fibers can raise back against the back wall of the pharynx to block off the nasal cavities. Because of this it is also known as the *velum,* from the Greek word for "veil." You can get a sense of the location and action of the soft palate if you say, over and over, "ng . . . gah, ng . . . gah, ng . . . gah."

Figure 3.8 shows the vocal tract and the main articulators.

From the discussion so far you know that resonation is the selective amplification of certain partials or overtones that exist in the complex tone set up at the vocal folds. You also know that the size, shape, length of opening, and texture of the walls of a resonating cavity are very powerful variables in determining which are selected and amplified.

Without delving into a complicated explanation of what actually happens with each of these conditions to reinforce some partials and damp (cancel out) others, it is helpful to remember that large cavities reinforce the rich lower over-

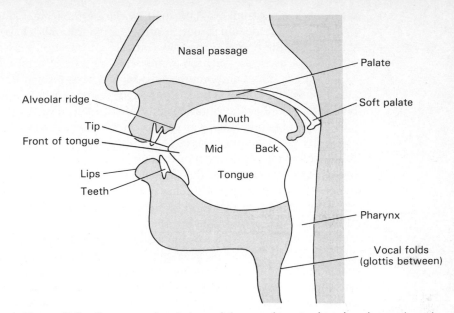

Figure 3.8 Cross-sectional view of the vocal tract, also showing main articulators

tones, as do loosely textured (not tense) walls, and such sounds are pleasing as underpinnings to a tone. With this as a framework, let us look at each of the resonators separately.

The pharynx

The pharynx is a vertical tube connecting the larynx and esophagus below with the nose and mouth above. Any number of changes in size, shape, and muscle tension take place when swallowing. To feel this, put your hand on your throat and swallow. You probably felt a good deal of tension, with the larynx shooting straight up. The front opening into the mouth can also be lengthened, shortened, or closed by the action of the tongue, and of course the upper portion can be blocked off by the action of the soft palate.

Most people will say, "Oh yes, I change my throat in all those ways to swallow, but the air just passes through automatically when I speak." Of course it does, but how?

The pharynx is not only an air passage; it is also a resonator for sounds. To work at its optimum to amplify a rich, mellow sound it needs to be easily open, with all muscles not directly and actively involved in phonation relaxed, because a relaxed throat creates a better-resonated sound than a tense one.

The nose

The nasal cavity is separated by the septum into two narrow, convol of about 4 inches in length. It allows very little change in the fac resonance. Some students claim that by flaring their nostrils they can change the shape of the openings, but in most people the only change that occurs is something quite beyond conscious control: An infection may alter the texture of the walls, as we are only too aware when we have a "stuffy nose."

Unlike the throat and mouth, the nose is a fixed resonator, like the box of a guitar or violin. On all sounds some slight resonation takes place in the nose, but on *m, n,* and *ng* the vibrating air is intentionally directed through it, the soft palate dropping out of the way to allow free passage directly from the throat.

One of the common misuses of the nasal passages is their *overuse* on many of the vowel sounds. If the mouth is not open enough to allow easy passage of the air, or if the closure of the soft palate is poor, vibrating air escapes up into the constricted passages of the nose, where most of it gets trapped, creating a resonance condition that amplifies the high, inharmonic partials, and an unpleasant, whiny, nasal sound results.

When the nose is intentionally used for the passage of air on the three sounds cited, the sound is a very pleasing one. Hum a protracted *mmmmmmmmmmmm* and *listen* to the sound. Place your fingers lightly on the upper part of your nose and cheeks as you do this and feel the covibrations that are part of the phenomenon of resonance. The optimum use of this cavity is achieved by capitalizing on it on the *m, n,* and *ng* sounds but being careful on all other sounds to maintain an open, large oral passage so that sound will not escape there inadvertently.

The mouth

The mouth, or oral cavity, is the most flexible of the three resonators and is capable of all kinds of modifications in size, shape, length of opening, and muscle tension of the walls. It also serves, with the parts within it and the tongue, the critical human purpose of articulation, stopping, hindering, or shaping sound into the phonemes of a particular language.

It contains the teeth and gums and is bounded by the lips in front, the cheeks on the sides, and the hard and soft palates above. In the back it opens into the pharynx, and the greater part of its floor is taken up by the tongue. Its structural base is the lower jaw, or *mandible.*

Few people without training have the flexibility in the jaw needed for good resonance, and many are what might be termed "lockjawers," "half-smilers," or "mask mouths," speaking always with the jaw held semirigid and the lips pulled slightly back. What happens to the resonance? First of all, the cavity never becomes large enough to reinforce the lower pleasing partials as it can when the jaw is easily dropped. The lips do not round and protrude on certain sounds, which is actually a way of increasing the mouth cavity length. Finally, the constant tension that it takes to hold the jaw in the fixed position transfers to the texture of the cheeks and, perhaps worse, radiates into the muscles that control the soft palate and the back of the tongue so that the air passage out the mouth is constricted and air can escape up into the nose.

To achieve clarity and good resonance, voice teachers often suggest that you imagine the oral cavity to be a megaphone. How can such an instrument work if you are squeezing the outer edges back in?

Also, attention should be on frontal placement of sounds—getting the sound out of the throat and the back of the mouth to give increased clarity.

For the mouth to work at its optimum as a resonator, then, there has to be great flexibility of the jaw, lips, and tongue and a focus on placing the sound well forward in the mouth.

ARTICULATION

It has been estimated that babies the world over, in the babbling, experimental prespeech stage, produce about 600 different sounds with their vocal apparatus. How interesting that the vast majority of these fade away and are never used— Bronx cheers and admiring whistles notwithstanding. A relatively few phonemes—experts estimate well under 100—are used as the basis of any language spoken in the world.

Voice sound is modified by the structures within the oral cavity primarily. The organs of articulation serve essentially as interrupters or stoppers of the vocal tone. Vowels are actually only a product of further refinement of resonance. Changes in the shape, size, and texture of the oral cavity working in conjunction with the tongue alter resonance features to produce what we perceive as *ee* or *ah* or *oo*.

By definition, the vocal tone is interrupted on consonants but not on vowels. Consonants are produced by bringing the movable parts of the oral cavity together to form a stoppage, with a resultant explosion, such as *b* or *g*, or into such close proximity that friction noise results, such as *z* or *v*, or just close together, as on *w*. Some consonants are the product of interrupting an airstream, not vocal tone, such as *p* or *s*.

The characteristics of each phoneme are based on the manner and place of articulation. Since the production of each one will be treated in detail later in the book, this section serves simply as an overview.

The articulators

The tongue is an organ of utmost importance not only in swallowing but also in speech, for it is used in producing most of the articulated sounds in a language, making contact or near contact with parts of the lips, teeth, gum ridge, hard palate, and soft palate. People can learn to talk with all kinds of vocal abnormalities, but never without a tongue.

The lips, too, are important in articulation, rounding, pursing, spreading. The teeth are used in articulating certain sounds, and the glottis also serves as an articulator for one sound in standard English, the *h*. Refer to Figure 3.8 for a diagram of the articulators.

Further explanation   The tongue is attached to the hyoid bone (to which the larynx is also fastened), the bone of the lower jaw, the inner wall of the chin, and the soft palate. It has both intrinsic and extrinsic muscles, the former shaping it and the latter positioning it.

For articulation purposes it is divided into the point (tip), blade, middle, and back.

Very important for articulation, the hard palate is divided into the gum ridge, *alveolar ridge,* the palate proper, and the soft palate. The gum ridge is the correct place of articulation with the tongue for many phonemes.

Optimum use of the articulators

The exact place of articulation is important in Standard American English, as is the manner of production. Also, 70 percent of the consonants, when correctly produced, are made in the front of the mouth with the lips, tip of the tongue, teeth, and gum ridge, so forward focus up out of the throat and to the front is essential for clarity of articulation.

Thus the articulators must be highly mobile and responsive, the tongue being the most flexible of all.

SUMMARY

Now that you understand the mechanisms involved and how the systems and muscles that control speech work, it is time to start exercising for mastery. But first, let us review.

The cerebrum is the coordinating and integrating center for speech.

Breathing for speech differs from breathing for life sustainment. For speech, in which it serves as a power source, breathing becomes a consciously controlled act, using a short inhalation and a prolonged exhalation. Abdominal control of the diaphragm and stomach muscles is crucial in using proper breath support for speech.

The larynx is the organ used to initiate sound. In addition to their biological function, the vocal folds draw together to create a fluttering pattern of vibrations, the basic sound wave pattern. Action of the intrinsic muscles allows breathing to occur as the vocal folds abduct, speech to occur as the folds meet at midline, and pitch of a voice to change through tension and relaxation; these muscles are controlled through the brain and ear. The extrinsic muscles position the larynx in the neck and throat area and *should be* under conscious control so that they are not allowed to tense and misposition the larynx.

Resonation, the selective amplification of certain partials in the complex tone set up at the vocal folds, takes place primarily in the throat, mouth, and nose. Variables that affect resonance that can be controlled in the mouth and throat include size, muscle tension, and shape and length of the opening, the goal being an open, large passage free of undue tension, with direction forward and out.

Articulation is the shaping, stopping, or hindering of sound into the individual phonemes that are the building blocks of speech. It occurs primarily in the mouth by bringing the movable parts into full or near contact with each other. The articulators are the tongue, lips, teeth, gum ridge, hard palate, soft palate, and glottis.

4

SUPPORT OF TONE: RESPIRATION

Lord what an organ is human speech when played
on by a master.

MARK TWAIN

Challenge exercise   Most of you are familiar with the portion of the famous
Mark Antony speech from *Julius Caesar* reproduced below. First, you are to
interpret it aloud (don't just run through the words, but convey the *ideas*) as if
you were addressing a large crowd and trying to sway them.

Friends, Romans, countrymen, lend me your ears;
I come to bury Caesar, not to praise him.
The evil that men do lives after them;
The good is oft interred with their bones.
So let it be with Caesar.
The noble Brutus hath told you that Caesar was ambitious.
If it were so, it was a grievous fault.
And grievously has Caesar answered it.

Now comes the real challenge. Do the same thing again, only this time *interpret
all eight lines on a single breath.*

Sound impossible? Some famous British repertory companies refuse to let an
actor even audition for a part in their company until he has demonstrated this
basic vocal control.

We are not suggesting that you are intending to be performers or that you
may ever be able to complete the Challenge Exercise, but the point behind such
a preaudition test is an important one. The company wants to be assured that
the actor has control of the power source, the air being exhaled from the lungs,
so that his total concentration will be on the meaning, emotion, and mood of
the lines he wishes to convey.

That is what we want for you: that you be in control of what you want to say
and able to convey the exact meaning you intend without any thought of fading
away or running out of breath in the middle. You will then be free to concentrate
on *ideas.*

GOALS FOR WORK ON BREATH SUPPORT

Now that your fitness program is beginning, what can you hope to achieve by the explanations and workouts in this chapter? The goals you set for yourself should include these:

1. To know how breath support and phrasing are coordinated
2. To understand the critical nature of breath control as the support underlying all voice and to recognize the faults that can occur because of lack of it[1]
3. To know how breath support actually works for you and to *feel* and *hear* the difference in yourself between a supported and an unsupported tone so that you have a basis of self-monitoring
4. To go step by step through exercises designed to help you gain ever increasing control of breathing for speech
5. To apply this control to practice materials of ever increasing complexity
6. To demonstrate your own control of breath support by successfully completing the final Checkpoint exercises

BREATH CONTROL AS IT RELATES TO MEANING

Let's say you were asked to say the following sentence:

> The woman on the diet said there was no way she could have gained 5 pounds this past week.

The way you pause and the way you emphasize certain words will determine the meaning your listener will get. For example, if you were to emphasize *no way,* one will assume the woman is denying such a possibility emphatically; if you emphasize *5 pounds,* the sentence will seem to mean that she's admitting she put on a bit of weight, but not that much.

Now suppose you know that the meaning you want to convey is that it is impossible that she put on that much weight this particular week. Ostensibly, you have to have such control of your exhaling air that you say the whole sentence while saving enough strong breath to pick up and emphasize the very last words, *this past week.*

Breath support is what this control of the power source, your exhaling air, is called, and it is aptly named, for once you have it, it supports whatever you want to say; it frees you to concentrate on ideas.

COORDINATING PHRASING WITH BREATHING

Later in this chapter we will suggest a variety of ways to gain increased control of the muscles involved in breathing for speech so that you can ultimately reach your goal of controlling the power source so that you always have a constant reserve of air that you can tap into effortlessly whenever the occasion demands.

---

[1] Readers who need more directed work on specific faults will find suggestions and additional exercises for correction later in this chapter.

But even before you develop this control, you can focus on conveying ideas by learning to coordinate your breathing with your phrasing.

In normal speech, one speaks in phrases, which are single ideas, and the separation between phrases is a pause. Pauses are the punctuation marks of speech. If we return to the sentence about the hapless dieter, the last few words *this past week* may be the most important part to emphasize, but there are several mini-ideas in there: *who* is saying it, *what,* and qualified by *when.* Thus the sentence could legitimately be broken into three parts:

> The woman on the diet said / there was no way she could have gained 5 pounds / this past week.

Each time you pause to separate a thought group you can take a quick breath if you need to. Coordinating your breathing with the phrasing will give you control over what you choose to emphasize, and no one will be able to tell whether you did it all on one breath or not.

FAULTS DUE TO INCORRECT BREATHING

Ideally, each phrase, each idea, should receive the nuance, color, and meaning that you, as the speaker, intend. The person who has not learned to control the power source may suffer from one of these problems:

- *Choppiness.* The speaker runs out of air and has to take another breath in the middle of a phrase, breaking up the logical thought.
- *Fading.* The speaker has too little air to sustain a strong tone through a phrase or sentence, so that toward the end the listener has a hard time hearing what is being said and loses part of the thought.
- *Glottal fry.* Toward the end of each phrase or sentence, an unpleasant sound, rather like rapidly popping corn, distracts the listener. This is an involuntary signal that the air pressure is too low, or it can also mean that a person is speaking in too low a pitch range.

Also, speakers who lack breath support will not be able to produce the rich clear sounds they want; straining and tension prevent it. Thus practically every unpleasant voice characteristic—strained, high-pitched, tense, and even nasal—can ultimately be traced to lack of correct breathing or breath support.

WORKING FOR GOOD BREATH SUPPORT

How do you work for good breath support? Simply remember the old phrase "Belt it out!" This is not to be taken in the sense of shouting! It is to give you a vivid image of where the activity for breathing for speech is centered.

As you know from Chapter 3, the lungs work on a simple vacuum principle: You *inhale* because the cavity of your chest has increased, and air rushes in to equalize pressure with the outside air. You *exhale,* because the cavity of your chest starts decreasing in size, and the air has to go out. This happens involuntarily, 24 hours a day, asleep or awake, to keep you alive.

But the minute you start to speak, the brain signals a change in what is basically the same pattern. The intake becomes quicker, however, and the muscles that relax on exhalation stay easily tensed. The cavity does not collapse as quickly, so the air escapes more slowly. The rate of inhalation to exhalation changes from a ratio of 1:1 to a ratio of 1:10 or so.

An important thing to keep in mind is that it isn't how much air you take in, it is what you do with the air you have, how you support it on the way out. The production of a clear, strong tone requires no more breath intake than a person can easily and inconspicuously manage.

Such knowledge is relatively recent, at least in musical circles. The idea used to be that the larger the chest, and by extension the greater the air volume intake, the stronger and better-supported the voice would be. Grand opera in the old days was cast with Amazons and human blimps. The voices were superb, and fortunately the opera audiences were ever so polite and rarely snickered at what looked like two beach balls trying to rotate toward each other in the love scenes. The voices today are still superb, but the casting has improved 100 percent. A slim little singer, Lily Pons, among others, took audiences by storm by showing that a person could have a grand voice and a small chest as well.

To be a bit more technical in explaining why you have most of the air you need anyway: The lungs remain partially inflated all the time, and if you were to inhale as deeply as you possibly could and then hook yourself up to a machine called a spirometer and measure the resultant maximum exhalation, you would arrive at a measure of the *vital capacity* of your particular lungs—the total amount of air you can hold. We can call that figure 100 percent. By the same token, if you were hooked up again to the same machine and were to measure your *tidal air,* the flow back and forth you use in normal respiration, you would find it to be only about 12 percent of the total capacity of your lungs, and in speaking you would find that you rarely used more than 20 percent.[2] In other words, you have plenty of air.

Think of it like a bank account in which you always maintain a balance of $100, dipping in to draw out small amounts of $12 to $20 but always replenishing the small amounts. That large reserve is there, to be tapped into for vigorous physical activity and for speaking when the demand arises.

As you also have already learned, although the chest can increase in almost all dimensions, *clavicular* (upper-chest) *breathing* is to be avoided for speech because the tension it produces radiates up into the general throat area and creates the very constriction you want to avoid. The principal expansion of the chest should be downward. The diaphragm on inhalation pushes down against the abdomen. When you breathe correctly, your stomach may protrude slightly, because the organs, pushed down from above, have no other direction in which to go. Also, as you breathe for good support, make sure the muscles of the lower chest that have increased the cavity outward do not relax, so that you have this extra air to work with, too. In breathing for speech, all attention is downward, in the abdomen and even back to the spine and buttocks.

---

[2] Hilda Fisher, *Improving Voice and Articulation* (Boston: Houghton Mifflin, 1975).

SOME IMAGES TO HELP WITH SUPPORT OF TONE

In perfecting a new skill, theory is important, but sometimes a random image can suddenly put things into clearer perspective. See if any of the following prove helpful.

- A singer acquaintance tells how as she breathes in, she pictures that the air is being brought into her stomach, inflating it all the way down to her groin and back up her spine.
- Dorothy Sarnoff, a leading speech consultant, suggests that you think of your lips down where your navel is and that you have to go all the way down there to get your voice.
- In her book *Speech Can Change Your Life,* Dorothy Sarnoff also shares the image that helped her most with support of tone. It came from Giovanni Martinelli, one of the great opera singers of all time. "Think," he would say, "of a ping-pong ball bobbing on the crest of a fountain. Imagine that the ball is your voice, and the fountain is the breath supporting it. If the support remains undiminished, the ping-pong ball will bob there indefinitely, but if the support slackens, the ball drops away."[3]
- A student who achieved a particularly strong and resonant voice described that he always thought of his throat as a wide tube lined with velvet, with the air gently smoothing the nap as it passed up all the way from the bottoms of his feet.

BUILDING MUSCLE AWARENESS

For some reason, when you are lying down, your breathing tends to be correct. Try doing this, with a book placed on your stomach, and watch the book rise with each inhalation.

A voice teacher we know holds a weight contest in her classes. The day she is planning to do this she asks students to bring extra books. The point is to see who can hold the greatest weight of books on the stomach and still have the pile rise. The tricky part is to make sure the books do not topple. The breathing has to remain very smooth, just as it does for speech.

It is harder to assume an erect posture, holding a book in the same position, and have the same thing happen. But that is what you are aiming for.

Here's another way to get the feel of the correct diaphragmatic breathing, or *abdominal breathing,* as it is more aptly called.

1. Stand up and bend over your desk. Leaning over in this position, hold the far edge of the desk with your hands, and slowly inhale a deep breath. You should feel a tightening in the belt area.
2. Count slowly aloud on that breath, and keep going until you run out of air. You should feel the belt area loosen the higher you count.

---

[3] New York: Dell, 1970, p. 29

Here is another way.

1. Standing up straight, place your hand in the triangle just above your belt where the rib cage splays out. Then stand a foot or so away from a wall, facing it, and with the other arm against the wall, try to push the wall down on a slow count of 5. This should give you a good idea of how those muscles tighten and continue to contract on back to the spine.
2. In the same position, whisper as loudly as you can, "Look out!" and feel how those muscles come into play!

So to support your breath, belt it out; feel the action in your abdominal area.

CONSERVATION AS AN ADDITIONAL KEY TO BREATH SUPPORT

Every singer, knows that it is important to learn to conserve the stream of air so that the musical phrase can be completed. Without this muscular control of the airstream, the singer may abruptly gasp for air in the middle of a phrase and thus interrupt the flow of the melody. The rhythm of the music is altered without an adequate breath supply, and even the lyrics may fade beyond recognition.

Such a singer will never succeed beyond the confines of his or her own shower. The same applies to the speaker.

LEARNING SELF-MONITORING

From the beginning of your exercises for breath support, you want to be able to monitor yourself in order to know if you are practicing correctly.

The first thing you need is an auditory reference, an example of what a well-supported voice sounds like, so that you will have something to aim for as you work. Your instructor can help you with this.

A tape recorder is a valuable aid. Listen to television and radio for voices that sound pleasing. Then tape your own voice and compare it to the others. The tape recorder is very useful as you are doing your exercises, especially when you are not quite sure how you sound. Then, too, a tape used throughout the course can provide feedback and a record of your progress.

From the beginning, your goal is to be able to step outside yourself and consciously *hear* and *feel* the correct and incorrect tones produced and feel the muscles involved. One of the best ways to do this is through negative practice countered immediately by positive practice.

1. On one breath, count clearly and distinctly until you feel your voice straining, tense, or fading. Stop. Note how far you got. This is your present ability, which will increase the more you do the exercises in this section.

   Use negative practice. On one breath, count again beyond ease of tone production. Hear the fading. Feel the throat muscles strain to push out the sound. Now do it again, making sure to stop the moment you hear or feel anything negative.
2. Get the feel of wasting air on words like *hit, home, half, hat, heat, hot, heavy,*

head. Now repeat the same words, trying to produce them all on the same breath, concentrating on efficient use of air.

WARM-UP EXERCISES

Support of tone

The proper stance is as important in speech as it is in doing physical fitness routines. For best results in voice production, follow these rules:

1. Maintain a comfortably erect posture (sitting or standing).
2. Inhale an easy deep breath.
3. Release the breath in a steadily controlled stream.

A. *Relaxation exercises*   It is always a good idea to start any workout with relaxation exercises in order to eliminate unwanted tension.

 1. Sitting comfortably, concentrate on each part of your body, beginning with the top of your head. Work your way down slowly to your toes, releasing any unwanted tension along the way.

 2. *Stiffen and relax*

    a. Sitting comfortably, stretch your arms out sideways, palms up, as far as you can. Stiffen and relax 3 times.
    b. Raise your legs and feet parallel to the floor. Stiffen and relax 3 times.
    c. Concentrate on your face and neck. Make a face, and stiffen and relax 3 times.
    d. Now do steps 1, 2, 3, together. Stiffen and relax 3 times.

    You should feel increased blood flow and relaxation throughout your body.

 3. Yawn 4 or 5 times, each time making the opening of the mouth wider. Feel the free flow of air as the throat opens up and relaxes.

 4. *Rag doll exercise* (This one has been around a long time, because it works.)

    a. Stand erect with feet apart about 6 inches.
    b. Drop forward from the waist, making sure your head, neck, and arms hang freely, letting your legs support your body.
    c. Slowly start to rise by first aligning your spine. Keep your head and arms relaxed.
    d. Finally, with head still forward on the chest and spine now erect, raise your head and neck to a standing position and slowly rotate your head around to the right and then to the left. Does your body feel relaxed? If not, repeat.

B. *Strengthening Breath Support*

 1. Phonate "ah" while maintaining the feeling of breathing against the belt and easily tensed abdominal muscles. On successive exhalations, phonate

and prolong "ah" with your ear as monitor to tell you when you begin to fade or when strain sets in. Work for clarity of tone and ease.

2. Can you increase the length of phonation of the clear "ah" with successive attempts? Practice successive countings on one breath using both a speaking tone and a singing tone, being conscious of the push from your abdominal muscles as the count extends. Try to stretch your count without forcing or fading. Practice daily and see how your muscular development lengthens your count.

3. *Cycle of breathing* This exercise is valuable for gaining depth and control. It is used by professional singers and actors as well as by athletes performing physical fitness routines.

   a. To a count of 6, inhale through your mouth, drawing your breath in evenly on all counts. Purse your lips so that you can hear the air rushing in.
   b. Hold the air in your lungs for a count of 6. Do not close the vocal bands so that the muscles of inhalation will do the work.
   c. Over a count of 6, exhale slowly and evenly, with lips pursed so that you can hear and monitor the outgoing stream.
   d. For a count of 6, hold in the exhale position. Again, do not close the vocal bands, requiring the muscles of exhalation to stay contracted.
   e. Repeat the cycle once or twice. Do not overdo, as you can temporarily overoxygenate your blood and become dizzy.

4. Repeat the following nonsense phrase over and over until you hear fading or vocal strain or are forced to inhale. Practice successive times. Can you lengthen the number of times you can say the phrase loudly and without vocal strain?

   Exercise works wonders if you . . . exercise works wonders if you . . . exercise works wonders if you . . .

ADDING ON FOR PROFICIENCY

Support of tone

1. Combine breathing with phrasing. The first time you read the following selections, pause and take a breath at each slash mark so that you can see how this can be done without the listener's awareness. The second time through, use the same pause marks, but inhale only as you need to. Beware of fading or strain the second time around.

   a. I can't believe he didn't see me / at least one / if not two / or maybe three times.
   b. The rolling surf swept up the beach, / leaving a dirty coating of foam / and a stray stone or shell.
   c. The exercise fanatic has built up enough strength to do 20, / sometimes 30 / or even 50 rounds of setting-up exercises.

2. Combine breath support with vigor and buoyancy. Tell a suspenseful story with a surprise ending using only one breath:

   1, 2, 3, 4, 5, 6, 7, 8, 9, . . . *10!*

3. Repeat the following phrases on one breath, making sure not to fade.

   a. I came; I saw; I conquered.
   b. Fiddle dee dee, Miss Melanie.
   c. I don't think we're in Kansas anymore.
   d. There's no place like home.
   e. A hero's path lies yonder.
   f. Dream on, dream on of rainbows.
   g. A moment on the lips, forever on the hips.

4. Try these longer sentences on one breath, keeping the sound projected on the same loudness level.

   a. My father always insists that I eat a good breakfast every day.
   b. Jogging with my Walkman on keeps me from feeling tired.
   c. Exercising can be fun, especially after studying for an exam.
   d. I wish my roommate were neater so that I could find my things.
   e. Before long I shall have to look the future in the face and get a job.
   f. Education is a sound investment yielding a high rate of interest.
   g. Polishing my rust-encrusted car, I dream about a shiny new one.
   h. Fantasy plants the seeds that make the imagination flower.

SUPER EXERCISES

Support of tone

A. *I went to registration*   Take a breath before the start of each beginning. How many courses can you add comfortably on one breath? Don't strain, but build up tolerance as part of your daily regimen.

   1. I went to registration and took one course in voice and diction.
      (Take a breath.)

   2. I went to registration and took one course in voice and diction and English literature.
      (Take a breath.)

   3. I went to registration and took one course in voice and diction, English literature, and experimental psychology.
      (Take a breath.)

   4. I went to registration and took one course in voice and diction, English literature, experimental psychology, and computer science.
      (Take a breath.)

   5. I went to registration and took one course in voice and diction, English literature, experimental psychology, computer science, and physical education.
      (Take a breath.)

6. I went to registration and took one course in voice and diction, English literature, experimental psychology, computer science, physical education, and music appreciation.
(Take a breath.)

7. I went to registration and took one course in voice and diction, English literature, experimental psychology, computer science, physical education, music appreciation, and art history.
(Relax.)

B. *Sound symphony*   Keeping the sound distinct, can you get all the way through this sound symphony on one breath?

Crack!
Plip plop plop smash
Tip
Tip tip tip
Too
Bongo bongo boom boom
Pit pat
Tik
Tikka
Tik
Shoosh
Mmmmmm mmmmmm
Swoop swoop
Clonk

C. The following selection is printed with no punctuation or capitalization. Read it through once this way, taking a breath only where you have to. Then divide it into phrases and read it for ideas with good breath support.

smog is everywhere it is upon the buildings upon the chimneys and shrouding the trees in murky haze what has our modern society created on the one hand we have ever stronger chemicals faster cars and superproducts on the other we have a landscape that makes clear blue sky and fluffy white clouds a reality mostly through pictures in magazines

D. *Soap opera synopses*   Take the role of an announcer with a strong supported voice throughout.

Good evening, America. For viewers who missed their favorite series this week, here is Soap Opera Update:

On *Tanglewood Vice,* the wisecracking team of Sergeant Joe and Lieutenant Sara has called in for questioning the call girl whom they believe to be the head of a munitions drop but who, unbeknown to anyone but Sergeant Joe, may also be his illegitimate daughter. Interrogation is interrupted by an all-precinct alert of a bomb threat at the SRO concert in progress at Symphony Hall.

County Wards found young doctors Chris and Doris coping with the victims of a tour bus and tractor trailer accident while desperately trying to contact the head of the hospital, Dr. Gerald, to warn him of an outbreak of Alaskan lung disease in the wards in which the air-circulating system is suspect. An empty gin bottle has been found in Dr. Gerald's desk drawer, but there is no clue as to his whereabouts.

In the elegant Fifth Avenue penthouse of Manley Atherton on *Off the Edge,* the theft of the Renoirs continues to occupy the police. Manley's wife finds a note that implies that Manley may have more than a passing interest in the college student who comes in to groom the poodles, and she is determined to confront him with her suspicions and then take her life by running her electric wheelchair into the shower.

E. Make up your own Soap Opera Update for *Sugar Plantation, As the Moon Turns,* and *Big Business Masquerade.*

F. Choose one of the following selections, and read it aloud with good breath support.

1. Mr. Goldin entered the inn, where a mighty fire was blazing on the hearth and roaring up the wide chimney with a cheerful sound. There was a large iron kettle shimmering and bubbling in the heat. And when the landlord lifted the lid, there was a savory smell. The glow of the fire was upon the landlord's bald head and upon his twinkling eyes. Mr. Goldin drew his sleeve across his lips and said in a murmuring voice, "What is it?"

   "It's stew of tripe," said the landlord. "And cowheel, and bacon," smacking his lips, "and steak and peas, cauliflowers, new potatoes, and sparrowgrass, all working together in one delicious gravy."

   CHARLES DICKENS, *Little Nell*

2. Dorian leaped up and cried, "You used to stir my imagination. Now you don't even stir my curiosity. You simply produce no effect. I loved you because you had genius and intellect, because you realized the dreams of great poets and gave shape and substance to the shadow of art. You have thrown it all away. You are shallow and stupid. My god! How mad I was to love you.

   OSCAR WILDE, *The Picture of Dorian Gray*

3. From under the roof of my umbrella I saw the washed pavement lapsing beneath my feet, the newsposters lying smeared with dirt at the crossing, the tracks of the busses in the liquid mud. On I went through this dreary world of wetness. And through how many rains and years shall I hurry down wet streets—middle aged, and then, perhaps very old? And on what errand?

   Asking myself this cheerless question I fade from your vision, Reader, into the distance, sloping my umbrella against the wind.

   LOGAN PEARSALL SMITH, *Trivia*

CORRECTING RESPIRATORY FAULTS

Once a person has learned to support a tone and has built awareness of any tendency to fade at endings, become choppy, or go into glottal fry, additional work may not be necessary. However, if you need further work, the following section will be useful for preventing choppiness or fading. Since an inappropriate pitch level is sometimes also associated with glottal fry, suggestions for correction of it will be found in the following chapter under the heading of Correcting Phonatory Faults.

Fading

Often the most important words in a sentence are the final ones. If you drop your voice at periods, as so many students were unfortunately taught to do in grade school to indicate finality, you will not get the meaning across. Even if the last words are not the most important, good speech is easily understood. If the meaning is confused or if it seems that the speaker doesn't care enough to make the effort to speak clearly, a listener may stop attending or even become annoyed.

In the exercises that follow, remember that exhalation must be controlled to the very end of a thought. Throughout, *support* is the key, and your ear is your guide.

WARM-UP EXERCISES

Preventing fading

1. Count to 15 on one breath slowly and distinctly. Did you start to fade toward the end?

2. Do the same thing again, only this time stop at whatever number you started to fade on. With repetitions, can you increase that count?

3. Start to read the paragraph right under the heading "Fading" above. On one breath, how far did you get before you started to fade? Repeat, stopping at the end of the first sentence but making sure you do not fade.

4. Rather than fading out as you do the following, purposely raise the volume slightly on each successive word in the phrase.

   a. Come in, come in, come in.
   b. Never, ever again should you do that.
   c. Please go and go right now.
   d. I hear wind and rain and now thunder.
   e. That is not what I want, not at all.
   f. He came, he saw, but he didn't conquer me.

5. To make sure you are not losing support because you are wasting breath early in a sentence, waste air purposely the first time you speak each of the following phrases, using up a breath a phrase. Then see how many times you can do each phrase on the same breath without fading.

    a. Who are you?
    b. What did he say?
    c. Has Sally come?
    d. What a sight!
    e. Half a pie is left.
    f. Put ham on the list.
    g. Whoopee!

ADDING ON FOR PROFICIENCY

Preventing fading

Now you take the important step of listening to yourself critically as you talk. Use a tape recorder for this.

1. Read the following paragraph, pausing at the phrase marks to take a quick catch breath. If you hear yourself fading before you can take a breath, put a pencil mark wherever you hear it happening, but do not stop to correct it.

    Part of the learning / and part of the fun of being in college / has nothing to do with what happens in classes. / The involvement in clubs, / the social events, / attendance at concerts and performances brought in from outside, / and, perhaps most of all, / talking with friends about this and that or nothing at all, / that's what's really important. / Yet the voice of reason keeps nagging, / "How are you going to get your schoolwork done?" /

2. Listen to the playback to check whether you heard yourself when fading set in.

3. Read the paragraph again, phrased as indicated for meaning, but this time take a breath on a pause only when you feel you need it rather than on every one. Make the same simultaneous judgment as before when you start fading, marking each instance. Again play back and check your judgment.

4. Continue this exercise until you can read the whole paragraph for meaning without ever fading or losing intensity.

SUPER EXERCISES

Preventing fading

Each of the following sayings is "loaded" because the meaning is made clear in the last few words. Read each, phrasing for meaning (the first few are done for you), making sure the voice is strong and clear right to the end. Remember that you can catch a breath whenever you stop for the slight pause between thoughts.

1. Some are weather-wise, / some are other-wise.
    BEN FRANKLIN

2. Work keeps at bay three great evils— / boredom, / vice / and need.
    VOLTAIRE

3. He who foresees calamities, / suffers them twice over.
   PORTEUS

4. The reason why worry kills more people than work, / is that more people worry than work.
   ROBERT FROST

5. The longer one lives, the less importance one attaches to things, and also the less importance to importance.
   JEAN ROSTAND

6. A man will sometimes devote all his life to the development of one part of his body—the wishbone.
   ROBERT FROST

7. A sharp tongue is the only edge tool that grows keener with constant use.
   WASHINGTON IRVING

8. There are no ugly women—there are only women who do not know how to look pretty.
   JEAN DE LA BRUYÈRE

9. Tact consists of knowing how far we may go too far.
   JEAN COCTEAU

10. "Oh Lord," he says, "let my words be tender and sweet, for tomorrow I may have to eat them."
    NORMAN VINCENT PEALE

Choppiness

Choppy speech can result when the speaker lacks an understanding of breath support. In the middle of a phrase, which is actually an idea, the speaker suddenly has to take a breath to replenish the power supply. The work you have done so far will do much to alleviate this fault.

However, some people speak choppily because they do not seem to think in ideas, let alone read in ideas. They speak in individual words, and if reading aloud, they tend to approach one word at a time rather than one whole thought at a time. For these people, some additional basic work on phrasing for ideas can be helpful, and such exercises follow.

It should also be noted that most of these exercises deal with *reading* ideas for phrases. It has been our experience that this is the critical first step. Once one can read aloud in phrase groups, blending the whole of each group, the technique begins to transfer over into more spontaneous speech.

WARM-UP EXERCISES

Preventing choppiness

If you go to the store, you don't ask for "a / loaf / of / bread," you ask for "a loaf of bread." If someone asks how the exam was, it was not "horrible / and /

absolutely / unfair," it was "horrible and absolutely unfair," and the gym is not "two / blocks / down / and / to / the / left" but "two blocks down and to the left." We speak in ideas, not individual words.

If someone says, "I'd like to come with you, but I have to study," the person is expressing two different thoughts: a desire to go and the impossibility of doing so. This distinction is indicated by a pause between the two thoughts. If someone else says, "My brother, who is actually my step-brother, will bring the food," there are of course three ideas: who, the relationship, and what the person is going to do, and there will be two pauses in the sentence to separate the individual thoughts.

1. Look at the sentences that follow and tell how many thoughts are in each. (Do not try simply counting commas. Sometimes ideas are not separated by commas.)

   a. I took the exam but I flunked.
   b. I have to pick up the mail, then I will stop for coffee, and perhaps I'll start my term paper after that.
   c. Turn left, no, I mean right, and then go straight for a mile.
   d. I'll take it, whatever it is and however it is served.
   e. Don't you ever dare say that to me again.
   f. I couldn't believe it not even if my life depended on it because it's plain silly, so there.

   a. 2; b. 3; c. 3; d. 2 or 3; e. 1; f. 4

2. Draw pause marks between each of the thoughts and then say the sentences aloud, supporting well.

ADDING ON FOR PROFICIENCY

Preventing choppiness

Some things that you will be reading are full of meaning although they may not take up much space in print. If the meaning is to come through to you as well as to others, ask yourself what is actually being said. What are the parts, the separate thoughts, that the sentence should be divided into?

1. Suppose you were to see the Milton Berle quote, "A committee is a group that keeps minutes and loses hours." Obviously, he is talking about how much time committees waste, and the sentence would be divided like this:

   A committee / is a group / that keeps minutes / and loses hours.

   As you read it aloud, think of each phrase as a continuous blended whole, much like a phrase in music.

   Here's a quote by Stephen Leacock: "I am a great believer in luck, and I find the harder I work the more I have of it." To convey his idea that opportunities do not just happen, this would be the phrasing:

I am a great believer in luck, / and I find / the harder I work /
the more I have of it.

Read the next quotes aloud, as marked.

The human mind / should be like a good hotel— / open the year round.

W. L. PHELPS

Oratory: / the art of making deep noises from the chest /
sound like important messages from the brain.

H. I. PHILLIPS

Adam ate the apple / and our teeth still ache.

HUNGARIAN PROVERB

2. Figure out the meaning of the following, mark the phrases, and blend together as in exercise 1.

   a. A man who has committed a mistake and doesn't correct it is committing another mistake.
      CONFUCIUS

   b. It destroys one's nerves to be amiable every day to the same human being.
      BENJAMIN DISRAELI

   c. Some people can stay longer in an hour than others can in a week.
      WILLIAM DEAN HOWELLS

   d. A pinch of probably is worth a pound of perhaps.
      JAMES THURBER

   e. The unfortunate thing about the world is that good habits are so much easier to get out of than bad ones.
      W. SOMERSET MAUGHAM

   f. If you have charm, you don't need to have anything else, and if you don't have it, it doesn't matter what else you have.
      J. M. BARRIE

SUPER EXERCISES

Preventing choppiness

Maintaining the same concentration on separating thoughts into well-blended phrases to transmit meaning, choose any of the literary excerpts in the Super Exercises for Support of Tone, and read aloud.

CHECKPOINT EXERCISES

Do you have it?

A. *Demonstrating knowledge of correct breathing for speech*   Place one hand on the triangular area of your upper abdomen where the rib cage flares out.

1. Slowly inhale. *You should feel your hand moving outward.*

2. Do the same thing again, noticing what is happening to your shoulders. *They should not move.*

3. Maintaining the same concentration on abdominal breathing and stationary shoulders, on one breath, count firmly and clearly at a measured pace to 25. *There should be no strain toward the end.*

B. *Combining breathing with phrasing*   Read and record the following Mark Twain quotation, taking a quick breath at every phrase mark.

The most striking difference / between a cat and a lie / is that a cat / has only nine lives.

Now read the same quote through again, breathing only as you need to but keeping emphasis on the ideas and giving strong support throughout.

C. *Demonstrating freedom from faults due to poor breath support*   If you have been working to free yourself of fading or choppiness, in your speech, consciously reproduce the fault in the following, and then provide strong support throughout.

"She's the sort of woman now," said Mould, . . . "one would almost feel disposed to bury for nothing: and do it neatly, too!"
CHARLES DICKENS, *Martin Chuzzlewit*

D. *Putting it all together*   Demonstrate that you can put all the techniques together in a longer selection. Choose one of the following. Phrase for ideas and read for total meaning, maintaining support throughout.

1. "I only took the regular course," said the Mock Turtle. "What was that?" inquired Alice. "Reeling and Writhing, of course, to begin with," the Mock Turtle replied, "and the different branches of Arithmetic—Ambition, Distraction, Uglification, and Derision."
LEWIS CARROLL, *Alice's Adventures in Wonderland*

2. We shall not flag or fail. We shall go on to the end. We shall fight in France, we shall fight on the seas and oceans, we shall fight with growing strength in the air, we shall defend our island, whatever the cost may be. We shall fight on the beaches, we shall fight on the landing grounds, we shall fight in the fields and in the streets, we shall fight in the hills; we shall never surrender. . . .
WINSTON CHURCHILL

3. How amazing is this spirit of man! In spite of innumerable failings, man, throughout the ages, has sacrificed his life and all that he held dear for an ideal, for truth, for faith, for country and honor. That ideal may change, but that capacity for self-sacrifice continues, and because of that, much may be forgiven to man, and it is impossible to lose hope in him.

    JAWAHARLAL NEHRU

5

ACHIEVING CLEAR SOUND: PHONATION

The majesty and grandeur of the English language
. . . [is] its extraordinary, imaginative, and
musical mixture of sounds.

GEORGE BERNARD SHAW

Challenge exercise With the tips of your fingers locate the thyroid notch of your larynx (women may need to hum up and down the scale or clear their throats.) With a finger placed firmly on the notch, shout the following commands as if you were calling to a group of people far outside the classroom:

LOOK OUT! READY! AIM! FIRE!

Was yours a "leaping larynx"? Did it rise straight up on each shouted command? Or did it stay pretty much in place? If it did the latter, you already have some control over the muscles needed for easy initiation of tone.

As you already know, sound is initiated when the vocal folds in the larynx are brought together at midline to create interference with the exhaling column of air. This resistance sets up the fluttering type of vibration, the basic sound wave pattern, which occurs instantaneously when you start to talk.

If you were reasonably successful with the Challenge Exercise, you were aware that the power for speech is related to the breathing muscles, not to the sound-producing mechanism itself. The increase in volume with the stronger column of air from your lungs required an increase of tension within the vocal folds, but you did not allow it to radiate into the extrinsic muscles that position the larynx on each shouted command. You obviously increased the tension in the abdominal muscles, where it belonged.

A leaping larynx is a sign that you still need to be aware of learning to relax the neck and throat muscles when you make demands on your voice. Some added attention is needed to maintain alignment against increased breath pressure. The truly well-trained voice can sustain high volume with no consequent change in quality or pitch. If you did the exercise alone and not with a classroom full of people, you probably noticed an accompanying strained or shrill sound.

GOALS FOR WORK ON PHONATION

With work on support of tone firmly established, set your sights in this chapter on achieving the following:

1. To understand how tone is easily initiated, how the vocal folds actually work, and what you can do to conserve your voice and use it to advantage
2. To know the difference between modal and optimum pitch and how to determine each in your own voice
3. To recognize the vocal faults that can result from poor phonatory habits[1]
4. To go step by step through exercises designed to help you produce a clear voice and to *feel* and *hear* the difference in yourself between a poorly and well-initiated tone so that you can monitor yourself
5. To practice materials of increasing complexity using a clear tone
6. To demonstrate control of phonation by successfully completing the final Checkpoint Exercises

AN EASILY INITIATED TONE

Voice is the product of integrated muscle activity, and nothing should interfere with the free, natural action of the vocal folds. They should come together with sufficient tension to maintain action through a forceful sustained column of air, but the important thing to focus on is not the mechanism itself but the *use* made of it. All too many people tighten the muscles in the neck and throat area the instant they begin to speak, mistakenly assuming that power is generated in this area. *It is not.* You don't squeeze a flute to get sound out of it! By the same token, you don't want to misposition the larynx through tension or obstruct the laryngeal opening through which the tone must pass.

Thus for easy initiation of tone what is needed is relaxation of all muscles not actively involved in phonation and an open throat for the free passage of tone.

MORE ABOUT THE VOCAL FOLDS AND TENSION WITHIN

Vocal fold vibrations are actually puffs of air produced when the pressure of the air below blows them apart. The reduction in pressure returns them to midline, only to have the pressure build up again and the cycle repeated. An increase in loudness results primarily from an increase in breath pressure. The natural elasticity of the folds returns them to midline, and the stronger the air pressure from below, the wider they are blown apart on each puff and the more the tension is needed to snap them back to the middle on each cycle. Therefore, the louder you talk, the more forcefully the vocal folds close. Conversely, the softer you talk, the more gently the vocal folds come together.

You already know that tension in the folds themselves is the main determinant

---

[1] Readers who need more directed work for specific phonatory faults will find suggestions and additional exercises later in this chapter.

of pitch, lengthening them and thinning out the edges. That is why when you go to a basketball game, for instance, and become too caught up in the excitement of cheering your team on to victory, your yell may turn into a shriek. You may make a high-pitched sound you didn't intend because the tension created by your volume has also affected the pitch.

By the end of the evening what has happened? Your voice has been reduced to a croak. The larynx has become so misaligned that you have to strain even harder to keep the sound coming. Although the vocal folds are covered with a protective coating of mucous membrane, the continual hard banging together of the folds has led to irritation and consequent swelling of the folds. You develop temporary laryngitis—and all because you wanted to help the team!

SAVING YOUR VOICE

Some important voice conservation principles are involved in the scenario just presented. A loud voice over a period of time, without careful controls, can irritate the vocal folds because they are being brought together from wider apart and thus are more subject to irritation as they are slapped or rubbed together. So if your voice feels strained, or if you have a cold, one of the best ways to conserve your voice when you do have to talk is to speak at a low volume. Many people find it helpful, too, to be mindful of their pitch if it seems high, keeping it comfortably lower but being careful to avoid any feeling of forcing the pitch down. And of course if the strain is bad, all vocalization should be stopped for a while.

Voice damage is an occupational hazard in certain lines of work, and cheerleading used to be in this category. Cheerleaders' stock in trade has to be loud volume—the stands will not be roused to fever pitch by a soft, well-modulated voice.

Before the introduction of voice coaching for cheerleaders, many of these crowd rousers suffered permanent damage to their vocal folds because the shouting led to the shriek, the shriek led to recurring bouts of laryngitis, and ultimately the body protected the area of constant irritation by growing small protective calluses known as *vocal nodes.*

Fortunately, larynx abuse is pretty much a thing of the past because now cheerleaders are not only taught to support a tone from the abdomen and keep tension from the muscles of the neck and throat, but they are also coached to cheer in abnormally low-pitched voices to counter the tension that is a necessary component of the loud volume.

PITCH

The vocal folds are highly elastic and capable of all kinds of pitch variations. However, each of us has a vocal range—an effective pitch range—within which we can comfortably alter the levels. This is because of the specific size and length of the folds in each individual and slightly different dimensions of the resonating tubes (mouth and throat).

This is not to say that some popular rock singers don't sing in every range, from falsetto down to bass and back to tenor, at a loudness level a drill sergeant would admire! But what is perhaps not so well known is how many of them end up with permanent damage to the vocal folds because of the strain in achieving levels that are not within their comfortable range, especially at shouting levels.

It has been said that the most beautiful singing voices ever heard were the haunting male soprano voices in the Baroque age of music. Fortunately, we will never hear them, for the possessors of these superb voices were castrati—boys with marked musical ability who had been subjected to castration.[2] Among the secondary sexual characteristics that the operation prevented was the enlargement of the male larynx during puberty. The boy sopranos never became baritones or bassos; the smaller vocal folds made the high pitch range their normal one into adulthood.

Some entertainers have tried to cash in on this phenomenon by using falsetto voices. However, prolonged use of the falsetto is also very bad for the vocal folds because of the inherent strain and tension involved in creating it, and many of these imitators, too, have paid for their short-lived successes with permanently damaged vocal folds.

Modal versus optimum pitch

We all have a pitch range that is natural for our particular vocal equipment. Within that total range, which in most people is more than two octaves when sung, there will be one pitch level, or possibly two, that we keep returning to when we speak. In normal conversation we do not go up and down the scale like a roller coaster, but rather we tend to favor one or two notes in our range. This is our habitual pitch level, a baseline from which we move up for emphasis or down to express finality. This level is called *modal pitch.*

Emotional state, imitation of faulty models, strain, nervous tension, and many other factors enter into a person's habitual pitch level. No generalizations can be made about the appropriate modal pitch for any one individual because each person's vocal equipment has different dimensions and the vibrating source needs to be in tune with its resonator. You will not achieve a mellower tone by transferring the strings of a cello to a violin!

What is important is that your modal pitch be the one that serves you best, for there is for every person a pitch level at which the voice works with maximum efficiency for speech, much like a car that runs most economically, with the least use of gasoline, at a certain speed. This level to which your particular equipment is tuned is called *optimum pitch.*

The ideal, of course, is that your modal pitch and your optimum pitch be the same, and in many of you this may quite unconsciously have occurred.

---

[2] An old 78-rpm record of what was probably the last true castrato, Allesandro Maoreschi, was found in the files of the Vatican not long ago. Although Maoreschi was very old when the record was cut and the sound-recording equipment was poor, Pavillion Records recently reissued the recording of his voice, and it is quite uncanny to realize that the haunting soprano was actually the voice of a man.

Symptoms of inappropriate modal pitch

Men particularly sometimes adopt a very low pitch range for a variety of reasons, not the least of which is the strong macho image depicted in television and movies. However, if the voice tends to fade out or go into glottal fry, that deep rattling sound, whenever the pitch lowers for finality or if the voice has a limited lower range and strain sets in when a lower note is attempted, one would suspect that the speaker is below optimum level.

Glottal fry has been mentioned as a problem in support of tone when the air pressure from below against the folds has been reduced too much, but an additional cause is the placing of the voice in too low a pitch register, where it is continuously "scraping against the bottom." If this has been identified as a problem for you, try to increase your pitch range upward, and do the exercises to correct glottal fry at the back of this chapter.

Because excitement, worry, nervous strain, improper breathing, and a tense throat all contribute to higher pitch in a voice, many experts observe that more voices tend to be too high than too low. A voice that sounds tense, shrill, metallic, or nasal would be symptomatic of this. Also, if a voice is generally weak and thin, and health problems or emotions are not a factor, one might presume this to be the case, because by definition optimum pitch is the level at which you get the greatest return for the least expenditure of energy. And even a small baby with tiny vocal equipment can make a very loud cry!

Determining modal pitch

Modal pitch is relatively easy to determine once people can cut through the natural tendency to think of their voices as a natural extension of themselves that just *are* and start really *listening.* Simply read aloud a paragraph or two of factual, unemotional material from a newspaper or textbook, for instance, and note carefully the pitch levels of your voice. You will begin to notice one, or possibly two, that you keep returning to for all the unimportant words—this is your modal pitch. This pitch will vary with fatigue, illness, and occasion. Even the unwelcome phone intruder ("Oh, did I wake you up?") notices the difference in your voice when he wakens you.

But under normal circumstances at a reasonable time of the day or, as the expression goes, other things being equal, this is the way to tell. Locate that particular level on the scale by humming it and then phonating *ah* enough times so you can identify it.

Starting from this level, sing note by note down the scale until your voice breaks or goes into glottal fry. Remember how many notes you could go down from there as you now go on to the suggestions for determining optimum pitch.

Determining optimum pitch

Different voices vary in the pitch to which they most easily and naturally respond. A pitch level that allows a strong voice with the least effort and allows adequate room for variation both up and down the scale for intonation is obviously optimum, or ideal. So is a voice that has a range of inflectional pitch changes.

Inflection is the melody pattern of the voice, used to underline and shade meanings. Studies have shown that people rated as good speakers tended to have a pitch range of at least an octave and a half and that they tended to use many different pitch levels, especially the upper ones, for emphasis. People rated as poorer speakers tended to have pitch ranges of only about half an octave. At the least, as you consider these exercises for pitch, think about the size of your range and see if you can't start to extend it. Many people are so caught in the rut of using few notes that to them it sounds natural.

Several methods of determining optimum pitch are presented here. You may wish to try each to see if any is of help to you. It must be cautioned that any substantive change in pitch level should be done under the direction of an expert because many factors have contributed to a habituated pitch level.

1. RANGE CALCULATION

One way to determine optimum pitch is based on first finding your total vocal range and then making certain calculations from this. To find your range, sing down note by note from wherever it is comfortable until your voice cracks or goes into glottal fry. Make note of that note, for that is the bottom of your range. (A piano will be a help in identifying notes.) For the top of your range, do the same thing going up the scale until your voice breaks or goes into falsetto. The number of notes in between on the musical scale is your total range. It will naturally be a great deal narrower for speaking until you have worked to extend it upward or downward.

Optimum pitch will always tend to be a third to a quarter from the bottom of your total range. Thus if your total range was 15 musical tones according to the musical scale, optimum would be about 5 from the bottom, so you simply make the mathematical calculation to find the pitch you should be using.

If, when you were determining modal pitch, you kept track of the number of notes you could sing down from there, you would ideally have at least four if modal were also optimum, and these you would use to go down at the ends of phrases or sentences when you were expressing finality, without becoming inaudible or going into glottal fry, leaving twice as many upper ones for color or emphasis.

It has been our experience that although this calculation is a valid means of determining optimum pitch, too many students have never experimented with their voices, nor do they have any idea of what their total range could be. So practically speaking, the suggestions that follow may be more useful.

2. THE "WHAT WORKS BEST" TEST

If by definition optimum is where your voice works best with the least amount of effort, you ought to be able to feel and hear it in yourself. Supporting a tone well, start to phonate an easy, open *ah* at whatever pitch level feels comfortable to you, and gradually increase the intensity, concentrating on the loudness and fullness of the sound. Now experiment. Repeat the same *ah* with the same increasing intensity on separate breaths as you move note by note down the scale and then back up the scale, repeating the whole thing a few times. You should discover that there is one note, or perhaps two, where that *ah* seems to ring out more loudly and clearly than on any of the others. This is your optimum pitch. Try to remember what the note is for further practice, or find it on the piano for easy reference.

3. THE "WHAT WORKS BEST" TEST ADAPTED TO A ROOMFUL OF PEOPLE

Stop up your ears completely with your fingers and repeat suggestion 2 substituting *mmmm* for *ah*. Experimenting up and down, you should be able to identify a note or notes where the sound seems to ring loudest in your head. Again try to identify where it is for further use.

Helping stabilize optimum pitch

If you have determined your optimum pitch and it is different from your modal pitch, your optimum pitch should feel a good deal easier to produce and should sound fuller to your ears. Only if this is true should you make any attempt to stabilize it; if it is not, what you judge to be optimum is obviously not.

First you will want to get used to the sound so you have a good auditory reference to help you hear in your mind as you speak, so continue phonating, gradually intensifying *ah* many times, and move into words, still chanting or singing on that one pitch. Count to 10. Experiment with your social security number, your address, the alphabet, the names of some of your textbooks.

Gradually move into normal speech by saying the sentences that follow, each of which starts on an unemphasized word. This is important, because you can slide into the optimal-modal pitch level easily and then be expressive in the rest of the sentence.

1. The telephone pole is beginning to fall.
2. It has been a long, dreary day.
3. In the closet, you will find the pail.
4. For the sake of the family, try to behave.
5. As you set the table, do it right.
6. In between the acts, we went out for a soda.

Now transfer the same concentration to some of the longer practice selections at the back of the chapter.

FAULTS DUE TO IMPROPER INITIATION OF TONE

As has been stated, nothing should interfere with the free and natural action of the vocal folds because the goal of phonation is that the folds meet easily along their entire length. Undue tension can constrict this free action, leading to a voice that is tense, harsh, or even strident. It may be hoarse, or there may be glottal attack. By contrast, if there is not enough tension to bring the folds together, the voice will sound breathy.

- *Harshness or tenseness*   If the folds are drawn too tightly together during phonation because of muscle constriction in the neck and throat, their free vibration is interfered with, and a hard, metallic, flat edge is heard in the sound. This strained sound may also be due to muscle tension mispositioning the larynx and constricting the free flow of the sound above. If the tension is extreme, resonance may also be affected, and the voice may sound strident, almost screechy, because of the tightened, compressed throat area.
- *Hoarseness*   When something interferes with the folds' meeting along their entire length, the typical raspy, strained sound associated with laryngitis results. Even among voice people, this is often confused with huskiness, but the main difference is that the hoarse voice sounds harsh, whereas the husky voice has a breathier, less strained quality to it.
- *Glottal attack*   Sometimes there is so much inherent tension in the folds that they stay rigid a split second too long on the onset of phonation and then blow apart with an explosive, clicking kind of sound. This harsh attack is particularly noticeable on words beginning with vowels.
- *Breathiness*   The folds have to be brought together with enough tension to remain closed during phonation, and if there is too little tension, the folds do not quite meet as they must, and a whispery, low-pitched voice results as unphonated air escapes.

WARM-UP EXERCISES

Initiating clear tone

1. Since it is very difficult to relax selectively just one part of your body on command, it is much better to start from total relaxation. Thus while you are aiming for the neck and throat muscles, start with total bodily relaxation. Refer to the exercises in Chapter 3, or do any of your own favorites, working toward progressive relaxation.

2. An important goal as you do the following is self-monitoring—*feel* how the neck and throat muscles are when they are tense and when they are relaxed. *Listen* to the difference in sounds produced. *You are aiming for the purest sound possible with the least amount of strain.*

3. *Head drop and head roll*   Once you are generally relaxed, sit or stand, shaking out the shoulders a few times to make sure they, too, are relaxed. With the chin muscles thoroughly relaxed, drop the head forward on the chest a few times, gradually lifting the head back to position. Then, with the head and jaw dropped forward, rotate the head back and forth easily between the shoulders.

4. *Add sighs and ahs*   Keeping the feeling of relaxation you have achieved and with your throat easily open, give yourself up to some deep sighs. Listen for easy voice sound. Change to *ah,* allowing the jaw to fall open on each vocalization.

5. *Yawn technique* Take a deep yawn, letting your jaw drop open and feeling the accompanying opening of the back of the throat on the end of the yawn. Do it a few times and then try to duplicate that easy back opening without actually yawning as you phonate an easy *ah* and try to prolong it, listening for clarity.

6. *Contrast tension and relaxation* Go back over exercises 4 and 5, tensing and saying *ah,* relaxing and saying *ah,* and hearing and feeling the difference.

7. *Adding more sounds* *Oh, ooh,* and *ah* are good vowel sounds for practice for a relaxed throat. Throughout the exercises that follow, good support of tone is basic. Add an *h* before each, easily prolonging the vowels here, and throughout the exercise so you can really *hear* how your voice sounds. First, sing the line, then speak it:

h-o-o-o-o-o-o-h
h-oo-oo-oo-oo-oo-oo
h-ah-ah-ah-ah-ah-ah

Listen, feel, and build into simple words, still prolonging the vowels:

home	who	how
hose	whole	house
homely	hope	hop

Now build these sounds into other words:

moan	nose	go
moon	mound	show
noon	moan	no
now	mole	toe

Now build them into simple phrases, concentrating on the feel and sound of the prolonged vowels:

Go home	Know no one
Know how to go home	How are you?
Hold out hope	Go now, Joe

8. If your are still having difficulty hearing your voice tension-free, especially if you are strident, repeat all of exercise 7 with your head tilted back at a comfortable angle, preferably resting it against a wall. Gravity will help drop the larynx back down into position, and this may help you get an auditory image of what your voice is capable of sounding like when constrictions are reduced.

ADDING ON FOR PROFICIENCY

Initiating clear tone

A. Study this quote from Longfellow:

The ocean old—centuries old,
strong as youth and as uncontrolled.

1. Read the quote aloud, dropping out all the consonants and vocalizing only the vowels, sustaining and listening to each one.

2. When the vowels sound completely pure, repeat, slipping in the consonants very lightly.

3. Finally, read the whole thing normally, but still concentrating on the sound of the vowels.

4. Do the same thing with these lines.

    a. Gold, gold, gold, gold—
       Hard to get and heavy to hold.

    b. Who are you sir, tell me who?
       What's that to you, sir? Who sir? You sir.
       What's that to who, sir? Who, sir? You!

B. *Contrasting tension and relaxation*

1. Each italicized word is to be said with as much tension as possible; the rest are to be tension-free.

    a. *Feed* food to all *people.*
    b. Cold *cream* and smooth *lipstick*
    c. *Free* tuition for all students!
    d. Buy the *cheapest* watch of all.
    e. He stole all the *scenes* in the last act.
    f. The book *seems* to have been stolen.

2. Read through the phrases again, trying to keep every word tension-free.

C. *Controlling tenser vowel sounds*

1. Locate the thyroid notch of the larynx. With your finger firmly on it, say the following pairs of phrases, making sure the larynx does not rise appreciably on the second one in each set.

    a. All aboard. Take your seats.
    b. You are cute. Kiss me quick.
    c. The room is gloomy. Light the lamp.
    d. Don't lose hope. Keep trying.
    e. Abuse the rule—and risk being punished.
    f. Joe's mood is rude. Squeeze him a lemon.
    g. Show us how. But please keep it simple.

2. Speak the same sentences again, raising your volume but keeping the larynx in place.

D. *Simultaneous speaking and self-criticism*   Read the following sets of sentences aloud, concentrating on tension-free, clear vowel sounds. (The second in each set will be more difficult than the first.) If you hear any impurities, continue right on, but mark each spot where you hear them. A tape recorder would be of great help in allowing you to go back and check your judgments.

1. The whole group of students is supposed to know the school song.
   But listen at any assembly; a few sing while the majority stand and look awkward.

2. The coach told the whole group to hold to the rules.
   Even so, three of the team members were given penalties.

3. Most of the courses in college are taught in large lecture halls.
   Seats in the rear seem conducive for sleeping.

4. Homework is something too often done at the last moment.
   This exacts a high price when a sneak quiz is given.

5. The old grads come back once again for reunion.
   It seems they get younger, or at least act younger, with each advancing year.

SUPER EXERCISES

Initiating clear tone

1. Rock groups seem to vie for outrageous names, probably to capture attention so you won't forget them. The Grateful Dead, Dead Milkmen, Strawberry Alarm Clock, Crowded House, Bananarama, and Psychedelic Furs are fairly representative.

   Make up some of your own, mixing and matching the left and right columns. Say them aloud, with a clear, pure sound.

Cool	Vacuum Cleaners
Groaning	Chicken Pickers
Oh-Boy-Oh	Nightmare Screams
Sobbing	Neon Rockets
Open	Parking Tickets
Wired	Cash Registers
Yellow	Deadhead
Sizzling	Fish 'n' Chips
Nuclear	Plates
Rude	Grasshoppers
Gorgeous	Knives
Honking	Cobwebs
Artful	George Washington Bridge

   Now take the role of a radio announcer, broadcasting to the public the 10 groups that will be on campus this year in the mellow, clear voice demanded of such a job.

2. Read the following excerpt from Oliver Goldsmith aloud, but stop the moment you hear any tension creeping into your voice, and start over. Can you get all the way through?

   A mandarin, who took much pride in appearing with a number of jewels on every part of his robe, was once accosted by a sly old bronze [beggar], who, following him through several streets, and bowing often to the ground, thanked him for his jewels. "What does the man mean?" cried the mandarin. "Friend, I never gave you any of my jewels." "No," replied the other; "but you let me look at them, and that is all the use you can make of them yourself; so there is no difference between us, except that you have the trouble of watching them, and that is an employment I don't much desire."

3. Choose one of the following and read it for beauty of vowels and tone.

a. A fool there was and he made his prayer
   (Even as you and I!)
   To a rag and a bone and a hank of hair
   (We called her the woman who did not care)
   But the fool he called her his lady fair—
   (Even as you and I!)
   RUDYARD KIPLING

b. Tread lightly, she is near;
      Under the snow,
   Speak gently, she can hear
      The daisies grow.
   OSCAR WILDE, "Requiescat"

c. Who walks with Beauty has no need of fear;
   The sun and moon and stars keep pace with him;
   Invisible hands restore the ruined year,
   And time, itself, grows beautifully dim.
   DAVID MORTON, "Who Walks with Beauty"

CORRECTING PHONATORY FAULTS

Once a person has become aware of how to support a tone and is working to achieve an open throat and relaxation of all muscles not actively involved in phonation, the voice will probably already sound clearer. However, for many, there is a lifetime habit to undo, and retraining will not happen overnight.

If you still need work on achieving clear tone because of a specific phonatory fault, refer to the appropriate exercises in the balance of this chapter.

Harsh, tense, or strident voice

Listeners, who are also self-appointed judges without realizing it, tend to associate this hard, strained voice with an aggressive, overbearing person, who by definition is always tense, scurrying to get ahead and stay ahead. What an unfortunate judgment, for it has been our experience that this is a fairly common fault in an untrained speaker of any personality type. Without knowledge of how to support a tone or where the power for speech comes from, such a person tenses the muscles in the neck and throat area in the mistaken notion that this will somehow help push the sound out. If the tension is extreme, resonance is affected, and the voice will sound strident.

The first step is understanding what is wrong and then knowing what to do about it. Review the exercises for clear initiation of tone, and as you keep doing them, ask yourself these questions each time;

1. Am I transferring tension where it belongs into the muscles of the stomach?
2. What about my habitual volume?
3. Is my pitch adjusted to a comfortable level—up if I am habitually too low or slightly down if I am too high?

Make haste slowly, as they say. Do not attempt the other exercises until you have achieved a clear tone in the warm-ups. This is particularly critical if your voice has been judged to be strident.

Then, as you start on the more difficult work in the proficiency section, it may help to do each exercise and sentence first with a consciously breathy voice and then trying to carry over some of that relaxed feeling into clear tone on the second trial of each.

Hoarseness

Is there anyone who has not been hoarse for a brief period of time? If so, you are one of the chosen few, endowed with perfect health and absolute emotional control.

When a person has a cold, the vocal folds may also be infected, causing them to swell, or mucus may lodge between the edges, preventing the vocal folds from meeting along their entire length, and the characteristic symptom of this impaired function, hoarseness, appears. Recurrent bouts of allergies can cause the same thing, and certainly most of us have had temporary bouts of laryngitis when we succumbed to shrieking and booing at our team's triumphs and tragedies over the course of a hotly contested game.

But nature heals.

The concern here is chronic hoarseness, with no infectious or transitory cause. What is interfering? Are the folds chronically inflamed from misuse by a person who always pushes from the throat, especially if the person is constantly under tension, using the voice a great deal, perhaps at high volume or an inappropriate pitch level? Is there something wrong with the folds structurally? Is a growth, a node or a polyp, interfering with the alignment of the folds?

If hoarseness is chronic, a laryngologist should be consulted. The folds will be examined with a special mirrored light and the cause of their impaired function seen and diagnosed.

Voice work can be a help to many people with hoarse voices if the cause is diagnosed as the result of continuous misuse. The contributing habits will be identified and minimized or eliminated as the person is retrained to speak more easily and efficiently.

Any substantive work for chronic hoarseness should be undertaken under the direction of a person trained in voice, so we purposely do not suggest exercises here. The goal of such exercises, however, would be similar to what is done for the harsh, tense voice: Every attempt is made to defer tension from the neck and throat area to where it more properly belongs, as pitch is adjusted if need be and a more relaxed initiation of tone is gradually adopted.

Glottal attack

Glottal attack often accompanies the harsh, tense voice, and alleviating the one sometimes helps the other. The hard click of glottal attack is natural when two vowels come together in a word and each is to be pronounced separately. We are re*ac*quainting you with what happens when two vowels co*i*ncide, you re*a*lize. But if this abrupt click is still fairly recurrent in your speech, especially on words beginning with a vowel, the important thing would be to try to get rid of the tension in the folds that is causing it. The suggestions for clear initiation of tone will be very useful in this.

In addition, you may need to work on the specific problem of words beginning with a vowel sound.

WARM-UP EXERCISES

Glottal attack

Think of sliding into each beginning vowel from the open vocal fold position of the *h*:

1. With nonsense words:

hhhocean	ocean	hhhokay	okay
hhhisn't	isn't	hhhact	act
hhhage	age	hhhonly	only
hhhopen	open	hhhever	ever
hhhan	an	hhhoff	off
hhhangle	angle	hhhother	other

2. With real words:

hold	old	harm	arm
hear	ear	heel	eel
hand	and	his	is
hate	ate	hedge	edge
had	add	heat	eat
hi	I	hat	at

3. Go back and say the second word in each pair in exercises 1 and 2 without the help of an *h* word before it, but keep the same sensation of sliding into the word rather than attacking it head on.

4. Try short phrases the same way.

han happle	an apple	hany hothers	any others
honly hours	only ours	haching	aching
		harm	arm
heat hout	eat out	hopen	open
		hended	ended
hancient harmor	ancient armor	hitching high	itching eye
han hegg	an egg	hevery heagle	every eagle

5. Instead of adding an *h* in front of the words in the phrases in exercise 4, try blending the words together by linking the end of one word to the beginning of the next, thus:

an apple

only ours

eat out

ADDING ON FOR PROFICIENCY

Glottal attack

1. As in Warm-up Exercises 4 and 5, first add an *h,* then blend the words together. The first is the model for the others.

   H-is h-Ann h-able?
   Is Ann able?

I eat everything.	I ate a lot.
All are eager.	Eight and eight
All right everybody	Oh all right, Arnold.
Up and about	Out and about
Up and out	It's always easy.

2. Speak all the phrases in exercise 1 without the help of either technique but being careful to slide into each word easily.

3. Here are simple sentences to try. If you hear glottal attack anywhere in them, go back to the techniques in exercise 1 before you try them again.

   a. Arnold and Amy are all ready to elope.
   b. Am I ever going to be able to eat alone?
   c. Around eight of us are in our awful old overalls.
   d. Everyone is awfully angry, it appears.
   e. Itching and aching, I arrived an awful sight.
   f. It is impossible and impractical to oblige everybody.
   g. Innocence is always in our eyes, but not in our minds.
   h. I'm able, available, and eager even if I am not about to arrive on time.

SUPER EXERCISES

Glottal attack

On the first sentence of each of the following paragraphs, purposely use glottal attack. Then start over, seeing if you can get all the way through with no trace of it.

1. Arthur Anderson and Eva Oldfield have just announced their engagement. Every opinion of Arthur's, Eva agrees with. Every action of Eva's, Arthur finds absorbing. Arthur is also always interested in Eva's every account of

her affairs, and Eva always asks Arthur every detail about his work. Each interprets the other's action as adorable, exciting, or even inspired.

Our opinion? *Ugh!*

2. In an old album are pictures that evoke images of events long forgotten: Uncle Adam atop an elephant in an Atlanta adventure park; Aunt Ann in an apron, embarrassed at opening an outrageous Easter outfit; our parents on an excursion in an appropriately old-fashioned Oldsmobile; ourselves on all fours on an April outing, absorbed in extracting ants out of an overturned apple pie—and each and every one evokes explicit memories and emotions.

Breathiness

Just as the harsh, strident voice carries the image of an aggressive, domineering person, the breathy, whispery-sounding voice is associated with the sex symbol. Yet one of the pushiest dragon ladies of our acquaintance has a breathy voice— so much for stereotyping!

Each time they are blown apart, the vocal folds must meet again at midline with enough strength and tension to set up the flutter type of vibration. In the breathy voice, there is not enough tension in the phonating mechanism to bring them quite together throughout vocalization, and thus unphonated air (breath) escapes, producing a fuzzy, low-pitched sound. Health and emotional state can contribute to breathiness, and if problems in either are a possible contributing factor, they should be investigated.

There are two types of breathiness, general and intermittent. The following comments apply to the general type.

1. Usually, increasing volume is a help because, as you already know, the louder the voice, the greater the tension within the folds.
2. Modal pitch should be checked because breathiness is usually accompanied by a low pitch, and a rise in pitch will also increase tension within the folds.
3. Attempts to increase laryngeal tension can be tried, such as speaking while pushing oneself up from a sitting position at a table with one's hands.
4. The exercises for intermittent breathiness will be useful, particularly if you concentrate on a louder, clearer sound throughout.

A far more common type of breathiness among college students is the intermittent kind. Too much breath is allowed to escape whenever a sound is made that uses only air, for example, *h, s, p, t,* or *k.* Air is simply wasted, and the following vowel can sound breathy, too.

Although people do not judge breathiness to be as annoying or grating as other vocal faults, it is nevertheless an inefficient way of speaking and for this reason alone should be attended to.

WARM-UP EXERCISES

Intermittent breathiness

1. Start with negative practice. Waste a whole breath on the word *hope,* noting how the *o* sounded breathy as well. Do the same with the following words.

hear	holy	hover	ham
hum	high	heat	handle
heavy	house	hose	hip

2. Be aware of spending air wisely. Go through the list in exercise 1, conserving the breath stream, and see how many times you can get through the list of words on one breath.

3. Pronounce each column of words wastefully, as you did in exercise 1; then pronounce each column economically as many times as possible, as you did in exercise 2.

sell	pots	tire	cat	shoes	fish	thanks
save	pans	time	couple	shape	feather	thumb
city	potatoes	tiptoe	company	sheet	five	three
century	pickles	tame	cash	shower	force	thousand
sight	peace	tease	cards	shove	firecracker	thunder

4. Pronounce these phrases wastefully, then economically.

a piece of apple pie	forty-four firefighters
porcupine quills	tiptoe through the tulips
cooking pots and pans	cold, hard company cash
pepper and salt	a feathered shower curtain
powerhouse force	powerful popping firecrackers

ADDING ON FOR PROFICIENCY

Intermittent breathiness

Read each set of simple sentences, being deliberately breathy in the first, considerably raising your volume on the second, and concentrating on a clear, unfuzzy tone at an appropriate volume on the third.

1. Pat put a firecracker in the can.
   The can exploded with a horrible clatter.
   Pat's parents put Pat in his room until supper.

2. Phil caught four sunfish.
   Sally caught two and a bad cold.
   On Sunday, Phil went fishing by himself.

3. Company came and so Thelma put the cat out.
   The cat slipped back into the kitchen and sampled the fish soufflé.
   The company complimented Thelma on her tasty supper.

4. A shower suddenly started and Paul was unprotected.
   He pulled a newspaper from the trash can and put it over his head.
   Too bad—he couldn't see, and fell into a huge puddle.

5. "Pat, this potato salad tastes blah," Sam said.
   She put in some pepper, some parsley, and a whole cup of celery.
   But only when she added two jars of pickles did Sam say, "Perfect."

6. The couples were playing canasta.
   "Someone cheated," cried Ted. "Someone peeked at my cards."
   "How do you know?" said his friends. "You were too busy peeking at ours."

SUPER EXERCISES

Intermittent breathiness

1. Here certain old tongue twisters will be useful. Work for accuracy, not speed. Your goal is to conserve breath and have a clear, strong voice sound throughout. A gauge of how well you are avoiding intermittent breathiness will be if you can get through each one at least two, if not three times.

   a. Peter Piper picked a peck of pickled peppers.
   b. Theopholis Thistle, the successful thistle sifter.
   c. She sells seashells by the seashore.
   d. Five flounders funnily flip flat feet.
   e. "Clip Clop" Kip clipped and clopped in clogs.
   f. The sixth sheik's six sick sheep.
   g. A too tricky toad tried to tow two toads to and fro.
   h. Stray cats, stay mats, stage cats, stage mats.
   i. Bat boy, boot boy, fat boy, foot boy, hat boy, coat boy.
   j. What a to-do to die today at a minute or two to two.

2. Choose one of the following to read aloud, demonstrating use of a clear, strong voice sound throughout.

   a. Professor Blacke of Edinburgh, being indisposed one day, caused to be posted on the door of his lecture room the following notice: "Professor Blacke will not meet his classes today."

      A student who was a bit of a wag erased the "c" in "classes." The Professor, hearing of it sent a messenger with instructions to erase the "l."

      "What's in a Letter?" *Modern Eloquence,* vol. 12

   b. "Papa is a preferable mode of address," observed Mrs. General. "Father is rather vulgar, my dear. The word papa, besides, gives a rather pretty form to the lips. Papa, potatoes, poultry, prunes, and prism are all very good words for the lips; especially prunes and prism. You will find it serviceable, in the formation of a demeanor, if you sometimes say to yourself in company—on entering a room, for instance—"Papa, potatoes, poultry, prunes and prism, prunes and prism."

      CHARLES DICKENS, *Little Dorrit*

   c. For rhetoric he could not ope
      His mouth, but out there flew a trope:
      And when he happened to break it off
      I' th' middle of his speech or cough
      H' had hard words, ready to show why
      And tell what rules he did it by.

      SAMUEL BUTLER, "The Pedant"

Glottal fry

As mentioned in Chapter 4, glottal fry is a fault resulting from too little air pressure in an individual's volume of air on exhalation or from using too low a pitch range, causing a popping or raspy sound, particularly toward the ends of phrases. The effect is a voice that lacks energy and is dull to listen to. If you still have a problem with glottal fry despite work on support of tone, the following exercises will be helpful—but first be sure to rev up your energy level.

WARM-UP EXERCISES

Glottal fry

1. Say each of the following words as if you were giving a command.

Eat!	Run!	Chew!	Fetch!
Jump!	Hurry!	Leap!	Attention!
Sit!	Stand!	Down!	Ready!

2. *Pitch awareness*   Start each of these words so low in your pitch range you hear the popping rumble of glottal fry, inflecting the pitch upward as you prolong the vowel until the sound is clear. Hold the clear vowel sound for at least a count of 3.

own	am	ease	how	can
open	ooze	each	has	hold
owl	off	eat	boot	hear
ask	home	it	beet	boat

3. Repeat the following phrases using appropriate inflection for meaning.

I *care!*	Liven *up!*
Please *stay!*	Use *energy!*
Catch *me!*	Be *quick!*
Watch *out!*	Shape *up!*
Get *down!*	Keep *fit!*
Don't *go!*	For crying out *loud!*

ADDING ON FOR PROFICIENCY

Glottal fry

1. Say the following phrases aloud energetically. Read with inflection appropriate to meaning using adequate breath support and a pitch rise on the final word.

   a. Give me a break!
   b. Will you leave me alone!
   c. Be quiet down there, will you!
   d. I'll buy a hundred shares!
   e. I saw that bargain first!
   f. Let's party all night long!

    g. Can you believe it!

    h. Oh how I love pizza!

    i. I found somebody's wallet!

    j. What a terrific new car!

    k. This is the last day of classes!

    l. I'm going to sun and swim all summer!

2. Read the following pairs of sentences aloud, maintaining the same high energy level and clear sound throughout.

    a. My friend thought I was being lazy.
       To tell the truth, she was right!

    b. Try turning up the amplification—I can't hear.
       Ouch! Now it's so loud I can't *hear!*

    c. Whom did I see you with at the Rathskeller last night?
       Last night? Nobody. That was just my sister.

    d. I love my new set of wheels, but I've got a problem—
       I can't keep up the car payments.

    e. I took the English poetry course pass-fail.
       Now I wish I hadn't. I'm doing really *well.*

    f. Exercises can make me feel great.
       It's getting myself to do them that is the problem.

SUPER EXERCISES

Glottal fry

Choose one of the following selections to read aloud, maintaining energy and enthusiasm as you monitor to be sure that the tone is always clear:

1. We should be careful to get out of an experience only the wisdom that is in it—and stop there; lest we be like the cat that sits down on a hot stove lid. She will never sit down on a hot stove lid again—and that is well; but also she will never sit down on a cold one any more.

    MARK TWAIN, *Pudd'nhead Wilson's New Calendar*

2. It is perfectly monstrous the way people go about nowadays saying things against one, behind one's back, that are absolutely true.

    OSCAR WILDE

3. Until he starts to sell, a writer is a bum to his family, a lazy lout to his friends, and a self-deluding parasite to his neighbors. When he becomes known he is "one helluva neighbor" to his neighbors, a genius to his friends, and a favorite cousin to his family. But none of them buy his books.

    CLIFFORD WELLES

4. May the road rise to meet you,
   May the wind be always at your back,

May the sun shine warm upon your face
And the rains fall soft upon your fields,
And, until we meet again,
May God hold you in the palm of his hand.
GAELIC PRAYER

CHECKPOINT EXERCISES

A. *Demonstrating relaxation of throat and laryngeal muscles*   Feel the larynx as you gradually build volume on the following commands:

Get out! Stand back! Watch out! Down in front!
It should not rise appreciably.

B. *Demonstrating adequate pitch control*   Read the following aloud, making sure you do not have an abnormally high or low pitch.

He had the kind of face that, once seen, is never remembered.
OSCAR WILDE

C. *Demonstrating initiation of clear tone*   Concentrating on the vowels, read and record the following, keeping clear tone throughout.

Four things come not back:
The spoken word; the sped arrow,
Time past; the neglected opportunity.
OMAR IBN AL-HALIF, "Aphorism"

D. *Demonstrating freedom from phonatory faults*   If you have been working on harsh or tense speech, breathiness, glottal attack, or glottal fry, consciously reproduce the fault on the following sentence, then demonstrate complete absence of that fault in the second selection.

1. Guess what! I almost won the lottery!

2. Times grew worse with Rip Van Winkle as years of matrimony rolled on; a tart temper never mellows with age, and a sharp tongue is the only edged tool that grows keener with constant use.
WASHINGTON IRVING, "Rip Van Winkle"

E. *Putting it all together*   Take on the role of a disk jockey broadcasting to the public that the rock groups Wired Deadheads and the Sobbing Cash Registers will be on campus at a certain time and date, using your best announcer's voice. You may wish to make up names for some of the band members and tell what they do. Your job is to sell the concerts to the campus.

6

RESONATION: IMPROVING QUALITY

There is a weird power in a spoken word. . . .
And a word carries far—very far.

JOSEPH CONRAD

Challenge exercise   You are punching buttons on your car radio, trying to find just the right station to listen to.

(Gravelly voiced boxer on an interview show) . . . Yeah, so I took, duh lef' to my cheek and duh right to my dose, and den duh ubpire, he . . . *CLICK*

(BBC announcer) . . . and this afternoon's concert at the Royal Albert Hall will have as guest conductor Sir Christopher Tittingale in an all . . . *CLICK*

(Whiny voice on a call-in show) . . . and doctah, I did everything for my boyfriend; I bought my own engagement ring, I didn't complain, doctah, I paid up his cah insurance, I didn't . . . *CLICK*

(Cavernous, hollow voice on a newscast) . . . and reporting live from two thousand feet under water may be distorting the clarity of the reception for those . . . *CLICK*

(High-pitched child's voice in a commercial) . . . Wowee! Yippee! A genuine talking, walking, burping doll in her very own telephone booth! And Mommy bought her just for . . . *CLICK*

(Syrupy-voiced storyteller) . . . and then, boys and girls, Aunt Harriet Crocodile did just the loveliest thing: She smiled so her seventy-nine pearly, pointed teeth . . . *CLICK*

(Back to the BBC) . . . And the audience has risen as the queen and members of the royal family enter the flag-draped center box. It would seem that Prince William is not at all pleased with . . . *CLICK* and OFF.

Now for the challenge: Can you do all the voices yourself, pausing no longer than the time the radio push-button *CLICK* would take between them?

Several schools of voice feel that experimenting with a variety of voice qualities is the first step in improving one's own vocal quality. If you were able to meet the challenge, you have taken that important first step.

Two things determine voice quality: the initiation of the original tone at the vocal folds and then, critically, what happens to that tone in the resonating cavities, principally those of the throat, mouth, and nose, through the process of selection, reinforcement, and enrichment.

Whether you were aware of it or not, you achieved the different voice qualities in the Challenge Exercise by altering those resonance cavities. By tightening and constricting the throat you adopt a shrill, strained tone; by letting the sound ride back in your mouth toward your tonsils you produce a muffled, cavernous quality; and by tensing and spreading the mouth and constricting it in back, air escapes into your nose and you sound whiny and nasal.

So, too, if you keep an open, relaxed throat and direct the sound purposely forward toward the front of your easily open mouth, you sound more like a professional speaker. Note that we say "more like, not exactly like." The structure and size of everyone's mouth, throat, and nose vary slightly, so no two people will sound exactly alike, ever. The goal of work on resonation is not to change your voice; it is simply to amplify what is already there that is pleasing and cancel out what is not.

GOALS FOR WORK ON RESONATION

If tone is supported and easily initiated, you should be well on your way to a pleasing voice quality. Your primary efforts in this chapter should center on the following:

1. To put in context what you already know about resonation
2. To recognize the faults that can result from misuse of the resonating cavities.[1]
3. To understand how to achieve improved oral resonance and to go step by step through exercises designed to help achieve this. These will include workouts for increased flexibility of the articulators, an easily open mouth, and forward focus and projection. Again you will work to build self-awareness so that you can monitor yourself.
4. To practice materials of increasing complexity using good oral resonance
5. To understand how to achieve good nasal resonance and go through the same progression in exercise material that you did for oral resonance
6. To apply what you have learned so far to increasing loudness should the occasion demand without incurring vocal strain or poor quality
7. To demonstrate control of vocal quality through successful completion of the final Checkpoint Exercises.

A CLOSER LOOK AT RESONATION

• The vocal folds produce a great number of simultaneous vibrations, and it is the function of resonating cavities to *resonate* ("sound again") *very selectively* only certain ones. Think of the tuning dial on your stereo receiver, which focuses on only a small number of all the radio waves out there in the atmosphere.

---

[1] Readers who need more directed work for specific resonance faults will find suggestions and additional exercises later in this chapter.

• The larger the cavity, the more its opening is elongated, and the less dense (less tense) its walls, the more the richer, deeper mellow sounds will be amplified. These are pleasing as underpinnings to a tone. In fact, the work in Chapter 5 that centered on keeping an easily open throat for the free passage of tone up and out should have already improved your pharyngeal resonance, and you will be doing more of this in the exercises for the easily open throat-mouth speech "megaphone" that are included in this chapter.

larger the size	deeper and mellower the sound
more elongated the opening	deeper and mellower the sound
more relaxed the walls	deeper and mellower the sound

• All three resonating cavities do not work equally at the same time. For most sounds the vocal tract consists of a long tube formed by the throat and mouth coupled in various ways in conjunction with the action of the tongue, with the nasal passages pretty much bypassed through the action of the soft palate. On *m, n,* and *ng* sounds, however, the soft palate is lowered, the oral cavity is blocked off, and the throat and nose become connected resonating tubes.

Since pharyngeal resonance has already been covered, we will concentrate in this chapter on improving oral and nasal resonance. This will include work on forward focus and projection, and making yourself easily heard (increasing loudness) as the demands of a situation warrant. For anyone who still needs help with specific faults, attention will be given later in the chapter.

FAULTS DUE TO IMPROPER RESONATION

• *Nasality.* If air is allowed to escape up into the nose on sounds other than *m, n,* and *ng,* either because the action of the soft palate is poor or because the mouth is kept too compressed and there is not an open, easy passage out, a whiny, annoying sound results.
• *Denasality.* If for some reason the vibrating air is not directed straight through the nose on the *m, n,* and *ng* sounds, a dull, cold-in-the-head quality results. Of course a cold or allergies can give you a stuffy sound, but adenoids, a deviated septum, or a broken nose can also block the nasal passages. Sometimes, too, it is simply a matter of directing the sound with enough energy.
• *Throatiness.* The cavernous, hollow sound made by a mummy in a horror movie is an exaggeration of the fairly common tendency speakers have for retracting the tongue and producing all sound farther back in the mouth than necessary, resulting in a dull, dark quality. Such speaking lacks the clarity and brilliance of a properly focused sound, although its generally low pitch may promote a macho image for some men.
• *Thinness.* The opposite of the throaty voice is the thin voice in which the tongue is positioned too far forward for all sounds, and thus the final small cavity reinforces a rather high-pitched sound, which to the speaker may suggest femininity but to the listener may connote childishness or immaturity.
• *Stridency.* The greater the tension in a person with a harsh, tense voice, the greater the tendency toward stridency. Undue tension pulls the larynx up into

the throat cavity, reducing its size and tensing its walls, among other negative things, thus creating a resonance condition that amplifies the high, inharmonic partials. This fault was considered in the exercises for the harsh, tense voice, so no further reference to it will be made in this chapter.

So far we have talked about the domino effect, whereby one thing sets off a chain reaction among seemingly unconnected things, in a negative way: Tension radiates, causing any number of vocal faults. This time, however, we wish to mention the domino effect in a very positive way: The resonance faults just listed were purposely prefaced by the statement that work would be provided later in the chapter "for anyone who still needs help."

The cavities of the resonance system do not work independently; their functions are coordinated and integrated to a degree, and a change in what occurs in one may affect the others. Thus in the process of working for improved oral resonance with an open oral cavity and relaxed lower jaw, nasality should be improved, for example, and working on forward focus should help minimize the fault of throatiness.

Since, as you will see, having flexible articulators is one of the requisites of good oral resonance, the directed exercises in this chapter should also make your overall articulation pattern sharper and clearer.

WORKING TO IMPROVE ORAL RESONANCE

Because of its variability in shape and size and its relationship to the other two resonating cavities, the mouth is not only the most flexible but also the most important of the cavities. Its function in resonance is to round out and build up the tone, and it is the chief outlet for sounds. But do not think of it in isolation; rather, think of it as the extension of the open tube started in the easily open throat. To achieve good oral resonance, remember these three points:

1. You should concentrate on projecting the tone to the front of the mouth.
2. Like the throat, the mouth should be easily open, selectively relaxed, and free of unnecessary tension.
3. The mouth, the lips, the jaw, and the tongue should be highly flexible and agile.

Each point will be considered separately in the Warm-up Exercises and then put together in the Adding On and Super Exercises. However, some comments are in order here on focus and projection.

All too often an untrained speaker makes one or both of these mistakes: allowing the sound to ride back in the mouth or tending to keep the teeth clenched, putting a barrier in the way of the clear tone. Players of wind instruments can intentionally create a temporary muffled effect by inserting something into the opening of their instruments. But speakers who commit the mistakes just mentioned create an unintentional muffled effect every time they speak. They must be taught to *project*.

Voice coaches and singing teachers variously exhort students on projection: "Focus your voice onto a pencil held eighteen inches from your mouth." "Project your voice to the farthest person in the room." "Think of each phrase as a ball that you are lightly tossing, projecting, to a basket on the wall." Plainly the voice cannot literally be projected out of the mouth in such a finite manner. Yet the images often help.

Focus and projection images may help you, too. They may make you open your mouth more widely than usual, and they may make you more conscious of using the front part of your mouth. As you do the exercises that follow, concentrate on these points, or if you are more practically minded, turn your energies to directing the tone forward against the front of your palate or the back of your top teeth. When you speak, the aim is always for *ease and naturalness*. However, in the warm-ups that follow, you will be asked to exaggerate certain jaw and articulatory movements. There are several reasons for this. The first is for feedback: to become aware of the *feel* of unexplored muscle potential and to *hear* the clarity of an unobstructed forward tone. Second, just as the baseball player practices with double weights on his bat, the intensified muscle effort will help build general muscle tone for when you do speak naturally.

WARM-UP EXERCISES

Oral resonance

Throughout, the throat and the back of the mouth should be free from strain. Support and easy initiation of tone are needed.

Start with general progressive relaxation exercises. Use those suggested in earlier chapters or ones of your own choosing; then move into the following exercises.

A. *Flexibility of tongue, lips, and jaw*

1. Clear movements of the articulators are essential if the tone is to reach the listener in all its beauty, crispness, and distinctness. Almost as if you were modeling clay, form a very clear *ah,* then *oo,* then *ee.* Notice the differences: the jaw dropping for the *ah,* the elongated pursed lips on the *oo,* the wide smiling motion on the *ee.* Repeat several times, being very aware of the different movements.

2. Do the same thing, adding to the wide lip movements of a *w* before each. Repeat 6 times with the same exaggeration:

   wah, woo, wee

3. Feel the tongue rise to make a firm contact with the alveolar ridge (gum ridge behind the upper front teeth) on *l.* Repeat 6 times:

   lah, loo, lee

4. Feel the lips make light but complete contact on *p.* With same exaggeration say 6 times:

   pah, poo, pee

5. Say the lines in succession, picking up speed if you can but never sac-

rificing the accuracy and feel of the exaggerated muscle movements and contacts. Repeat over and over:

wah, woo, wee
lah, loo, lee
pah, poo, pee

6. Count very slowly up to 8, exaggerating every articulatory movement and concentrating on the sound. Imagine that you are programming a robot so every movement must be very deliberate and clear.

7. In a mirror, say the following word pairs, noting the changes in lip and jaw position:

too	bake	far	cry
hot	food	fat	seat
neat	sight	lumpy	goo
coffee	break	pit	stop
no	way	so	please

8. "How now brown cow . . ."   The old-time elocution teachers have gone the way of the dodo, but this old standby of theirs is still an excellent exercise if done with complete exaggeration. Notice how in the first part of each diphthong (two vowels coming together without a break in between) the jaw moves from an open position into a lip-pursed position with no break in the vowel sound:

Haaaaaaoooooo   naaaaaaoooooo . . .

9. Keep the same exaggeration in the following phrases, also noting carefully articulatory contacts.

a town mouse	down and out
a town house	brown out
a town louse	sound out
a town souse	drown out
a town spouse	found out

10. *Negative contrast*   Say the following sentence, first with very little lip and jaw movement, then with exaggerated movement, and the third time trying to use the contacts and muscles in a normal fashion.

We shall fight on the beaches, we shall fight on the landing grounds. . . . We shall never surrender.

B. *Keeping mouth and throat easily open and free of unnecessary tension*   You are now more aware of the need for movement of the tongue, lips, and jaw and accuracy of shaping and contacts.

1. *Contrast tension and relaxation*   Tense your whole jaw and throat as if to swallow, intoning *ah*. Now relax the whole back as if for a yawn, drop the jaw, and do the same sound. Go back and forth. You should *feel* and *hear* a large difference.

2. Tense, bunch your tongue toward the back of the mouth, and intone *ah.* Relax, drop the jaw easily, keep the back of the tongue down and the top behind your front teeth, and intone again, noting the differences.

3. Keeping the back of the tongue easily down with no undue tension, think of a megaphone formed by your easily open throat and mouth. Concentrating on purity of tone, say *ahmmm* 5 times, holding both sounds for at least a count of 3. Do the same with *oo,* then *oomm,* then *moon.* Intone *ho,* thinking of shaping the tone into the rounded vowel. Do the same with *who* and *home.*

4. To exaggerate mouth opening, drop the jaw down toward your chest, saying *ah.* Can you hold two fingers sideways between the cutting edges of your front teeth? With an open throat and relaxed lower jaw, repeat the following 3 times each:

   mah, bah, fah, lah, yah, nah

5. Do the same thing, checking with the two fingers on the first sound of each of these words. (Be careful not to force the opening, but have the image in mind.)

opera	are	almond
ox	alms	ark
oxen	argue	Arthur
olive	army	

6. Keeping the open-tube megaphone in mind, say the following phrases, dropping the jaw on the italicized sounds as much as you can without forcing.

d*a*rk h*a*rbor	r*o*b a p*o*cket
an al*a*rmed gu*a*rd	g*o*t a b*a*rgain
sm*a*rt p*a*rtner	st*a*rt to *a*rgue
h*a*rmful c*a*rgo	qu*a*lify to p*a*rk

7. *Negative contrast*   If a tape recorder is available, record and listen to the difference. Say the following sentence the way you normally would. Then say it with as much constriction of the throat and mouth as possible, and the third time with the open-tube megaphone and easily dropped jaw on the vowel sounds.

   Arthur ought to stop arguing with his partner.

8. The jaw opening may not be as simple on the following titles, but open as much as you can on each vowel.

The Wayward Bus	*The Razor's Edge*
The Grapes of Wrath	*Look Back in Anger*
Gone with the Wind	*Raisin in the Sun*
Look Homeward, Angel	*The Last Days of Pompeii*
Catcher in the Rye	*The Old Man and the Sea*

C. *Forward focus and projection*   Now that you are aware of the need for flexibility and the open-tube megaphone, concentrate on projecting the tone forward with clear movements of the articulators.

1. *Arriving at forward focus*   Hum *nnn* for a count of 3, noting how your tongue nestles up just behind your upper front teeth. Repeat several times. Then on a count of 2, intone *nnn* and gradually drop the jaw into *ah* for the second count of 2. Alternate back and forth, *ah-nnn-ah-nnn-ah,* being very aware of where your tongue tip is just as it is about to slide from *nnn* to *ah.* Keeping that as a point for concentration, slowly intone the following words 3 times.

not	near	knack
note	knee	need
neat	night	know

2. Keep your focus right here. Say the following words, concentrating on the articulatory contacts up front.

eat	see	feet	pet
heat	seat	fit	pen
team	beat	pit	pat

3. Prolong *ah,* then *ee.* Note how much farther to the front *ee* is produced. Without tensing, try to move the sound in the second word in each pair up closer to the first.

ear	are	seen	soon
beet	bar	fix	fox
feet	far	fill	fall
get	goat	tan	tone
heat	hope	been	bone

4. If the focus is up front, your whole sound has more clarity and precision. With focus on the back of your upper teeth or gum ridge and with articulatory precision, say the following:

light and delicate	petty person
a little too tense	pretty person
twice-told tales	a tight little spot
tip to toe	bright white light

   and this nonsense phrase:

   little, bottle, bat-a-pit

5. In these triplets, the first phrase will be easier to keep up front than the following two, but try to maintain the same clarity and firmness throughout all three.

   a. tea and green beans, oatmeal and raisins, corn on the cob
   b. a despicable scene, an old garden, a gloomy day
   c. clean the street, mop the floor, dust the house

    d. see TV, go to the movies, take in a concert

    e. sleep and dream, walk and look, climb and turn

6. *Negative contrasts*   Listen and feel the difference as you say each sentence first back toward your tonsils and then up front where the focus is.

    a. I don't eat meat very often.

    b. It is hard to settle down to study.

    c. I wish I were anywhere but here.

ADDING ON FOR PROFICIENCY

Oral resonance

1. The British are known for their precision of articulation. We do not suggest that you in any way adopt a British accent, but these exercises from a British manual for speech improvement are excellent for increasing agility of the articulators and thus promoting energetic forward focus and projection of tone.

    a. Two toads totally tired of trying to trot to Tetbury

    b. Lots of hot coffee in a proper coffeepot

    c. Pimlico, Pamlico, pumpkin, and peas,
       Pepper them properly else you will sneeze;
       Pop in a pipkin and leave them 'til one,
       Pimlico, Pamlico, then they'll be done.

    d. If to hoot and to toot, a Hottentot tot
       Were taught by a Hottentot tutor,
       Should the tutor get hot, if the Hottentot tot
       Should hoot and toot at the tutor?

    e. Say each 3 times:

       international intermonetary fund
       interplanetary auditory discrimination

2. With the same focus and flexibility and open throat, concentrate on shaping each sound as you read at a slow rate so you can really listen.

    a. *There was*—and O! how many sorrows crowd
       Into those two brief words!
         WALTER SCOTT

    b. Gold! Gold! Gold! Gold!
       Bright and yellow, hard and cold,
       Molten, graven, hammered and rolled;
       Hard to get and heavy to hold;
       Hoarded, bartered, bought and sold,
       Stolen, borrowed, squandered, doled:
       Spurned by the young, but hugged by the old
       To the very edge of the churchyard mold.
       Gold! Gold! Gold! Gold!
         THOMAS HOOD

3. Feel and hear the relaxation of the open-tube megaphone as you form, rather than just say, the sentences in these pairs. Try to keep the second as far front as the first.

   a. We each picked flowers in the public park.
      Did we know we shouldn't? Of course. But we did it anyway.
   b. Many people say that seeing is believing.
      But Joe is from Missouri. He doesn't believe even what he's shown.
   c. His greed exceeded his need and his reach.
      Too bad. Now his home has iron bars.
   d. To feel really tip-top you need to exercise.
      But your old bones don't always agree.
   e. We seem to have reached a dead end.
      Don't tell us. We know. We should begin all over.
   f. It seems that vacation will never begin.
      Now that it's come, it's as though it would never end.
   g. Please put out the cat.
      How can I? He's already outside.
   h. A stitch in time, they say, saves nine.
      But who likes to sew?

SUPER EXERCISES

Oral resonance

1. To demonstrate energetic forward focus, say the following sets of words with your back turned so that a listener can clearly distinguish them. Keep the throat relaxed.

   a. cents, thence, tense, hence
   b. bought, brought, bossed, tossed
   c. froth, fought, frost, fraught
   d. wise, wives, wife's, white
   e. buffs, bus, buts, busts
   f. griefs, grease, greets, greased
   g. lease, least, leaf, leaves
   h. lifts, lists, Liz, lives
   i. mouse, mouth, mouths, mound
   j. dose, doze, dotes, don'ts

2. *Definitions of nonsense words*   Pronounce each word. Then make up a definition for it and use it in a sentence. Throughout, keep the open-tube megaphone and clear forward focus.
   Example: tittlebot. You might decide that a tittlebot is a kind of salamander, so you define it that way. Then your sentence might be, "I turned over the stone and there was a nest of tittlebots." Or it might be, "Certain tribes consider tittlebots a delicacy."

petteet	littabit	pleek
papatit	betbeet	beelee

teetertet   manana   eeneen
fafata   leeleet   ipple

3. Gilbert and Sullivan are known for their patter songs. Every word must have good oral resonance and forward focus, or a listener would lose some of the meaning, because the words are meant to be delivered at a rapid rate. However, do not sacrifice precision and fronting for rate. Choose one:

a. Here's a first-rate opportunity
To get married with impunity,
To indulge in the felicity
Of unbounded domesticity.
You shall quickly be personified,
Conjugally matrimonified,
By a doctor of divinity
Who resides in this vicinity.

b. And I'm a peppery kind of a king
Who's indisposed to parleying;
To fit my wit to a bit of a chit—
And that's the long and the short of it.

c. A magnet hung in a hand-worn shop,
All around was a loving crop
Of scissors and needles, nails and knives,
Offering love for all their lives;
But for iron the magnet holds no whim—
Though he charmed the iron, it charmed not him.
From needles and knives and nails he'd turn,
For he'd set his love on a silver urn.

4. Put it all together in reading these opening lines of Dickens's *Tale of Two Cities.* But first, take a tip from a London acting school: To get the focus and the precision, mouth the first several lines with no sound, just concentrating on the enjoyment of the tactile sense of where each contact is made. If you really concentrate, it works!

It was the best of times, it was the worst of times, it was the age of wisdom, it was the age of foolishness, . . . it was the season of Light, it was the season of Darkness, it was the spring of hope, it was the winter of despair, we have everything before us, we had nothing before us, we were all going direct to Heaven, we were all going direct the other way. . . .

WORKING TO IMPROVE NASAL RESONANCE

On three sounds, *m, n,* and *ng,* the soft palate is lowered, the oral cavity is blocked off, and the sound is purposely reinforced in the nasal cavities, although in many people's speech there may be some slight nasal reinforcement on all sounds. To feel how the oral cavity is blocked variously on these three sounds, hum *m* and notice that that oral cavity is blocked off only at its exit by the lips. For *n* it is blocked with the tongue raised behind the upper front teeth, and for *ng* it is blocked by the back of the tongue in contact with the soft palate. The differences in sound in these three consonants is due to these modifications in the oral chamber, because for all three the vibrating air is energetically directed through the nasal passages.

If full nasal resonance exists on just three sounds, why bother to set aside space to specifically work on this kind of resonance? Because such resonance makes for fullness and beauty of tone as well as carrying power.

WARM-UP EXERCISES

Nasal resonance

1. Hum *m* up and down the scale until you can feel tingling in your lips and vibrations in the upper part of your face.

2. Feel the vibrations as you do the same thing with *n* and *ng*.

3. Stay very aware of the vibrations as you say the following nonsense syllables, prolonging the nasal sounds.
   a. ahmm-ahmmm-ahmmmmah-ahmmmah-ahmmmahmmm-ahmmmmahmmm
   b. eennn-eennn-eeennneee-eeennnneee-eeeennneennn-eenneennn
   c. ahng-ahng-ahngah-ahngah-ahngahng-ahngahng

4. If a person does not have enough nasal resonance (see the discussion of denasality), *m* will sound rather like *b*, as in *bay* for *may*; *n* will resemble *d*, as in *dose* for *nose*; and *ng* will sound like *g*, as in *sig* for *sing*. To contrast lack of nasal resonance compared to its presence, slightly prolong the nasal sound in the second word of each pair and listen for the difference.

bat, mat	dough, no	bag, bang
bowl, mole	dip, nip	rag, rang
bee, me	Dee, knee	rig, ring
by, my	deck, neck	sag, sang
boat, moat	deal, kneel	hug, hung
bay, may	day, nay	tag, tang

5. Prolong the nasal sounds in the following words, first in an exaggerated fashion and then just so they can really be heard.

running	comfort	remembering
coming	welcoming	clanging
maybe	turning	numbering
never	spinning	encumbering
tongue	dreaming	numbing

ADDING ON FOR PROFICIENCY

Nasal resonance

1. Since the nasal sounds add beauty and carrying power to your speech, you want to sustain them slightly longer as you speak, particularly as they come toward the end of a syllable, so that the flow of a word will not be interrupted.

Notice the musical quality you will adopt by doing this. We purposely exaggerate the first for you:

gleaming moon: gleammmminnnng moonnnn

on wings of song	angry ocean
moaning wind	calling soon
streaming sand	thundering storm
murmuring stream	welcoming arms

2. *Contrast exercise* On these, purposely have little nasal resonance the first time you read each sentence; the second time through use good nasal resonance and sustain each nasal sound slightly.

   a. I am not going to come home again.
   b. The wind is howling and the night will be long.
   c. I seem to be always coming or going.
   d. To err is human; to forgive, divine.
   e. November brings the end of autumn.
   f. Again and again he watched the strange scene.
   g. Morning is the time for watering the garden.
   h. Moaning and groaning, he complained once again.
   i. The woman and the man were arguing for the umpteenth time.
   j. Nearly everyone envies an eminent person's mind.

3. Read the following quotes, using good nasal resonance.

   a. The time to stop a revolution is at the beginning, not the end.
      ADLAI STEVENSON

   b. I kissed my first woman and smoked my first cigarette on the same day. I have never had time for tobacco since.
      ARTURO TOSCANINI

   c. If a man fools me once, shame on him. If the same man fools me twice, shame on me.
      ASIAN PROVERB

   d. An asylum for the insane would be empty in America.
      GEORGE BERNARD SHAW

   e. One should always get even in some way, else the sore place will go on hurting.
      MARK TWAIN

SUPER EXERCISES

Nasal resonance

1. *Using nasal resonance* To get you used to capitalizing on nasal sounds in your conversational speech, formulate a sentence for each of these phrases and say it aloud.

changing scene	main plan
moving reading	hidden meaning
strange plan	plain cotton
human emotion	simple definition
again and again	fine example
open-ended	wrong turning

2. Choose one of the following to interpret with full nasal resonance.

a. The cataract strong
    Then plunges along
    Striking and raging
    As if a war waging
    Its caverns and rocks among;
    Rising and leaping,
    Sinking and creeping,
    Swelling and sweeping,
    Showering and springing,
    Flying and flinging,
    Writhing and ringing,
    Eddying and whisking,
    Spouting and frisking,
    Turning and twisting,
    Around and around
    With endless rebound.
      ROBERT SOUTHEY, "The Cataract of Lodore"

b. Once upon a midnight dreary, while I pondered weak and weary,
    Over many a quaint and curious volume of forgotten lore;
    While I nodded, nearly napping, suddenly there came a tapping,
    As of someone gently rapping, rapping at my chamber door.
    " 'Tis some visitor," I muttered, "tapping at my chamber door—
        Only this and nothing more."
      EDGAR ALLAN POE, "The Raven"

c. When, in the course of human events, it becomes necessary for one people
to dissolve the political bands which have connected them with one another, and to assume among the powers of the earth the separate and equal
station to which the Laws of Nature and of Nature's God entitles them,
a decent respect to the opinions of mankind requires that they should
declare the causes which impel them to the separation.
      THOMAS JEFFERSON

d. We are the music-makers,
      And we are the dreamers of dreams,
    Wandering by lone sea-breakers,
      And sitting by desolate streams;

    World-losers and world-forsakers,
      On whom the pale moon gleams:

Yet we are the movers and shakers
Of the world for ever, it seems.
ARTHUR O'SHAUGHNESSY, "Ode"

MAKING YOURSELF HEARD: INCREASING LOUDNESS

It is only at this point in the text that such a topic belongs. Of course we all can and do increase loudness with no training. "Look out!" we shriek. "Watch it!" "No! *No!*" "Look behind you! *Look!*" And by the time we finish, our throat feels offended and our voice has a high grate to it. But we have certainly increased our loudness.

Most people have adequate volume for daily interchanges with their family and friends. Some, for psychological, health, or cultural reasons, may speak so softly that they are constantly being admonished to speak up, and such causes should be explored. Most people, however, manage, until they suddenly find themselves in a situation where their voice really needs to carry.

The reason that such a discussion belongs at this point in the text is that although most of us can be heard when the occasion demands, we pay for it with a shrill, high-pitched, strangled sound. To increase volume and still maintain clear voice is a bit of an art. It presupposes certain knowledge that by now you should have:

- Support your breath.
- Don't tighten up your throat.
- Keep the pitch from rising.

You already know about forward focus and projection; to increase loudness, the following may also help.

- If you speak loudly, you are "tossing" your voice in a general direction and over a general area with sufficient strength and power so that most people present can hear and understand what you are saying. If you are projecting your voice, you are beaming your voice to a particular individual or group or to a rather specific area.
- Projection is a difficult term to define, and it is all but impossible to approach it from a "scientific" point of view. Here is one authority's definition:

Projection is controlled energy that gives impact, precision, and intelligibility to sound. On the part of the speaker, it also involves a deliberate concentration and a strong desire to communicate with the listeners.[2]

- Certain sounds have more carrying power: *m, n,* and *ng,* and also the vowels, which are shaped in your oral resonating cavity. A slight sustaining of these sounds thus becomes important in "filling out" the tone so that it is carried. Shouting to someone, "Come down" would carry better if it were "Cuuhmm daahooonnn."
- Of course an increase in loudness requires an increase in energy. The degree of loudness should be dictated by the size of the room and the number of people.

---

[2] Lyle V. Mayer, *Voice and Diction,* 7th ed. (Dubuque, Iowa: Brown, 1985), p. 175.

WARM-UP EXERCISES

Increasing loudness

Use breath support, open-tube resonance, and open feedback channels.

1. Say *ah* at a low volume with the mouth wide open. Gradually increase the intensity until it is louder than your conversational voice and then gradually reduce the loudness until very soft again. Monitor that you feel no tension and that your pitch did not rise. Repeat several times.

2. Count to 6. With each count you are reaching someone farther back in a hall. Watch that the pitch does not rise.

3. Count to 6 again, consciously shaping and elongating the vowels and nasals, with a strong volume but one that you can do without tension.

4. Say the following phrases, energetically, each on a single breath, with no rise in pitch at the end of the phrase.

   a. Not now, please!
   b. Up this way!
   c. Come on!
   d. I don't understand!
   e. Bring it here!
   f. That's not it!
   g. Try the other one!
   h. I just can't hear you!
   i. This won't do!
   j. Please be quiet!

5. Go back and say the phrases in exercise 4 again, this time shaping and sustaining the vowels and nasals.

ADDING ON FOR PROFICIENCY

Increasing loudness

1. Obviously as the demands increase for your need to be heard, so too do those for precise articulation and forward fronting. The intelligible and forceful projection of speech sounds will get your message across, sometimes even without increased intensity. Imagine that the phrases that follow are a code; it is critical to get every single sound across to someone listening across the room, but in the interests of secrecy you cannot raise your voice above a low conversational level.

   a. Test the paper packet practically.
   b. Clamp the question box smartly.
   c. Twist strong strings for strength.
   d. Fill Bill's metal flask.
   e. Click silk heels briskly.
   f. Think every sixth blink.

g. Clasp contact's metal sink.
h. Pull forth swizzle sticks.
i. Drive west to Tunbridge Wells.
j. Cross out lists for posts.
k. Take fifths and quarters off.

2. You are in three different situations:

A small room chatting with friends
A classroom addressing 25 classmates
A lecture hall of 100 people

Repeat the following sentences 3 times, adjusting for the differing demands. Be sure to monitor your focus.

a. What will we talk about this morning?
b. This seems a good idea to me.
c. How are you going to vote in the next election?
d. I feel very strongly about the awful parking situation.
e. The year is almost over and there are still things to do.
f. I find TV addictive.
g. I can't wait for school to be out.

3. Add one more situation to the three in exercise 2: a gymnasium that holds 500 people. Speak the following short phrases all four ways. For the demands of the fourth, *move.* Physicalize the sound. Monitoring now becomes critical as voice quality should not be affected.

a. Stop now.
b. Give me your attention.
c. Quiet over there!
d. Calm down!
e. Give me a break!
f. One thing, please.
g. Just listen.
h. Not *yet!*

SUPER EXERCISES

Increasing loudness

1. Role-play the following situation. The sound system has suddenly gone out at a large basketball game. You are the captain of the home team, so it is up to you to go to the middle of the floor and get the following across to the stands:

a. They have to quiet down for a minute.
b. Can you be heard?
c. Apologize for the disruption.
d. Assure them the sound system will soon be functioning.
e. The game will continue in the meantime.

2. With careful monitoring, assume all three roles in this mini-drama.

   VILLAIN (*forcefully*):   I've come to get the rent, the rent, the rent.

   HEROINE (*softly*):   But I haven't the rent, the rent, the rent.

   VILLAIN (*forcefully*):   But I want the rent, the rent, the rent.

   HEROINE (*plaintively*):   But I haven't the rent, the rent, the rent.

   HERO (*grandly*):   I will pay your rent, your rent, your rent.

   HEROINE (*softly*):   My hero!

   VILLAIN (*loudest of all*):   *Curses! Foiled again!*

3. Sometimes in reading something aloud the meaning will be lost unless there is a sudden dramatic rise in volume to underscore what is happening or being said. Choose one of the following to read aloud, with clear tone throughout, even on the volume rise.

   a. Suddenly the eyes of the crowd in the amphitheater beheld, with ineffable dismay, a vast vapor shooting from its summit in the form of a gigantic pine tree; the trunk, blackness, the branches, fire—a fire that shifted and wavered in its hues with every moment, now fiercely luminous, now of a dull and dying red, that again blazed terrifically forth with intolerable glare!

      EDWARD BULWER LYTTON, *The Destruction of Pompeii*

   b. The trumpet's loud clangor
          Excites us to arms
      With shrill notes of anger
          And mortal alarms.
      The double double beat
          Of the thundering drum
          Cries, "Hark! the foes come;
      Charge, charge, 'tis too late to retreat!"

      JOHN DRYDEN, "A Song for Saint Cecelia's Day"

   c. For suddenly he smote on the door, ever
      Louder and lifted his head:
      "Tell them I came and no one answered,
      That I kept my word," he said.

      WALTER DE LA MARE, "The Listeners"

   d. At length the sexton, hearing from without
      The tumult of the knocking and the shout
      And thinking thieves were in the house of prayer,
      Came with his lantern, asking "Who is there?"
      Half choked with rage, King Robert fiercely said,
      "Open: 'tis I, the King! Art thou afraid?"

      HENRY WADSWORTH LONGFELLOW, "King Robert of Sicily"

CORRECTING RESONANCE FAULTS

Lifetime habits are hard to break, and for those of you who still need work on specific faults, the following sections should prove helpful.

Nasality

A certain amount of confusion justifiably exists about the quality fault termed nasality. From our discussion so far, you know that when the soft palate is dropped to create a passage through the nose and the oral cavity is blocked off, the sounds we recognize as *m, n,* and *ng* are created. These phonemes are described as "musical" and as possessing extra carrying power. So the question arises, if the nasal passages can amplify such pleasing sounds, why can their excessive use cause something that is described as an annoying fault?

The important thing to remember about the production of *m, n,* and *ng* is that the oral cavity is blocked off entirely, so that the vibrating air is *forced* all the way through the nasal passages. On all other sounds, the oral passageway is open, and the sound is primarily being resonated there. But if the oral cavity is not open enough, especially in the back, some vibrating air will escape up into the nose as well. This creates an entirely different resonance condition from what we have described for the three nasal sounds. The narrow convoluted passages trap the air. Some gets through, but most "dead ends" on itself. Such a resonance condition is called *cul-de-sac resonance,* and this amplifies inharmonic partials, resulting in a quality that we describe as whiny or nasal. It is unfortunate that over the years this label has been hung on a fault that should more properly be called dead-ending or cul-de-sac.

Why does the fault of nasality occur? A combination of factors may be responsible. As you already know, the soft palate (velum) rises to shut off the nasal passages (see Figure 3.8 in Chapter 3). Among the factors at fault may be any of the following:

1. The soft palate does not rise sufficiently to close off the nasal chamber.
2. The tongue tenses and humps back in the rear of the mouth, thus blocking the sound from an easy, open passage, and some of it "backfires" up into the nose.
3. The mouth does not open sufficiently overall because the jaw is held rigid and the teeth may be clenched or nearly closed. Again, all the vibrating air cannot get through easily, and some is forced up into the nose.

KINDS OF NASALITY: GENERAL, PHONEMIC, AND ASSIMILATION

In our experience, in a normal population, tension, habit, and clenched jaw for the most part produce *general* nasality, a slight whining undercurrent throughout a person's speech. Work on maintaining an open jaw and flexible articulation should improve this. Other people may exhibit *phonemic* nasality in which, predictably on just certain vowel sounds, that whiny sound can be heard. Most often those vowels are the ones that occur in the following sample words: *class* or *hat, time* or *light, brown* or *down,* and *boys* or *noise.* We use relatively few phonemes in our overall speech, but because we use them over and over, the presence of nasality on even one of them recurs like a crack in a broken record.

Some people avoid general nasality and phonemic nasality but fall prey to *assimilation* nasality, which occurs on predictable vowel sounds when a legitimate nasal sound comes before or after it because the switching of passages is not completely accomplished. Thus a person might not nasalize the *a* sound in *hat* but might on *hand* or *mat.* Some speakers exhibit assimilation nasality if the vowel is tense, like *ee* or *ay,* because they allow the tension to affect the easy closure of the soft palate.

WARM-UP EXERCISES

Eliminating nasality

Concentrate throughout on strong oral direction of sound through an easily open passage.

1. *Feeling soft palate action*   Open your mouth wide, keeping the back of the tongue down out of the way. Feel the action of the soft palate. Say *ng* (the palate is down); say *ah* (the palate is up). Alternate back and forth, *ngah, ngah, ngah,* until you really feel its action.

2. *Negative contrast*   Our experience shows that most nasality occurs because of misplaced tension and a constricted oral passageway. Clench the back of the teeth and say the word *man* as nasally as you can. Next relax all tension in the back of the throat, drop the jaw wide, and say the word again. Concentrate on *feeling* and *hearing* the difference as you alternate slowly back and forth several times.

3. *Pull-outs*   Start extremely tense and constricted at the back of the mouth saying the word *class* as nasally as you can. This time, only gradually relax and gradually drop the jaw as you keep repeating the word and notice the clearing of the sound as you feel the tension lessening. Many people also notice that their pitch sounds lower on the final repetitions.

4. *Concentrating on being nonnasal*   Relieve any back-of-the-tongue tension or humping, drop the jaw, and think that you are molding the following sounds in an exaggerated manner and that it is your ear that is guiding you.

that class	high and dry
out and about	noisy toys
cat in the hat	noisy boys
bright light	high tide
fast class	shout and pout

5. *Eliminating assimilation nasality*   Using your best oral resonance and dropped jaw, say the following sets of three words. Prolong the vowel sound every time so that you can really hear it. Notice that the second in each set is the difficult one, so as you do the first in each set, listen and feel so that you can transfer that exact same sound to the second one and then on to the easier third one. *There should be no change in vowel sound at all in any of the triplets.*

be, me, see	bay, may, pay
beet, meet, beer	date, mate, late
seat, meat, street	sail, mail, pail

seal, seen, seep   Kate, came, cape
seer, seem, seed   fate, same, shade

at, and, add   brow, brown, browse
sat, sand, sad   cow, now, how
bat, band, bag   doubt, down, dowdy
had, hand, lag   arouse, around, abound
lad, land, lap   south, mouth, souse
sag, sang, sat

pie, my, die   toys, noise, boys
tight, time, tile   joy, join, coy
light, line, lisle   choice, moist, soil
fight, fine, file   destroy, employ, enjoy
sight, sign, sigh   oil, point, toil

ADDING ON FOR PROFICIENCY
Eliminating nasality

1. *Checking for nasal escape*   The following commands are phonemically controlled so that there are no *m, n,* or *ng* sounds in them. Theoretically, then, the nose is not being used as a resonator. Say the phrase aloud with your best oral resonance; then lightly pinch your nose with thumb and forefinger and repeat the same phrase. There should be no appreciable difference in sound or feel.

Class is excused.   Shut up all desks.
Wipe the blackboard.   Sweep up the floor.
Pick up all the papers.   Erase today's date.
Pass out the chalk.   Set out fresh paper.
Close up the closets.   Put out the trash.
Pull up the shades.   Flick off the light.

2. The following phrases are to be read aloud as pairs. Keep the second one as free from nasality as the easier first one.

   a. What's for lunch?
      Have half an apple.
   b. Let's go on a picnic.
      I don't want ants in my sandwich.
   c. It's getting late.
      Mind the time.
   d. Would you like some Pepsi?
      Wine when I dine is fine.
   e. How about a spin?
      Andy has the last dance.
   f. Is your mother here?
      About now she'd be way down town.
   g. How did your date go?
      Ooh dandy! I had a fine time.

    h. Let's turn on the stereo.
       Enjoy the noise.
    i. Did you like the concert?
       Oh boy! I'll say! It was noisy.
    j. You don't know anything.
       But I can cram for the exam.

3. *Simultaneous speaking and listening for nasality*   Tape the following sentences. Once again you will be marking each spot where you hear yourself becoming nasal, but you will not stop. You will continue to the end of each set. Then go back and play the tape and see if you heard yourself every time you became nasal. The second time through, go as slowly as you need to, but concentrate on not being nasal. Taping and replaying will help here too. In each set, the sentences become progressively more difficult.

    a. Two coeds studied together. "Let's share crib sheets," said the first.
       "Good idea," said the second. "Only we can't. I've nothing to share."
       "My exams are anatomy, algebra, and life science, and I haven't any
         answers."
    b. "Let's pick places for a holiday. How about Hawaii or Jamaica?"
       "Too resorty. I'll take Cape Cod, New Orleans, or Fire Island any time."
       "Too trendy. Japan, Canada, San Francisco, or Scandinavia is where the
         action is."
    c. The food at the cafeteria has gone from bad to horrible.
       There used to be occasional ham for breakfast, and fresh fruit.
       Now, nine times out of ten, there is mashed mystery meat and canned
         applesauce.
    d. It is difficult to get excited about this year's carnival.
       Sack races are old hat, and there are too many pitch-a-ball games.
       Antigambling laws have outlawed bingo, and the bandstand needs brand-
         new night lights.
    e. Last year's season had several good plays.
       There was *Our Town, My Fair Lady,* and *Night Rider.*
       But this year's was absolutely fantastic with *Man of La Mancha, Hamlet,*
         and *Animal Farm.*
    f. The college authorities say they may abolish fraternities.
       Among the reasons for banning them: They no longer serve a purpose.
       Also, one of the pranks last initiation night led to an untimely accident.

SUPER EXERCISES

Eliminating nasality

1. *Mishmash recipes*   Choose at least five of the words in the following list to combine in a recipe of your devising, the crazier the better. *Example:* One student suggested combining two plastic bags with a candied apple in a large plastic bowl, adding animal crackers, pizza snacks, and a daffodil, turning it all into a cement mixer, and baking for one hour. Serve on your best china.

    The important thing is that you monitor yourself to be free of nasality throughout.

Tab	campfire	baked Alaska
Tropicana	pancakes	striped bass
black pepper	pineapple	baggage claim
grand canal	Spanish olives	black beans
amino acids	mashed bananas	wax beans
ambrosia	apple brown Betty	road map
anchovy	casserole	hamburger
canapés	cranberry	cabbage rolls
ham	No-Cal	daffodil
caviar	apple pan dowdy	espresso
lamb tidbits	apricots	Caesar salad
crabmeat	clams	raspberry sauce
black-eyed Susan	tomato aspic	cat food
piano music	life raft	garbage bags

2. *Making up commercials*   If there is a particular phoneme that you tend to nasalize (*a* in *man, i* in *fine, ow* in *now,* or *oi* in *noise,* for example), make up the name of a product that is loaded with that sound, and use it as many times as you can in the sales pitch you make for the product. Read it first with the strongest nasality you can command. Then read it absolutely perfectly. If there is no one particular problem, choose one. *Example:* A student who knew he was prone to nasality on the *i* sound as in *fine* composed the following:

Hi! I'm Miles Klein, founder and president of Klein's Fine Vine Wines. We use only the finest grapes taken from our vines in The Argentine and Versailles. These vines, I might add, are mine. Klein's Fine Vine Wines are great to imbibe as you dine. Klein's Fine Vine Wines are only $9.99 a bottle. And remember our slogan: "Only a swine would sell a fine wine before its time."

3. If you can get through the following selection with no trace of nasality, you are well on your way to control—at least when you stay conscious of it.

Amanda Mandelheim wanted to go to the dance. "It's my chance to get to know Marvin!" she pleaded with her mother.
"My! Such a time to be thinking of dancing!" answered her mother. "Why, in my time we couldn't go dancing after nine at night."
"Now, Ma," said Amanda, "this is a fine time to be telling me when my young man will be joining me around now. Can't I please go? What harm will it do? Besides, you'll be charmed by Marvin Nartfine."
"Charmed, shmarmed. Amanda, you are mine to bring up. I want none of these fancy ideas. Marvin Nartfine can come in for a glass of wine, and then you two can play cards, and that's that."
And since this is an old-time story, that *was* that.

Denasality

The exercises for improving nasal resonance are the same as we would suggest for you who are denasal. The only additional suggestion would be to exaggerate and prolong the nasal sounds, especially in the Warm-up and Adding On for Proficiency exercises.

If after turning back and repeating them this way you still exhibit noticeable denasality, you should seek professional advice. Unknown to you, you may have a deviated septum, a growth, allergies, or some other condition that needs attention.

Throatiness

If you have the dull, dark sound that is associated with the voice "that rides back toward the tonsils," the exercises for forward focus and projection in the section on improving oral resonance should have helped you a good deal. If you still need work, review them and do the condensed exercises that follow with these suggestions in mind.

1. A retracted tongue position is the most common cause of throatiness. (a) Is the middle or front of your tongue humped up too far back in your mouth? (b) Look at yourself in a mirror. As you speak, does your chin tend to be pulled down toward your neck? If so, "Chin up!" is the advice for you. In either or both cases, make every attempt to move that focus forward.
2. Sometimes a person's voice is throaty because the person has adopted an abnormally low pitch, for one reason or another, and holding the tongue back helps keep that dark, low sound on all the vowels. For this, also review the work on modal versus optimum pitch.

WARM-UP EXERCISES AND ADDING ON FOR PROFICIENCY

Eliminating throatiness

1. *Negative contrasts* Say each phrase twice. The first time, deliberately retract the chin and feel the sound riding back on your tonsils. The second time, hold your chin up and feel that your production of all the sounds is exaggeratedly far forward in your mouth.

read the speech	leave the scene
heat the meat	peel a peach
believe Pete	hide a pill
steal secrets	live in a city
beat the heat	hidden eggs
bittersweet	sell ten pens

2. Keep every sound in these sentences as far forward as the second attempt on each of the phrases in exercise 1. Each sentence will be harder toward the end.

    a. The leaves were eaten by some horrible tree blight.
    b. Illegal deeds are outlawed by the law.
    c. Excessive sleeping is a sign of some illness.
    d. Expressing feelings is a relief for an overburdened conscience.
    e. Greens fees are charged at public golf courses.

f. Steel beams are more durable than iron ones.

g. Speed freaks get there faster—if they get there.

h. He who believes he can achieve often does so.

SUPER EXERCISE
Eliminating throatiness

Can you get all the way through the following movie review without once riding back in your mouth?

Beach Street Secrets

Pete Zeller and Bee Bee Green steal the scene from leading man Neil Hinton in the new smash hit *Beach Street Secrets,* playing at the Bijou on East Thirteenth Street. Portraying sneaky thieves who snitch apples and milk from the Beach Street Deli with as practiced ease as when they lift cash from pedestrians, their secret weapon is the ear-splitting sneezing routines Bee Bee slips into, distracting the innocent victims for the time needed for Pete to complete his heist. Neil Hinton as the chief of police seems as believable in his role as Bee Bee's adopting an antihistamine regime. Rated PG.

Thinness

The person with the high, thin voice often lacks sufficient strength, and the listener often feels goaded to interject, "Speak up, *speak up!*" In keeping the tongue so far forward that the final resonating cavity is always small, such a speaker often maintains a tense half-smile while speaking, with almost no lip or tongue activity. The work on the easily open speech megaphone and exercises for tongue, lip, and jaw agility in the section on oral resonance should have helped. If you still need work, do the condensed exercises that follow with the following suggestions in mind.

1. Check that breath support is strong. Rev up your energy.

2. Use exaggerated lip activity at first, keeping the throat easily open.

3. Check your pitch level.

WARM-UP EXERCISES AND ADDING ON FOR PROFICIENCY
Eliminating thinness

1. Exaggerate the lip activity on *w* and listen for the fullness of back vowels that you purposely sustain.

want a wash	wooden woman
wind wool	Whoa! Watch out!
wash the walk	awoke wanly
wander away	warp and woof
wide wharf	wobbly window

2. The first time through, exaggerate the lip opening and rounding of the vowels. The second time, speak in a normal conversational manner, but listen carefully for the fullness of back vowels while providing good support.

   a. Oh, no! Who told Homer to go?
   b. Cold potatoes are no joke.
   c. Joe's look showed only gloom and doom.
   d. Sue hooked a cookie from the cookie jar.
   e. Who threw the soup spoon in the stew?
   f. Most of the gold and jewels were stolen from the vault.
   g. June and July are too humid and hot.
   h. Only a fool would sue over a rumor.

SUPER EXERCISE

Eliminating thinness

Stay aware of good lip and jaw activity as you concentrate on the rich sound of the back vowels in the following movie review.

Wholesome Corners

   The goose that laid a golden egg was one up on the movie that opened at the Oldtown Music Hall on Tuesday: It wasn't rotten. Joe Marrow's bold direction of *Wholesome Corners,* the story of the reunion of the 22 boys who grew up in an orphanage of that name, could not rescue an outdated script and characters that were about as moving as cold glue. Only Lou Cooper as the saloon owner who blew up Grober's Take-out Juice 'n Booze and Roy Doogan, portraying the former steward who crooned his way to fortune in the Hollywood musical *Mule Canoe,* were noteworthy. Don't go. Costly boredom. Mature audiences only.

CHECKPOINT EXERCISES

Vocal Quality

A. *Demonstrating good oral resonance*   Read the following poem aloud with *forward focus.*

A centipede was happy quite
Until the toad in fun
Said, "Pray which leg goes after which?"
Which worked her mind to such a pitch
She lay distracted in the ditch
Considering how to run.
     EDWARD CRASTER

B. *Demonstrating nasal resonance*   Read these two sentences aloud for musical quality and carrying power.

1. Soon, too soon, the old man's home will tumble into dust.
2. Alone, all, all alone, by the glow of the silvery moon.

C. *Demonstrating increasing loudness*   While maintaining good vocal quality, read the following critical information to a crowd of 200.

Would all guests please stay in their seats. Repeat: *Do not leave your seats.* We will soon know what the difficulty is.

D. *Demonstrating freedom from quality faults*

1. *Nasality*

a. *General*   Read the following sentence twice: the first time with your best oral resonance, the second time with your thumb and forefinger pinching the bridge of your nose. There should be no appreciable difference in sound or feel.

TV soaps provide escape, but they are also addictive for those who choose to avoid a dull research paper.

b. *Phonemic or assimilation*   You are to be marooned alone on an isolated desert island. You may take with you only *two* of the following items. Choose, and then tell why.

home handyman's guide	hammer and nails
matches	automatic signal light
bandages and iodine	manual of desert survival
ham radio set	case of canned apple juice

2. *Denasality*   Repeat exercise B, purposely sustaining the nasals.

3. *Throatiness*   With clarity and focus far forward, read this poem aloud:

And here's the happy bounding flea.
You cannot tell the he from she.
The sexes look alike you see;
But she can tell, and so can he.
ROLAND YOUNG

4. *Thinness*   With energy and support, and resonant rounded vowels, read this excerpt from Tennyson's "Brook":

Clear and cool,
Clear and cool,
By laughing shallow and dreaming pool . . .

E. *Putting it all together*   You are being interviewed for a job as anchorperson on the televised campus news program. To determine your speaking style, you have been asked to think of one noteworthy event that happened on campus this year and then to tell about it as if you were actually on the air.

7

ACHIEVING AN EXPRESSIVE VOICE: VOCAL VARIETY

Let your speech be always with grace, seasoned with salt.

COLOSSIANS 4:6

Nothing great was ever achieved without enthusiasm.

RALPH WALDO EMERSON

Challenge exercise   Script for a Chip-Brains commercial.

Students, are you frazzled, overworked, or just plain depressed about passing final exams?

Send your brain on vacation, and let Chip-Brains do the work!

Chip-Brains is a personalized 200-IQ robot programmed to get an A in all college subjects. Guaranteed to look exactly like you—our makeup department makes a computer duplicate of your face so exact that your own mother couldn't tell the difference.

So while you party or lie in the sun, let Chip-Brains sit in class for you, ready with all the answers. Only $270,000, delivered to your dorm. Credit cards accepted.

Buy in complete confidence: Only your mechanic knows for sure.

First, read the commercial with *no expression whatsoever.* Then read it again, really trying to sell the product and using full vocal expression to that end.

Which was more difficult, the first reading or the second? For those of you whose vocal expressiveness has been on automatic pilot for many years, the first reading may have proved more of a challenge. Did becoming aware of the need to remove all variety from your voice make you feel self-conscious?

In any event, are you able to analyze what you took out in your first reading or what you added in the second—what the components of an expressive voice are?

What really conveys the meaning when you speak is the sum of your parts, your enthusiasm, your whole *affect:* facial expression, posture, gestures, stance, along with how you color what you say by varying the tools at your disposal, which are the basic components of sound:

- *Pitch:* inflection and intonation pattern, how and where you go up or down the scale for stress and emphasis
- *Rate:* pacing, where you speed up, where you slow down, where you pause for emphasis or between thoughts
- *Volume:* where and how you increase or decrease the loudness of your voice to emphasize key points
- *Quality:* use of breathiness, stridency, thinness, and other vocal characteristics for dramatic effect

The blending of those elements brings the message alive, underscores the meaning, shades nuances, and makes you an expressive speaker.

It has been estimated that in a face-to-face situation, over 90 percent of the message is communicated without words—or you might say *despite* the actual words. For instance, take the three words "I like biology." Ostensibly these seem to mean that whoever said them finds biology a subject that is appealing.

But suppose these same words were actually said in the following ways:

"I likc biology?"   (Who says I do!)
"I *like* biology?"   (You're out of your mind.)
"I like *biology?*"   (I like some of my subjects, but not this one.)

Are you beginning to get it?

Even this line could be uttered in ways that have little to do with the simple question intended, "Do you understand?"

"*Are* you beginning to get it?"   (I have some doubt.)
"Are *you* beginning to get it?"   (Others have, but what about you?)
"Are you *beginning* to get it?"   (I know it's a hard concept but perhaps a bit is sinking in.)

Try a few yourself. Give at least three different meanings to the following sentences just by how you color and emphasize the words:

I like my instructor.
School is easy.
Jack's a really nice guy.
That's a neat new shirt.

Or just take one little word: *yes.* Can you say it to mean these five things?

1. I'm not sure.
2. Of course.
3. Regretfully, I'll do it.
4. I thought you'd never ask me!
5. I'll do it, but I'm furious I have to.

Your reaction to all this may be, "Well, of course I do that naturally as the emotion moves me, but I can't fake it. I'm not an actor after all. So what does it have to do with me?" Quite simply stated, the overall aim of the work in this chapter is to demonstrate to you the potential within your own voice. It's there. Listen to it. Then, ultimately, the end result is naturalness, not artificiality.

GOALS FOR WORK ON VOCAL VARIETY

1. To build awareness of the potency of the message that you convey through your total affect and through color or lack of it

2. To explore all the ways at your disposal to enhance, underline, or detract from a message

3. To go through a variety of exercises that will allow you to hear your own voice doing things you may not consciously have heard it do before, because self-awareness is a big step

4. To break out of your accustomed mode. Some of the exercises will seem crazy—for a good reason: Once people stop thinking, "This is just the way I talk," they are often amazed at what they can actually do with their voices.

5. To apply these skills to interpreting the written word more effectively. There will be suggestions for putting more vocal variety into your daily communication, but the main point of concentration in the chapter will be interpreting the words of others, because once you can color someone else's ideas and bring out the inherent shades and nuances, it will be much easier to transfer the skill to your own speech.

Can vocal expressiveness be taught?

Of course vocal expressiveness can be taught. Remember, though, that speech is interwoven into the whole self—general physical and mental health and overall self-image. For the majority of people, however, lack of adequate vocal color is simply habit, lack of awareness, and lack of training. This chapter will attempt to change all that.

Perhaps it will help to think of all this from the following perspective. The vast majority of us are visually oriented. We take for granted punctuation marks in print that help divide the thoughts to convey the meaning.

We never expect to see:

Madgemyhalfsistertoldmetobecarefullastnightjustatsuppertimeshesaid . . .

We expect:

Madge, my half-sister, told me to be careful. "Last night, just at suppertime," she said, . . .

Obviously, when we hear the same thing spoken it will not be:

Madge, comma, my half hyphen sister, comma, told me to be careful, period. Quotation marks, last night, comma, . . .

But what we do to punctuate what we say—to express ourselves, to make ourselves interesting and listened to by other people—can be much more powerful than any symbols set down in black and white. They are fixed. We can transcend them in any number of ways, as we hope the examples earlier in the chapter made clear. And that is the purpose of this chapter: to make you aware of how you punctuate your speech and how you come across to others.

Just as a painter has to learn the possibilities inherent in each color and then how to mix colors, so, too, must speakers explore the potential in the colors at their disposal—pitch, rate, volume, and quality—and then combine them. Each of these properties of sound will be treated separately with Warm-up Exercises, although in actuality these components work together, each dependent on the other, so the chapter will conclude by putting them all together with Adding On for Proficiency and Super Exercises combined.

PITCH

Do you control your speaking pitch, or does it control you? Here are two mini-challenges for you to try. For these exercises especially, it would be a good idea to use a tape recorder so you can get feedback and determine exactly what you did.

1. Sing up and down the 8-note scale of an octave. (This should be relatively easy unless you are tone deaf.) Now use your speaking voice: *Say,* do not sing, the numbers in the pitch progression as follows:

<pre>
                    4
        3   3
    2   2
1   1
</pre>

2. Most of us can follow a simple tune as we sing. With your speaking voice, can you follow the pitch progressions and changes indicated in the following pitch contours?

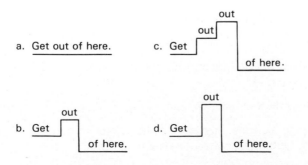

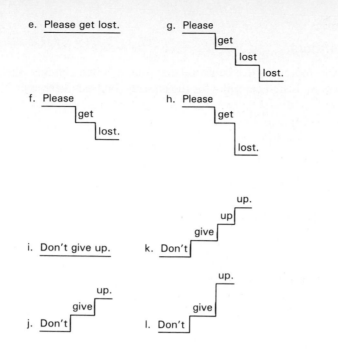

e. Please get lost.

f. Please
   get
      lost.

g. Please
   get
      lost
         lost.

h. Please
   get
      lost.

i. Don't give up.

j. Don't
      give
         up.

k. Don't
      give
         up
            up.

l. Don't
      give
         up.

Both of these challenges underline an irony: Most of us take it for granted that we can control the pitch of our singing voice, but how many of us have thought about doing the same for our speaking voice? After all, one speaks, not sings, one's way through life!

Pitch changes as we speak in a variety of ways. As you already know, everyone has a modal pitch (that is hopefully optimum) from which one moves up or down for emphasis. The overall melody of pitch changes in a sentence is known as *intonation. Inflection* is a pitch change within a single uninterupted sound, like this:

   at? Oh, th
  a   a
Wh   a
                 at.

A *step* is a pitch change between syllables that is done for emphasis:

    this or like
like   that.

Stress is the prominence given to a syllable or word through pitch change (and of course rate or volume change), and *emphasis* is the same as stress on words

   a whole thought
or   group.

WARM-UP EXERCISES

Playing with pitch contours

To gain more practice controlling and using pitch changes, speak these pairs of sentences. Listen carefully for the contrast between each pair.

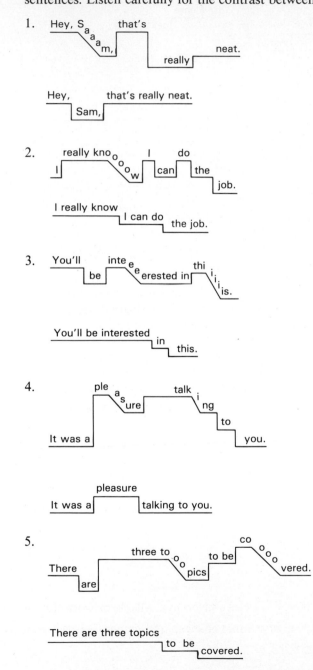

1. Hey, S^a_a_am, that's really neat.

   Hey, Sam, that's really neat.

2. I really kno_o_ow I can do the job.

   I really know I can do the job.

3. You'll be inte^e^eerested in thi_i_iis.

   You'll be interested in this.

4. It was a ple^a_sure talkⁱng to you.

   It was a pleasure talking to you.

5. There are three to_o_opics to be co_o_overed.

   There are three topics to be covered.

6.

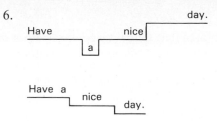

In no way are we suggesting that you become overanimated with excessive pitch changes throughout your speech, but a certain exaggeration is good in a warm-up session to build awareness. More to the point, how many of you recognized your customary speaking style in the second example in each pair? Far too many people have a narrow three- or four-note range, and it is stereotyped besides, tending predictably to go down at the end.

A good deal of the problem of extending a usable speaking pitch range is for the individual to accept the need to do so. As stated earlier, a good speaker should have a usable range of an octave and a half.

Extending usable pitch range

1. Count to 5 in a monotone at a comfortable pitch level. Raise it two whole notes and repeat; two more, and repeat; and even two more. Go back to the comfortable level for the count of 5, then down two notes and down two more.

2. Repeat the phrases "That's okay," "I don't think so," and "That's better," varying the levels up and then down exactly as you did in exercise 1, only this time do not use a monotone. Hit the intended level with some portion of each phrase.

3. *Experimenting with exaggerated pitch changes*   Try dramatically different pitch patterns in the following sentence. Can you do at least six?

   I never want to repeat such a performance—not ever.

4. Let the meaning in the following help you alter pitch levels.
   a. "Start high," the voice coach demonstrated. "Then go a little higher still; now very low; now very high; higher still; and back to where it's comfortable."
   b. The little girl chanted in rhythm with her swinging, "I go up in the swing and back down; up, up, and back down, up up *UP* and back down; up, up, up, *UP* and back down; and stop."
   c. Jamie showed his father a mark on the wall. "Now I am this big. In another year I will be *this* big." He pointed to a spot up higher. "But when I'm grown up, I will be *thi-i-i-s* big," he said on tiptoe, stretching as high as his hand could reach.

   Intonation and inflection can alter meaning. A rising tone implies a question, uncertainty, or perhaps unfinished business. A falling tone signals finality.

Altering pitch to change meaning

1. Say each of the phrases that follow twice, first with a falling inflection and then with a rising inflection. Can you tell how the meaning changed each time?

Not now	I know
Perhaps later	Knock it off
Please don't	I guess so
Any time	Stay outside
Good-bye	Practice here

2. Now do the same with these bumper stickers and notice still another change in meaning.

Feed a crocodile.	Kiss a porcupine.
Ride a giraffe.	Play house with a gorilla.
Hug a lion.	Cuddle a yak.

Thus far, the exercises have aimed to help you explore a variety of pitch change situations and hear your voice doing so. All were admittedly contrived. The important thing, now that you know what changes you are capable of, is to apply this naturally to the content of the ideas you want to get across or the emotion you want to convey in your everyday life. Let that be your guide in doing the exercises that follow.

Pitch changes in everyday phrases

Speak each line in each of the ways suggested. Try to let the emotion you might feel guide you.

1. Please give me a break.

   a. You are waiting your turn to look at some family photographs.
   b. Someone has said something stupid to you.
   c. You are asking a professor to let you retake an exam.

2. That's very interesting.

   a. Your friend is a bore and you are just keeping the conversation going.
   b. Someone has told a juicy bit of news about a mutual friend.
   c. An experiment that you started has worked.

3. I feel confident about this.

   a. You are buying a lottery ticket.
   b. You are about to ask your parents for more allowance.
   c. You are telling a prospective employer you can handle the new job.

4. Thank you for seeing me.

   a. To the nurse, since you are next in line at the infirmary.

b. Your note at the stage door has resulted in your entry into your idol's dressing room.

c. You are concluding a job interview.

5. This is really wonderful.

a. You've just bitten into a soggy pizza.
b. You're on a roller coaster swooping downhill.
c. You're thanking your 5-year-old niece for the picture she's painted you.
d. The interviewer has told you you've just landed the job.

Pitch changes are important in interpreting or in reading aloud to highlight the meaning or emotion intended.

Using pitch changes in interpreting the printed word

1. Consciously think of what you can do with pitch in each of these quotations.

a. People don't ask for facts in making up their minds. They would rather have one good, soul-satisfying emotion than a dozen facts.
     ROBERT KEITH LEAVITT

b. A highbrow is the kind of person who looks at a sausage and thinks of Picasso.
     SIR ALAN HERBERT

c. When our first parents were driven out of Paradise, Adam is believed to have remarked to Eve: "My dear, we live in an age of transition."
     W. R. INGE

d. It was one of those cold, clammy, accusing sort of eyes—the kind that makes you reach up to see if your tie is straight: and he looked at me as if I were some sort of unnecessary product which Cuthbert the Cat had brought in after a ramble among the ash-cans.
     P. G. WODEHOUSE

2. Do the same with these descriptions by Dickens. He was known for them, and they deserve every bit of nuance you can give them.

a. In came a fiddler—and tuned like fifty stomachaches. In came Mrs. Fezziwig, one vast substantial smile.
b. With affection beaming in one eye, and calculation shining out of the other.
c. Skewered through and through with office pens, and bound hand and foot with red tape.
d. That vague kind of penitence which holidays awaken next morning.
e. He had but one eye, and the popular prejudice runs in favor of two.
f. It was as true . . . as turnips is. It was as true . . . as taxes is. And nothing's truer than that.

RATE

Mini-challenge. Here are three sentences:

He bought purple boys' shorts.
Rose admired the man-eating tiger.
Let's eat, boys and girls.

As you already know, pauses are the punctuation marks of speech that separate thoughts. Read these same sentences aloud, as phrased for you:

He bought purple boys' / shorts.
Rose admired the man / eating tiger.
Let's eat boys and girls.

You can see how critical pauses in speech are in conveying meaning!

Pausing is just one of the ways that rate in speech varies. Individual phonemes and syllables can vary in length, as you already know, as well as the number of the pauses and the length of the pauses, for silences are just as much a part of speech as vocalizations.

Here's another mini-challenge. As the old saying goes, "Silence is golden." Yet for some reason most of us are afraid of letting the pauses stand, feeling we have to fill them up with some sort of sound: "errrr" or "uh" or "ummmm" or "you know" or "like."

Try to do this with a whole group, appointing someone with a second hand on a watch to be timer. Each person is to recommend (or not) a recent film, TV show, or book for the group. But the moment a silence is "embellished," the speaker is through. How long did each one last? (A real champion might last 60 seconds.)

To heighten your awareness of how individual phonemes and syllables can be varied in length and contribute greatly to the shading and underlining of what you say, try the following exercises.

WARM-UP EXERCISES

Obtaining word color by varying phoneme and syllable length

1. Concentrate on re-creating the image each of the following words can evoke.[1]

huge	melodious	cold	terrifying
smooth	clanking	boring	lazy
tiny	thunderous	coarse	cool
brisk	hot	frantic	dumb

2. Say the following sentences twice. The first time give the italicized word normal length; the second time, a much longer length. Note what happens to the meaning each time.

---

[1] Here and throughout the exercises, although rate is the component to vary consciously, it will be impossible to exclude some pitch and volume changes.

   a. The lecture was *boring.*
   b. That lead drummer is *cool.*
   c. I'm in a *huge* amount of trouble.
   d. Wow! That's *hot!*
   e. She gave me a *horrible* look.
   f. I'm *frantic.*
   g. This *rhythm* is smooth.
   h. You *fiend!*

3. Very often in trying to interpret a poem or re-create a scene, word color is essential to convey the picture intended. Here are phrases from poems. What can you do with them?

   a. swirling wrecks
   b. young leaves murmuring thirstily
   c. rosy-fingered dawn
   d. yellow, and black, and pale, and hectic red
   e. pestilence-stricken multitudes
   f. whirled all about, dense, multitudinous, cold
   g. most radiant, exquisite, and unmatched beauty
   h. they're crammed and jammed in busses, and they're each of them alone
   i. the city now doth, like a garment, wear the beauty of the morning, silent, bare

Pausing for emphasis or suspense

Not only do pauses to differentiate between thoughts vary in length and number, but they can also be used for something altogether different. They can be used to heighten suspense—to keep the listener hanging on what comes next. Such a technique, however, should be used rather sparingly, or like the boy in the fairy tale who cried "Wolf!" too often, it will lose its effectiveness. Here are a few examples, each successive version showing how a pause heightens interest.

Right there on Main Street in plain sight was a gila monster.
Right there on Main Street in plain sight was . . . a gila monster.

I looked behind me and there was a man with a mask.
I looked behind me and . . . there was a man with a mask.
I looked behind me and . . . there was a man . . . with a mask.

You have just won $100.
You . . . have just won $100.
You . . . have just won . . . $100.

Other ways in which speech rate can vary

Speech can also vary in the overall rate a person uses. A few speakers are like trip-hammers, exploding along in high-speed, staccato fashion, while some others speak so slowly you want to shake them. If you are a trip-hammer, go back to the vowel prolongation exercises in Chapter 5 and consciously overdo the stretching out of everything; then review the smooth phrasing exercises for the choppy voice in Chapter 4. If listeners fall asleep waiting for you to finish speaking, daily practice reading aloud from a newspaper with good phrasing may help. Since the "average" speaking speed is 150 to 180 words a minute, time yourself and see if you can consistently meet that time or even beat it. Then try to transfer that rate to your everyday speech.

Personality, regional background and nervousness all contribute to the overall rate. Most people fall within acceptable limits—but they are not necessarily off the hook. One of the biggest problems with speaking rate is its lack of variety. A predictable pattern, which need not be as dramatic as a singsong, soon lulls a listener. Take a tip from the ancient rug artisans of the Near East. They purposely wove a flaw into the design of every Oriental rug they produced; they knew that perfection needed variety!

Basically, the material should determine the rate. See what happens in the following exercises.

WARM-UP EXERCISES

Effects of rate on meaning

1. Read the following sentences at a rate completely opposite to the meaning.

   a. I'm tired, discouraged, and thoroughly blue.
   b. I'm so excited. It's just too good to be true!
   c. The sense of loss is more than a person can bear.
   d. Never, ever, do I want to go through such an experience again.
   e. I won the lottery! I won the lottery!
   f. Slow down—easy does it.

2. The following passages were written by students. The assignment was to compose a short paragraph in which the meaning would dictate a rate change. Read them aloud. Then write one of your own.

   a. It was cold, impossibly cold. I was frozen, miserable, shivering, shaking, and so rigid with the freezing temperature that my feet moved like they were massive steel rods—ever so slowly and deliberately—one step; one step; one . . . Whoa! What's the deafening noise? An avalanche! From the roof of the warehouse! I'll be buried alive! Run!
   b. Slowly, ever so slowly, they inched their way forward to escape detection. Suddenly the search light fell squarely on them, and they turned and ran, their feet barely touching the ground. The police! The police!
   c. She was sitting quietly on the park bench observing the pigeons gingerly eating the bread crumbs that she had spread before them. An elderly man was limping toward her. She watched him carefully placing each step. Suddenly, behind the man, she saw two teenage boys on skateboards zooming down the hill. She sat up rigidly and helplessly watched the boys approaching the man. Instinctively she covered her eyes. She missed wit-

nessing the boys veering away from the man. When she opened her eyes, she saw the man carefully moving on, step by step by step. She sat back, sighed, and relaxed.

In important, serious, or thought-provoking material, the rate obviously needs to be slower, with more and longer pauses so that listeners can digest what they have heard, whereas anything that is light, repetitive, or unimportant can rather literally rip along. Good speakers are always on the alert for both, so that their speech will have that very special ingredient, variety.

Variety in rate

1. Literally warm up by trying the following two selections at the rather obvious rates they dictate.

   a. At the heart of the matter, the very future of the United States, indeed of the whole free world, is at stake.
   b. It was just like any other class picnic: the beer, the sodas, the pretzels, the potato chips, the crumpled paper cups, the curled paper plates, the candy wrappers dotting the ground around the barbecue pit . . .

2. These will be more difficult, for it is up to you to decide how they should be varied in rate.

   a. Why should U.S. citizens be concerned about the coffee blight in Brazil? Corn fields have had borers, wheat fields have been decimated by droughts, whole harvests of oats have been wiped out by floods, and tomato patches the same. So what's all the cry about? And who needs to drink coffee anyway?

      The issue, quite simply, is not the product itself. The issue is the whole future economy of one of our good neighbors to the south, whose financial well-being depends on it for survival.
   b. There is something awe-inspiring and a little frightening about standing in the moss-covered ruins of an amphitheater that was built over 20 centuries ago. More than half the stone seats have crumbled and weeds stand in place of spectators, yet with the slightest stretch of the imagination one sees the vendors hawking their wines, the crowd roaring as the star gladiator makes his entrance, the children pleading with their parents for one more souvenir, the man shouting at the late group "down in front." And one has to ask oneself: How far have we actually come in these 2000 years?

Using the various components of rate

Concentrate on how you can bring the following selections alive through rate changes of all the kinds discussed. Do not forget word color as a tool.

1. This excerpt is a description of an impending tornado from Lafcadio Hearn's *Chite.*

   For over a moment there was a ghastly hush of voices. And through that hush there burst upon the ears of all a fearful and unfamiliar sound, as a colossal cannonade—rolling up from the south, with volleying lightnings. Vastly and swiftly, nearer and nearer it came—a ponderous and unbroken thunder roll, terrible as the long muttering of an earthquake.

2. Amy Lowell in "The Precinct—Rochester" is describing a moment near an old wall.

The pear trees press their branches against it
And feeling it kindly,
The little pears ripen to yellow and red.
They hang heavy, bursting with juice,
Against the wall.
So old, so still!
The sky is still.
The clouds make no sound.
As they slide away
Beyond the Cathedral Tower,
To the river
And the sea
It is very quiet
Very sunny.

3. In "The Coming Out of Maggie" by O. Henry we come into the story where Maggie stops a fight at a dance.

But Maggie was off, darting zigzag through the maze of dancers. She burst through the rear door into the dark hall and then threw her solid shoulder against the door of the room of single combat. It gave way. And in the instant her eye caught the scene . . . Dempsey Donovan in his shirt sleeves dancing, light-footed, with the wary grace of the modern pugilist, Terry Sullivan standing with arms folded and a murderous look in his dark eyes. And without slackening the speed of her entrance she leaped forward with a scream—leaped in time to catch and hang upon the arm of O'Sullivan that was suddenly uplifted, and to whisk from it the long, bright stiletto that he had drawn from his bosom. . . .

VOLUME

Mini-challenge: Read the following paragraph, using *only* increased loudness to emphasize the words in italics.

Hurry, hurry, hurry! *Last chance* to buy *Margaret's Snake Oil. Guaranteed* to put *hair back on your head.* In *under* 30 days. Applied to your face, acne *dissolves;* freckles *vanish.* Taken internally, headaches *disappear.* Your money back *if not fully satisfied.*

Did you like the way you sounded?

Unfortunately, many people achieve stress and emphasis by the hit-'em-over-the-head routine: If it's important, talk louder; if it's really important, bellow.

As we hope you have realized, there are many subtler ways to emphasize what needs pointing up. Rate changes, dramatic pauses, intonations, and inflections are all far more powerful than raising your volume— and more interesting to listen to.

This section on volume changes will be a good deal shorter than the two preceding ones because almost everyone knows how to emphasize an important word by getting louder. However, there are times when the meaning or mood will be lost if a volume change isn't used, and these are what you should be on the lookout for.

WARM-UP EXERCISES

Volume changes

1. *Changing volume to reflect meaning*   Here are more paragraphs written by students to read aloud. In each the volume needs to change to enhance the content.

   a. The quiet in the motel room was punctuated softly by the faucet dripping— plop, plop, plop, plop. In the far distance a muted horn honked. Suddenly, bright lights, noise, confusion. "This is a raid. Open up."

   b. The cat inched through the grass, noiselessly, paw in front of soft padded paw, eyeing its prey, calculating each move, until, one rapid pounce, a loud screech, a wild flutter of feathers . . . and the hunt was done.

   c. We were hiding in the darkened room. No one dared to make a sound. It was then that we heard the screech of car brakes. Someone was coming to the door! We crouched back behind the furniture and held our breaths. The doorknob twisted and opened. Soon the room was full of light. "Happy birthday!" we all cried.

   d. "It's tripendicular to the max, like totally, for sure!" squealed the Valley girl. "Sit down and don't make another sound," said the stern teacher, the softness of her voice with an edge of steel to it.

2. *Changing volume for dramatic effect*   In these selections, the meaning or mood will not come across unless the volume is purposely made softer or louder.

   a. This is the dramatic scene from "The Captain's Daughter" by James Fields.

   > And thus we sat in darkness,
   >   Each one busy with his prayer,
   > "We are lost!" the captain shouted
   >   As he staggered down the stairs.

   b. Totally different is this description of a grave from Oscar Wilde's "Requiescat."

   > Tread lightly, she is near
   >   Under the snow,
   > Speak gently, she can hear
   >   The daisies grow.

All her bright golden hair
Tarnished with rust,
She that was young and fair
Fallen to dust.

c. Ahab thinks of his nemesis, the great white whale, in Herman Melville's *Moby Dick*.

All that most maddens and torments; all that stirs up the lee of things; all truth with malice in it; all that cracks the sinews and cakes the brain; all the subtle demonisms of life and thought; all evil to crazy Ahab, were visibly personified, and made practically assailable in Moby Dick. He piled upon the whale's white hump the sum of all the general rage and hate felt by his whole race from Adam down; and then, as if his chest had been a mortar, he burst his hot heart's shell upon it.

d. In *The Last Lesson* by Alphonse Daudet, a schoolmaster in a town on the border of Alsace-Lorraine tells the class that French may no longer be spoken in the village.

At the same moment, the trumpets of the Prussians, returning from the drill, sounded under our windows. M. Hamel stood up, very pale in his chair.

"My friends," said he, "I— I" But something choked him. He could not go on.

Then he turned to the blackboard, took a piece of chalk, and bearing down with all his might, he wrote as large as he could:

"Vive la France!"

Then he stopped and leaned his head against the wall, and, without a word, he made a gesture to us with his hand:

"School is dismissed—you may go."

QUALITY

Mini-challenge: Read the first selection as if you were doing it in at least two of the following ways:

1. To a child who revels in gory stories
2. To a child who likes happily-ever-after stories
3. As Dan Rather reporting a news brief
4. As someone who has never heard this before and is surprised by everything

It was the ugliest and most horrible sight you ever would see. It came crawling out of the swamp with slime and blood oozing out of its creepy body. It had six bulgy eyes and huge green teeth as sharp as knives. . . .

Now comes the real challenge: Read the next selection in exactly the same manner as you read the first.

I receive a disability pension from the federal government in addition to a small pension from the state. My house has a second mortgage on it, and I am concerned about keeping up the payments on it. . . .

To succeed in any measure at the mini-challenge, you had to use quality changes in your voice. Change in voice quality is the fourth component of sound that can be used to achieve variety. However, it is used primarily for dramatic material, where character voices are needed. Lily Tomlin, Whoopi Goldberg, and Rich Little are masters at this, their solo shows peopled with a whole cast of characters. Vocal changes also serve the purpose of extra shading when you are building suspense or trying to create a very special mood.

WARM-UP EXERCISES

Changes in voice quality

1. Here are more scenes written by students to be read aloud. Use changes in quality to enhance the character's voices.

   a. "Coffee, sir?" the waitress asked the elderly gentleman. "What's that you say, Missie?" inquired a squeaky, shaky voice. "Would you like some coffee?" she repeated, shouting. "No thank you, young lady, I can't chew. Ain't got no teeth . . . ! See . . . !

   b. "Laryngitis." Max pointed to his throat as he forced his raspy voice to work. Nurse Smith purred, "No need to talk, Max, just use the pen and pencil." But his friend's deep voice roared with amusement. "Motormouth Max can't talk!"

   c. "I love Mary, I love her very much," crooned the young man.
      His mother whined, "What do you see in her? How can you do this to us? How will we survive?"
      "Oh, leave him alone. We'll get along. Let the young man have his fling," growled the grizzly grandfather.

2. Read aloud this scene between Alice and the Cheshire Cat from Lewis Carroll's *Alice's Adventures in Wonderland.* Experiment with changes in quality to achieve a more dramatic effect.

   Alice asked the cat another question. "What sort of people live about here?"
   "In *that* direction," the cat said, waving its right paw around, "lives a hatter; and in *that* direction, lives a March hare. Visit either you like: They're both mad."
   "Oh but I don't want to go among mad people," Alice remarked.
   "Oh you can't help that," said the cat. "We're all mad here. I'm mad. You're mad."
   "How do you know I'm mad?" said Alice.
   "You must be," said the cat, "or you wouldn't have come here."

3. Here is part of the witches' scene from *Macbeth* to be interpreted with appropriate vocal quality.
   WITCH 2:   Eye of newt and toe of frog
   Wool of bat and tongue of dog
   Adder's fork and blind-worm's sting

Lizard's leg and howlet's wing,
For a charm of powerful trouble,
Like a hell-broth boil and bubble.
ALL: Double, double, toil and trouble; fire burn and caldron bubble.

4. As you read the following aloud, use quality changes for special shading of meaning or mood.

a. Edgar Allen Poe describes an indescribable horror in "The Fall of the House of Usher."

Nor hear it?— Yes, I hear it, and have heard it. Long— long— long— many minutes, many hours, many days, have I heard it— yet I dared not— Oh pity me, miserable wretch that I am— I dared not— I dared not— I *dared* not speak! *We have put her living in the tomb!*

b. In "Ozymandias" by Percy Bysshe Shelley, the ancient words are starkly contrasted with all that remains of him, a broken statue.

And on the pedestal these words appear:
"My name is Ozymandias, king of kings.
Look on my works, ye Mighty, and despair!"
Nothing beside remains. Round the decay
Of that colosssal wreck, boundless and bare
The lone and level sands stretch far away.

c. Edgar Allen Poe's poem "The Bells" is well known for his description of the "tintinnabulation" of the silver bells. For the bronze, the mood dramatically shifts:

. . . clang, and clash, and roar! . . .
Yet the ear, it full knows.
        By the twanging—
        And the clanging—
How the danger ebbs and flows;
Yet the ear distinctly tells—
        In the jangling
        And the wrangling
How the danger sinks and swells,
By the sinking or the swelling in the anger of
        the bells.

PUTTING IT ALL TOGETHER FOR AN EXPRESSIVE VOICE

Now that you have explored the potential inherent in pitch, rate, volume, and quality changes, try putting them all together in interpreting selected literary selections. We do not expect you to be professional actors when it comes to reading someone else's words aloud to others, but here are some pointers to help you understand the meaning, mood, or intent of a piece so that you can convey it. And remember that being expressive in reading someone else's thoughts aloud to others is the bridge to being more so in your own speech.

Interpretation tips

Before reading any selection, ask yourself these important questions:

1. Who is speaking in the piece: a man, a woman, a mother, a father, a child, or simply the author?
2. To whom is the person speaking, another person or persons or a general audience?
3. What is the point of view of the person speaking or the author? What is the *intent:* to set a mood or capture an emotion, to tell a story, to share a point of view, to create a word picture, to inform?
4. What is the dominant mood or emotion: informative, sad, nostalgic, angry?

ADDING ON FOR PROFICIENCY AND SUPER EXERCISES

Vocal variety

Glance through the following selections and choose those that you can relate to. Apply the tips for interpretation; then practice using whatever mixture of the tools of vocal variety that will most enhance the meaning of what you want to convey, and read each selection you chose aloud.

1. In "The Tragedy of a Comic Song" by Leonard Merrick, a young woman contemplates how to get rid of her fiancé and profit from it at the same time.

   They sit at a café table, and he talks, the fiancé, of the bliss that is to come. She attends to not a word, not a syllable. While she smiles, she questions herself, frenzied, how she can escape. She has commanded a *sirop.* As she lifts her glass to the syphon, her gaze falls on the ring she wears—the ring of their betrothal. "To the future, *cher ange!*" says the fiancé. "To the future, *chéri!*" she says. And she laughs in her heart—for she resolves to sell the ring!

2. "Résumé" by Dorothy Parker hardly needs explanation.

   Razors pain you;
   Rivers are damp;
   Acids stain you;
   And drugs cause cramp.
   Guns aren't lawful;
   Nooses give;
   Gas smells awful;
   You might as well live.

3. Edmund Rostand's play *Cyrano do Bergerac* remains a classic. Its central character, Cyrano, a gallant, eloquent knight, is cursed with an overly large nose, which causes him no end of anguish. In this speech, he is reacting to someone's comment about it.

   My nose is very large? Young man, you might say many other things, just by varying the tone. For example— *Aggressively:* "Sir, if I had such a nose, I'd cut it off!" *Friendly:* "You have to drink from a tall goblet or your nose would dip into it." *Descriptive:* "'Tis a rock! . . . a peak! . . . a cape, a cape! forsooth! 'Tis a peninsula!" *Graciously:* "Are you so fond of little birds you offer them a roosting place to rest their little feet?" *Quarrelsome:* "When you smoke a pipe and the smoke comes out your nose, doesn't some neighbor shout, 'Your chimney's on fire!'?" *Warning:* "Be careful, or its weight will drag you down on your head and stretch you prostrate on the ground!" *Tenderly:* "Have a large umbrella to hold over it, lest its color fade in the sun." *Dramatic:* "'Tis the Red Sea when it bleeds!" . . .

4. In four simple lines in "The Chimney Sweep," William Blake presents a poignant case history:

When my mother died I was very young,
And my father sold me while yet my tongue
Could scarcely cry, "'weep! 'weep! 'weep! 'weep!"
So your chimneys I sweep, and in soot I sleep.

5. This deceptively simple "Parable of Life" by an unknown author is very much what its title suggests, on several levels.

One day, when the birds had sung themselves quite weary, a long pause ensued, broken at last by a philosophical chaffinch in these words: "What is life?"

They were all rather startled at this interruption, but a little warbler answered at once, "Life is a song."

"No, it is a struggle in darkness," said a mole who had just succeeded in getting his head above the ground.

"I think it is development," said the wild rose bud, as she unfolded her petals one by one to the delight of a butterfly who came to kiss her and exclaimed, "Life is all enjoyment."

"Call it a rather short summer's day," hummed a little fly as it passed by.

"I cannot see anything but hard work," lamented a small ant as she struggled with a straw ever so much too big for her.

The magpie only laughed to cover his own poverty of thought. . . .

Meanwhile it had grown dark, and a practically minded goldfinch proposed that they go to rest. And the night wind rustled softly through the branches, "Life is one long desire ever unfulfilled."

"It is the eternal mystery," whispered the newborn morning breeze.

Then suddenly a rosy light spread over the horizon and singed with its glow the tops of the forest trees as it rose in the sky. And as the morning kissed the awakening earth, a mighty harmony rang through the world: "Life is a beginning."

6. One marvels at how much Lucille Clifton has compressed into the 18 spare lines of "Miss Rosie."

When I watch you
wrapped up like garbage

sitting, surrounded by the smell
of too old potato peels
or
when I watch you
in your old man's shoes
with the little toe cut out
sitting, waiting for your mind
like next week's grocery
I say
when I watch you
you wet brown bag of a woman
who used to be the best looking gal in Georgia
used to be called Georgia Rose
I stand up
through your destruction
I stand up

7. Anyone who has read to a young child knows that vocal variety is essential. Imagine a kindergarten class in front of you as you read "How the Elephant Got His Trunk" from *Just So Stories* by Rudyard Kipling.

Then the Crocodile winked the other eye, and lifted half his tail out of the mud; and the Elephant's Child stepped back most politely because he did not wish to be spanked again.

"Come hither, Little One," said the Crocodile. "Why do you ask such things?"

"'Scuse me," said the Elephant's Child most politely, "but my father has spanked me, my mother has spanked me . . . so if it's quite all the same to you, I don't want to be spanked anymore."

"Come hither, Little One," said the Crocodile, "for I am the Crocodile." And he wept crocodile tears to show it was quite true.

The Elephant's Child grew all breathless, and panted, and kneeled down on the bank and said, "You are the very person I have been looking for all these long days. Will you please tell me what you have for dinner?"

"Come hither, Little One," said the Crocodile, "and I'll whisper."

Then the Elephant's Child put his head down close to the Crocodile's musky, tusky mouth, and the Crocodile caught him by his little nose, which up to that very week, day, hour, and minute, had been no bigger than a boot, though much more useful.

"I think," said the Crocodile . . . and he said it between his teeth like this . . . "I think today I will begin with . . . Elephant's Child."

8. In "Ambiguous Lines" by an unknown author, strive for variety as you re-create each image.

I saw a peacock with a fiery tail.
I saw a blazing comet pour down hail.
I saw a cloud all wrapt with ivy round.
I saw a lofty oak creep on the ground.

I saw a beetle swallow up a whale.
I saw a foaming sea brimful of ale.
I saw a pewter cup sixteen feet deep.
I saw a well full of men's tears that weep.
I saw wet eyes in flames of living fire.
I saw a house as high as the moon and higher.
I saw the glorious sun at deep midnight.
I saw the man who saw this wondrous sight.
I saw a pack of cards gnawing a bone.
I saw a dog seated on Britain's throne.
I saw King George shut up within a box.
I saw an orange driving a fat ox.
I saw a butcher not twelve months old.
I saw a great-coat all of solid gold.
I saw two buttons telling of their dreams.
I saw my friends who wished I'd quit these themes.

9. In "Sing a Song of the Cities," Morris Bishop suggests several moods and emotions by stringing together place names in a dialogue.

"Towanda Winooski? Gowanda!"
   Rahway Setauket Eugene.
"Watseka? Warc! Tonawanda!"
   Flushing Modesto DeQueen."

"Wantagh Revere Petaluma!
   Pontiac! Rye! Champaign!
Kissimmee Smackover! Yuma!"
   Ossining, Waverly Kane!

"Rockaway! Homestead! Tacoma!
   Neenah Metuchen Peru!
Oswego Moberly Homer!
   Dover Andover Depew!"

10. When you read "The Highwayman" by Alfred Noyes, convey a sense of the dark, cold, suspenseful night.

The wind was a torrent of darkness among the gusty trees,
The moon was a ghostly galleon upon the cloudy seas,
The road was a ribbon of moonlight over the purple moor,
And the highwayman came riding—Riding—riding—
The highwayman came riding, up to the old inn-door.

11. In reading Fyodor Dostoevsky's "Notes from the Underground," communicate the anger and hurt.

    The frightened and wounded expression on her face was followed by a look of sorrowful perplexity. When I began calling myself a scoundrel and a blackguard and my tears flowed (the tirade was accomplished throughout by tears) her whole face worked convulsively. She was on the point of getting up and stopping me; when I finished she took no notice of my shouting: "Why are you here, why don't you go away?" but realized only that it must have been very bitter to me to say all this.

12. Reading Elinor Wylie's "Velvet Shoes," try to create a mood of stillness.

Let us walk in the white snow
    In a soundless space;
With footsteps quiet and slow,
    At a tranquil pace.
    Under veils of white lace.

I shall go shod in silk,
    And you in wool,
White as a white cow's milk,
    More beautiful
    Than the breast of a gull.

We shall walk through the still town
    In a windless peace;
We shall step upon white down,
    Upon silver fleece,
    Upon softer than these.

We shall walk in velvet shoes:
    Wherever we go
Silence will fall like dews
    On white silence below.
    We shall walk in the snow.

8

AN INTRODUCTION TO PHONETICS AND THE IPA

One's eyes are what one is, one's mouth what one becomes.

JOHN GALSWORTHY

Challenge exercise Read the following verse aloud, rhyming the last word of each line with the word *dove*.

A pure white dove
Downward dove
And alighted on my love.
I watched but dared not move.

As you can see, this is a challenge that no one can meet! Although the last word of each line ends in *-ove*, they are obviously not pronounced the same.

Suppose you saw the following sentence:

Phrank's pnews is knot phunny, ewe no.

Or you tried to figure out why *ghoti* can be pronounced "fish."[1]

Or take the words *daughter* and *laughter*. Both have eight letters, yet *laughter* has five sounds when spoken (*l, a, f, t, er*) while *daughter* has only four (*d, au, t, er*).

Everyone will agree that English spelling is very difficult. In fact, how any of us ever learn to read is a mystery in itself. By now you must have realized that the English language is not always phonetic—meaning that it is not always pronounced the way it is written. The reasons for this can be traced back to the origin of written languages and the nature of language itself.

---

[1] *gh* as in *laugh, o* as in *women, ti* as in *nation*.

128

GOALS FOR READING THIS CHAPTER

As a background for work on your own articulation patterns, the following goals will be helpful:

1. To understand the development of written language and to be aware that language is characterized by change
2. To know the distinction between an accent and a dialect
3. To appreciate the need for a phonetic system and the International Phonetic Alphabet and how it can be helpful
4. To be aware of the major dialects spoken in the United States and the three American standard ones and to understand why the use of General American will give you the most career mobility
5. To understand how substitutions, omissions, additions, and distortions cause articulation errors
6. To know how sounds are classified in the IPA and how assimilation works in connected speech
7. To begin to become familiar with the IPA

LANGUAGE AND THE ALPHABET

Language scholars agree that our alphabet originated around 4000 years ago when the Phoenicians modified the Egyptian hieroglyphic pictograms and designated one symbol for each consonant sound in that early language. This "alphabet" was then copied by the Romans and then the Greeks, who added vowel representations. Somewhere along the line, however, these letters were doomed to fail as an accurate representation of the sounds of each language. Fourteen vowel sounds in English came to be represented by only five vowel symbols. What is more, invasions of the British Isles by Teutons, Celts, Jutes, Angles, Saxons, Romans, and Normans added new words and sounds to English and wreaked havoc with English pronunciation. But an alphabet, engraved in stone or set in print, is very hard to change. So all the various influences, symbols, and sounds were compressed into a form that was often inaccurate and in some cases quickly outmoded.

The fact that a language is spoken causes it to change constantly—unlike a "dead" language like Latin, which is no longer spoken by any population and therefore remains fixed in form and pronunciation. To illustrate how rapidly a spoken language changes, think of the words that have been added only recently due to the influences of television, space, and technology. In the film *Back to the future,* a young man is miraculously transported back in time to his hometown 30 years earlier. At first, before "tuning in" to the language, he has a difficult time communicating his needs because certain technologies hadn't been invented yet. He goes to a coffee shop and asks for a "Tab." The man behind the counter says, "I don't give you a tab until you order something." The young man then asks for a "Pepsi Free," to which the man behind the counter says, "You want me to give you a Pepsi for free?" Exasperated, the young man finally says, "Well, give me anything without sugar." He gets a cup of black coffee. This young man of the 1980s would not have been able to have a "blast" of a party by showing his 1950s ancestors "freeze-framed" scenes of his childhood, "videotaped" with his own "minicam." By labeling and describing changes in a society, language parallels social change.

Not only does such labeling change rapidly in attempting to keep up with an ever-changing world, but so also do expressions that are used by a particular class or group. These sets of idioms are referred to as *argot,* originally the jargon of the underworld. *Slang* is a form of argot referring to the nonstandard vocabulary of a given culture or subculture. Most often these figures of speech are coined and popularized almost overnight. The majority tend to become old hat and disappear as swiftly as they were formulated.

DIALECTS AND ACCENTS

The *American Heritage Dictionary* defines a *dialect* as "a regional variety of a language, distinguished from other varieties by pronunciation, grammar, or vocabulary" and as "the spoken language peculiar to the members of an occupational or professional group, a foreign-born or minority group, or a particular social class." An *accent* is defined as "a characteristic pronunciation: . . . determined by the regional or social background of the speaker . . . [or] by the phonetic habits of the speaker's native language carried over to his use of another language."

We might hear an accent in the dialect of a speaker whose pronunciation may be influenced by these factors:

1. Occupation
2. Social class
3. Region
4. Origin of parents and grandparents

Accents and dialects occur in the speaking of any language by virtue of the fact that it is *spoken* and natural changes take place along lines of least resistance. For example, sounds that are difficult to pronounce, either because of a foreign-language background or for some other reason, are gradually changed to similar sounds that are easier to pronounce. A modern example of this principle is the tendency of people to say "shtraight" instead of "straight." The combination of consonant sounds *shtr* takes less effort to pronounce than the combination *str.*

PHONETICS AND THE IPA

The language of every culture was spoken long before it was ever recorded in written form, and American English too has undergone many sound changes in its short evolutionary history. Recognizing that sounds spoken by cultures everywhere undergo changes and that their written form in most cases had not kept pace, scholars and linguists in the latter part of the nineteenth century formed the International Phonetic Association. They saw that the world was becoming smaller—a steamship could cross the Atlantic in a mere three weeks, and a trip from London to Paris took merely days! Convinced of the growing need for people to learn languages other than their native ones, the scholars and linguists convened a congress in Vienna in 1888 to formulate an International Phonetic Alphabet (IPA). This alphabet consisted of an international dictionary of sounds taken from the spoken languages of the Western world. The founders designated a symbol for every recognizable sound in the various languages, along with a description of where in the mouth or throat this sound was made and in what manner the sound was produced—where it was stopped, constricted, shaped, directed through the nose, hissed, clicked, whispered, voiced, or hindered in order to achieve its unique character. These sounds were called *phonemes,* and the collection of each distinctive one, regardless of language of origin, made up the IPA.

To illustrate further what is meant by a phoneme: the word *bought* has six letters but only three phonemes: [bɔt].[2] The term *phonetics* refers to the sounds of the spoken language; phonemes make up the phonetics of what is heard.

Further discussion in this book will be confined to the phonemes in the IPA that occur in American English.

THE MAJOR DIALECTS OF AMERICAN ENGLISH

Do you drink a "soda," "tonic," or "pop"? You may refer to that drink in any one of those ways depending on the part of the country you come from. You may also pronounce the first as "soder" instead of "soda," "tawnic" rather than "tahnic," and "pawp" in place of "pop." Pronunciation and word usage vary with region in the United States. These variations are caused by the dialectal differences referred to earlier.

Language scholars have speculated that the English spoken in Appalachia is probably very close in construction to the English spoken in Shakespeare's day. This is probably due to the fact that the population of the original people who migrated to that part of the country has not been altered by too many outside influences and therefore tends to sound old-fashioned in relation to other parts of the United States.

Although the influence of television has tended to reduce regional dialects, one can still hear different dialectal patterns throughout the United States. These differences can be attributed to three factors: region, ethnicity, and education.

GEOGRAPHIC DIFFERENCES

There are five major American linguistic regions:

1. Eastern (New England and parts of New York and New Jersey)
2. Middle Atlantic (Pennsylvania, Delaware, and parts of New Jersey)
3. Appalachian (Tennessee and Kentucky)
4. Southern (Alabama, Mississippi, Louisiana, Virginia, West Virginia, and parts of Florida and Texas)
5. General American (Midwest and Far West)

---

[2] Phonetic respellings using IPA symbols are traditionally enclosed in slashes, or, as in this book, brackets.

The recent migration patterns of Eastern Americans to parts of the Sunbelt have lessened the distinction of former regional patterns in some cases.

ETHNIC DIFFERENCES

The United States is truly a "melting pot" of many nationalities, all having contributed something of their own heritage to American English. Five ethnic backgrounds have had a significant influence on our language:

1. European
2. Black American
3. African
4. Hispanic
5. Asian

EDUCATIONAL DIFFERENCES

Three types of speech can be differentiated in American English:

1. The speech of the educated
2. The speech of the self-educated
3. The speech of people with limited education

STANDARD AMERICAN ENGLISH

Although regional dialects may vary, due to the differences we have mentioned, it is usually agreed that there are three major regional American dialects or standards, defined as the speech of the majority of the educated in an area. Boundary lines are hard to define and overlap. These are the Standard American dialects:

- *General American* (spoken in most of the country—the Midwest, the West, and parts of the Southwest)
- *Eastern* (spoken in New England and parts of the Middle Atlantic states)
- *Southern* (spoken south of the Mason-Dixon line in the region that was the old Confederacy)

Students often want to know if there is a correct dialect that is preferred over the others. To this we can only respond that General American speech devoid of any geographic labeling is spoken by the greatest number of people in the United States. This is the dialect sometimes referred to as "broadcast speech" used by network television and radio announcers and most television, stage, and film actors. We recently witnessed an audition for a television commercial. After being interviewed by the casting director and reading the commercial copy, one young actor was told, "You're a wonderful type for commercials, but you have an accent that you'll have to get rid of if you want to be cast in commercials. You have to sound completely nonregional."

In the film *Trading Places*, two elderly commodities brokers revive the Pygmalion theme when one brother bets the other that he could take any street-wise con artist out of the gutter and pass him off as an investment executive. They find the appropriate derelict, clean him up, dress him in a business suit, and educate him on the dealings of the stock market. The derelict soon begins to discard his "street talk" along with his old clothing and makes a meteoric rise to success. Of course this example is a movie fantasy, but we would like to emphasize that using Standard American speech will indeed give you the most mobility in terms of job interviews, social engagements, and employment possibilities.

Learning the International Phonetic Alphabet will enable you to identify the sounds of Standard American English and compare your production of those phonemes with the norm. The IPA thus becomes a valuable tool in attuning your ear to the sounds of Standard American English.

DEVIATIONS FROM STANDARD AMERICAN

Phonemes can differ from those used in Standard American English in four ways: through substitutions, omissions, additions, and distortions.

Substitutions

Imagine Hamlet, the aristocratic Prince of Denmark, contemplating suicide in this fashion:

> To be, or not to be—*d*at is *d*a question.
> Whe*d*er 'tis nobler in *d*a mind to suffer
> *D*a slings and arrows of outrageous fortune,
> Or to take arms against a sea of troubles
> And by opposing end *d*em. To die, to sleep—
> No more, and by a sleep to say we end
> *D*a heartache and *d*a *t*ousand natural shocks
> *D*at flesh is heir to . . .

Would you think that this Hamlet's accent sounded princely? Probably not. What makes the difference? This Hamlet has *substituted* the phonemes [d] and [t] for the words that contain [th] sounds.

Other examples of substitution errors include the [w] substituted for the phoneme [r], so that the listener would hear a person who had "p*w*oblems p*w*o-nouncing co*ww*ect" [r] phonemes. Or someone who didn't like getting a "too*f*-brush for his bir*f* day." This example shows the substitution of [f] for the [th] phoneme.

Omissions

Can you figure out this well-known quotation of President Kennedy?

> Asna wa ya cunri c'n do f'you—
> Aswa you c'n do f'ya cunri!

Here is a translation into Standard English:

Ask not what your country can do for you—
Ask what you can do for your country!

Notice how many sounds, mostly consonant sounds, were left out in the first example of the quotation and how difficult it would be to understand someone who spoke like that all the time. Thus *omitting* phonemes where they should be pronounced is another source of pronunciation errors. Regional dialects, for example in various parts of the Northeastern United States tend to omit [r] sounds at the end of words, like the "New Yawkah" or the Bostonian whose "cah" is "pahked." Omitting [r]'s at the ends of words is considered Standard British among the English "uppah class."

Additions

Another example of how accents are produced is by the *addition* of a phoneme where it should not be sounded:

Americ*er,* Americ*er,*
God shed his grace on thee.
And crown thy good
With brotherhood,
From sea to shining*k* sea.

Try reading this example aloud and notice that simply *adding* the sound of [r] at the end of *America* and a [k] at the end of *shining* creates an impression of an accent. In many places in the English-speaking world, you might hear someone order "a scotch and sod*er,*" adding a phoneme where it should not be and illustrating another example of how mispronunciations occur.

Distortions

Earlier in this text it was mentioned that good speech should not call attention to itself, meaning that the listener should focus attention on content and not on pronunciation. A *distortion,* however, calls attention to the process of articulating speech. Unlike the other three categories of pronunciation faults, no phoneme is substituted, omitted, or added. The listener can still recognize the desired phoneme, but something about the way it is pronounced distorts the sound of what is heard, creating an unwanted accent.

The most common distortions occur on vowel sounds, which may tend to sound nasal and whiny. The vowel sounds in the following sentence are prone to this kind of nasal distortion:

*O*ften S*a*mmy c*a*n't st*a*nd to take Fr*a*n d*ow*ntow*n.

Another distortion that should be mentioned is called *dentalization.* It is heard on the pronunciation of *d, t,* and *s* phonemes, which in most languages other than English are pronounced with the tip of the tongue against the inside of the teeth rather than elevated to the alveolar ridge.

REGIONAL DIFFERENCES IN STANDARD PRONUNCIATION

Although General American will be the model for all articulation work that follows, it should be noted that minor variations in pronunciation occur across the country. For example, though many phoneticians say that it is no longer important to differentiate between the *wh* in *whether* and the *w* in *was,* many sections of the country have yet to concur. Also, the *a* in *ask* and *dance* can vary from a tense, front sound, particularly in the Midwest, to a more relaxed, slightly lower version of the same sound that is heard on both coasts and among trained speakers. It is never, however, the "veddy British" back *a* of "bahth" or "I cahn't."

There is general agreement across the country that the *r* that begins a word such as *ready,* the medial *r* that is followed by a vowel as in *occurring,* and the *r* blend words such as *pretty* and *bread* should all be pronounced with a strong *r* sound. However, Southerners and Easterners allow considerable variation in the pronunciation of a final *r* or an *r* that is followed by a consonant as in *park* or *farm.*

These few examples should suffice to illustrate the point that Southern and Eastern standard speech may vary slightly from what is presented in this text, and if you speak either one, let your ear guide you to the norm of what is used by the majority of the educated speakers in your area.

CLASSIFICATION OF SOUNDS IN THE IPA

In grade school we all had it drummed into us that the vowels are "*a, e, i, o, u,* and sometimes *y.*" Forget it—or rather think of that litany as a handy way of describing the five or six *written* symbols that so imperfectly represent the 14 vowel sounds of our *spoken* language,[3] which are the concern of the next chapter. Phonetics classifies all sounds (phonemes) into three categories (vowels, diphthongs, and consonants) and defines them thus:

1. *Vowels are shaped sounds*—sounds that are totally a product of resonance due to alterations in the size, shape, and texture of the oral cavity.
2. *Diphthongs are a blend of two vowels* coming together with no break in between. For instance, listen to the two vowel sounds in the words *boy, my,* and *now.* A *triphthong is a blend of three vowels* that appears in some dialects, particularly Southern ones, where a simple word with one vowel like *sit* expands into "sijuht."
3. *Consonants are sounds that have been stopped* (as in [p] or [d]) *or hindered in some fashion* (as in [z] or [f]) *by the articulators.* Some are *voiced* (the vocal bands are vibrating) and other are *unvoiced* (produced on the outgoing breath stream). Contrast the difference between [z], which is voiced, and [s], which is unvoiced.

---

[3] Take the alphabet symbol *a:* What sound does it represent? Compare *ate, any, at, car, taught, tear, fail.*

In addition, it is important to know that phonetics recognizes the existence of *allophones* in connected speech, which are *variations of individual phonemes.* For instance, if you listen for the [s] sound in the words *save* and *lists,* you will notice that it sounds more whistly on the second one. If you compare the [p] in *pie* with the one in *cup,* there is more of a puff of air on the first than on the second. Many voiced sounds become partially unvoiced if an unvoiced consonant precedes them. Notice the difference in the [n] in *now* and *snow.* However, when these legitimate slight variations within a phoneme go beyond what is naturally heard in connected speech and call attention to themselves, they become distortions and are considered incorrect.

ASSIMILATIONS IN CONNECTED SPEECH AND SPEECH STANDARDS

Assimilation is the effect of one sound on a neighboring sound. When we speak, we may be uttering as many as 25 phonemes in a single second, so "the movements required to make a sound will have to accommodate the movements required for the sounds that precede, follow, or overlap the sound."[4] *Eh-v-uh-er-ee* (every) *s-ah-oo-n-d* (sound) cannot maintain intact all the features it has in isolation. The speed of our mechanism just isn't up to it—nor would we want it to be, for we speak in phrases, in a connected flow, not in individual phonemes.

Assimilation operates to promote ease and naturalness in articulation. The problem becomes determining what is acceptable and what is not. For instance, the word *stopped* is correctly assimilated by all of us to something that sounds like "stopt" rather than the more difficult "stopd" or "stop-ped." *Soldier* was originally a mouthful to pronounce, "sold-ee-er," and assimilation has long since justified the simplification of the middle sounds to the pronunciation we know.

But if someone "ast" you if you "wanna sam'ich," you would have to agree that "ast" is easier to say than "askt," "wanna" than "want to have," and "sam'ich" than "sandwich," but such assimilations are considered too far from the norm of acceptable speech and thus nonstandard.

So what are acceptable assimilations and what are not? There is no absolute rule of good speech at all times in every section of the country; we are back again to what was stressed in the first chapter. Appropriateness and unobtrusiveness should be your guide: *Whom* are you talking to (what is their usage)? *What* is the occasion? What is your *role* as communicator? What is your *objective* in this role?

Throughout the work on articulation that follows, some of the more commonly accepted assimilations will be mentioned.

COMMON AMERICAN ENGLISH PHONEMES AND THEIR IPA SYMBOLS

Tables 8.1 through 8.3 show the common phonemes of American English with a comparison of the dictionary symbol and its IPA equivalent. Key words are

---

[4] Robert G. King and Eleanor DiMichael, *Articulation and Voice: Improving Oral Communication* (New York: Macmillan, 1978), p. 255.

TABLE 8.1   Consonants

IPA symbol		Dictionary symbol	Key words		
p	_p_	p	_p_ick	ha_pp_y	cli_p_
b	_b_	b	_b_et	a_b_out	kno_b_
t	_t_	t	_t_oe	li_tt_le	nes_t_
d	_d_	d	_d_o	en_d_ow	a_dd_
k	_k_	k	_k_ey	a_c_tor	as_k_
g	_g_	g	_g_o	su_g_ar	lo_g_
f	_f̶_	f	_f_ly	su_ff_er	loa_f_
v	_v_	v	_v_iew	a_v_ow	lo_v_e
θ	_θ_	th	_th_in	me_th_od	my_th_
ð	_ð̵_	th	_th_e	fa_th_er	ba_th_e
s	_s_	s	_s_ea	pe_s_t	ki_ss_
z	_z_	z	_z_oo	ea_s_y	pha_s_e
ʃ	_ʃ_	sh	_sh_oe	mi_ss_ion	plu_sh_
ʒ	_ʒ_	zh	_g_enre	trea_s_ure	rou_ge_
h	_h_	h	_h_ow	be_h_ave	—*
tʃ	_tʃ_	ch	_ch_ew	a_ch_ieve	i_tch_
dʒ	_dʒ_	j	_j_oy	a_dj_oin	e_dge_
m	_m_	m	_m_e	a_m_ong	so_m_e
n	_n_	n	_n_o	a_nn_oy	wi_n_
ŋ	_ŋ_	ng	—	fi_ng_er	cli_ng_
l	_l_	l	_l_ove	fe_ll_ow	pu_ll_
hw	_hw_	hw	_wh_at	some_wh_ere	—
w	_w_	w	_w_ing	s_w_ell	—
r	_r_	r	_r_un	t_r_ee	tea_r_
i	_j_	y	_y_outh	on_i_on	—

* A blank space indicates that the particular sound does not appear in that position in any word in English.

specified to help you identify each phoneme as it appears in various positions—initially, in the middle, or at the end of a word.

For students for whom English is a second language and who wish to work on American English pronunciation in depth, an additional chapter, "A Guide for the Foreign Speaker of American English," has been added to supplement the work in the next two chapters and to identify the features of English that may present difficulties.

In school you learned the _orthographic_ alphabet, the written form used for spelling in the traditional way. For many of you, learning the _phonetic_ alphabet will have a practical benefit in addition to its value as a tool in learning Standard American English pronunciation. Acting students find it a boon in mastering the sound changes of learning stage dialects, while singers find it valuable in helping them to pronounce the various foreign languages they need to sing in. Broadcast majors use it for ready transcription of complicated or unfamiliar names or places in reporting the news, interviewing, or announcing. And for everyone, knowledge of the phonetic alphabet will prove an additional plus in jotting down the exact pronunciation of an unfamiliar-sounding name or place.

TABLE 8.2   Vowels

IPA symbol		Dictionary symbol	Key words		
i	ɩ	ē	*e*ach	f*ee*t	*see*
ɪ	ɪ	i, ĭ	*i*tch	f*i*t	min*i*
e, eɪ	e, eɪ	ā	*a*che	c*a*ke	s*ay*
ɛ	ɛ	e, ĕ	*e*ver	m*a*ny	—
æ*	æ	a, ă	*a*sk	f*a*ncy	—
u	u	o͞o	*oo*ze	f*oo*d	t*oo*
ʊ	ʊ	oo	—	f*oo*t	—
o, oʊ	o, oʊ	ō	*o*kay	v*o*te	l*ow*
ɔ	ɔ	ô	*aw*e	t*a*lk	l*aw*
ɑ	ɑ	a	*o*n	f*a*ther	p*a*pa
ɝ, ɜ	ɝ, ɜ	ur	*ear*th	w*or*ld	occ*ur* (stressed)
ɚ, ər	ɚ, ər	ər	—	p*er*form	sist*er* (unstressed)
ə	ə	ə	*a*llow	s*ea*son	pizz*a* (unstressed)
ʌ	ʌ	u, ŭ	*u*p	l*o*ve	— (stressed)

* [a] is a lower-tongue variant of [æ] used in some parts of the country.

TABLE 8.3   Diphthongs

IPA symbol		Dictionary symbol	Key words		
aɪ	aɪ	i	*i*ce	sm*i*le	s*igh*
aʊ	aʊ	ou	*ou*nce	d*ow*n	n*ow*
ɔɪ	ɔɪ	oi	*oi*l	v*oi*ce	t*oy*

Starting to read phonetics

Now that the alphabet is before you, can you figure out who these famous people are?

[me wɛst]   [bɑb hop]
[mɪki maʊs]   [brus sprɪŋstin]
[krɪstəfɚ kəlʌmbəs]   [ebrəhæm lɪŋkən]
[kliopætrə]   [wɪljəm ʃekspiɚ]
[ɛlvɪs prɛzli]   [lusil bɔl]

Vacation time. Where would you like to go?

[həwaɪi]   [ɪtəli]
[bɚmjudə]   [skændəneviə]
[ɪŋglənd]   [dɪznilænd]
[mɛksɪko]   [grænd kænjən]
[naɪægrə fɔlz]   [fræns]

SUMMARY

Spoken language changes constantly, but the written form, being fixed, does not keep pace. Thus spelling in English (and in other language systems) is often not representative of pronunciation. The International Phonetic Alphabet (IPA) was developed toward the end of the nineteenth century as a means of helping people learn languages other than their own. The place and manner of production of each separate phoneme was analyzed, and a fixed symbol was assigned to each distinctive one.

Dialects and accents persist in speakers from different parts of the United States due to a number of factors including regional and ethnic background, but there are three accepted standards countrywide: General American, Eastern, and Southern. General American is recommended because it is used by most of the people in the country and will give the user the greatest mobility with the least labeling. The IPA can be used as a tool to compare speech with the standard. Any fairly consistent substitutions, additions, omissions, or distortions can be identified and then corrected.

Phonetics recognizes three classes of sounds: vowels, diphthongs, and consonants, with allophones (accepted variations) in each. To promote ease and naturalness of articulation, a certain amount of assimilation (change in sounds) is normal in connected speech, but the problem becomes determining what is acceptable and what is considered nonstandard.

9
VOWELS AND DIPHTHONGS

"Remember that you are a human being with a
soul and a divine gift of articulate speech; that
your native language is the language of
Shakespeare and Milton and the Bible; and don't
sit there crooning like a bilious pigeon."

GEORGE BERNARD SHAW, *PYGMALION*

Challenge exercises

1. Say the following sentence with your fingers lightly placed on the bridge of your nose. The challenge is to say the sentence without feeling any vibrations on your fingertips.

   "Hi!" she cried aloud to the class as they laughed back at her.

2. Each of the vowels in the following sentence should be pronounced *without the addition of extra sounds.*

   As a rule, in school, it is an off day when I feel stale and so I fail.

Vowels are not as easy to pronounce purely as one might think. Two problems are particularly recurrent: Either they become nasalized, or they are subject to impurities, with extra sounds added. If you felt any vibrations in your fingertips on the first challenge sentence, there was some nasalization. On the second sentence, if even one word sounded as written below, you were adding sound that didn't belong:

   As a ru*wuh*l, in schoo*wuh*l, it is an *oowuh*ff day when I fee*yuh*l sta*yuh*l and so I fai*yuh*l.

Vowels

As has already been stated, vowels are shaped sound, totally a product of resonance. In the chapter on resonance you learned that a modification of the resonating chamber will alter the pattern of overtones and therefore will alter the quality of the sound. The changing movement of the articulators to vary the size and shape of the mouth, and the jaw, the lips, and the humping of the tongue change the overtones being reinforced, producing vowel sounds.

In fact, vowel phonemes are pure sound, although the quality of the sound can be pleasant or whiny, depending on how the articulators are modified. Vowels carry the sound of your voice, and how you want your vowels to sound is dependent on how you shape your articulators.

Diphthongs

Diphthongs, as defined earlier, are two vowels coming together without a break between; they are phonemes that begin the resonating characteristics of one vowel sound and glide toward the resonating characteristics of another vowel sound. There are two types. In *phonemic* diphthongs, both vowels have to be included or the meaning of the word changes or is lost; [aɪ] as in *fight,* [aʊ] as in *down,* and [ɔɪ] as in *join* are phonemic diphthongs. Notice that if the second vowel in *fight* [faɪt] is removed, it becomes a different word, *fat* [fat]. Experiment by doing the same with the other two.

In *nonphonemic diphthongs,* the second vowel *can* be removed without significantly altering the meaning of the word. In American English, [eɪ] as in *plate* [pleɪt] is commonly used in the stressed syllables of words rather than the pure vowel [e], and the same is true of [oʊ] instead of [o] in such words as *home* [hoʊm]. Notice that if you take the second vowel out in either of these examples, the word sounds clipped off, but there is no question as to its meaning.

CLASSIFYING VOWEL PHONEMES

All vowels are voiced, which means that the air has been set into vibration at the vocal bands. Vowels may be classified on the basis of five characteristics: position of the tongue, height of the tongue arch, muscle tension, lip rounding or spreading, and duration.

Position of the tongue

If the tongue is theoretically divided into three parts, the *front, center,* and *back,* the vertical movement of the tongue shifts from front to middle to back, or vice versa, depending on which vowel sound is being articulated. For example, notice the shifting of the tongue movements from the front of your mouth to the back as you say *only* the vowel sounds in the words *seep, sup,* and *soup.* According to tongue position, we divide vowel phonemes into three groups: *front, central,* and *back.*

1. [i, ɪ, e, ɛ, æ] are called *front vowels* because the tongue is active in the front of the mouth upon production of the sound.
2. [ʌ, ə, ɝ, ɚ] are called *central vowels* because the tongue shifts to the center of the mouth upon production of the sound.
3. [u, ʊ, o, ɔ, ɑ] are called *back vowels* because the tongue activity shifts to the back of the mouth upon production of the sound (see Figure 9.1).

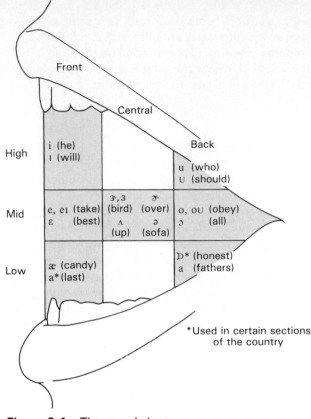

Figure 9.1   The vowel chart

Height of the tongue arch

Look in a mirror and notice the change in jaw position when you pronounce *only* the front vowel sounds in the following sentence:

He will take best candy.

The height of the tongue arch gradually diminishes as the jaw lowers. This changes the shape of the resonating chamber (in this case, the mouth) as you move from sound to sound. Thus a second way to classify vowel phonemes is as *high, mid,* and *low.*

Muscle tension

The tongue is a powerful instrument of muscle fibers. If you say the vowel sounds *only* in the two phrases *he is* and *who would* while holding your fingertips directly under your chin, you will notice a change in muscle tension as you shift from one sound to another. Therefore, a third way to classify vowels is according to whether the tongue is *tense* or *lax* upon production.

Lip rounding or spreading

Look in a mirror again to notice the differences in lip rounding or lip spreading during the articulation of vowel phonemes. Refer to Figure 9.1 to help you identify the placement of vowel phonemes. You will notice that front vowels exhibit various degrees of lip spreading as you pronounce them. The back vowels, with the exception of [ɑ], exhibit various degrees of lip rounding. The central vowels tend to be neither rounded nor spread. Vowels also have differing degrees of jaw opening.

Duration

How long a vowel is held, in English, can sometimes change its sound. This is dependent on two factors: first, by the nature of the vowel itself—some vowels, like the [i] sound in *meet,* are held longer than the [ɪ] sound in *hit*—and, second, by whether the vowel occurs in a stressed or unstressed syllable. As an example, in the word *beneath,* the stress is on the second syllable, giving the first syllable a short vowel sound [bɪniθ].

THE FRONT VOWELS: [i ɪ e ɛ æ]

[i]

fonɛtɪk trɪviə

Which of these would you *not* eat?

[mit, krimtʃiz, piz, fliz, otmil, gris, pitsə, triz]

Say the following sentence aloud both ways, exactly as written:

1. I f*eeyu*l that price is a r*eayu*l st*eayu*l.
2. I f*ee*l that price is a r*ea*l st*ea*l.

The phoneme [i] is an easy sound for anyone to produce, but it is subject to careless addition errors, as in sentence 1.

FACTS

Technical description: [i] is a high, front, unrounded, tense vowel of long duration.
Correct production: The tongue is arched high toward the front of the mouth. The tongue is tensed, the upper and lower teeth are close together, and the lips are spread.
☆ *Spellings: e* as in *me, ee* as in *seek, i* as in *marine, ea* as in *meat, ie* as in *achieve, ei* as in *deceive, eo* as in *people, ey* as in *key.*
Standard variations: In certain parts of the United States [i] becomes [ɪ] in final unstressed positions, so *pretty* is not [prɪti] but [prɪtɪ].

IN USE

Each *e*vening p*eo*ple m*ee*t to exchange s*ea*son's gr*ee*tings.

Check yourself on words from each list.

eat	please	three
east	seal	flee
easy	believe	see
eager	achieve	be
Easter	real	tree
even	meat	key
ear	ravinc	me
eel	feel	glee
evil	repeat	agree
each	conceive	he

PROBLEMS TO AVOID

1. Addition of "uh" [ə] or "yuh" [jə].

☆[1] **2.** Substitution of [ɪ] as in *hit* for [i] as in *heat.*

Each problem is analyzed in greater detail. Concentrate on your area of weakness.

1. Added sound or sounds   [i] is particularly prone to addition error if it is followed by [l]. It is [sil], not [sijəl], one syllable, not two.

Say the following pairs of words, keeping the second as free from additions as the first.

feet	feel	peat	peal
reap	real	meat	meal
deep	deal	keep	keel
squeak	squeal	weep	wheel
steep	steal		

Warm-up phrases for practice: a green automobile, squeaky wheels, weep real tears, seem to feel it, an even keel, meaty veal, steep heels, shady deals, sleeping seals, please peel it

☆ **2. [ɪ] for [i]**   People for whom English is a second language may confuse [ɪ] in *in* with [i] in *seen.*

With your hand under your chin, feel the tension as you say [i] in *be, me, see* [bi, mi, si]. Contrast that with the lack of tension as you say the short [ɪ] in *in, sin, thin* [ɪn, sɪn, θɪn]. Note also that your tongue is higher in your mouth for [i] than for [ɪ].

Contrast the following pairs of words for differences in tension, sound, *and* meaning:

---

[1] The symbol ☆ is used to designate material specifically intended for nonnative speakers of English.

[i]	[ɪ]	[i]	[ɪ]
seat	sit	keep	clip
beat	bit	steep	stiff
feet	fit	reap	rip
meat	mitt	sweet	swift
deep	dip	deem	dim

Warm-up phrases for practice: a pleasing view, season meat well, a dreamy scene, a cheese pizza, green beans, means to please

Use care in the following phrases, for both sounds are in each: see it, a squealing pig, a thin tree, will agree, skinned his knee, a sleeping prince, a ticket to Greece, lift the ceiling

ADDING ON FOR PROFICIENCY

1. Read the following sentences aloud, pronouncing clear [i] sounds and avoid adding extra sounds.

   a. In the evening I need to feel the wheels of stress unwind.
   b. In the scene, the people screamed and squealed.
   c. We feel the need to eat three meals a day.
   d. The fields yield plenty of greens.
   e. He concealed his need for petty stealing until he was seen.
   f. She conceived a new deal to achieve real freedom for the people.
   g. Please peel a green plum for me.
   h. He healed the evil people of their evil deeds, or so he feels.
   i. The movie's reel ended with the dream sequence scene.

☆ 2. *For nonnative speakers*   Keep clear long [i] sounds in the following sentences.

   a. The heel on my shoe seems loose.
   b. A deep seat feels comfortable.
   c. We eat a meal each evening.
   d. Speaking English clearly is easy to achieve.
   e. She cleaned the machine.
   f. I feel sleepy at three in the afternoon.
   g. My feet squeak on the shiny, wet street.
   h. I believe in planting fresh green seeds.
   i. Steven eagerly reads to meet his needs.
   j. Peace and quiet seem ideal.

SUPER EXERCISES

☆ 1. *Using* [i] *correctly in conversational speech*   Once you have mastered the warm-up and proficiency exercises, make the transition to everyday speech. Create a sentence around each of the following words or phrases; then use the sentence in conversational speech without writing it down.

evenings	seasons of the year
Easter time	cleaning
monthly meetings	green beans
TV	cheese
dreams	beefburger

☆ 2. *Travelogue*   You can only visit places that contain [i] in their names. How many of the places listed can you travel to? Say them aloud; then assume you are a travel agent and make a "sales pitch" for each place whose name contains [i].

Greece	West Indies	Reno
Minnesota	Alaska	Atlantic City
Disneyland	Sweden	Queens
Greenland	Boston	Argentina
Bermuda	Palm Beach	Italy
Seattle	Mexico	Egypt

[ɪ]

fonɛtɪk trɪviə

Which of the following is *not* an animal?

[tʃɪmpænzi, mɪŋk, dʒɪræf, diɚ, kɪtən, sɪŋk, bigəl]

Say the following sentences aloud exactly as written:

1. Th*ee*s *ee*s M*ee*s S*ee*mpson.
2. Th*i*s *i*s M*i*ss S*i*mpson.

The most prevalent and recurring problem with the phoneme [ɪ] is heard among nonnative speakers of English who tend to substitute [i] for [ɪ].

FACTS

Technical description: [ɪ] is a high, front, unrounded, lax vowel of short duration.
Correct production: The tongue is arched slightly lower and a little farther back in the mouth than for [i]. The tongue is relaxed, the upper and lower teeth are close together, and the lips are spread.
☆ *Spellings: i* as in *fit, e* as in *refer, u* as in *busy, o* as in *women,* any vowel in an unstressed syllable that may be pronounced [ɪ] or [ə]
Standard variations: In words ending in *y,* the final sound is pronounced as [i] or [ɪ] depending on the part of the United States you live in. Either is considered standard pronunciation.

IN USE

Mr. Fl*i*nt bl*i*nked his eyes *i*n the m*i*st.

Check yourself on words from each list:

if	pick	debate
ill	city	defer
is	stick	believe
it	think	receive
important	lift	resist
impossible	gift	beneath
in	mint	demand
intuition	pink	before
instead	visit	devise
insist	will	remove

PROBLEMS TO AVOID

☆ **1.** Substitution of [i] for [ɪ]. As mentioned before, this is a very common problem for people who learn English as a second language.

2. Diphthongation or triphthongation of [ɪ] so that *sit* becomes "si-uht" [sɪət] or "si-yuht" [sɪjət].

3. Substitution of [ɛ] for [ɪ]. Although this is not a common substitution, it is heard in certain parts of the United States.

Each problem is analyzed in more detail. Concentrate on your area of weakness.

☆ **1. [i] for [ɪ]**   *This* is [ðɪs] not [ðis]. Notice the slight shift in tongue movement backward and decreased muscle tension as you shift from [i] to [ɪ]. Your ear will be your greatest guide. Follow a good American model.

Contrast the difference in sound *and* meaning in the following word pairs.

[i]	[ɪ]	[i]	[ɪ]
sleep	slip	seal	sill
peach	pitch	beat	bit
creep	crib	ease	is
cheap	chip	meet	mitt
leap	lip	deep	dip
each	itch	neat	knit
heat	hit	steel	still
eat	it	meal	mill
sheep	ship	peal	pill
feet	fit	feel	fill

Warm-up phrases for practice: fifty things, include it in, if it fits, quick pick-me-ups, insist on it, impress him with it, indent the margins, silly bit

2. Added sound   Say the following words without adding any extra sounds so that diphthongs are not created out of vowels meant to remain pure. If this is one of your problems, it helps to shorten the vowel sound and move on more quickly to the following consonant.

quit	quick
chip	pitch
bring	sick
sing	list
tint	miss

Warm-up phrases for practice: thrift institutions, simple hints, limited vision, visiting the Quinns, bringing in tins, rich living, shipping him gin

3. [ɛ] for [ɪ]   This substitution occurs infrequently, but if you say "set" instead of "sit" contrast the words listed below to become aware of your pronunciation.

[ɪ]	[ɛ]
hill	hell
pick	peck
quill	quell
lit	let
sill	sell

Practice the warm-up phrases under point 2 as well.

ADDING ON FOR PROFICIENCY

1. Say the following sentences using clear [ɪ] sounds.

   a. You need to slim if you can pinch an inch.
   b. He swims even with his limited vision.
   c. Liz is interested in silver rings.
   d. Dip the dishes in the sink.
   e. Prince sings and sprints in the music video.
   f. Bill is visiting with Jim in Kensington.
   g. Tim will inherit everything.
   h. Vincent fills the vial to its lip with pills.
   i. Dennis still likes to lick icicle sticks.
   j. Venice is a city splendid enough for kings.

☆ 2. *For nonnative speakers*

   1. Say the following sentences aloud with clear [ɪ], not [i] sounds.

      a. The list is in English.
      b. Children live in a hillside inn.
      c. Bill is visiting his six sisters.
      d. Quick, bring him some gin!
      e. Tim is hitting Mister Flynn.
      f. Kids swim in the river.

2. Now say the following phrases, which contain both [ɪ] and [i].

city streets	a real hit
rich cream	meet traffic
feel sick	discount jeans
silver earrings	meaty dishes
keeping fit	minty green

3. Read the following sentences aloud using clear [ɪ] sounds.

a. Lynn thinks often of him.
b. The liquid dripped from the rim of the glass.
c. He dipped his fingers into the ink.
d. Little things swim in the river.
e. Pick the twins to sing the hymns.
f. Tim hit himself in the chin.
g. The immigrant intended to improve his English.
h. Milk over fish is a favorite dish.
i. Bill is still ill.
j. The liquid spilled on the window sill.

SUPER EXERCISES

☆ 1. *Using* [ɪ] *correctly in conversational speech*   Once you have mastered the warm-up and proficiency exercises, make the transition to everyday speech. Create your own sentence around each expression and say it aloud at a normal conversational rate. For example, if the expression is "think and wish," you might use it this way: "I think of spring and wish for it every day." Do not write your sentences down.

cities	children
I will	business
paying bills	I will finish
women	inch by inch
This is	pretty

☆ 2. *Finish the scene*   Cast two people in the roles of Linda and her husband, Tim, and then let the class participate in finishing the scene.

In a Minute, Tim

SCENE: A motel room. Tim is out on the front stoop calling through the door to Linda, who is still in the bathroom.

TIM: The airport limousine has just pulled up, Linda.
LINDA: In a minute, Tim.
TIM: It's picking up passengers. Come on!
LINDA: In a minute, Tim.
TIM: We'll miss it if you don't come *quickly!*
LINDA: In a little minute, Tim. I'm finishing my lips.

TIM: Women! *Skip* the lipstick! (*angry*) Not a single minute more, Linda. *Linda*!

LINDA: (*appearing on the stoop*) See—the minute's up. Finished. Let's go!

TIM: (*sitting wearily*) Skip it. We've missed the limousine. In a million years I'll never figure women out. . . .

LINDA: Missed the limousine? You idiot—why didn't you . . .

[e] or [eɪ]

fonɛtɪk trɪviə

Which of the following is not in the United States?
[meɪn, ɪndiænə, gris, mɪsɪsɪpi, ɪtəli, ʃɪkɑgo, mɪniæpəlɪs, rino]

Say the following sentence aloud and listen to whether you keep the vowel pure or whether you add an extra sound to extend it into a diphthong:

Jane's baby remains dismayingly plain.

If you are American-born, you undoubtedly made each of the vowels into the diphthong [eɪ], which is the way this vowel is most often pronounced in American English. If you are a nonnative speaker, you may have kept the vowel pure, which calls attention to your speech as being slightly "foreign."

FACTS

Technical description: [e] is a mid-front, unrounded, tense vowel of long duration in stressed syllables. The diphthong [eɪ] is almost always heard for this sound in American English in stressed syllables. The pure vowel [e] is heard in unstressed syllables, which occur less frequently.

Correct production: The tongue is in the middle in the front of the mouth, slightly lower than for [ɪ]. The lips are spread. The tongue muscles are tense.

☆ *Spellings: a* as in *fame, ay* as in *away, ea* as in *break, ai* as in *claim, ei* as in *vein.*

IN USE

The tr*ai*n was del*ay*ed *ei*ght hours in the st*a*tion today.

Check yourself on words from each list.

aid	made	play
ache	take	say
ape	baby	today
eight	remain	obey
agent	blame	away
able	same	okay
ace	tame	gray
ale	sane	may

aimed	stain	ray
age	drain	pay

PROBLEMS TO AVOID

1. Addition of [ə] to [eɪ] so that *game* [geɪm] becomes "gayuhm" [geɪəm] or [geɪjəm].

2. Nasalization of [eɪ] when preceded or followed by *m* or *n,* so that the velum (soft palate) is raised for the sound on a word such as *aim.*

☆ **3.** Substitution of [e] or [ɛ] for [eɪ] so that *take* [teɪk] becomes "tek" [tek] or [tɛk].

Each problem is analyzed in greater detail. Concentrate on your area of weakness.

1. Added sound   Say the following words without adding any extra sounds so that triphthongs are not created. If this is your problem, shorten the duration of time spent on [eɪ] and move on more quickly to the following consonant sound.

pale	scale
chain	bake
vein	crate
remain	await
break	wake

Warm-up phrases for practice: plain strain, pale veins, remains the same, bake the grain, crochet a chain, attain a name, explain the drain, take a cake

2. Nasalization of [eɪ]   If you tend to keep your velum lowered on vowel sounds before or between nasal consonants, try these exercises to create awareness of velar movement. Place your fingertips lightly on the bridge of your nose. You should feel no vibration as you say the first word of the pair. Then try to duplicate that same freedom from nasality as you pronounce the vowel in the second word of each pair.

ate	mate	aid	mane	ache	aim
ape	nape	ace	maim	fate	fame
say	same	tray	train	date	dame
cape	came	clay	claim	rate	rain
late	lame	ail	snail	skate	snake

Warm-up phrases for practice: aping games, amazing gains, grains of maize, mailing to Maine, mistaking the claim, the stranger entertained, blaming the tame, mating the strain

☆ **3. [e] or [ɛ] for** [eɪ]   This is a common problem for nonnative speakers and native speakers of English outside America.

  a. If you substitute [e] for [eɪ], prolong the [e] and add an [ɪ] right after it with no break between the sounds. It may help to exaggerate the added vowel sound at first, making *play* into "playee" [pleɪ . .] or [pleɪ . .] and *stay* into "stayee" [steɪ . .] or [steɪ . .]. Go back to the earlier word lists in parts 1 and 2 and practice each this way; then do the warm-ups that follow part b.

b. If you substitute [ɛ] for [eɪ], contrast the difference in sound *and* meaning between the following, being sure to prolong and exaggerate the added vowel sound in the second word in each pair.

get	gate	lest	laced
met	mate	test	taste
rest	raced	bet	bait
west	waist	let	late

Warm-up phrases for practice: saving your pay, paving the way, a safe that won't fail, aim for the base, a day in May, bet on eight races, a cake display, a paper plate

ADDING ON FOR PROFICIENCY

1. Say the following phrases with clear [eɪ] sounds.

   a. taking the train to Maine
   b. claiming fame for the game
   c. paying for insane gains
   d. training the pale cranes
   e. taking the stains away

2. Practice saying these sentences.

   a. Blake awaits the tourist train in Spain.
   b. Lazy David's wages are insane.
   c. Ray aims to engage other forms of play.
   d. Fame is to blame for the drain in creative talent.
   e. Dainty Fay will stay that way if she maintains her weight.
   f. May strays along the bay on lazy summer days.
   g. The tamer made a change in the way he trains the animals.
   h. The paper saints were made to look quaint by using paint.
   i. Sailors sail away before the break of day.
   j. Dame Elaine retains her name even when living in Maine.

☆ 3. *For nonnative speakers*   Say the [eɪ] diphthongs clearly.

   a. I always say, "Today is the day to make changes."
   b. The dating game is often played.
   c. Aspirin makes the pain go away.
   d. David changed the pace of the race.
   e. Mavis blamed Jane for throwing grain down the drain.
   f. Changing your ways may save the day.
   g. Lorraine may faint when you explain your delay.
   h. Abe gave his name to the baby without any shame.
   i. That vein takes the blood away from the brain.
   j. Amy portrays a crazy lady in the play.

SUPER EXERCISES

☆ 1. *Using* [eɪ] *correctly in conversational speech*   Once you have mastered the warm-up and proficiency exercises, make the transition to everyday speech. Create your own sentence around each expression and say it aloud at a normal conversational rate. For example, if the expression is "makes stains," you might say, "Bleach makes stains disappear." Do not write your sentences down.

plain paper	frames
changes	stained teeth
tasty bits	The United States
Today I . . .	my favorite place

2. *Finish the scene*   Cast two people in the roles of the Maid and Madame Renée; then let the class participate in finishing the scene.

Backstage at the Algonquin

SCENE: Madame Renée's dressing room backstage.

MAID: Madame Renée, wake up! It's time to awake. Your public awaits you onstage for the matinée.

MADAME RENÉE: (*grandly*) Go away! I shall not play upon the stage today.

MAID: But Madame Renée, please don't delay any longer. It's getting very late.

MADAME RENÉE: (*loudly*) I say that I'll not play today. I'm in a rage over Elaine. That dame upstages me at every matinée.

MAID: Madame Renée, please get into your makeup for the matinée. It would be such a shame to let Miss Elaine lay claim to your place on the stage—not to mention your fame and your well-known name. . . .

[ɛ]

fonɛtɪk trɪviə

Which of the following would you not drink?

[lɛməneɪd, ti, mɪlk, geɪtɚeɪd, ɪŋk, pɛpsi, wɪndɛks, frɛskə]

Say the following sentences aloud exactly as written.

1. *A*yvery *A*murrican should *i*njoy eating *a*ygs.
2. *E*very American should *e*njoy eating *e*ggs.

Although [ɛ] is relatively easy for most people to produce and therefore presents no major problem in terms of communication, it is nevertheless a sound prone to substitutions.

FACTS

Technical description: [ɛ] is a mid-front vowel of short duration.
Correct production: The front of the tongue is raised midway toward the palate.
The tongue muscles are lax, and the lips are spread only slightly.

☆ *Spellings: e* as in *get, ea* as in *head, ie* as in *friend, eo* as in *leopard, a* as in *any,
ai* as in *said, u* as in *bury, ae* as in *aesthetic*

IN USE

The b*e*st def*e*nse every *e*nemy uses is s*e*lf-def*e*nse.

Check yourself on words from each list:

egg	leg	said
every	test	dreamt
etch	met	led
energy	tent	any
elevate	set	guess
edge	bet	buried
empty	merit	many
edit	merry	says
exercise	fend	friendly

PROBLEMS TO AVOID

1. Substitution of [ɪ], [eɪ], or [æ] for [ɛ] so that *pen* [pɛn] becomes "pin" [pɪn],
   egg [ɛg] becomes "aygg" [eɪg], and *any* [ɛni] becomes "anny" [æni]. These
   substitutions occur frequently in certain parts of the United States.
2. Substitution of [ɝ] for [ɛ] when followed by *r* so that *very* [vɛri] becomes
   "vuhry" [vɝi].

Each problem is analyzed in greater detail. Concentrate on your area of
weakness.

1. [ɪ], [eɪ], or [æ] for [ɛ]   Contrast [ɛ] with [ɪ], [eɪ], and [æ] in the words listed
here. Notice that compared to [ɛ], [ɪ] has much more lip spreading and a slightly
higher tongue position, [eɪ] has more lip spreading and tenser tongue muscles,
and [æ] has a more open mouth and lowered jaw position.

Contrast the difference in sound *and* meaning in these pairs, concentrating
on the substitution you make.

[ɪ]	[ɛ]	[eɪ]	[ɛ]	[æ]	[ɛ]
pin	pen	pain	pen	and	end
win	when	wait	wet	aster	Esther
tin	ten	gate	get	lap	let
kin	Ken	take	tech	bad	bed
mint	meant	rake	wreck	shall	shell
sit	set	date	debt	capped	kept
fit	fetch	paste	pest	fast	fest

mit	met	mate	meant	mass	mess
knit	net	rate	rest	vast	vest
lift	left	baste	best	crass	cress

Warm-up phrases for practice: pink pencil, ten pins, Kenneth's kinfolk, twin tents, physical wreck, seven sins, gate legs, lap desk, excellent inns

2. [ɝ] for [ɛ] when followed by r   Contrast the sounds in the following pairs:

merry	Murray
very	worry
American	murky
bury	Burry
ferry	furry

Warm-up phrases for practice: many Americans, buried berries, very best, merry men, ten ferries

ADDING ON FOR PROFICIENCY

1. Repeat the following phrases aloud using clear [ɛ] sounds, building up speed but not at the expense of accuracy.

   a. energetic exercise bends
   b. ten and twenty pens
   c. blended eggs with lentils
   d. a very merry American
   e. better library dictionaries
   f. pretending to spend tens

2. Read the following sentences aloud, taking care to pronounce clear [ɛ] sounds. Avoid substitutions in place of [ɛ].

   a. Edward left his best friend in debt after his death.
   b. Hedy enjoys strenuous exercise at every session.
   c. Get me the red pen from the table next to my desk.
   d. Treasure hunts bring a measure of pleasure to Betty, who gets a kick out of them.
   e. Plenty of men spend just as much money on dressing trends as women do.
   f. Dentists tell everyone how to cleanse dentures properly.
   g. Senator Brent attempted to get reelected by his constituency.
   h. Edna felt the empty nest syndrome when Peggy and Ted left home.
   i. The chef's expertise in cookery experimentation involved breads and eggs.
   j. It's best not to send so heavy a desk for fear of bending the legs.

SUPER EXERCISE

Create your own recipe using at least *five* of the following ingredients, the crazier the better. Sample start: "Take a pheasant and put it in an electric mixer with ten cherries. . . ."

Jell-O	jelly beans
peppermint	pheasant
wet bread	seven eggs
hens	electric mixer
recipe cards	cherries
sesame seeds	heavy cream
relish	empty pan
melted cheese	

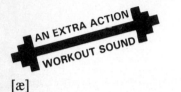

[æ]

fonɛtɪk trɪviə

Which of the following would you *not* plant?

[kærəts, spɪnətʃ, sændwɪtʃɪz, pəteɪtoz, pænkeɪks, mærɪgoldz, lɛtəs, sidz]

Say the following words aloud, trying to keep the vowel sounds the same and free from nasal distortion.

Add, act, acid, after, apple, and, ant

Although [æ] is subject to a number of problems, the most common one is nasalization. Of all the vowel sounds, it is the one that is most frequently distorted in this way.

FACTS

Technical description: [æ] is a low front unrounded vowel of medium duration.
Correct production: The tongue is forward but low in the mouth. The muscles of the tongue are lax, and the lips are neither spread nor rounded but wide open and relaxed.
☆ *Spellings: a* as in *at, au* as in *laughter, ai* as in *plaid*
Standard variations: In certain parts of the United States, most commonly in the Northeast, [æ] is pronounced as the lower allophone [a], which has a slightly lower tongue position than [æ] and a wider open mouth position.

IN USE

*A*gnes *a*dds a lot of *a*ction to her cl*a*ss d*a*nce *a*ctivities.

Check yourself on words from each list.

as	man	jam	sandwich
act	can	class	apple

add	stand	flag	angry
am	fan	annual	random
active	land	slam	answer
actor	pass	chance	lack
at	sank	began	package
ask	thank	path	candy
after	hat	bad	track
attic	traffic	fact	ham

PROBLEMS TO AVOID

1. Nasal distortion of [æ], especially when [æ] is preceded or followed by *m, n,* or *ng,* thus allowing air to escape through the nose on the vowel sound.

2. Substitution of [ɛ], [ɪ], or [ʌ] for [æ] so that *pan* sounds like *pen, pin,* or *pun.*

3. Addition of an extra sound so that [æ] becomes a diphthong.

☆ **4.** Substitution of [ɑ] for [æ] by nonnative American English speakers, although in certain words this is sometimes a substitution that speakers of other English dialects wish to retain.

Each problem is analyzed in greater detail. Concentrate on your area of weakness.

1. Nasal distortion In phonetics, such a distortion is marked with a wavy line ~ over the symbol. Thus to avoid [æ̃], drop the jaw and keep the *back* of the tongue lowered as much as you can. Both actions will make for a larger, less constricted oral passageway for the existing air so that there will be less likelihood of its escaping up into the nose.

Also, to avoid nasalizing [æ], especially before or between [m], [n], or [ŋ], learn the feeling of raising and lowering the velum (soft palate) in order to close off the nasal passage on the vowel sound.

First, say *nn-gah* 3 times to get the feeling of raising and lowering the soft palate.

Next, do these transfer exercises. Listen carefully as you say the following words aloud. Try to produce the same clear [æ] consistently and free from nasality in every word.

a. bat, bag, bad, ban, bland
b. fat, fast, frat, fan, frank
c. cab, clap, chap, can, candy
d. last, lass, laugh, lamb, lamp
e. tack, tad, tap, tan, tank
f. sad, sat, staff, slap, sandy
g. chap, chat, chatter, champ, chant
h. grab, grass, grabbed, gram, grand
i. rat, ran, rant, ramp, rang
j. man, mangle, rack, angry, fancy

Warm-up phrases for practice: chanting chap, fancy dance, tacky candy, ranting man, trapped tramp, grand lass, manage fans, hanging hats, anxious aunts, matching grants

2. [ɛ], [ɪ], or [ʌ] for [æ]   Contrast [æ] with each of the other sounds in the list, paying particular attention to the substitution you make. Notice the difference in sound and meaning.

[æ]	[ɛ]	[ɪ]	[ʌ]
fan	fen	fin	fun
Dan	den	din	done
sand	send	sin	sun
tan	ten	tin	ton
ban	Ben	been	bun
mass	mess	miss	muss

Warm-up phrases for practice: happy Betty, sand in the sink, dandy drink, tanning suns, chancy check, pat the pet, crafty tints, last leg, fabulous fun

3. Added sound   In each word, keep the vowel clear without adding any extra sounds, as happens sometimes in some Southern or Mountain dialects.

can't	ant
man	grant
tram	stand
stamp	black
chant	sack

Warm-up phrases for practice: can't stand, dramatic act, black ants, fantastic dance, bland Spam, chanting fans, glass lamps, chance glance

☆ **4. [ɑ] for [æ] or [a]**   In certain contexts it is important to use the [æ] sound in order not to confuse meaning. For example, *flag* [flæg] not "flahg" [flɑg], which would be *flog,* "to whip someone." However, whether you say "can't" [kænt] or "cahn't" [kɑnt] does not change the meaning of the word *can't;* it simply depends on how American you wish to sound.

Contrast [æ] with [ɑ], noticing the difference in sound *and* meaning.

[æ]	[ɑ]	[æ]	[ɑ]
tap	top	swam	swan
hat	hot	ran	Ron
band	bond	chap	chop
slap	slop	smack	smock
flap	flop	jab	job

Warm-up phrases for practice: swam past Sam, tanned hand, grand land, bran and jam, active man, black bag, the last bandstand, that van, pass my exams

ADDING ON FOR PROFICIENCY

1. Repeat the following phrases aloud using clear [æ] sounds. Build up speed, but not at the expense of accuracy.

   a. flagging the black cab
   b. active grand slams
   c. standard canned hams
   d. added a last chance
   e. tangy fancy apples
   f. sanded the damp land

2. Read the following sentences aloud, taking care to pronounce clear [æ] sounds, free from nasality. Avoid substitutions or adding extra sounds to [æ].

   a. Andy flew to Atlanta on Transatlantic Airlines this afternoon.
   b. Sandy sat on the fat Santa's lap and asked for fancy toys.
   c. Fran glanced at the handsome Anthony from under her glasses.
   d. Alan crammed to pass his last academic exam.
   e. Cassandra's language was stamped with epigrams and slang.
   f. Dr. Diane managed to activate a gram of DNA strands.
   g. Captain Anderson carefully planned the attack on the land.
   h. Abby drank apple juice for her snack and ate some crackers with jam.
   i. Dan added to his salary when he landed that contract.
   j. Samantha laughed as the camera panned to catch her fabulous act.

SUPER EXERCISES

1. *Using [æ] in conversational speech: A "Something's Wrong" Story* Read the following story; then discuss all the errors it contains. There are eight errors in this story. (Subsequent Something's Wrong Stories will be more difficult as we will not tell you how many errors to be on the alert for.)

   Angela and Andy were getting married at last. They had been childhood sweethearts and had met for the first time at a single's club last January. They had a large church wedding, and Angela looked radiant as she walked down the grass of the aisle on her father's arm as the organ music soared in the familiar bridal march, "The Star-Spangled Banner." The groom gave Angela away as the minister clapped. At the conclusion of the ceremony, Angela unstrapped her veil so that Andy could kiss her. They were husband and wife!

   All the guests gathered in the church vestry room for cake and toasted the happy couple with cans of champagne. Then Angela and Andy left for their honeymoon, a camping trip in lower Manhattan.

2. *Pack the Sack* Divide the class into two teams. You are participating in a Pack the Sack Supermarket Contest. Each team gets a chance, one at a time, to pack the sack with products that contain [æ] sounds. Each must be said aloud. If a member of one team mispronounces the [æ] sound in the product,

the other team says "stop" and scores a point, and then takes a turn at packing the sack. The team with the most products in its sack wins. Have a recorder, one for each team, and write the packed products on the board. Here's a start. You add the rest.

champagne   aspic   apples
applesauce   anchovies   plastic bags
Band-Aids   bananas   after-shave

3. *Finish the scene*   Cast two people in the roles of Officer Daniel and Mrs. Appleton. Let the class decide how to finish the scene.

Police Protection

SCENE: The front door of Mrs. Appleton's house. Mrs. Appleton has just opened the door to officer Daniel's ring.

OFFICER DANIEL: All right, Mrs. Appleton, what happened this time?

MRS. APPLETON: That man! There— (*pointing*) standing on the corner. He's planning to kidnap me.

OFFICER DANIEL: Now Mrs. Appleton, that man is selling chances for the Saint Anthony's church fair. I know him.

MRS. APPLETON: But that can he's holding—there's a dragon in it.

OFFICER DANIEL: Come now, Mrs. Appleton . . .

MRS. APPLETON: Don't "Mrs. Appleton" me—you know I'm Queen Anne and I'm going to be held for ransom.

OFFICER DANIEL: (*wearily*) Mrs. App— uh, I mean Queen Anne, last Saturday you were Mata Hari and you called us because a spy ring had planted a bomb in your bathroom.

MRS. APPLETON: I pay my taxcs! Are you going to catch that man who's planning to kidnap me?

OFFICER DANIEL: . . . And the Saturday before, Prince Andrew was planning a bachelor party in your yard and you asked for police protection. *Andrew's married!*

MRS. APPLETON: Stand back—the dragon's out of the can. He's landed in my pansy patch! Grab your gun! His flag is flapping. . . .

CHECKPOINT EXERCISES

Front vowels

Demonstrating clarity and forward focus on the front vowels   Listen to your production of the front vowels as you interpret at least two of the following selections. Record them for playback. Mark any front vowels you produce incorrectly *as you are doing the reading;* then use the recording to check your self-judgments. Note any errors you still make on the table that follows the readings.

Adam and Eve had many advantages, but the principal one was that they escaped teething.

MARK TWAIN

Great rats, small rats, lean rats, brawny rats,
Brown rats, black rats, grey rats, tawny rats . . .
From street to street he piped advancing,
And step for step they followed, dancing.

    ROBERT BROWNING, "The Pied Piper of Hamelin"

The Moving Finger writes; and having writ,
Moves on; nor all your Piety nor Wit
Shall lure it back to cancel half a line
Nor all your tears wash out a word of it.

    EDWARD FITZGERALD, "Omar Khayyam"

'Tis an old maxim in the schools
That flattery's the food of fools;
Yet now and then you men of wit
Will condescend to take a bit.

    JONATHAN SWIFT, "Cadenus and Vanessa"

In Xanadu did Kubla Khan
    A stately pleasure-dome decree:
Where Alph, the sacred river, ran
Through caverns measureless to man
    Down to a sunless sea.

    SAMUEL TAYLOR COLERIDGE, "Kubla Khan"

Substitutions, additions, and distortions still needing work

[i] as in *heat* _____

[ɪ] as in *hit* _____

[e] as in *collate*; [eɪ] as in *hate* _____

[ɛ] as in *met* _____

[æ] as in *hat* _____

THE BACK VOWELS: [ɑ ɔ o ʊ u]

[ɑ]
_____

fonɛtɪk trɪviə

Which of the following is *not* Italian?

[pɑstə, hægɪs, tʃɪli, pitsə, spəgɛti, fɛtutʃini, mɑrinɑrə, ʃnɪtsəl]

Say the following sentences aloud exactly as written.

1. My c*o*re was p*o*rked behind the g*o*rebage truck.
2. My c*a*r was p*a*rked behind the g*a*rbage truck.

[ɑ] is an easy vowel for most people to pronounce correctly since it is a sound that is found in all languages. However, it is sometimes subject to substitutions.

FACTS

Technical description: [ɑ] is a low back vowel of long duration.

Correct production: The tongue is at its lowest, and back in the mouth. The tongue muscles are lax, and the mouth is wide open. The lips are neither spread nor rounded.

☆ *Spellings: a* as in *father, o* as in *opera, ea* as in *heart.*

Standard variations: The phoneme [ɑ] is sometimes substituted by its allophone [ɒ], a higher and shorter sound made with a slightly less open mouth. In certain regions this sound is heard in such words as *not* or *pot.* [ɔ], the mid-back vowel with rounded lips, is also used interchangeably in certain regions and is heard in such words as *orange* and *Florida.*

IN USE

It's *o*dd *a*rt leads observers to either *a*rdor or *a*rgument.

Check your pronunciation of [ɑ] on words from each list:

on	balm	blah
arc	calm	hurrah
art	hot	market
are	slop	partner
arch	chop	alarm
honest	psalm	heart
otter	lobby	charm
octave	want	farm
obvious	harm	carbon
arm	bother	start

PROBLEMS TO AVOID

1. Substitution of [ɔ] for [ɑ] so that *park* [pɑrk] becomes *pork* [pɔɚk]

2. Substitution of [æ] for [ɑ] so that *hot* [hɑt] sounds like *hat* [hæt].

Each problem is analyzed in greater detail. Concentrate on your area of weakness.

1. [ɔ] for [ɑ]   A helpful rule to remember is that with the exception of words beginning with *war* (*warn, warm,* etc.), the spelling *ar* in English is pronounced [ɑ].

Contrast [ɑ] and [ɔ] in the words that follow. Be sure to keep the lips unrounded on [ɑ]. Notice the difference in sound and meaning:

[ɑ]	[ɔ]	[ɑ]	[ɔ]
barn	born	char	chore
bar	bore	Mark	Mort
far	for	darn	dorm

car	core	knot	naught
star	store	cot	caught

Warm-up phrases for practice: (Note that both [ɑ] and [ɔ] occur in each phrase.) quality store, calming song, hard core, a harmless bore, bargained for, born a star, darn the torn carseat, charred corn

2. [æ] for [ɑ] Contrast [ɑ] with [æ] in the following pairs. Notice the difference in sound and meaning.

[ɑ]	[æ]	[ɑ]	[æ]
pot	pat	mop	map
lock	lack	cop	cap
block	black	shock	shack
cot	cat	rock	rack
sock	sack	stop	stab

Warm-up phrases for practice: black pot, rotted shack, spotted cat, map stop, flat rock, sacked cop

ADDING ON FOR PROFICIENCY

1. With widely open mouth, repeat these phrases, building up speed but not at the expense of accuracy.

   a. father's charming farm
   b. watch the hot pot
   c. modern drama farce
   d. garbage for garden plants
   e. a lot of rotted spots

2. Read the following sentences aloud, making sure you drop the jaw on all [ɑ] sounds.

   a. Arnold sang harmony for the barber shop octet.
   b. Father promised to take Tom to the park.
   c. Poppies grow ardently in a lot of garden spots.
   d. That charming old barn on the Johnsons' farm was demolished.
   e. Mom wanted Donna to wash the car.
   f. Donald's heart nearly stopped from the shock of that alarming noise.
   g. Barbara remained calm even after hearing an ominous knock.
   h. Apart from one forgotten lie, Bob was always honest.
   i. "Nonsense," said Dr. Thompson to Grandma, "your heart is as strong as an ox's."
   j. Wanda loves to eat spaghetti marinara, especially when it's hot.

SUPER EXERCISE

Read the following commercial aloud, or write your own featuring the sound of [ɑ].

Hello, this is Rob Snodgrass of the Garden Hot Spot. Do you have a problem with garden goblins? Do they rob your garden of its crops? Are the marguerites gone when you go out to pick them? Then get snodspot, the balm that keeps garden enemies apart from your garden. It deposits a scent that your goblins detest, so they depart from your garden without doing any more harm, and the crops that you plant can prosper.

That's Snodspot—the garden tonic for your backyard farm.

[ɔ]

fonɛtık trɪviə

Which of the following does *not* describe size?

[smɔl, greɪt, kɑtən, midiəm, tɔl, bɔl, æmpəl, lɑɚdʒ, pɔɚtli]

Say the following words aloud, trying to keep the vowel sounds pure, consistent, and free from nasal distortion.

*aw*ning, t*a*lk, d*aw*n, d*au*ghter, l*aw*, f*ou*ght, s*aw*

[ɔ] is particularly prone to distortion or the addition of extra sounds.

FACTS

Technical description: [ɔ] is a tense, mid-back, rounded vowel of long duration.

Correct production: The tongue is in the back of the mouth at mid-height. The lips protrude and are rounded, but not as much as for [o]. The tongue is tense, and the tip is behind the lower teeth.

☆ *Spellings: aw* as in *raw, au* as in *fault, ou* as in *cough, o* as in *office, a* between *w* and *r* as in *warm.*

Standard variations: As mentioned previously, the low back vowels of [ɑ] and [ɒ] are used interchangeably with [ɔ] and vary according to region. The appropriate choice depends on what is most often heard in your part of the United States. However, in the case of words spelled *ar,* [ɔr] should not be substituted for [ɑr].

IN USE

The st*or*m was str*o*ng, lasting l*o*ng after d*aw*n.

Check your pronunciation of the words on each list.

awning	fawn	law
all	lawn	saw

always	bought	flaw
awkward	cough	jaw
awe	loss	claw
awesome	toss	paw
off	soft	raw
ought	morning	gnaw
or	pawn	call
order	thought	yawn

PROBLEMS TO AVOID

1. [ɔ] can be distorted by too much tension of the lips with the resultant addition of extra sounds, so that *coffee* [kɔfi] becomes "kaw-uh-fee" [kɔwəfi].
2. Substitution of [aʊ] for [ɔ] so that *off* [ɔf] sounds like "owf" [aʊf], sometimes heard in certain Southern dialects.
☆ 3. Substitution of [o] for [ɔ] by foreign speakers of English if [ɔ] does not exist in the native language. Therefore *tall* [tɔl] becomes toll [tol].

Each problem is analyzed in greater detail. Concentrate on your area of weakness.

1. Distortions of [ɔ] **through addition**   Listen carefully as you say the following words aloud. Try consistently to produce the same clear [ɔ] or the optional, more open [ɒ]. Avoid nasality and the addition of any extra vowel sounds after [ɔ]. Round but do not tense your lips too much.

    a. fault, assault, taught, caught, bought
    b. door, store, sore, tore, pour
    c. hall, tall, call, mall, small
    d. clause, cause, pause, applause, jaws
    e. wrong, long, song, strong, belong
    f. off, office, cough, coffee, toffee
    g. talk, walk, stalk, chalk, caulk
    h. dawn, fawn, tawny, pawn, lawn
    i. fall, ball, hall, recall, squall
    j. short, port, more, core, adore

Warm-up phrases for practice: soft ball, glorious songs, fought along, port in a storm, short or small, autumn or fall, wrong office, saw squalls

2. [aʊ] for [ɔ]   Contrast [ɔ] with [aʊ] in these words. Notice the difference in sound and meaning.

[ɔ]	[aʊ]
all	owl
fall	fowl
tall	towel
ball	bowel
call	cawl

Warm-up phrases for practice: (Notice the occurrence of both [ɔ] and [aʊ] in each phrase.) small towel, faulty towers, call out, strong spout, all about, cough aloud, because he's out, hall fountain

☆ **3. [o] for [ɔ]**   Contrast [ɔ] with [o] in these words. For [ɔ], use less lip rounding and lip tension than for [o]. Notice the difference in sound and meaning.

[ɔ]	[o]	[ɔ]	[o]
law	low	chalk	choke
bought	boat	lawn	loan
slaw	slow	fawn	phone
call	coal	hall	hole
taught	tote	caught	coat
walk	woke	malt	molt

Warm-up phrases for practice: (Notice the occurrence of both [o] and [ɔ] in each phrase.) photo call, over the wall, slow to fall, growing tall, sew a shawl, go for walks, alone in August, blow a horn

ADDING ON FOR PROFICIENCY

1. With widely open mouth, repeat the following phrases, building up speed but not at the expense of accuracy.

   a. talked up a storm
   b. called the office
   c. soft water wash
   d. naughty dog's paw
   e. long and short costs
   f. warm chocolate sauce

2. Read the following sentences aloud without adding additional sounds to [ɔ].

   a. Dawn adored eating the soft toffee she bought in Florida.
   b. The lawyer taught a course on the use of force.
   c. Fawn took a long walk just for the sport.
   d. Too much strong coffee can be awfully wrong.
   e. Orange juice can help you perform more in the morning.
   f. George saw a small flaw in the store-bought saw.
   g. The storm tore down all the trees along the shore and lawns.
   h. Every fall Paul sought to reorganize his office.
   i. The audience lauded Morgan with applause after his performance.
   j. Gloria scalded her jaw because the water was too warm.

☆ 3. *For the nonnative speaker*

   1. Read the following phrases aloud, making sure that you do not substitute [o] for [ɔ]. Try to build up speed, but never at the expense of accuracy.

      a. awful storm
      b. all talk

    c. had a ball
    d. call along
    e. wrong form

2. Read the following sentences aloud.

    a. Paul tossed the ball to Norman.
    b. My office is across the hall.
    c. She wore a warm shawl.
    d. This morning's coffee was too strong.
    e. I lost my dog when I went for a walk.
    f. It can be very warm in August.
    g. Corn is a form of vegetable.
    h. Gloria was born in Boston.
    i. Don't give me more chocolate.
    j. My boss lost his job.

SUPER EXERCISES

1. *A Something's Wrong Story* Can you identify the errors in the following story? Read the story aloud; then discuss the errors.

    Maude was being entertained for tea by the royal family. She held her bone china coffee cup in her lap just so and made polite conversation about the cost of the tea set as she copied the way the princess sucked the hot liquid up through the straw in small sips. She was offered a plate of tempting watercress sandwiches, and just as her mother had taught her, she carefully put four back. The butler then passed a silver tray of chocolate mints, and in the British tradition, she took one on her plate and carefully ate it with a fork. Then she put the plate in her pocketbook, crossed her legs, and got up to bid the prince and princess an appreciative farewell as the footman helped her off with her coat.

2. *Create a recipe* To develop practice in using correct [ɔ] sounds in conversational speech, create a recipe from the following list of words. Use at least five ingredients.

sauce	porridge	toss
moth balls	chocolate	malted milk
frothy	broth	cornflakes
corn	form	celery stalks
warm	port	forty
short	snort	four

3. *Finish the scene* Cast two people in the roles of Paul and Dawson; then let the class finish the scene.

Pawning It All

SCENE: Dawson's Pawn Shop.

PAUL: (*embarrassed, trying to appear "cool"*) Uh, hello. I don't really have any use for all this stuff. I'd like to pawn all of it.

DAWSON: (*looking at the items*) Well, kid, let me see what you've got. Hmm. These are all war items: a torpedo shell, a grenade that looks like it had been lost—and look at this, an army knife with a worn-out blade and an army uniform. (*looks at it closely*) Hey, this cloth is full of moth holes!

PAUL: Gee, I'm awfully sorry. I thought they were all right. (*takes something else out of his pocket*) I have an autographed baseball. Can I pawn that?

DAWSON: No, kid, not interested.

PAUL: Oh, well. Here. (*opens a satchel*) How about two automatic pistols? They're in perfect working order.

DAWSON: (*looks at Paul suspiciously*) Just where did you get this stuff, and why are you so eager to pawn it? I ought to toss you out or call the police. . . .

PAUL: No, please, Mr. Dawson, don't call the police! I only thought . . .

[o] or [oʊ]

fonɛtɪk trɪviə

Which of the following would you *not* have in your home?

[boʊt, foʊn, soʊfə, toʊd, goʊt, wɪndo, hotɛl, piæno, koʊm]

Say the following sentence aloud exactly as written.

1. D*o-wuh*nt be opp*o-wuh*zed to *o-wuh*ld cl*o-wu*ths.
2. D*o*n't be opp*o*sed to *o*ld cl*o*thes.

[o] or [oʊ], when well rounded, adds beauty to speech. However, [o] can be carelessly articulated or subject to addition errors.

FACTS

Technical description: [o] is a mid-back, rounded, tense vowel of long duration in stressed syllables.

Correct production: The tongue is in the back of the mouth, raised at mid-height toward the palate. The lips are more rounded than for [ɔ]. Both the lips and the tongue muscles are tense. The jaw is half lowered.

☆ *Spellings: o* as in *old, ow* as in *grow, oe* as in *toe, ou* as in *boulder, oa* as in *loaves, ew* as in *sew, oo* as in *brooch*

Standard variations: When [o] occurs in stressed syllables, it is pronounced as the diphthong [oʊ], the nonphonemic allophone of [o]. In certain regions, standard pronunciations vary between [ɔ] and [o] when followed by *r*.

IN USE

Fl*o* l*oa*thes to g*o* h*o*me al*o*ne, s*o* she m*oa*ns a l*o*t.

Check your pronunciation of [o] on the words on each list.

old	home	no
oak	roam	show
ode	stole	blow
oaf	vote	sew
okay	bone	toe
oboe	clone	row
Ozarks	phone	bow
own	nose	glow
owe	moan	stow
only	coat	low

PROBLEMS TO AVOID

1. Addition of sounds that distort. For example, *gold* [goʊld] becomes "go-wuhld" [gowəld] or *low* [loʊ] sounds like the phrase "Let go" without the *t* and *g* [lɛoʊ].

2. Substitution of [ə] for [o] in unstressed syllables, so that *obey* [obeɪ] becomes "uh-bey" [əbeɪ].

☆ **3.** Substitution of [o] for [oʊ] in stressed syllables, sometimes heard in foreign speakers of English, so that *home* [hoʊm] is shortened to "hom" [hom].

Each problem is analyzed in greater detail. Concentrate on your area of weakness.

1. Added sound Say the following words without adding any extra sounds either before or after the vowel. Each word has *one* syllable.

old	sewn
bowl	moan
cold	told
grown	scold
tone	fold

Warm-up phrases for practice: old gold, home grown, own a phone, scolding tone, float a loan, roam alone, a Poe poem

2. [ə] for [o] Pronounce [o] correctly in the following words.

okay	hotel
obey	yellow
obese	window
omit	piano
ovation	fellow

Warm-up phrases for practice: (Notice that both [o] and [ə] occur in each phrase.) hotel in a hut, tub for the obese, funny phone, avert the overt, hum at home, muddy mode, club code, love the location

☆ **3. [o] for [oʊ]**   Pronounce the following words. Note that the American [o] becomes a diphthong (two vowel sounds in succession) in stressed syllables. The [o] sound is extended and glides toward a [w] sound before the following consonant is pronounced. It is elongated, as in *home* [hoʊm], not shortened as in [hom].

bone [boʊn]	blow [bloʊ]
phone [foʊn]	glow [gloʊ]
cone [koʊn]	stove [stoʊv]
alone [əloʊn]	slow [sloʊ]
atone [ətoʊn]	stone [stoʊn]

Warm-up phrases for practice: (The following [o] sounds are all in stressed syllables and are therefore pronounced as diphthongs.) Coca-Cola, slow motion, scolded so, closed her coat, so-so, a blow to the toe, most stoves, sold soap

ADDING ON FOR PROFICIENCY

1. Repeat the following phrases aloud, building up speed but not at the expense of accuracy.

   a. horned toe growths
   b. toasty glowing stoves
   c. showing grown posies
   d. home-blown rogues
   e. roaches, moles, and toads

2. Read the following sentences aloud, taking care not to add extra sounds that might distort the [oʊ] sound.

   a. Drive slowly as you go home on the toll road.
   b. Only older oak trees grow in Oklahoma.
   c. Joan loaned Tony her only telephone.
   d. Zoë chose a bowl of home-grown roses for the show.
   e. Flo could smell the aroma of cloves that arose from the stove.
   f. Joe wrote a glowing letter home about the snowblower.
   g. Is it okay to open the only note that Otto wrote?
   h. The ghost floated up over the moat, but only its bones were soaked.
   i. Coca-Cola was Mona's favorite cold soda, which she hated to forgo.
   j. Do you know along which toll road Rose drove to go to Ohio?

☆ 3. *For the nonnative speaker*

   1. Say the following phrases using the [oʊ] diphthong.

      a. blow your nose
      b. sew a golden cloak
      c. rowed to the boat
      d. a loaf of dough
      e. show the boat

2. Read the following sentences aloud.

    a. Tony's coat was old and worn.
    b. Don't throw stones at the oaks.
    c. No one likes to go home alone.
    d. Joan knows all about old gold.
    e. Joe towed his boat to a cove.
    f. Rome was her only home.
    g. He is going to Ohio to open in a show.
    h. Sofia wrote a note home.
    i. My piano's tone sounds old.
    j. A bowl of cold Cheerios was on the stove.

SUPER EXERCISES

☆ 1. *Using* [ou] *correctly in conversational speech*   Once you have mastered the warm-up and proficiency exercises, make the transition to everyday speech. Create a sentence around each expression on the list; say it aloud at a normal conversational rate. For example, if the expression is *motorboat,* you might use it this way: "I rowed my motorboat over to the other side of the lake." Do not write your sentences down.

phoning home	sold
Roman togas	baloney
bonus	ghosts
doughnuts	Coca-Cola
ocean	voting
throne	throw stones

2. Read the following commercial aloud, or write your own featuring the sound of [ou].

Do you have a cold?
Do you always have to blow your nose?
Does your nose glow from blowing too much?
Then you need Cold-Go,
The cold medicine that coats your nose.
You see, tiny drops roll into your nose to end colds, sneezing, and blowing.
So get Cold-Go—the *only* medicine for your nose.
It keeps you from being indisposed.

3. *Finish the scene*   Cast two people in the roles of Rhoda and Tony; then let the class decide how to finish the scene.

I Sold the Home

SCENE: Sloane's Realty Office.

RHODA: (*angrily*) Tony, did you show the Jones house to Mr. Coe?
TONY: Yes, I did, Rhoda, and I sold it, too.

RHODA: (*louder*) What do you mean *you* sold it! I sold that home also, and what's more, I sold it two days ago!

TONY: (*emphatically*) That home was *not* sold two days ago. The owners told me so.

RHODA: Well, I took Mrs. Rose there only two days ago, and she made an offer to the Joneses.

TONY: That bid didn't hold, Rhoda, so I showed the Joneses' home to Mr. Coe today.

RHODA: (*furious*) But Tony, you can't show a home that I already sold! That's . . .

[ʊ]

fonɛtɪk trɪviə

Which of the following would you *not* find on a safari?

[bʊl, æntəlop, bʊldɔg, sprɪŋbak, zibrə, bʊʃɪz, ɛləfənt, gəzɛl]

Say the following sentence aloud both ways exactly as written:

1. P**oo**l or p**oo**sh but don't l**ooo**k.
2. P**u**ll or p**u**sh but don't l**oo**k.

The biggest problem with [ʊ] occurs in nonnative speakers. Lacking such a phoneme in their own language system, they tend to use one they are familiar with in its place.

FACTS

Technical description: [ʊ] is a high, back, rounded, lax vowel of short duration.

Correct production: The back of the tongue is high up toward the palate. The lips are rounded, slightly more than for [o] but less than for [u]. The muscles of the tongue are lax.

☆ *Spellings: u* as in *put, oo* as in *good, ou* as in *could, o* as in *wolf.*

IN USE

Mrs. B**oo**k's c**oo**k c**oo**ked up a f**u**ll-bodied p**u**dding.

Check your pronunciation of [ʊ] in the words on each list.

look	would	full
shook	could	pull
cook	should	bull
book	stood	wool
foot	hood	sugar

PROBLEMS TO AVOID

☆ 1. Substitution of [u] for [ʊ] by nonnative speakers of English so that *cook* [kʊk] becomes "kook" [kuk].

2. Substitution of [ʌ] for [ʊ] so that *book* [bʊk] sounds like "buck" [bʌk].

Each problem is analyzed in greater detail. Concentrate on your area of weakness.

☆ 1. **[u] for [ʊ]**   Contrast [ʊ] with [u] in these words. Notice that the lips are less rounded for [ʊ] and the tongue muscles are more lax than for the [u]. Ask an American model to monitor your pronunciation. The words in the two lists differ in pronunciation and meaning. Be aware of the difference.

[ʊ]		[u]	
wood	[wʊd]	wooed	[wud]
soot	[sʊt]	sued	[sud]
could	[kʊd]	cooed	[kud]
pull	[pʊl]	pool	[pul]
good	[gʊd]	goose	[gus]
hood	[hʊd]	hoot	[hut]
should	[ʃʊd]	shoot	[ʃut]
book	[bʊk]	boot	[but]
look	[lʊk]	lewd	[lud]
stood	[stʊd]	stewed	[stud]

Warm-up phrases for practice: pulling wool, sugar cookies, looking good, push and pull, cookery book, put a foot, hooked the wool

2. **[ʌ] for [ʊ]**   Keep [ʊ] words well rounded, because [ʊ] is the second most rounded vowel sound. *Look* is [lʊk], not *luck* [lʌk]. Notice, too, that [ʊ] is made in the back of the mouth, whereas [ʌ] is a central vowel. Contrast the difference in sound *and* meaning in the following pairs.

took	tuck	could	cut
shook	shuck	book	buck
hook	Huck	stood	stud
put	putt	should	shut

Warm-up phrases for practice: (Each phrase contrasts both [ʊ] and [ʌ].) cookie cups, took supper, pull and touch, look at much, foot on the clutch, put such, wooden hutch, full of nuts

ADDING ON FOR PROFICIENCY

1. Say the following phrases using well-rounded [ʊ] sounds. Try to build up speed, but never at the expense of accuracy.

a. stood on the wood
b. shook the bush
c. put down the book
d. butchers and cooks
e. overtook the crook
f. look at my foot

☆ 2. *For nonnative speakers*   Read the following sentences aloud, making sure that you do not substitute the long, tense [u] for the short, lax [ʊ].

a. He took another look at that book.
b. She pulled her foot away from the sooty fireplace.
c. Could I please have pudding and cookies for dessert?
d. The hood was knitted out of lamb's wool.
e. I feel so full after eating all those goodies.
f. Should I put the books away?
g. Mr. Brooks shook the crook that tried to push him.
h. He pulled Mrs. Wood away from where I stood.

SUPER EXERCISES

☆ 1. *Packing for a trip to the moon*   In packing for your trip to the moon, choose *only* items that contain [ʊ] sounds. Repeat the items aloud using good lip rounding on [ʊ].

cookbook	wool socks	cushions
map of outer space	a pound of sugar	matches
pudding mix	mirror	a bushel of apples
recent movies	cookies	flashlight
NASA bulletins	toothpaste	football
footstool	winter coat	space suit

2. *Commercials*   Make up your own commercials for the following books. Say your commercials aloud, using good lip rounding on all [ʊ] sounds.

a. *The Would-Be-Good Cookbook*
b. *Mrs. Hood's Sugar Cookies* (for dieters)
c. *Whoopie Cushions* (party favor suggestions)
d. *The Push-and-Pull Exercise Book*
e. *Wolves I Have Known* (a best seller)
f. *I Would If Only I Could* (an inspirational book)

[u]
_____

fonɛtɪk trɪviə

Which of the following has *nothing* to do with singing?

[kul dʒæz, krunɪŋ, nun, tun, mjuzɪk, bluz, mɛlədiz, mun]
_____

Say the following words aloud, trying to keep the vowels sounds rounded and pure.

B*oo*t, p*oo*l, f*oo*d, f*oo*l, m*oo*n, sp*oo*n, sch*oo*l

[u], the most rounded of all the vowel sounds, can add beauty to speech if given full resonant value.

FACTS

Technical description: [u] is a high, back, rounded, tense vowel of long duration.
Correct production: The back of the tongue is raised very high toward the palate. The lips are very rounded, slightly more than for [ʊ]. The muscles of the tongue are tense.
☆ *Spellings: oo* as in *too, ue* as in *clue, u* as in *June, ew* as in *blew, oe* as in *shoe, o* as in *move, ui* as in *suit.*
Standard variations: A few words spelled with the double *o,* such as *room, roof, root, coop, hoof,* and *broom,* may be pronounced with either [u] or [ʊ]. In more formal usage, as well as British English, and in certain parts of the country, [j] as in *yet* is inserted before the [u] following *n, t,* or *d.* Thus *news* is pronounced [njuz] and *duty* becomes [djuti]. Let your ear be your guide in determining the standard pronunciation in your area.

IN USE

H*ugh* bl*ew* on the s*oup* sp*oo*n to c*oo*l the st*ew.*

Check your pronunciation of [u] in words on each list.

ooze	moon	too
groom	roost	slew
dune	pool	blue
June	fool	sue
boom	cool	chew
loom	stoop	grew
noon	rule	do
broom	dupe	zoo

PROBLEMS TO AVOID

☆ **1.** Substitution of [ʊ] for [u] by nonnative speakers of English so that *shoe* [ʃu] becomes [ʃʊ].
2. Addition of [ə] or [wə] to [u], creating nonstandard diphthongs out of the pure vowel [u].

Each problem is analyzed in greater detail. Concentrate on your area of weakness.

☆ **1.** **[u] for [ʊ]**   Contrast [u] and [ʊ] in the word lists. As in the section on [ʊ], notice that the lips are more rounded for [u] than for [ʊ], the tongue muscles are more tense for [u], and the sound of [u] is held longer than [ʊ].

[u]		[ʊ]	
loot	[lut]	look	[lʊk]
tool	[tul]	took	[tʊk]
wooed	[wud]	would	[wʊd]
fool	[ful]	full	[fʊl]
pool	[pul]	pull	[pʊl]
ghoul	[gul]	good	[gʊd]
shoot	[ʃut]	should	[ʃʊd]
suit	[sut]	soot	[sʊt]
boot	[but]	book	[bʊk]
stewed	[stud]	stood	[stʊd]

Warm-up phrases for practice: soup spoon, a June moon, foolish move, choosing tunes, loosing a tooth, cool pool, blue shoes, beautiful movie

2. Diphthongization of [u] by the addition of [wə] or [ə]   One or both sounds can be added, making *cool* [kul] sound like [kuəl] or [kuwəl]. Keep the following words pure without adding any sounds.

school	pool	route
rule	brood	flute
tool	crew	you
truth	fuse	soon
stool	loom	true
foolish	food	excuse

Warm-up phrases for practice: blue pool, a crude stool, truthful youth, moon route, gloomy noon, see you soon, moody music, super bloom

ADDING ON FOR PROFICIENCY

1. Say the following phrases using pure [u] with good rounding.

   a. to a new moon
   b. food on a spoon
   c. shooting at noon
   d. cool musical mood
   e. you grew too
   f. flew to the zoo

2. Say these sentences. Make sure you keep the [u] pure and well rounded. Do not add extra sounds to make it a diphthong or triphthong.

   a. As a rule, rules in school are for a pupil's own good.
   b. Drew read the eulogy to the gloomy few who attended the funeral.

c. At two minutes to two every afternoon, the noon whistle blew out of tune—and out of phase!

d. Each raw recruit was asked to introduce himself with "Who are you, and what do you do?"

e. "Yoo hoo!" Hugh called to Sue. "You're a fool, Hugh," Sue coolly called back.

f. The lagoon took on the beautiful hue of a bright blue day in June.

g. Ruth foolishly fell in the pool and was soaked through and through.

h. "Who wants to hear of a future full of gloom and doom?" hooted the rude audience member.

☆ 3. *For nonnative speakers.* Say these sentences. Make sure you do not substitute short, lax [ʊ] for long, tense [u].

a. Sue chewed and chewed the food.
b. Lou flew on through to Timbuktu.
c. Lucy spooned the soup into her mouth.
d. It was much too soon to plant new blooms
e. Do you choose to be amusing, or do you refuse?
f. The blueberries bloomed beautifully every summer.
g. Judy crooned a tune about the moon.
h. Who are you, and what do you do?

SUPER EXERCISES

☆ 1. *Choosing tunes*   Select and repeat aloud only the song titles that contain [u] sounds.

a. "The Moon Is Blue"
b. "Excuse Me for Loving You"
c. "I'm a Fool to Care"
d. "Row Your Boat to Heaven with Me"
e. "Cruising on the Danube"
f. "Love Bloomed Early This Year"
g. "Warm as Toast in Your Arms"
h. "I Choose You over Food"
i. "Doomed to Loving You"
j. "Soon You Will Be True to Me"
k. "Let's Dance Together Soon"
l. "Two Foolish Hearts in Tune"
m. "Close Those Eyes While We Kiss"
n. "Who Knew I'd Fall for You?"
o. "I Hadn't a Clue that You Loved Me"
p. "It's Gloomy Without You"

2. *Stocking the library*   Make up book titles to stock your library shelves. You may keep only titles that contain [u] sounds. Here are a few examples; you make up the rest. Say your titles aloud.

      a. *Fooling Your Stomach Without Food*
      b. *How to Groom Your Guru*
      c. *Choosing Comfortable Stools*
      d. *Tattoos Without Ado*

CHECKPOINT EXERCISES

Back vowels

Demonstrating purity and beauty of tone on the back vowels   Listen to your production of the back vowels as you interpret at least two of the following selections. Record them for playback. Mark any back vowels you produce incorrectly *as you are doing the readings;* then use the recording to check your self-judgments. Note any errors you still make on the table that follows the readings.

> How dreary—to be—Somebody!
> How public—like a frog—
> To tell one's name—the livelong June—
> to an admiring Bog!
>
>   EMILY DICKINSON

> She left the web, she left the loom,
> She made three paces through the room,
> She saw the water lily bloom,
> They saw the helmet and the plume—
> She looked down to Camelot.
>
>   ALFRED, LORD TENNYSON

> Man's fascination with Tomorrow is as old as man himself.
> From the dawn of his imagination, he has tried to peer
> behind the "curtain's magic fold" to where Bret Harte
> said "the glowing future lies unrolled" . . .
> And sometimes, he has, indeed, looked into Tomorrow.
>
>   ORVILLE FREEMAN

> Marley was dead, to begin with. There is no doubt whatever about that. The register of his burial was signed by the clergyman, the clerk, the undertaker, and the chief mourner. Scrooge signed it. And Scrooge's name was good upon 'Change for anything he chose to put his hand to.
> Old Marley was dead as a doornail.
>
>   CHARLES DICKENS, *Martin Chuzzlewit*

> Roaming in thought over the universe, I saw the little that is Good steadily hastening toward immortality, and the vast that is Evil I saw hastening to merge itself and become lost and dead.
>
>   WALT WHITMAN

Oh, this is the joy of the rose:
That it blows,
And goes.

WILLA CATHER

Substitutions, additions, and distortions still needing work

[ɑ] as in *far* _____

[ɔ] as in *law* _____

[o] as in *piano*; [oʊ] as in *home* _____

[ʊ] as in *pull* _____

[u] as in *too* _____

THE CENTRAL VOWELS: [ʌ ə ɝ ɚ]

[ʌ] and [ə]

fonɛtɪk trɪviə

Which of the following would *not* eat pet food?

[pʌpi, kɪtən, hʌni biz, goʊldfɪʃ, dʌk, bigəl, mɪŋk, mʌt, klæm]

Say the following sentences aloud exactly as written.

1. Don't give me m*ah*ch s*ah*pper; I'm not h*ah*ngry.
2. Don't give me m*u*ch s*u*pper; I'm not h*u*ngry.

[ʌ] and [ə] represent the same vowel sound. The first symbol [ʌ] is used by the IPA to designate the sound in a stressed or accented syllable, as in the word *love* [lʌv]. The second symbol [ə], called the *schwa* (from the German *schwach*, meaning "weak"), is used to represent the same vowel sound in unstressed or unaccented syllables, as in the word *about* [əbaʊt]. This vowel does not occur in many languages, and thus nonnative speakers predictably may have difficulty with it, as in the sample sentence above.

FACTS

Technical description: [ʌ] and [ə] are mid-central vowels. The accented version [ʌ] has a longer duration than the unaccented [ə], which has more of a neutral quality. In English any unstressed vowel will often become [ə] in connected speech. [ə] is thus the most frequently heard vowel sound.

Correct production: The central part of the tongue is lifted midway toward the palate. The lips are unrounded. The muscles of the tongue are lax.

☆ *Spellings:* In stressed syllables, *u* as in *cup*, *o* as in *some*, *ou* as in *double*, *oo* as in *blood*, *oe* as in *does*. In unstressed syllables, *a* as in *about*, *o* as in *collect*, *u* as in *circus*, *e* as in *apparent*, and almost any vowel in an unaccented syllable.

IN USE

I abs*o*lutely *a*dore that l*o*vely new l*u*gg*a*ge I j*u*st bought.

Check your pronunciation of the words on each list.

	[ʌ]			[ə]	
cup	bump	mother	appoint	afford	above
love	funny	brother	annoy	miracle	soda
supper	luck	hungry	around	potato	assist
stuff	summer	but	occur	parade	agree
club	one	us	afraid	poem	alone

Notice that [ʌ] always represents the neutral vowel in a stressed syllable.

Self-check for the difference between [ʌ] *and* [ə]. In the following sentence, write the symbol [ʌ] over each syllable in which it belongs.

The sisters were not opposed to their brother's opinions.[2]

☆ **FURTHER CLARIFICATION OF THE SCHWA**

In English, unlike many other languages, in words of more than one syllable, only one syllable receives stress (force and slight prolongation); the others are spoken more rapidly, and their vowels often lose their identity and become [ə]. Unfortunately, English spelling cannot help you determine how very often the neutral schwa occurs.

To give you more of an idea of this, look back at the "self-checking" sentence at the end of "In Use." *Opinions* does not keep equal weight on all three syllables: ó pín ións. Rather, it is [əpɪnjənz]. By the same token, *sisters* is [sístəz] and *opposed* is [əpóuzd].

A good American model and a pronouncing dictionary will help you with this.

COMMON MISPRONUNCIATIONS

The schwa is a simple sound to produce. The only problems the native speaker may encounter are mispronunciations of certain common words.

1. *Omissions.* Check that you include [ə] in these words:

poem	cruel	riot	naturally	editor	liable
poetry	jewelry	terrible	police	miracle	similar

2. *Additions.* None of these words has a medial schwa:

evening	ticklish	hindrance	business	lightning
bracelet	athlete	burglar	disastrous	

---

[2] There should be a mark over only the first syllable of *brother's*.

PROBLEMS TO AVOID

☆ *Substitution of* [ɑ] *for* [ə] *or* [ʌ]. *cup* should be pronounced [kʌp], not as *cop* [kɑp]. Since [ɑ] occurs in all languages, this is the sound that nonnative speakers generally substitute, but it could also be [ɔ] as in *talk* or [o] as in *omit*.

Suggestions   Think of the schwa as a new but very easy sound to produce. Start with "Huh?" which you might say if you did not understand someone, and simply take the initial [h] away: "uh." Go back to the [ʌ] and [ə] word lists and practice them using this sound. Then contrast the differences in sound *and* meaning in the following word lists.

[ʌ]		[ɑ]	
cup	[kʌp]	cop	[kɑp]
luck	[lʌk]	lock	[lɑk]
suck	[sʌk]	sock	[sɑk]
Chuck	[tʃʌk]	chock	[tʃɑk]
rub	[rʌb]	rob	[rɑb]
some	[sʌm]	psalm	[sɑm]
nut	[nʌt]	not	[nɑt]
stuck	[stʌk]	stock	[stɑk]
cluck	[klʌk]	clock	[klɑk]

Warm-up phrases for practice: dust again, just occur, afraid of, official money, someone's mother, lovely summer, come and jump, love enough

These contain both [ɑ] *and* [ʌ]: smart brother, father's uncle, charm us, calm enough, not much of a bargain, another job, stop us, large supper

ADDING ON FOR PROFICIENCY

☆ 1. Say the following phrases aloud for clear [ʌ] sounds. Try to build up speed, but never at the expense of accuracy.

    a. struck by a truck
    b. double or nothing
    c. cover the rug
    d. a country lunch
    e. a fussy uncle
    f. hungry for supper

☆ 2. Read these sentences aloud, being sure to pronounce [ʌ] and [ə] correctly. The final five contain other vowel sounds spelled like those pronounced [ʌ]. Can you recognize which are which?

    a. Last Monday was a lovely summer day.
    b. Just the two of us will go away.
    c. Tina suspected the hungry man of stealing her money.

d. My brother loves bananas and cucumbers.

e. Will you come for lunch at one?

f. Nora was Edna's blood relative.

g. Must I fill the mugs up again?

h. There was dust under the rug.

i. The test was no trouble for us, and we scored one hundred.

j. I wonder who won the discussion.

k. The thunderclouds alarmed everyone on the farm.

l. My young son tossed the rock up and down.

m. The butter and honey in the pot were hot.

n. Arthur stopped having lunch at the country club.

o. He didn't qualify for the sudden success.

SUPER EXERCISES

☆ 1. *Packing a lunch bucket*   Pack your lunch bucket only with foods from the list that contain [ʌ] or [ə], and say them aloud as you pack. Hearty appetite!

crunchy peanut butter	fried chicken wings
double chocolate fudge	donuts for dunking
lemon meringue pie	a cup of coffee
tuna sandwiches	a veal cutlet
summer salad	ice-cream cake
a hot fudge sundae	hard-boiled eggs
piña coladas	bananas
lumpfish caviar	mushrooms

Can you add some of your own that contain [ʌ] and [ə]?

☆ 2. *Finish the scene*   Cast two people in the roles of Captain Buddy and Gina Plummer; then let the class finish the scene.

The Love Tub

SCENE: The deck of *Captain Buddy's Tub.*

GINA: (*sweetly*) Oh, Captain Buddy, may I have a word with you?

CAPTAIN BUDDY: Why of course, Mrs. Plummer. What can I do for you?

GINA: Well, Captain, I'm supposed to be on my honeymoon, but this tub of yours is far from being the Love Boat.

CAPTAIN BUDDY: Why, Mrs. Plummer, I'm stung by your remarks. Don't you and your husband find your accommodations satisfactory?

GINA: (*getting louder*) Captain Buddy, your pamphlet led us to believe this tub was a luxury liner; instead it looks more like a garbage dump. My husband and I are constantly seasick. (*She starts to weep.*) This is some honeymoon! Supper was disgusting tonight and— (*pause*) well, we just want to get off this tub!

CAPTAIN BUDDY: But Mrs. Plummer, that's impossible. We're in the middle of the Pacific Ocean. There is no way to get off this tub right now. It's just impossible (*splash!*) Mrs. Plummer, *Mrs. Plummer!* . . .

[ɝ] and [ɚ]

fonɛtɪk trɪvɪə

Which of the following is *not* a profession?

[mɝtʃənt, æktɚ, titʃɚ, loufɚ, sɝkəs klaʊn, pɝsən, bɝdwɑtʃɚ]

Say the following sentences aloud exactly as written:

1. I h*uh*d the b*uh*d ch*u*p just as my sist*ah* t*uh*ned the key in the do*ah*.
2. I h*ear*d the b*ir*d ch*ir*p just as my sist*er* tu*rn*ed the key in the do*or*.

[ɝ] and [ɚ] are two symbols used to represent the same vowel sound. [ɝ] is used by the IPA to represent that sound in the accented or stressed syllable of a word, as in *bird* [bɝd]. [ɚ] is the same sound in an unaccented or unstressed syllable of a word, as in *sister* [sɪstɚ]. [ɝ] and [ɚ] are vowel sounds with an *r* coloration. If you are aiming for General American pronunciation, do not omit the *r* coloration.

FACTS

Technical description: [ɝ] and [ɚ] are mid-central *r*-colored vowels. Because [ɝ] occurs in stressed syllables, it has a longer duration than [ɚ].

Correct production: The central part of the tongue is lifted mid-high toward the palate. The tip of the tongue is curved up toward the palate. The lips are neither rounded nor spread, and the muscles of the tongue are tense.

☆ *Spellings:* In stressed syllables, *ir* as in *bird*, *ear* as in *heard*, *ur* as in *murder*, *er* as in *serve*, *or* as in *work*, *our* as in *journal*. In unstressed syllables, *or* as in *doctor*, *er* as in *father*, *ar* as in *cellar*, *ure* as in *measure*, and *ur* in *murmur*.

Standard variations: Certain Eastern dialects and standard Southern dialects pronounce this sound without *r* coloration, represented as [ɜ] by the IPA. Let your ear be your guide to the standard spoken in your area.

IN USE

H*er*man s*ear*ched all ov*er* the *ear*th in ord*er* to find his real moth*er* and fath*er*.

Check your pronunciation of [ɝ] and [ɚ] in words on each list.

[ɝ]		[ɚ]		[ɚ] + consonant	
person	urge	tenor	labored	part	barn
clerk	certain	writer	chiropractor	cart	worn
service	search	bigger	senator	bargain	board
earn	curve	better	actor	chart	dark
merge	burst	braver	senior	farm	war
church	germ	clever	October	smart	guard
term	hurry	harder	easier	lark	park
rehearse	nervous	flavor	saver	art	sword

PROBLEMS TO AVOID

1. Substitution of [ʌ] or [ɔɪ] for [ɝ] so that *bird* [bɝd] sounds like "buhd" [bʌd] or "boyd" [bɔɪd].
2. Omission of [r] before a final consonant or at the end of a word so that *clerk* [klɝk] sounds like "cleuhk" [klɜk] or *stir* [stɝ] sounds like "stuh" [stʌ].
☆ 3. Substitution of [ɛr] or [ɑ] for [ɝ] by foreign speakers of English for whom [ɝ] is not a phoneme so that *word* [wɝd] becomes [wɛrd] (usually with a trilled *r*) or [wɑd].

Each problem is analyzed in greater detail. Concentrate on your area of weakness.

1. [ʌ] or [ɔɪ] for [ɝ] Say these words, making sure to retract your tongue to the center of your mouth for correct [ɝ] sounds.

serve	merger	clergy	girdle
birth	hermit	termite	hurdle
circle	sir	verse	curdle
dirty	clerk	worse	lurch
third	turkey	curl	perch
turban	person	first	quirk

Warm-up phrases for practice: perfect service, personal merger, Kermit's curfew, perky turkey, serve turnips, return to learn, permanent curls, church sermon

2. Omission of [r] Let your ear be your guide as to whether the standard in your area "drops" the [r] in words like *mother* [mʌðə] rather than [mʌðɝ]. However, General American, due to the influence of national television media, does include *r* colorations, so if you move from an area that is *r*-less, this omission will be noticed.

Here are some suggestions for improvement.

a. Listen for the [r] sound as you say the words *door, car, her, are, near.*
b. Take a number of adjectives like *big, tall,* and *small,* and add the comparative *-er: bigger, taller, smaller,* and so on.
c. Be just as careful in words that have a consonant after [r], such as *harm* and *park.* Practice these in the word lists already given.

Warm-up phrases for practice: appear near, pair of stairs, part carbon, the greener park, a charming sister, another brother, a major fear, near beer, we are here, we are there, her poor car, hear her louder cheer

☆ **3. [ɛr] or [ɑ] for [ɝ]** Check the directions for production of [ɝ], and select a good American model to follow. Be careful to not trill the sound.

If you can make a strong [r] at the beginning of a word, capitalize on this by saying the following word pairs, prolonging the joining of the two words. Then isolate the resultant [ɝ] sound.

hear rumors	are ready	car radio	were right
hair ribbon	wear red	far Rockies	near riot

Practice these words in addition to words on earlier lists.

[ɝ]				[ɚ]	
birth	[bɝθ]	girl	[gɝl]	teacher	[titʃɚ]
heard	[hɝd]	serve	[sɝv]	picture	[pɪktʃɚ]
learn	[lɝn]	early	[ɝli]	perform	[pɚfɔɚm]
earth	[ɝθ]	nurse	[nɝs]	mother	[mʌðɚ]
perfect	[pɝfəkt]	bird	[bɝd]	father	[faðɚ]
burn	[bɝn]	dirty	[dɝti]	sister	[sɪstɚ]
curtain	[kɝtən]	first	[fɝst]	brother	[brʌðɚ]
hurt	[hɝt]	nerve	[nɝv]	helper	[hɛlpɚ]
turn	[tɝn]	verb	[vɝb]	dollar	[dɑlɚ]
third	[θɝd]	worst	[wɝst]	builder	[bɪldɚ]

Warm-up phrases for practice: birthday girl, early bird, certain person, first purchase, third brother, inner and outer ear, clever mother, serve dinner

ADDING ON FOR PROFICIENCY

1. Say the following phrases aloud without omitting *r* colorations or substituting other vowels for [ɝ] or [ɚ]. Repeat 3 times, building up speed, but never at the expense of accuracy.

    a. perfect corner cupboard
    b. bigger turkey servings
    c. searching for furniture
    d. learning to impersonate characters
    e. earning bigger salaries
    f. working for rounder curves

2. Read these sentences aloud, listening for correct pronunciations.

    a. Early on Thursday mornings, Shirley turns her attention to learning how to perform culinary wonders.
    b. Bernard turned the corner and took a circular route in order to avoid the inner-city traffic.
    c. The barber had a hard time persuading Junior to let the man cut off the youngster's perfect curls.
    d. Kurt Berger became the world's most popular writer of murder mysteries.
    e. Ambassador Murphy served the entire earth on his mission for world peace.
    f. That is a hard part for a lesser actor to play.
    g. There was carbon in the carburetor, and the car sputtered but wouldn't start.
    h. "Better late than never" is one of the poorer excuses we've heard.
    i. When the farmers in the north started to fertilize their corn, the ears grew larger.
    j. The weather report said it would be partly cloudy and rather warm.

☆ 3. *For nonnative speakers*

1. Continue to practice the American [ɝ] sound as you say the following phrases aloud.

   a. surf and turf
   b. third-world merchant
   c. search and serve
   d. perfect summer term
   e. First Jersey teller

2. Say these sentences to practice [ɝ] and [ɚ].

   a. The color of the earth looked purple at sunset.
   b. Were you ready for exercises so early?
   c. Learning new words can open up new worlds.
   d. Many birds were perched above the church door.
   e. She served Bermuda onions with the hamburgers.
   f. Don't be nervous about the purpose of these drills.
   g. His concern was over passing the term.
   h. Herbert's birthday is on November third.
   i. The girl got hurt by the strong waves of the surf.
   j. Make your first turn down the dirt road.

SUPER EXERCISES

1. *Create a story*   Using at least seven of the words listed, or adding your own containing [ɝ] and [ɚ] sounds, create a short story.

sermon	murder	paper
furniture	reserve	razor
person	curfew	Hercules
lurked	senator	burst
blur	miner	vermin
flirt	neighbor	urchin

2. *Soap opera update*   Read the following synopsis aloud.

   In our last episode of *The Perfect Murder,* Reverend Peter Herbert had just finished his weekly sermon when Bertha Curtis let out a scream, which abruptly ended the church service. Bertha had seen old Mr. Herman clutch his throat and slump over in the first pew. Reverend Peter Herbert rushed to the first pew and discovered that Mr. Herman had been murdered! A curved dart had entered his throat. Myrtle Burns smirked a satisfied smile in the third pew, and the church cat, Bertie, was heard purring.

CHECKPOINT EXERCISES

Central vowels

Demonstrating control of central vowels   Listen to your production of the central vowels as you interpret at least two of the following selections. Record them for playback. Mark any central vowels that you produce incorrectly *as you are doing the readings;* then use the recording to check your self-judgments. Note any errors you still make on the table that follows the readings.

> Then to the lips of this poor earthen urn
> I learned, the secret of my life to learn;
> and lip to lip murmured, "While you live,
> Drink! for once dead you never shall return."
>
> EDWARD FITZGERALD, "Omar Khayyam"

"I only took the regular course," said the Mock Turtle. "What was that?" inquired Alice. "Reeling and Writhing, of course, to begin with," the Mock Turtle replied, "and the different branches of Arithmetic—Ambition, Distraction, Uglification, and Derision."

> LEWIS CARROLL, *Alice's Adventures in Wonderland*

> Courage is the price that life exacts for granting peace.
> The soul that knows it not, knows no release
> From little things;
> Knows not the vivid loneliness of fear,
> Nor mountain heights where bitter joy can hear
> The sound of wings.
>
> AMELIA EARHART PUTNAM

I'm shuddering all over, but I just can't go away. I'm afraid to be quiet and alone. I was born here. . . . My only son was drowned here. Oh don't be so rough on me, Peter. I love you as though you were one of us. I'd gladly let you marry Anna—only you do nothing. You're simply tossed from place to place. Strange, isn't it? And you must do something with your beard to make it grow longer. You look so funny.

> ANTON CHEKHOV, *The Cherry Orchard*

Love is the delightful interval between meeting a beautiful girl and discovering that she looks like a haddock.

> JOHN BARRYMORE

Omissions, substitutions, additions, and distortions still needing work

[ʌ] _____

[ə] _____

[ɝ] _____

[ɚ] _____

THE PHONEMIC DIPHTHONGS: [aɪ, aʊ, ɔɪ]

A diphthong is a vowel sound composed of two vowel sounds in succession. The phoneme begins with the sound of the first vowel element and then shifts or glides to the second vowel element, which in all three cases involves a lifting of the tongue. Remember that with a phonemic diphthong, both vowels must be included or the meaning will change.

[aɪ]

fonɛtɪk trɪvɪə

Which of the following would you be *unlikely* to use in the description of a person?

[haɪt, weɪt, wɑtʃ, ʃuz, ʃeɪp əv aɪz, kʌlɚ əv aɪz, smaɪl, tiθ, hæɚ kʌlɚ]

Say the following sentences aloud exactly as written.

1. *Ah* tr*ah* to sm*ah*l when *ah* fl*ah* even though *ah*m fr*ah*tened.
2. *I* try to sm*i*le when *I* fl*y* even though *I*'m fr*i*ghtened.

In [aɪ], if you eliminate the shift to the second vowel element, [ɪ], as in the first sentence, you will sound as if you speak with a Southern accent.

FACTS

Technical description: [aɪ] is a phonemic diphthong consisting of two vowel elements, shifting from [a] to [ɪ], but considered a single phoneme in American English.

Correct production: [aɪ] begins with a low-front tongue position and glides upward to a high-front tongue position. The lips shift from a spread position at first to an unrounded position as the sound glide occurs. The muscles of the tongue are lax.

☆ *Spellings: i* as in *fine, y* as in *cry, uy* as in *guy, ie* as in *pie, ei* as in *height, eye* as in *eye, aye* as in *aye, ui* as in *guide.*

Standard variation: [ɑɪ] is an optional standard variation. The sound begins with the tongue positioned farther back.

IN USE

Try to cl*i*mb the h*i*ghest peak to give your *eye*s the best s*i*ght of the hor*i*zon.

Check your pronunciation of [aɪ] in the words on each list.

I	time	my
I'm	tide	buy
idea	write	cry
ivory	night	sigh
eye	arrive	shy
ice	light	dry
island	blind	wry

PROBLEMS TO AVOID

1. Substitution of [aə] for the diphthong [aɪ] so that *I'm* [aɪm] sounds like "ahm" [aəm] or [ɑm].

2. Substitution of [ɔɪ] for [aɪ] so that *mine* [maɪn] sounds like "moyn" [mɔɪn].
3. Nasalization of [aɪ].

Each problem is analyzed in greater detail. Concentrate on your area of weakness.

1. **[aə]** **for** **[aɪ]**   This problem can also be perceived as a prolongation of [a] and omission of the glide to [ɪ]. Be careful to *complete* the diphthong as you say each word.

sigh   kind
buy   dime
I   fine

Keep the articulation of the diphthong complete and consistent as you read the following rows aloud.

a. sigh, slime, find, while
b. shy, mine, climb, drive, strive
c. file, quite, bright, might, blight
d. why, whine, wine, vine, nine
e. ride, pride, right, rhyme, crime

Warm-up phrases for practice: right time, find a dime, night light, vile slime, iced lime, Idaho prime, nice style, high dive

2. **[ɔɪ]** **for** **[aɪ]**   Drop your jaw for correct [aɪ] production. Do not round your lips. Say each word aloud.

side   bite
grime   fight
shine   height

Keep your lips spread, not rounded, at the start of the sound of [aɪ] as you say the words in each row.

a. nine, pine, time, I'm, lined
b. like, rind, grind, archive, alive
c. eyed, acquire, fry, tied, lied
d. type, tire, stripe, tiger, mile
e. deny, guy, high, nice, lice

Warm-up phrases for practice: spicy life, bye and bye, flight time, write a sign, devise a rhyme, I'm fine, fight fire, wide line

3. **Nasalization**   [aɪ] is particularly prone to nasality [ãɪ]. If a speaker has the tongue already lifted for [ɪ] as the first vowel [a] is being produced, the oral passage is narrowed, and air escapes up into the nose. To overcome this, artificially separate the two vowels in the diphthong, holding the first as a pure [a] with the dropped jaw for a count of 2, and only then lift the tongue to complete it with [ɪ]: *light* is pronounced [la . . . ɪt], *fine* is [fa . . . ɪn], *sign* is [sa . . . ɪn], and *time* is [ta . . . ɪm]. Gradually reduce the amount of time you hold the first sound, still keeping it pure. Practice production of [aɪ] by repeating the word lists in parts 1 and 2.

ADDING ON FOR PROFICIENCY

1. Say the following phrases aloud using clear [aɪ] diphthongs. Build up speed, but not at the expense of accuracy.

   a. wild lively time
   b. shy delighted smile
   c. shiny Irish eyes
   d. finding bright ties
   e. tying wires tight
   f. sighing light sighs

2. Say each sentence, being careful to pronounce [aɪ] correctly.

   a. Liza took the skyline drive along the tree-lined highway.
   b. I find Simon's smile very beguiling.
   c. Stars appear to shine very brightly in the sky on ice-cold nights.
   d. I took my time in finding the right road to Route 95.
   e. While climbing higher, I noticed little white edelweiss growing on the mountain.
   f. Dining with white wine adds a certain style to a fine meal.
   g. Times have gone by when I could buy something fine for a dime.
   h. Try to decide why I should fly instead of drive to the island.
   i. Michael often tried to act like a tyrant.
   j. Slice limes on edible vines for a divine appetizer.

SUPER EXERCISES

1. *A Something's Wrong Story*   Identify and discuss the errors in the following story as you read it aloud.

   The night flight took off from Hawaii en route to China flying high over the Alps. Myra could scarcely contain her excitement. She had never been to the Orient before, and as the plane landed, she shut her eyes so she could really take in all the delights of the bustling, unfamiliar scene. It was noon when she cleared customs, and the quaint streets were bathed in moonlight. When she arrived at the hotel, she set right off on a sightseeing expedition, camera clutched in hand so she could buy some choice snaps to take home. She was delighted by the constant silence on the streets and the firecrackers popping all around, and she even dared to step into a pantomime theater where she could listen to lines spoken in Chinese.

2. *Finish the scene*   Cast the following scene and read it aloud. Then let the class discuss how to finish the scene.

   SCENE: Home Buying Time, a cable TV shopping program

HOST: Hi, everyone. This is Mike Lyons, your host on Home Buying Time. I've got something very exciting for you to buy—at a *very special price!* Hi there! Who am I talking to?

CALLER: Hi, Mike. My name is Dinah Tyler, and I'm from North Carolina. This is my first time on the air. I'm so excited!

HOST: Hi, Dinah Tyler. Here's what I've got for you—I've got a pair of fine white diamond earrings to offer at the very special price of only $999!

CALLER: Oh, Mike, what a buy! What a price! $9.99 for diamonds. I'll buy five pairs at that price and give them to my family and special friends for Valentine's Day.

HOST: Great! You're wise to grab five pairs at this price—just $999. Just give us your credit card number and you'll own five pairs of gorgeous diamond earrings for only $999.

CALLER: Wow, what a deal! My credit card number is . . .

[aʊ]

fonɛtɪk trɪviə

Which of the following is *not* usually associated with money?

[əmaʊnt, fi, əlaʊəns, daʊt, əkaʊnt, sæləri, tæksɪz, paʊnd, faɪnæns]

Say the following words aloud, trying to keep the diphthongs pure, consistent, and free from distortion.

h*ow*, all*ow*, v*ow*, n*ow*, b*ow*, c*ow*, br*ow*

Of the three diphthongs presented in this section, [aʊ] is the one most often distorted in regions of the country. When distorted, it can sound very unpleasant.

FACTS

Technical description: [aʊ] is a phonemic diphthong consisting of two vowel elements, shifting from [a] to [ʊ] but considered a single phoneme in American English.

Correct production: [aʊ] begins with a low-front tongue position and glides to a high-back position. The lips shift from unrounded to rounded. The muscles of the tongue are relaxed.

☆ *Spellings:* ou as in *house,* ow as in *now.*

Standard variation: [ɑʊ], an optional standard variation, begins the sound with a low-back tongue position.

IN USE

I live d*ow*nt*ow*n in the br*ow*n h*ou*se by the S*ou*nd.

Check your pronunciation of [aʊ] in each list.

ounce	power	pow
owl	clout	couch
out	shout	ground
ours	bound	found
ouch	clown	plow

PROBLEMS TO AVOID

1. Distortion by adding nasality [aũ]. This is often accompanied by an extra vowel [æ] before [a] so that *house* [haʊs] sounds like [hæãʊs].
2. Lack of lip rounding on [ʊ] so that the diphthong [aə] or [ɑə] or even the phoneme [ɑ] is substituted. *Our* [aʊɚ] sounds like *are* [ɑɚ].

Each problem is analyzed in greater detail. Concentrate on your area of weakness.

1. Nasality and possible distortion   The key to correct pronunciation is relaxation and easy dropping of the jaw when you begin to articulate the first vowel element of the diphthong.

Nasality may occur because the tongue is raised for the second element [ʊ] even as the first [a] is being produced. It may therefore help to separate the two vowels, holding [a] for a count of 2 before allowing the tongue to rise for [ʊ], pronouncing *how* [ha . . . ʊ], *count* (ka . . . ʊnt], and *mouse* [ma . . . ʊs]. Gradually reduce the amount of time you hold [a], but always keep it pure.

Practice the words listed in "In Use" this way. Keep the same purity as you articulate the first vowel element of each word in each of these rows.

a. chow, round, down, mound, bow
b. doubt, bout, pout, lout, drought
c. mouse, douse, grouse, browse, frown
d. shout, sound, mount, hound, ground

Warm-up phrases for practice: downtown, loud sound, countdown, pound hound, cowled blouse, bounding clown, mounted crown, ground round

2. [aə], [ɑʊ], or [ɑ] for [aʊ]   Substitution occurs particularly when [ɚ] or [l] follows [aʊ]. To produce the sound correctly, drop your jaw to pronounce [a]; then shift your tongue up and back as you glide into [ʊ], *rounding your lips on the second element.*

a. our, ours, sour, hours, flour
b. bower, flower, power, glower, shower
c. towel, dowel, foul, jowl, scowl
d. owl, growl, prowl, trowel, vowel

Warm-up phrases for practice: flower power, sauerkraut, power outage, vowel sounds, pounds of flour, our house, glowering scowl

ADDING ON FOR PROFICIENCY

1. Say the following phrases aloud using clear [aʊ] diphthongs. Try to build up speed, but not at the expense of accuracy.

a. bound to sound loud
b. proud to shout out
c. hours of sour scowls
d. thousands of flower bowers
e. glowering brown hound
f. lousy grouse fowls

2. Read these sentences aloud, being careful to pronounce [aʊ] correctly.

a. Don't count on browsing through these books when there are hours of reading to do.
b. Turn down the house lights and let the sounds of the overture begin.
c. I could down a thousand pounds of chocolate mounds, but I would end up very stout.
d. Clouds of rain finally doused the awful drought down South.
e. Howard astounded everyone with his amount of power and political clout.
f. Loud shouts were heard outside and around the mountain.
g. Mrs. Powell found a brown silk gown at Howe's department store downtown.
h. A house becomes more of a house with beautiful grounds around it.
i. The brown couch was rounded out around its outer edges.
j. He wiped his brow and found himself in the tower surrounded by iron gates.

SUPER EXERCISES

1. *A Something's Wrong Story*   Identify and discuss the errors in the following story as you read it aloud.

Have you ever been in the Deep South—somewhere around the states of Colorado and Utah? They have rodeos almost every week, and you can watch the cowboys rounding up the cattle. Sometimes you can watch them chase a steer and rope it as it flies around the rodeo grounds. Other times you can see the mounted bulls trying to rope a cowgirl as the crowd shouts encouragement. The losers are announced at the beginning, and as they step up to get their trophies, a giant bonfire is lit for a cookout. Sides of beef are roasted over the fire and then eaten in the typical cowboy fashion, raw. Everyone drinks steaming mugs of coffee grounds, and someone usually gets out a guitar and everyone sings around the glowing embers of the dying fountain.

2. *Soap opera update*   Read the following soap opera update aloud.

In our last episode of *Fountain Spout,* we found out Mr. Townsend, the town's chief councilor, had become drowsy after downing too many drinks laced with poisoned powder, which caused him to drown in the town's great fountain. Countess Mountbank had counted on Townsend's clout to win her bout against bankruptcy. But now the countess floundered about as to what her next move would be and cursed the town fountain where Townsend's corpse had been found.

[ɔɪ]

fonɛtɪk trɪviə

Which of the following is *not* a natural substance?

[ɔɪl, fɔɪl, sɔɪl, dɝt, sɪlvɚ, goʊld, kɑpɚ, stil]

Say the following sentence aloud exactly as written.

1. I t*oyuh*l and t*oyuh*l to av*oyuh*d sp*oyuh*ling my b*oyuh*s.
2. I t*oi*l and t*oi*l to av*oi*d sp*oi*ling my b*oy*s.

The diphthong [ɔɪ] is prone to distortions or additions of extra sounds.

FACTS

Technical description: [ɔɪ] is a phonemic diphthong consisting of two vowel elements, shifting from [ɔ] to [ɪ] but considered a single phoneme in American English.

Correct production: [ɔɪ] begins with a mid-back tongue position and glides forward to a high-front position. The lips change from rounded to unrounded as the sound glide occurs. The muscles of the tongue are lax.

☆ *Spellings:* oi as in *boil,* oy as in *toy.*

IN USE

I enjoy v*oi*ce lessons but am c*oy* and av*oi*d singing in public.

Check your pronunciation of [ɔɪ] in words on each list.

oil	Troy	boy
oyster	moist	toy
joy	rejoice	soy
boil	soiled	noise

PROBLEMS TO AVOID

1. Addition of [ə] or [jə] between [ɔɪ] and a following [l] so that *oil* [ɔɪl] becomes "oyuhl" [ɔɪjəl].
2. Substitution of [əɪ] or [ɜɪ] for [ɔɪ] due to lack of lip rounding on the first part of the diphthong so that *join* [dʒɔɪn] becomes [dʒəɪn] or [dʒɜɪn].
3. Substitution of [ɝ] for [ɔɪ] so that *spoil* [spɔɪl] becomes "spurl" [spɝl]. This is no longer a very common substitution, but it may still be heard in parts of the South or New York City. If this is your problem, follow the exercises in sections 1 and 2 below.
4. Nasalization of [ɔɪ]. As with [aɪ] and [aʊ], the diphthong [ɔɪ] may be distorted by raising the tongue too soon on [ɔ], thus narrowing the oral passage and allowing air to escape up into the nose. Follow the directions for separating

the vowel elements and prolonging the first as suggested in the sections on [aɪ] and [aʊ]; then do the exercises in sections 1 and 2 below.

The first two problems are analyzed in greater detail. Concentrate on your area of weakness.

1. Addition of [ə] after [ɔɪ]   Read the words that follow, first separating the diphthong into two syllables and then blending it together into one syllable in order to avoid adding extra sounds.

a. to . . . il, toil
b. aw . . . il, oil
c. baw . . . il, boil
d. caw . . . il, coil
e. saw . . . il, soil

Warm-up phrases for practice: toil the soil, broil in foil, oily soil, coiled coil

2. [əɪ] or [ɜɪ] for [ɔɪ]   Read the following word series aloud, making sure to round your lips as you begin to articulate the first vowel element in each word.

a. joys, coy, boys, soy, Roy
b. join, moist, poise, noise, doily
c. oyster, boil, broils, coins, royal

Warm-up phrases for practice: royal poise, broiled oysters, moist pork joint, oinking noise, joyful toys

ADDING ON FOR PROFICIENCY

1. Say the following phrases aloud using clear [ɔɪ] diphthongs. Try to build up speed, but not at the expense of accuracy.

a. boys toiled the soil
b. toys bring joy to Roy
c. purloined coins
d. avoid oily poisons
e. adjoining coiled foils

2. Read these sentences, being careful to pronounce [ɔɪ] correctly.

a. Don't destroy your appetite by eating before I serve the roast loin of lamb.
b. Poisonous coils of steam roiled up from the moist soil.
c. Troy avoided joy by being boisterous and noisy.
d. Poison is the name of a new perfumed bath oil.
e. I have no choice but to voice my disappointment.
f. As a boy Roy enjoyed all types of toys.
g. Boiling the soil acts as a foil against impurities.
h. Mrs. Doyle pointed her finger at the pearl found in the oyster bed.
i. Sirloin is a joy to eat when broiled on the grill.
j. Ahoy, mates, let's hoist the sails and point them to the south.

SUPER EXERCISE

1. Read the following commercial aloud, or write your own featuring [ɔɪ] sounds.

   Are you spoiled? Do you like to do things that give you joy? Then try Dr. Joyce's Oil of Poison—the moist spray that rids your house of embarrassing odors! Just open the foil packet and watch the moist spray coil out to scent your home from foyer to attic. Remember, don't be coy about household odors. Get Dr. Joyce's Oil of Poison and enjoy, enjoy your odor-free home. Oh boy!

2. *A job interview*   Choose one person to play the applicant, Roy or Joy Floyd, a designer of cowboy costumes, and another person to play the interviewer, Mr. or Miss Boyd. There is an opening for promotion within the Happy Noise Toy Company to director of the Employee Suggestions Department. Applicant must demonstrate loyalty to the company and knowledge of the entire line the company makes. In addition, applicant must have an idea of a brand-new toy that the company might profitably produce and market over TV. Have the actors role-play the interview. Let several pairs of students take the roles.

CHECKPOINT EXERCISES

Phonemic diphthongs

Demonstrating control of the phonemic diphthongs   Listen to your production of the phonemic diphthongs as you interpret at least two of the following selections. Record them for playback. Mark any diphthongs that you produce incorrectly *as you are doing the readings;* then use the recording to check your self-judgments. Note any errors you still make on the table that follows the readings.

To everything there is a season, and a time to every purpose under the heaven:

A time to be born, and a time to die;
A time to plant, and a time to pluck up that which is planted;
A time to kill, and a time to heal;
A time to break down, and a time to build up;
A time to weep, and a time to laugh;
A time to mourn, and a time to dance;

   ECCLESIASTES 3:1–4

And when he fell in whirlwind, he went down,
As when a lordly cedar, green with boughs,
Goes down with a great shout upon the hills,
And leaves a lonesome place against the sky.

   EDWIN MARKHAM, "Lincoln, the Man of the People"

Thanksgiving, like ambassadors, Cabinet officers, and others smeared with
   political ointment,
Depends for its existence on presidential appointment.

   OGDEN NASH

Annual income twenty pounds, annual expenditure nineteen six, result happiness. Annual income twenty pounds, annual expenditure twenty pounds ought and six, result misery.

CHARLES DICKENS, *David Copperfield*

He who doubts from what he sees
Will ne'er believe, do what you please.
If the sun and moon should doubt,
They'd immediately go out.

WILLIAM BLAKE, "Auguries of Innocence"

Another said—"Why, ne'er a peevish Boy
Would break the Bowl from which he drank in Joy;
Shall He that *made* the Vessel in pure Love
And Fancy, in an after Rage destroy?"

EDWARD FITZGERALD, "Omar Khayyam"

Substitutions, additions, and distortions still needing work

[aɪ] as in *my* _____

[aʊ] as in *how* _____

[ɔɪ] as in *joy* _____

10

THE CONSONANTS

The flowering moments of the mind drop half of
their petals in our speech. Talking is one of the
truly fine arts . . . and its fluent harmonies may
be spoiled by the intrusion of a single harsh note.

OLIVER WENDELL HOLMES

Challenge exercise   There are 10 errors in the following challenge passage. Can
you find all 10 and correct them?

Spencer wen out wif his new rifle. De neighbahs down his shtreet noticed
him walkin by and aksed him if he had any idear what he was gunnin foah.

Here are the correct answers:

1. *wen* for *went:* omission of a [t] sound
2. *wif* for *with:* substitution of [f] for [θ]
3. *de* for *the:* substitution of [d] for [ð]
4. *neighbahs* for *neighbors:* omission of an [r] sound
5. *shtreet* for *streeet:* substitution of [ʃ] for [s]
6. *walkin* for *walking:* substitution of [n] for [ŋ]
7. *aksed* for *asked:* reversal of [s] and [k]
8. *idear* for *idea:* addition of an [r] sound where it does not belong
9. *gunnin* for *gunning:* the substitution of [n] for [ŋ]
10. *foah* for *for:* omission of a final [r] sound

Notice that three of the four possible sources of error in articulation appeared
in the challenge: substitution, omission, and addition. Distortion was the only
one that did not occur.

Just how important is it to pronounce consonants clearly in terms of the
overall comprehension of an individual's speech pattern? It has been estimated
that consonants make up about 65 percent of an individual's total speech output.
Thus clear articulation of consonants is a key factor in being understood.

CLASSIFYING CONSONANTS

Consonants, which you know by definition are stopped or hindered sounds, are
classified on the basis of three characteristics: voice, place of articulation, and

manner of production. These classifications distinguish the consonants from one another; they are also helpful as a guide in learning how to pronounce each one correctly.

Voice

You learned in the chapter on vowels that all vowels are voiced. This is not always true of consonants. Say [h] as in *how* and notice that it is produced simply on the outgoing breath. In fact, many of the consonants come in voiced/unvoiced pairs called *cognates:* Two distinctly different phonemes are produced in exactly the same manner with the same placement of the articulators; the only thing that distinguishes them from each other is the presence or absence of voice— that is, whether the exiting air has set the vocal bands into vibration or not. Here is a list of cognates in English. Place your fingertips lightly on your larynx in order to feel the presence or absence of voiced sound as you say each consonant.

Voiced	*Unvoiced*
[b]	[p]
[d]	[t]
[g]	[k]
[v]	[f]
[ð] as in *them*	[θ] as in *thumb*
[z]	[s]
[ʒ] as in *measure*	[ʃ] *she*
[dʒ] as in *jar*	[tʃ] *chip*

Place of articulation

Starting from the front of the mouth and moving back, there are seven different possible places of articulation: at the two lips (bilabial), at lower lip and upper teeth (labiodental), with tongue to teeth (linguadental), with tongue to gum ridge (alveolar), with tongue to hard palate (palatal), with back of tongue to soft palate (velar), and at the vocal folds (glottal). See the chart in Table 10.1 for the correct placement of each consonant and compare them with your own.

Manner of production

Consonant sounds can be classified according to how the outgoing airstream is stopped or hindered when the sound is formed. For example, [d] and [t] are called *plosives* ("exploders") because the breath stream is stopped and then re-leased with a slight explosion as these two sounds are made. There are six such categories of sounds:

1. *Plosives* are sounds that involve a stopping and then releasing of the breath stream. They are also known as *stops* or *stop-plosives.* [p, b, t, d, k, g]
2. *Fricatives* are produced by narrowing the outgoing breath stream so much that friction noise can be heard. [f, v, θ, ð, s, z, ʃ, ʒ, h]

TABLE 10.1   Articulation of Consonant Sounds in English

	Bilabial	*Labiodental*	*Linguadental*	*Alveolar*	*Palatal*	*Velar*	*Glottal*
Plosives	p b − +			t d − +		k g − +	
Fricatives		f v − +	θ ð − +	s z − +	ʃ ʒ − +		h −
Affricates					tʃ dʒ − +		
Nasals	m +			n +		ŋ +	
Lateral				l +			
Glides	hw ʻw − +				r j + +		

− indicates without voice
+ indicates with voice

3. *Affricates* are created by the stopping of the breath stream and the release of it as a fricative. The sound thus formed is perceived as one phoneme. There are only two in English. [tʃ, dʒ]
4. *Nasals* are created when the outgoing breath stream is directed through the nose rather than the mouth. [m, n, ŋ]
5. *Laterals* are produced when the breath stream is emitted at the sides of the tongue (that is, laterally). There is only one lateral consonant in English.[1] [l]
6. *Glides* are produced by a slight narrowing of the oral cavity as the articulators stay in motion, gliding toward the position of the vowel sound that follows. [hw, w, r, j]

THE PLOSIVES

The production of all six plosives [p, b, t, d, k, g] assumes the raising of the soft palate so that air does not escape up into the nose. Plosives at the beginning of a word have a more explosive sound than those at the end of a word, and the three voiced consonants [b, d, g] do not have the breathy release of their cognates [p, t, k].

ACCEPTED ASSIMILATIONS FOR THE PLOSIVES

Although the stop contact for the articulation of the plosives is made in *all* circumstances, if a plosive is followed by another consonant in the very next syllable, there is no breath release after the first plosive. Instead, the plosive is held momentarily and then its release is blended into the following sound.

---

[1] Because there is only one lateral consonant in English and because it has much in common with the glides, [l] will be discussed with the latter.

Examples

breakfast	hop down
popcorn	buck private
actor	hat check
cupcake	crab tracks

[p] and [b]

fonɛtɪk trɪviə

How many pickled peppers did Peter Piper actually pick?

[pitɚ paɪpɚ dɪd nɑt pɪk ə pɛk əv pɪkļd pɛpɚz. hi oʊnli pɪkt wʌn kwɔɚt ænd ðɛn hi kwɪt bɪkɔz hi sɛd ðə peɪ wʌz nɑt gʊd ɪnʌf]

Say the following sentences aloud exactly as written.

1. O'viously, you pro'ly won't try to remem'er my num'er.
2. Obviously, you probably won't try to remember my number.

Although the [p] and [b] sounds are relatively easy for most people to produce, they tend to get slighted in some words or disappear entirely in others because of overassimilation. Correct production will add a sharpness to your speech.

FACTS

Technical description: Both are bilabial plosives. [p] is unvoiced and [b] is voiced.
Correct production: The lips are brought lightly but firmly together to block momentarily the outgoing airstream, and when the lips part, a slight explosion occurs. [p] has an airy quality; [b] does not.
☆ *Spellings:* Usually as each appears. There are two exceptions, however:

1. If an *m* comes before a *b* at the end of a word or before a suffix, the *b* is silent. *Examples:* thumb, comb, plumber.
2. If *n, t,* or *s* follows *p* at the beginning of a word, the *p* is silent. *Examples:* pneumonia, ptomaine, psyche.

IN USE

Applause pleased Pam as she practiced the high jump for the Olympics.
Bryan was disturbed that the borrowed cab had a blind number plate.

Check your pronunciation of [p] and [b] in the words on each list.

pun	happy	mop	bough	harbor	crab
pool	proper	cop	boy	stable	grab
pull	hoping	drop	buy	crumble	sob
pan	appeal	rope	ball	somber	tribe
pope	staple	slope	bird	anybody	stab
path	ample	skip	burst	nobody	cube

paper	apple	ship	busy	symbol	web
paid	happen	grope	bunch	public	bulb
price	topple	group	bulk	ability	disturb
popular	simple	sleep	banner	habit	tube
police	respect	wrap	bandage	number	
please	prize		black	bright	
play	practice		blue	brown	
plan	proud		blister	bread	
plate	pray		blush	brick	
place	pretty		blame	brought	

Contrast these word pairs:

pang	bang	staple	stable	cup	cub
pie	buy	simple	symbol	sop	sob
pump	bump	ample	amble	tripe	tribe
pair	bear	roped	robed	lope	lobe

PROBLEMS TO AVOID

1. Slack articulation of [p] and [b], with incomplete closure of the lips.
2. Omission of [b] in certain contexts so that *member* [mɛmbɚ] becomes "mem'er" [mɛmɚ].
☆ 3. Substitution of [p] for [b] or [b] for [p] so that *cup* [kʌp] becomes *cub* [kʌb] and *rib* [rɪb] becomes *rip* [rɪp].
☆ 4. Substitution of [v] for [b], particularly in the middle of a word so that *habit* [hæbɪt] becomes *have it* [hævɪt].

Each problem is analyzed in greater detail. Concentrate on your areas of weakness.

1. Slack articulation   By definition, [p] and [b] are made by stopping the air with the two lips, and whether the sound explodes or not, this closure must be firmly but lightly made or the sound will not be articulated.

a. Do you feel a complete stop in each of the following?

popcorn	bobby pin
paper	pepper
porpoise	happy
pumpkin pie	dribble
baby	bubble

Warm-up phrases for practice: baby's bib, up and about, a helping of pot pie, popping popcorn, ripped balloon, baby baboon, cheap plastic bubble, rubber basketball

b. If [f] or [v] follows [p] or [b], there may be a tendency for the plosive to be assimilated into the fricative. This must be avoided; for example, *stop first* must be pronounced [stɑpfɚst], not [stɑfɚst]. Read each of the following words aloud, carefully pronouncing *each* consonant.

capful	tubful
hopeful	subvert
top value	obvious
helpfulness	job file

Warm-up phrases for practice: bob for apples, cheap vacation, help find it, stop flirting, rob vaults, hope for, jump fast, disturb Frank, sob forever

2. Omission of [b]   Such omission often occurs if *b* is preceded by *m*. Read each word, pronouncing *each* consonant clearly.

December	somebody
September	cucumber
combination	symbol

Warm-up phrases for practice: an optimum number, a contemptible member, limbering up, probable combinations, comparing memberships, cucumbers in December, somebody's emblem

☆ **3.** [p] **for** [b] **and** [b] **for** [p]   Some nonnative speakers confuse these two sounds, particularly at the beginnings of words, although they can occur at the end as well. It is important to remember that words written with the letter *p* are voiceless, and the sound is produced just with air; those written with *b* are voiced, so less air is emitted.

Pronounce these words all with the "airy" [p]:

pie	paper	up
pill	upper	cup
pole	happy	wrap
policeman	popcorn	keep

Pronounce these with the heavier [b]:

baby	maybe	rob
bite	habit	crib
buttons	number	robe
bowl	grumble	rib

Contrast the difference in sound *and* meanings in these pairs:

pig	big	pay	bay	rip	rib
pail	bail	poor	boor	mop	mob
pin	bin	pump	bump	cap	cab

Warm-up phrases for practice: (Be careful, because both sounds occur in each phrase.) a bad person, poor babies, a big park, stop the cab, pink beads, busy people, disturb the cop, keep a Band-Aid, put it back, up and about, step back, peel a banana, rob a bank, a simple symbol, Mabel's maple syrup

☆ **4.** [v] **for** [b] **in medial position**   Some languages have a sound that does not exist in English, a friction noise made by the two lips that sounds rather like [v], and so, particularly in the middle of a word, a native speaker of one of those languages may substitute the more familiar sound. Be very careful to close the lips to make a *stop* when pronouncing [b].

rubber   crumbled
table   sober
rubbish   noble

Warm-up phrases for practice: a head of cabbage, babbling brook, somebody's table, a noble habit, rubber ball, disturbing rubbish, dabbling in hobbies

ADDING ON FOR PROFICIENCY

1. With light but absolutely firm contacts, repeat these phrases 3 times, building up speed, but not at the expense of accuracy.

   a. pepper pie
   b. happy pippin
   c. pink pea bulbs
   d. boy baboon baby
   e. proper double bubbles
   f. bib bop bap

2. Read the following sentences aloud, pronouncing [p] and [b] clearly and monitoring yourself to make sure you avoid errors.

   a. Betty had an unbelievably horrible experience on her blind date with Peter.
   b. The baseball player fumbled the ball and was booed by a number of people in the bleachers.
   c. Why do professors say a B is a respectable grade when we believe we have put in appropriate work for an A?
   d. A champion who is caught napping may pay the price of being labeled a past champion.
   e. Ping-Pong players are particularly nimble and adept at lobbing balls from peculiar positions.
   f. Why do people believe that apes and baboons are particularly partial to bananas?
   g. A popular pastime at breakfast is sleeping in bed that extra precious hour before class begins.
   h. Pizza, popcorn, and potato chips may be labeled junk foods, but they appeal to the appetite.
   i. If there's soda *pop, pop* guns, *pop* art, *pop*corn, and *pop* music, why do I call my father "pop"?
   j. Reports and term papers take application, preparation, and prayer!

☆ 3. *For nonnative speakers*   Read these sentences aloud, pronouncing each consonant clearly.

   a. Paul paid me a number of compliments.
   b. I hope I pass the test for obtaining citizenship papers.
   c. It is my responsibility to be prompt in keeping appointments with professors.

d. Buses and cabs are public means of transportation.
e. Apple pie is a particularly American dish.
f. Pizza is popular in the snack bar on campus.
g. Peace is a popular topic of discussion.
h. "Be prepared" is better practical advice for taking tests than "Hope."
i. Paper plates, paper cups, and paper napkins are useful on picnics.
j. A map can explain where a particular place is.

SUPER EXERCISES

☆ 1. *Using* [p] *and* [b] *correctly in conversational speech*   Once you have mastered the warm-up and proficiency exercises, make the transition to everyday speech. Create a sentence around each of the words and phrases that follow, and say it aloud at a normal conversational rate. *Do not write the sentence down.*

Example: If the phrase were *a passing term paper,* you might say, "I hope I submit a passing term paper" or "Preparing a passing term paper takes more than just luck."

pizza	newspapers
a simple problem	lucky numbers
parking spaces	playing baseball
opportunity	a bad habit
a popular professor	surprises
a big problem	

2. Take the role of announcer with superbly fluent articulation in one of the following newsbreaks.

This is Paul/Paula Appleton for cable station WPOP's *Popular Newsbreak.*

A pair of prisoners has escaped from the Minneapolis prison in Black Pit County. The pair appears to have driven openly out of the prison grounds in the warden's private car, dressed as state troopers. Peter Paxton, also known as Rubber Mouth, and Bobby Poole, alias Baboon, worked in the prison's tailoring shop and obviously made the escape outfits there. They were so believable in their roles that a lady stopped them beside the outer prison gate to report a missing dog. They are armed and believed dangerous. Be on the lookout.

Human interest: Park Slope Primary School in neighboring Pinehurst held its annual Perfect Pet Contest last Saturday. Entrants included a tame robin, four guinea pigs, a pure-blooded show poodle held tightly by a parent, a bowl of tadpoles, five pigeons, and a stuffed rabbit. Tabby Peters, owner of the toy, staunchly defended her entrant as the Perfect Pet. "He requires no upkeep and sleeps patiently beside me in bed. Besides, my parents don't always bug me to feed him."

Employees of the Top Price supermarket in Paduca, Pennsylvania, had a near riot on their hands this past week. The local newspaper published an ad for prime lamb chops at $.29 a pound. A 4 before the decimal point had been omitted—$4.29 a pound was the way the ad was supposed to appear.

This explanation did not appease the impatient crowd of bargain hunters. Apollo Papadopolis, supermarket manager, sold the chops at the published price only after the paper promised to make up the difference. "At least I didn't have to give them Green Stamps," a weary Papadopolis reported.

☆ 3. *Finish the scene*   Cast two people in the roles of Betty and Mabel[2] and then let the class decide how to finish the scene.

The In-Laws Are Coming

SCENE: Kitchen. Betty is cooking as she gets directions over the phone from her friend Mabel, who is heard but not seen.

BETTY: How much butter did you say, Mabel?
MABEL: Half a pound.
BETTY: Got it. Half a pound. This butter's like a brick. How am I supposed to stir it?
MABEL: Betty, butter for pie is always meant to be at room temperature.
BETTY: Oops! Too late now. I'll put it on the burner to melt. How many cups of flour?
MABEL: One cup. And then cut up ten apples.
BETTY: *Ten* apples? But I only have three apples, Mabel.
MABEL: Then make a small apple pie.
BETTY: But Bob's parents have big appetites and they're so particular. Perhaps I could put in a can of pineapple as well?
MABEL: No pineapple. And Betty, what about the butter on the burner?
BETTY: (*small scream*) That's where the black smoke is coming from! It's burnt. It's ruined. Help, Mabel, help. I hear the buzzer. Bob's parents are here! . . .

[t] and [d]

fonɛtık trıviə

Which one of these people was *never* photographed?

[grɛtə gɑˑbo, tɛdi rouzəvelt, wɔlt dızni, mɑrtın luθɚ kıŋ, krıstəfɚ kəlʌmbəs, ðə bitlz, tɛd kɛnədi]

Mini-challenge: This is a cumulative exercise in absolute precision. If you successfully complete step 1, repeat it before going on to step 2; repeat steps 1 and 2 before going on to step 3, and so on. However, you are finished the moment

---

[2] Feel free to substitute Bob for Betty or Mark for Mabel.

you (a) omit a final [t] or (b) substitute a [d] for a [t] in the middle of a word. How far can you get?

1. Potatoes
    2. Potatoes are mostly water.
        3. Potatoes are an important food.
            4. Hot and buttered they are totally delicious.
                5. Little bits of grated cheese make them even better.
                    6. But last, do not forget to add a little packet of buttered croutons.

The sounds [t] and [d] tend to be slighted. In rapid speech they have a way of disappearing at the ends of words, and in the middle of words [d] often replaces [t] because of assimilation. The mini-challenge should help build self-awareness. Being more precise with these sounds will sharpen your whole diction pattern.

FACTS

Technical description: Both are alveolar plosives. [t] is unvoiced and [d] is voiced.
Correct production: [t] and [d] are produced by lifting the tongue tip to the gum ridge behind the front teeth in a lightly held contact and then releasing it with a resultant slight explosion. If you hold your wrist in front of your mouth, [t] can be felt as a puff of breath. Check that the tip of the tongue is touching the gum ridge, *not the upper teeth,* and that the tongue does not slide forward, making a [ts] sound.
☆ *Spelling:* As is, or doubled, *tt* or *dd.* However:

1. In words ending in *-tle* or *-ten,* if *t* is not doubled, it is silent. *Examples:* castle, thistle, hasten, listen.
2. In some words (no rule seems to exist), *t* and *d* are silent. *Examples:* Christmas, mortgage, handsome, Wednesday.

Standard variations:

1. Some phoneticians feel that the medial [t] as in *letter* or *little* may acceptably be pronounced somewhere between [t] and [d]. However, the substitution of pure [d] is still unacceptable, so for practice purposes it is best to aim for a clear [t], as assimilation will weaken it in connected speech anyway.
2. Assimilation sometimes makes the suffix ending *-ed* into [t] according to rules outlined in detail in Chapter 11.

IN USE

The *t*ired mo*tt*o "Be*tt*er la*t*e than never" is no*t* necessarily *t*rue.
It was a *d*ismal, *d*ank *d*ay, and *D*iane shu*dd*ered at the *d*readfully col*d* win*d*.

Say some words from each list:

tune	into	cat	do	hiding	had	trick	dress
top	beating	coat	die	reading	did	treat	drip

tooth	hating	put	deck	seeding	Dad	tree	drive
task	rating	bet	door	loading	mad	trash	drink
tell	coating	wet	dim	fading	rode	tribute	dread
time	sitting	mate	dark	riding	wide	try	drip
team	writing	root	doll	feeding	need	train	dream
tired	little	but	dead	garden	food	trifle	dry

PROBLEMS TO AVOID

There are many possible problems with [t] and [d].

1. Omission of the [t] or [d] at the ends of words so that *last night* [læst naɪt] becomes "las nigh" [læs naɪ].
2. Substitution of [d] for [t] in the middle of a word so that *writing* [raɪtɪŋ] becomes *riding* [raɪdɪŋ].
3. Omission of [t] or [d] in the middle of certain words so that *enter* [ɛntɚ] becomes "enner" [ɛnɚ].
4. Omission of [t] in final consonant clusters so that *lists* [lɪsts] becomes "liss" [lɪs].
5. Substitution of a sound resembling *chr* [tʃr] for *tr* [tr] so that *tree* [tri] becomes "chree" [tʃri].
6. Substitution of a sound resembling *jr* [dʒr] for *dr* [dr] so that *drain* [dreɪn] becomes "jrain" [dʒreɪn].
7. Substitution of a glottal stop for medial or final [t] so that something like a click in your throat replaces [t] as in *little.*
8. Overpronunciation of medial [t].
☆ 9. Distortion due to dentalization so that a slight spitting sound accompanies [t] and [d].
☆ 10. Distortion due to excessive tongue contact.

Each problem is analyzed in greater detail. Concentrate on your areas of weakness.

1. Omissions at the ends of words   Read each word aloud, pronouncing all finals.

taught	did
what	that
but	first

Warm-up phrases for practice: that is it, it is good, not bad, put it back, it could be, night light, what a sight, ate it up, a tight fit, not a lot, get it back, sweet but not neat

2. [d] for [t] in the middle of a word   Say each word, pronouncing each medial [t] clearly.

pretty	little
letter	metal
later	written

Contrast the difference in sound *and* meaning:

tide	died	latter	ladder	hat	had
tell	dell	boating	boding	mat	mad
team	deem	rating	raiding	wrote	rode

To help achieve a clean medial [t], try the trick of adding a very slight [h] right after it:

fat her	fatter	set hing	setting
wit he	witty	pat hing	patting
bet her	better	get hing	getting
sit he	city	it his mine	it is mine
writ hen	written	what ha treat	what a treat

Warm-up phrases for practice: a pretty little girl, a metal medal, a metal bottle top, settle it by letter, a rotten little brat, settle it later, a flower petal and a bicycle pedal, a bitter note, do as bidden so you won't be bitten

3. Omission of [t] **or** [d] **in the middle of words**   When [t] or [d] follows another consonant, it may tend to be omitted. Say the following words without omitting medial [t] or [d].

understand	correctly
enter	exactly
older	wonderful
fastest	western

Warm-up phrases for practice: handling your children, a hundred twenty, forty-four forty or fight, a frantic interest, entering correctly, wondering about the ending, starting at midnight

4. Omission of [t] **in final consonant clusters**   Say the following words without omitting [t].

wrists	costs
corrects	respects
accepts	conducts

Warm-up phrases for practice: the latest tests, highest costs, neatest lists, respects the facts, coldest frosts, out in the wilds, accepts helping hands, spends wildly

5. [tʃr] **for** [tr]   Good diction requires that *tr* be pronounced [tr]. Say these words carefully and correctly.

try	trip
treat	tree
triumph	truck

Warm-up phrases for practice: a true treat, trying traffic, try out the truck, trip over the trunk, untrustworthy tramp, trick or treat, trash your trash

6. [dʒr] for [dr]   The [d] sound must remain identifiably a *d*, not a [dʒ]. Read these words aloud, correctly.

drip   dribble
drunk   dry
droop   dream

Warm-up phrases for practice: dribble as you drink, a dreadful driver, droopy drawers, dream about driving, dread fixing the drip

7. Substitution of a glottal stop for [t]   [ʔ] is the IPA symbol for the glottal stop, a clicking sound from your throat, at the end of words or more often in the middle of words in place of the [t]. You can tell if you have a tendency to do this by placing your hand on your larynx as you say "little Italy's bottle." If you felt any clicks, you are undoubtedly doing it, and need to set about correcting it. For instance, *kettle* is pronounced [kɛtl] not [kɛʔl]. Say the following words without using [ʔ].

metal   battle
utmost   total
written   kitten

Warm-up phrases for practice: an important battle, metal kettle, settle in Italy, a metal rattle, startle the kitten, Itty's new mittens, patterns on bottles, whittle a little

8. Overpronunciation   In an attempt to pronounce a medial [t], some people tend to stress it too much. To avoid this, do not remove the tongue tip from the gum ridge, but go straight into the following sound without putting a vowel in between. *Kitten* is pronounced [kɪtn̩], not [kɪtən]. Say the following words without overemphasizing medial [t].

little   bitten
rattle   rotten
fatten   whittle

Warm-up phrases for practice: Use the phrases for problem 7.

☆ **9. Distortion due to dentalization**   In phonetics, dentalization is written with a small mark under the sound, [t̪] or [d̪], to indicate the distortion. *Hat* is [hæt], not [hæt̪].

Dentalization is due to incorrect tongue placement. If the tongue tip is allowed to rest down against the teeth, a dull spitting sound will be heard on [t] and [d]. This is because the stop contact for the explosion of the sounds is being made with the whole front of the tongue thrust up against the front of the hard palate while the tip stays lodged against the teeth. This is in marked contrast to its correct production in which the tip of the tongue rises to make contact with the gum ridge.

Many foreign languages include dentalization as a feature of correct production of [t] and [d], but in English such production is considered nonstandard. In large metropolitan areas that are "melting pots" of first- and second-generation immigrants, dentalization is particularly prevalent as a holdover from the original languages.

Here are some suggestions for improvement.

a. Go back and check correct production. Make up nonsense words with [t] and [d] in combination with the various vowels, monitoring your tongue position each time (using a mirror will help): aht-aht-aht, eet-eet-eet, awt-awt-awt, oot-oot-oot, and so on.

b. Contrast wrong and right:

time is [taɪm], not [t̪aɪm]
dash is [dæʃ], not [d̪æʃ]
what is [hwʌt], not [hwʌt̪]
eight is [eɪt], not [eɪt̪]
medal is [mɛdl̩], not [mɛd̪l̩]
widen is [waɪdn], not [waɪd̪n̩]
hot is [hɑt], not [hɑt̪]

c. Apply the correct production of [t] and [d] to the other word lists in this section.

Warm-up phrases for practice: tic-tac-toe, high tide, tell the time, take the total, a dark sight, light the light, take sides, dash ahead, mind Tom's advice, took time, need a dime.

☆ **10. Distortion due to excessive tongue contact** [t] and [d] are light, delicate sounds, particularly [t], which is just a light puff of air. In fact, as you pronounce words beginning with [t], hold the back of your hand near your mouth and feel the light explosive burst of air. This will also help you avoid substituting a sound resembling [d] for [t].

Refer to the word lists earlier in the section for practice. Follow a good American model to help you train your ear.

ADDING ON FOR PROFICIENCY

1. With light but absolutely firm contact with the tip of the tongue to the gum ridge, repeat the following phrases 3 times, building up speed, but not at the expense of accuracy.

   a. what a to-do today
   b. contented, tired, and hot
   c. a bit of better butter
   d. Hottentot tutor
   e. hidden tulip garden

2. Read the following sentences aloud, pronouncing [t] and [d] clearly and monitoring yourself to be sure you avoid all the errors outlined.

   a. Didn't you tell Tom he couldn't train on the team?
   b. Dina lifted ten-pound weights.

  c. Lester placed twenty bets on the latest lottery.
  d. Waxed dental floss lets Steven maintain his white teeth.
  e. Trevor drove his truck into the tree and stripped it of bark.
  f. Wouldn't you like to come for tea at two today?
  g. Betty was totally rattled at the prospect of settling down.
  h. Wanda's best bottle of ketchup won the first award.
  i. Mr. Hunter washed the cleanest windows with his fists.
  j. "Don't do it!" shouted Mr. Winters. "You'll get caught!"

3. Practice saying these sentences.

  a. Last summer Hester expected to collect antiques on Cape Cod.
  b. She rejects only a few of the metal parts she inspects all day.
  c. "Get out, get out," insisted the rotten old lady in the haunted house.
  d. What a pity Martin tries to act like a little boy.
  e. That is easy, thought Betty as she washed the dirty pots.
  f. Life in the city is better in the winter despite the traffic.
  g. The ancient lady delicately handed her sister the artist's paints.
  h. She asked if the poet entered his works in the contest.
  i. My sister's vision is 20/20, but she seems blind most of the time.
  j. Put out the light and let in a little of the nighttime breezes.

☆ 4. *For nonnative speakers*   Keep each [t] and [d] light and delicate, making sure you do not dentalize. Read these sentences aloud.

  a. What happened to the audience in the last act of the play?
  b. "That product is the greatest," said the city official.
  c. According to the committee, the meeting will be at two this afternoon.
  d. An important advantage of real art is its lasting beauty.
  e. Betty entered the hospital to take a much needed rest.
  f. Winter is not exactly my favorite time of the year.
  g. It is important to try to practice writing that material.
  h. Most students with ability are introduced to mathematics at a young age.
  i. That sentence was particularly hard to interpret.
  j. Kitty had heard exactly what was said.

SUPER EXERCISES

A. The physical fitness enthusiast practices with ever heavier weights to build extra endurance and muscular control. So, too, the good speaker exercises his or her articulatory muscles beyond the demands of ordinary conversation for true proficiency.

  The Super Exercises continue with more step-up exercises similar to the Challenge Exercise that began this section.

 1. What a hot spot.
  2. It was a pothole on a paved asphalt road.
   3. Automobiles bumped into it with monotonous regularity.
    4. Pedestrians and motorists complained loudly and bitterly.

5. Later, residents of the city also complained loudly and bitterly.
6. At last, a citizens' board raised a fund and had it fixed.

1. Tetbury is a British city.
2. Elephant and Castle and Tottenham Court are London underground stops.
3. The British watch their favorite bird, the tawny pippet.
4. They like crumpets and hot buttered buns.
5. Tittingham and Tottle are British family names.
6. Altogether the British speech is clipped and better than ours.

1. Patterns on bottles
2. Intricate patterns, beautifully wrought
3. What an art form is bottle art.
4. Twisted patterns, pretty patterns, and patterns matched left and right
5. Mustard bottles, crystal bottles, and bottles of bright plastic
6. All are made light and decorative because of pattern bottle art.

B. Here are sentences loaded with [t] and [d] sounds in polysyllabic words that are a challenge to master at a conversational rate.

1. Amongst the thickly stalked cottonwood trees on the contessa's estate, it was discovered that twenty-two hundred of the prime experimental specimens had unfortunately been destroyed.

2. The archaeologist gets historical assistance every time he descends to the strata of the prehistoric past.

3. Articulating distinctly and lightly with an optimum rate pattern characterized the customary conversation of the inhabitants of the outer Antarctic islands.

4. The democratic constituents of the greater metropolitan area will congregate to formulate an opportune slate of candidates for the Democratic Party in the next election.

5. Dramatic literature of the Restoration Period had limitations placed on it by the intricacies of the intrigues rampant in court affairs.

6. Domesticated water birds, when liberated, have an unfortunate tendency to revert to the idleness civilization has imposed on them.

7. Proportional representation is an ideal attribute to strive for in the formulation of totally new constitutions for emerging states.

8. The automobile has created the unfortunate situation of putting pedestrians on notice that they must be observant at all times when strolling on heavily trafficked streets.

9. An optimistic biologist assumes automatically correct labeling on the specimens placed in laboratory test tubes.

10. A particularly drastic cut in expenditures seems a necessity if a balanced budget is to be met within the next decade.

C. *Soap opera practice*   Cast three people as Kitty, Burt, and the announcer, and present this script as a radio play.

ANNOUNCER: In our last episode of *General Waterworks,* Burt, frustrated in his attempts to show that an incestuous relationship had grown up between Kitty and Martin, threw dynamite into the water turbines, destroying eight-tenths of the plant and throwing the town of Hattersville into turmoil. Kitty, afflicted with the rare disease of toeitis, must bathe in a full tub of fresh, temperature-controlled water every two hours or risk total paralysis. With her water tanks empty, she pleads with Burt in his flooded Watertown factory.

KITTY: Burt, how *could* you? This is the most insane act yet, and all for what?

BURT: To get you to admit to your illicit arrangement with Martin, my dear Kitty. . . .

KITTY: But to have destroyed the waterworks and plunged the town into its worst crisis in twenty years . . . !

BURT: Justice must be served. Until you admit your guilt, Hattersville will just have to do without water.

KITTY: Fiend. Sadist. Don't you mind that my left foot is already dragging without my water treatment?

BURT: Admit your guilt, and the repair teams will be at the turbines.

KITTY: My right foot! My right foot is getting numb!

BURT: I repeat. I am waiting. . . .

ANNOUNCER: And as Burt waits and Kitty's feet become increasingly paralyzed, we take leave of *General Waterworks.* . . .

D. *Composing commercials*   Create a commercial for the following products, using the name of your product at least three times.

Red Hot Tomato Paste
Tom Thompson's Automotive Parts
A Tickle-in-Time Throat Medicine
Toasty Tidbits Kitty Food
A Practical Traveler's Pamphlet to Lost Cities
Doctor Foster's Denture Toothpaste
Tap and Toe Practice in Patents and Satins
Diet Delight for Fatties

☆ E. *Finish the scene*   Cast three characters in a restaurant—Matt and Betty sitting at a table and a waiter standing over them—and have them act out this scene. Let the class decide how to end it.

BETTY: Matt, that was the best meal I've ever had.
MATT: Glad you liked it.

WAITER: Excuse me, but the restaurant has closed. I'm waiting for you to pay the bill: forty-two dollars and twenty cents.

BETTY: Matt, even though this is our first date, you spent a lot on me.

MATT: You haven't seen anything yet, baby. Stick with me, and you'll go first-class—the best way.

WAITER: Forty-two dollars and twenty cents, please.

MATT: Later, waiter, later.

BETTY: And you picked such a great restaurant.

WAITER: *The restaurant has closed.*

MATT: Uh— Betty, I seem to have lost my credit cards. And my wallet— it *was* in my front pocket. Uh— Betty, could you lend me fifty dollars? Just until tomorrow . . .

[k] and [g]

fonɛtık trıviə

Which are the two fictitious characters?

[kærəlaın kɛnədi, kıŋ hɛnri ði eıθ, gılbət ænd sʌlıvən, vınsənt væn goʊ, kælvın kulıdʒ, kıŋ kɑŋ, kıt kaəsən, mʌðə gus]

Say the following sentences aloud exactly as written.

1. She ast if I reconized the estent of the estra damage.
2. She as*k*ed if I re*c*o*g*nized the e*x*tent of the e*x*tra damage.

The common problems most people have with [k] and [g] are due to careless articulation. The stop contacts may be incomplete, resulting in a fuzzy sound, or assimilation may lead the sound to be omitted. A crisp speaking pattern comes with crisp articulation of the plosives.

FACTS

Technical description: Both are velar (tongue–to–soft palate) plosives. [k] is unvoiced and [g] is voiced.

Correct production: The back of the tongue presses lightly but firmly against the soft palate, blocking the air. When the back of the tongue drops, there is a sudden slight explosion of air from the buildup pressure. (Check that the closure is complete.) [k] has an airier quality than [g].

☆ *Spellings:* Usually as each appears. There are exceptions, however:

1. A *c* at the beginning of a word is pronounced [k] if followed by *a, u,* or *o*. *Examples:* cat [kæt], come [kʌm], cut [kʌt].
2. If *n* follows *k* or *g* at the beginning of a word, these sounds are silent. *Examples:* knee, knife, gnaw, gnat.
3. If the letter *g* comes before *m* or *n* at the end of a word, it is silent. *Examples:* sign, diaphragm.

4. Occasionally, *ch* is pronounced [k] and *gh* [g]. *Examples:* chorus [kɔrəs], chemical [kɛmɪkəl], ghetto [gɛto], ghost [goʊst].

Assimilation note: Vowels are all voiced, so if *x* [ks] comes before a vowel, *x* takes on the voiced sound of [gz]. *Examples:* exact, exam, exotic.

IN USE

After *K*ate's tur*k*ey dinner, *C*laude's stoma*ch* a*ch*ed again, but he was *c*areful not to *c*riticize.

*G*reta could always re*c*o*g*nize a *g*littering bargain among the tired sales *g*oods.

Check your pronunciation of the words on each list.

cool	become	lake	geese	again	rig
key	because	rake	gum	begin	rug
cave	baking	back	gift	begging	hog
caught	bacon	hook	get	regard	rogue
kettle	require	stork	gap	forget	snug
chord	token	stake	guilt	signal	rag
cope	weaker	fork	guest	tiger	dig
kill	wicked	pink	give	disguise	dog
call	turkey	cork	guide	haggard	egg
coffee	asking	cook	guess	bogus	plague
curb	looking	book	gone	digging	bag
coach	naked	fake	gauze	vaguely	vogue
queen	enquire	brick	gate	regulate	

class	crowd	glad	grass
clan	creep	glass	great
clap	crate	glimpse	grip
cloud	crush	glaze	grub
close	creature	globe	groan
clipper	cripple	glow	growl
clam	crayon	gland	group

Contrast the following word pairs:

crime	grime	stacker	stagger	leak	league
clue	glue	locking	logging	hawk	hog
cave	gave	meeker	meager	luck	lug
cause	gauze	tricker	trigger	queue	ague

PROBLEMS TO AVOID

1. Articulation of [k] and [g] may be slack because of inadequate closure between the tongue and velum.
2. [k] and [g] may be omitted entirely in some words so that *lecture* [lɛktʃɚ] becomes "lecsher" [lɛkʃɚ] and *recognize* [rekəgnaɪz] becomes "reckanize" [rɛkənaɪz].

☆ **3.** Nonnative speakers may substitute [k] for [g] and vice versa so that *came* [keɪm] becomes *game* [geɪm] and *gold* [goʊld] becomes *cold* [koʊld]. Each problem is analyzed in greater detail. Concentrate on your areas of weakness.

1. Slack articulation   By definition, [k] and [g] are stop sounds, but if an imprecise closure is made, they may sound more like guttural fricatives. This happens particularly in the middle of a word. Check in pronouncing the following words that the closure is complete.

chicken	giggle
market	linger
pickle	burglar
coconut	cookies
turkey	tiger

Warm-up phrases for practice: liquor basket, clucking chickens, ragged beggar, quacking ducklings, a misguided struggle, disgusted and angry, tucked-up pockets

2. Omission of [k] **and** [g]   These sounds may be omitted if they come before other consonants. *Exact* is pronounced [əgzækt], not [əzækt] or [əzæk].[3]
Pronounce each word carefully and correctly.

explore	ignition
blackboard	picture
recognition	

Warm-up phrases for practice: asked the extent, expressed excitement, significant exploration, extra recognition, a stag party, exports disk brakes, explains the significance, escapes detection
   The sounds [k] and [g] are also often omitted when they come at the ends of words, particularly before -*s* and -*ed* endings. *Asked* is [æskt], not [æst].[4]
   Say the following words correctly.

attacked	hugged
taxed	begged
thanks	

Warm-up phrases for practice: asks and begs, picks out bricks, makes stacks of socks, smoked and cooked, asked the extent, asked and asked, looked under rugs, critics of sex, provoked mean jokes

☆ **3.** [k] **for** [g] **and** [g] **for** [k]   Speakers of some European languages confuse the two sounds, substituting one for the other. It is important to remember that words written with the letter *k* are *voiceless,* while words written with *g* are voiced, so there is a greater emission of air on [k]. This confusion occurs more at the end of words, but can be heard in all positions.

---

[3] The word *escape* is prone to the faulty *addition* of [k], resulting in the incorrect pronunciation [ɛkskeɪp] rather than the correct [əskeɪp].
[4] This word seems to cause havoc: It is also heard as [ækst] or [æskdɪd].

Pronounce all these with the "airy" [k].

cat	local	back
came	bacon	take
keep	package	pick
coat	taken	tack

Pronounce these with the heavier [g].

get	bigger	bag
give	tiger	dog
gold	anger	frog
goal	beggar	but

Contrast the difference in both sound and meaning in these pairs:

coast	ghost	racket	ragged	hack	hag
class	glass	ankle	angle	back	bag
		stacker	stagger	sack	sag

Warm-up phrases for practice: (Be careful, because both sounds occur in each phrase.) take it back, a big pig, pack your bag, a good book, pick again, begin counting, forget to look, came to the game, jog back again, tack on the tag, cold gold

ADDING ON FOR PROFICIENCY

1. With light but absolutely firm contacts, repeat these phrases. Build up speed, but never at the expense of accuracy.

   a. bigger beggar's bag
   b. cigar tobacco package
   c. plastic picnic basket
   d. snugger rug bug
   e. six sick chickens
   f. dog tag taker

2. Read the following sentences aloud, monitoring yourself for sharp [k] and [g].

   a. A cat may look at a queen, but the queen doesn't have to look back.
   b. Credit cards are plastic money, which we too often forget requires paying back!
   c. Ignoring regulations again, Carl asked for an extra week's vacation.
   d. It is a good idea to respect the instructor's lecture material when taking examinations.
   e. Singles clubs have certain aspects in common with meat markets: In each the goods are on display for inspection.
   f. "All that glitters is not gold" and "The grass is always greener on the other side" are quaint, timeworn expressions.
   g. Mickey talked so much as he walked he forgot what direction he was going in.

h. A groom grasps the gold ring—and courteously gives it away again.

i. The lackluster actor began to lose the crowd a quarter of the way into the first act.

j. It was the biggest, hungriest, ugliest tiger that had yet to escape from its cage—thank goodness!

☆ 3. *For nonnative speakers.* Say each sentence carefully and correctly.

a. The college orchestra and chorus are quite good.

b. Exam questions are easy to forget, afterwards.

c. Bacon and eggs are common for breakfast in America.

d. Do you like sugar and cream in your coffee?

e. It is the custom to eat turkey, cranberry sauce, and pumpkin pie on Thanksgiving.

f. Directions on campus were difficult to learn in the beginning.

g. Do you have credit cards in your country?

h. It looks like the stack of books is growing bigger every week.

i. Graduation is a good goal to work for.

j. Required courses must be taken.

SUPER EXERCISES

☆ 1. *Using* [k] *and* [g] *correctly in conversation speech*   Create a sentence around cach word or phrasc and say it aloud at a conversational rate. *Do not write the sentence down.* For example, if the phrase were *a broken record,* you might say, "I hate to find a broken record" or "The lecturer sounded like a broken record."

lucky	a big crowd
college campus	credit cards
a good example	jogging
Thanksgiving	cookbook
going home	questions
quiet	difficult class
my country	a future goal

2. Choose a portion of this newscast to read aloud as an announcer.

This is E. J. Pickens for station WKOK Nightly Newsbreak.

Human interest: Lincoln Park is guaranteed its place in the *Guiness Book of World Records.* Local citizens in their Milk Cartons for Charity campaign have collected enough used cartons to make a 60-foot pile covering the entire town square. Local pride in the $6000 dollars thus collected is undimmed by a recent unexplained outbreak of cockroaches in buildings next to the square.

A man's home is his castle, but what about his flag pole? Chuck Foxx, who has lived on the top of his for the past six weeks, refuses to vacate. Increasingly large and unruly crowds have gathered in Coggle Berg, Kansas, to gape at his makeshift home in the sky, and his continued stay there has been declared a public nuisance by the town selectmen. His only megaphone response to the selectmen's edict: "Consult my attorney."

Election notes: The October 6th election of Caleb Huxley as mayor of Carleton, Oklahoma, is being hotly contested by a concerned citizens' graft-in-elections committee. The final count of 6000 votes for the incumbent is 60 more than the number of citizens registered to vote in Carleton. Mayor Huxley was on vacation and unavailable for comment.

3. *Finish the scene*   Cast two people in the roles of Kiki and the radio doctor. Involve the whole class in taking roles to finish the scene.

A Tricky Boyfriend

SCENE: Kiki Singleton on the telephone with a radio call-in adviser, Dr. Gold.

KIKI: Oh, Dr. Gold, I can't believe I got through to you.

DR. GOLD: And what can I do for my good radio caller?

KIKI: It's Cab, my boyfriend. We're engaged. We've gone together for six years. I kind of wonder if he's beginning to play tricks on me.

DR. GOLD: Going together for six years gives you a good idea of a person. What kinds of tricks?

KIKI: Maybe monkey tricks. Doctor, last week I caught him with a girl in his apartment. Two weeks ago I caught him with *two* girls there. The girl last week was wearing only a blanket.

DR. GOLD: How did he explain the girl and the blanket?

KIKI: I asked. He said her clothes were stolen on campus and he was being kind to rescue her. Oh, he is kind, Doctor. . . .

DR. GOLD: And the two girls two weeks ago?

KIKI: I found them naked in the kitchen.

DR. GOLD: How did he explain that?

KIKI: I asked. He claimed they broke the lock on the kitchen door and sneaked in to use the automatic washer. Doctor, his automatic washer does clean clothes extra, extra well. I could believe that also. . . .

DR. GOLD: So what kinds of tricks can he be playing on you?

KIKI: Doctor, get this: Last night I came in to catch him with a girl in a bikini.

DR. GOLD: His explanation?

KIKI: I asked. He said she was an acrobat in a circus taking a coffee break. Doctor, I'm not dumb. I was in the Girl Scouts! Acrobats don't drink coffee. Coffee isn't good for their coordination. What kind of trick can he be pulling on me? . . .

CHECKPOINT EXERCISE

Plosives

Demonstrating precision and delicacy on the plosives   Listen to your production of the plosives as you interpret at least two of the following selections. Record them for playback. As you read, mark any plosives that you produced incorrectly;

then use the recording to check your self-judgments. Note any errors you still make on the table that follows the selections.

"I saw you take his kiss!" "Tis true."
"O modesty!" "'Twas strictly kept:
He thought me asleep—at least, I knew
He thought I thought he thought I slept."
COVENTRY PATMORE

"I'm so excited," said Mrs. Haddock, as the time for departure drew near. "I've never been on a boat before."

"You'll be very seasick," said Aunt Flora. "The Quetches were never good sailors except your half-brother Edmund who was drowned at that picnic thirteen years ago next July fourth."

"Drowned people can be raised to the surface by firing guns over the river," said little Mildred.

"People who are drowned at sea," said Aunt Flora, "are never recovered."

"I should think," said little Mildred, "that if you fired a big enough gun over the Atlantic Ocean you could bring a lot of interesting things to the surface."
D. O. STEWARD, *Mr. and Mrs. Haddock Abroad*

Sow a thought, and you reap an act;
Sow an act, and you reap a habit;
Sow a habit, and you reap a character;
Sow a character, and you reap a destiny.
ANONYMOUS

The codfish lays ten thousand eggs,
The homely hen lays one.
The codfish never cackles
To tell you what she's done.
And so we scorn the codfish,
While the humble hen we prize,
Which only goes to show
That it pays to advertise.
ANONYMOUS

I went to the woods because I wished to live deliberately, to front only essential facts of life, and see if I could not learn what it had to teach, and not, when I came to die, discover that I had not lived.
HENRY DAVID THOREAU, *Walden*

Omissions, substitutions, additions, or distortions still needing work

[p] and [b] _____

[t] and [d] _____

[k] and [g] _____

THE FRICATIVES

Nine consonants are produced by forcing air through a very narrow space between the articulators. All of them are produced orally, with the soft palate raised to block passage into the nose. It is important with each to *hear* and *feel* the continuous air flow, with its frictionlike sounds.

There are four cognate fricative pairs:

[f] as in *fish*   [v] as in *vine*
[θ] as in *thin*   [ð] as in *them*
[s] as in *see*   [z] as in *zoo*
[ʃ] as in *she*   [ʒ] as in *treasure*

The ninth fricative is [h] as in *how*.[5]

[f] and [v]

fonɛtɪk trɪviə

[fækt: fræns ɪz ə kʌntri ɪn jurəp
fækt: vil ɪz ə kaɪnd əv mit
fækt: filədɛlfiə ɪz ə sɪti
fɪkʃən: fɪʃ sɪŋ ænd flaɪ]

Say the following sentence aloud exactly as written.

1. Belie'me, you can gimme a lotta work to do if you hafta.
2. Believe me, you can give me a lot of work to do if you have to.

Although [f] and [v] are relatively easy for native speakers to produce, they tend to get slack in some words, and in careless speech the final [v] can disappear entirely.

FACTS

Technical description: Both are labiodental (upper teeth and lower lip) fricatives. [f] is unvoiced and [v] is voiced.
Correct production: Bring the cutting edge of the upper teeth and the lower lip together and force the air out audibly.
☆ *Spellings:* Usually as each appears. There are two exceptions, however:

1. [f] is sometimes spelled *ph*. *Examples:* philosophy [fɪlɑsəfi], photo [foʊto].
2. [f] at the end of a word is sometimes spelled *gh*. *Examples:* cough [kɔf], enough [ɪnʌf].

---

[5] Some phoneticians include [hw] as in *when* because of the [h], but most include it with its glide cognate [w].

IN USE

Hal*f* of *Ph*illip's co*ff*ee cup was *f*ull of rou*gh* grounds.
An a*v*id tra*v*eler lo*v*es to *v*isit e*v*ery a*v*ailable place.

Check your pronunciation of the words on each list.

favor	defeat	rough	Vaseline	television	alive
fashion	afford	graph	valentine	avoid	thrive
fake	soften	beef	virtue	invite	grieve
fame	refuse	chief	vacuum	lovely	shove
phobia	confuse	cuff	variation	evil	dive
fire	effect	off	valuable	cover	prove
future	effort	if	vital	event	live

flat	flirt	fry	free
flower	fly	freeze	front
flip	flicker	fresh	freight
floor	flame	fruit	frame

Contrast both the sound and the meaning of these word pairs:

fault	vault	define	devine	serf	serve
fender	vendor	refuse (*verb*)	reviews	fife	five

PROBLEMS TO AVOID

Although native speakers have little difficulty with these sounds, they may make
two kinds of errors:

1. Slack articulation of [f] and [v].
2. Omission of [f] and [v] before other consonants so that *have some* [hæv səm]
   becomes "ha some" [hæ səm].

Foreign speakers may make three kinds of errors:

☆ 3. Substitution of [f] for [v] and [v] for [f] so that *vast* [væst] becomes *fast* [fæst]
   and *file* [faɪl] becomes *vile* [vaɪl].
☆ 4. Substitution of [b] for [v] so that *vote* [voʊt] becomes *boat* [boʊt].
☆ 5. Substitution of [w] for [v] so that *vine* [vaɪn] becomes *wine* [waɪn].

Each problem is analyzed in greater detail. Concentrate on your area of
weakness.

1. Slack articulation of [f] **and** [v]   A speaker must make sure that the teeth
and lips touch. Check your articulation in the following words.

every	avoid
laughing	marvel
fair	twelve
tough	half
glove	visit

Warm-up phrases for practice: every evening, footloose and fancy free, resolve to improve, five cups of coffee, forever forgetful, carefully efficient, half a loaf

2. Omission of [f] or [v]   This occurs particularly before another consonant. For example, *leave me* is pronounced [liv mi], not [limi]. Special mention must be made of one word: *of.* It is pronounced [ʌv], and the [v] should not be omitted.

Say the following expressions carefully and correctly.

cough syrup	believe me
twelfth	kind of good
sort of nice	bag of candy

Warm-up phrases for practice: half the time, five of them, I've done it, enough of that, give me some, I've tried, lots of times, love me or leave me, bag of clothes, two-fifths, one-twelfth.

☆ **3. [f] for [v] and [v] for [f]**   People from a non-English-speaking background tend to confuse [f] and [v] at times, substituting the one for the other. Remember, if it is spelled with an *f* (or *ph* or *gh*), it is produced entirely with air; if it is spelled with a *v,* voice is present. Thus *leave* is [liv], not [lif]. The sole important exception is *of,* pronounced with [v] [ʌv].

Say each phrase, using [v] in *of.*

cup of coffee	can of beans
pack of matches	piece of pie
bowl of soup	

Pronounce all these words with the "airy" [f].

full	laughing	half
fit	effort	stiff
fan	coffee	enough
fork	defend	safe

Say these with the voiced [v].

very	given	live
visit	having	give
vowel	every	move
vote	even	above

Contrast the difference in sound *and* meaning in these pairs:

feel	veal	shuffle	shovel	half	have
fine	vine	surface	service	leaf	leave
few	view	rifle	rival	safe	save

Warm-up phrases for practice: (Be careful, because both sounds occur in each phrase.) a fast visit, drive halfway, have a fight, love at first sight, have five of them, leave the leaf there, proof of its value, view of a few

☆ 4. [b] **for** [v]   Make sure that your *upper teeth* touch the lower lips. *Very* is pronounced [vɛri], not [bɛri]. And remember that in English the letter *v* can signal only the [v] sound.

Say each word carefully and correctly.

value   vine
valley   rival
verse   victory

Contrast the difference in sound and meaning in these pairs:

van   ban   vase   base
very   berry   vanish   banish
vote   boat   vow   bow

Warm-up phrases for practice: a very big value, bought every bargain, be above it, various bad voices, volume of books, a very vocal baby, voting booth

☆ 5. [w] **for** [v]   In English *v* never signals any sound but [v]. Make sure the upper teeth touch the lower lip in all *v* words. *Very* is pronounced [vɛri] not [wɛri].
Say each word carefully and correctly.

visit   variety
vowel   veal
verb   vinegar

Contrast the difference in sound *and* meaning in these pairs:

verse   worse   vest   west
vine   wine   vent   went
very   wary   vet   wet

Warm-up phrases for practice: visit Will, went to vote, wound very tightly, a warm evening, wonderful voices, a willing visitor, wash off varnish, wipe off the vase

ADDING ON FOR PROFICIENCY

1. Articulating each [f] and [v] clearly, repeat these phrases 3 times, building up speed, but never at the expense of accuracy.

    a. fifth floor
    b. twelfth night
    c. video viewers
    d. flat fat flounders
    e. a variety of virtues
    f. full-fledged movie star

2. Read the following sentences aloud, monitoring your production of [f] and [v].

a. Believe me, if I don't have to visit Aunt Fanny for twelve more years, I won't be grief-stricken!

b. Valerie swerved into the curve as the nervous driving instructor valiantly tried to cover his fear.

c. Vera had a lot of fine clothes she couldn't afford and a lot of shelved bills she could live with.

d. The cover girl moved, and the photographer vowed after this to only photograph still-lifes.

e. Being flirtatious and having an affair are about as different as seeing a fish and actually serving it in your frying pan.

f. I have to believe that was the funniest film I have ever laughed my way through.

g. Fans raved, "Fantastic, marvelous, ravishing, lovely, fabulous," in reference to Mrs. Foster's fudge cake.

h. If we have to save money, we will have to live very differently and not feel virtuous.

i. If an elevator elevates, a gravitator gravitates, and a levitator levitates, what vegetates?

j. If—fish had feet, calves had feathers, and fowl had fingers, what would elephants have?

☆ 3. *For nonnative speakers.* As you practice [f] and [v] in the following sentences, note that sentences *g* through *l* contrast [v] and [b] and *m* through *v* do the same with [v] and [w].

a. Fast foods are a way of life in America.

b. Which of our customs feels most foreign to you?

c. Driving takes a lot of skill—and nerve!

d. They say, "To have half a loaf is better than to have none."

e. Television shows are not always worth viewing.

f. Do you live on or off campus?

g. Some stores have better values than others.

h. What is the best vacation you have ever taken?

i. Buying video equipment can prove quite expensive.

j. It is better to have a good voice than to have a big voice.

k. Victor banged into the van. Lesson: Beer and driving don't mix.

l. The newspaper gave valuable advice about buying veal.

m. I believe in reading the reviews before viewing the movies.

n. Having a bicycle in a big city can prove to be of questionable value.

o. It is valuable to wait as long as it is not in vain.

p. Do they have many volunteer workers in your profession?

q. I was relieved: That girl's voice is worse than mine.

r. Wine varies from vineyard to vineyard.

s. Will violence on TV never be banned?

t. Advertisements work if they sell goods or services.

u. Have you ever visited the West?

v. What we want and what we have are very different things.

SUPER EXERCISES

☆ 1. *Using* [f] *and* [v] *in conversational speech.* Create sentences around the following words and phrases. Say each at a conversational rate.

a habit I have	travel
a famous TV star	I would like to have . . .
saving money	I have to have . . .
photographs	invitation
breakfast food	future plans
traffic	a big fear
visit	flying

2. Read the following commercial aloud at a conversational rate.

Value Vacations

Friends, are your nerves frayed? Do you need a break from it all? Value Vacations is the outfit for you! Value Vacations provides private villas in a fabulous resort area. Fulfill your wildest vacation fantasies at prices everyone can afford. Our reservations clerks are standing by to reserve that vacation of your dreams. Phone (800) 555-4545 and say you want to reserve your very own Falkland Island Hideaway. Plane fare is extra.

3. *Finish the valentine messages.* Some messages on valentines can be straight, some sickly sweet, and some downright ridiculous.

The words needed to complete the messages are at the bottom of the page (or use your own). Complete a valentine and then read it aloud.

Oh, you cute devil!
Are you on the _____ ?

I'll be your slave
If you'll only _____ .

As cows like grass
And polar bears, ice
I'm drawn to you
For you're my _____ .

I'd give up my life
If you'd be my _____ .

Never say never!
We'll cuddle _____ .

You make my heart move.
We're right in the _____ .

My heart's on my sleeve.
Don't ever _____ .

You're mine
Like grapes on a _____ .

vine, wife, forever, vice, behave, level, groove, leave

AN EXTRA ACTION WORKOUT SOUND

[θ] and [ð]

fonɛtɪk trɪviə

Which of these would you *not* like to attend?

[fɔrθ əv dʒulaɪ pəreɪd, θæŋksgɪvɪŋ dɪnə, ə bɜθdeɪ pɑrti, ə θiətə mætɪneɪ, ə tuθ puliŋ æt ðə dɛntɪsts ɔfɪs, ə θɜtiəθ ænəvɜsəri sɛləbreɪʃən]

Contrast the phrases said both ways.

I'll go wit'cha	I'll go wi*th* you
nuttin' doin'	no*th*ing doing
bofe of 'em	bo*th* of *th*em
over dere	over *th*ere

Some linguists consider [θ] and [ð] "unnatural" phonemes because they exist in so few languages other than English. Nonnative speakers usually have trouble with them, and native speakers can be careless in their articulation of them.

FACTS

Technical description: [θ] and [ð] are linguadental (tongue-teeth) fricatives. [θ] is unvoiced and [ð] is voiced.

Correct production: The blade of the tongue should be placed lightly against the cutting edge of the upper teeth.[6] The characteristic fricative quality is achieved by forcing air through this barrier. (Make sure that the sound is *fricative,* not *plosive.*)

☆ *Spellings:* Both [θ] and [ð] are spelled *th,* and most native speakers have learned which is which without conscious thought. However, for the nonnative speaker, there is only one rule to help tell which is which, and that is of very limited use: If a word ends in *-the,* the sound is [ð]. *Examples: breathe* [brið], *clothe* [kloʊð]. Trial and error and a good ear are your only reliable guides, but the lists under "In Use" will help.[7]

IN USE

[θ]: The tru*th* is I was *th*oroughly *th*irsty, and I *th*ought no*th*ing would satisfy me.

[ð]: *Th*ere *th*ey were, over *th*ere with *th*eir bro*th*ers, arguing about the wea*th*er.

Check your pronunciation of [θ] and [ð] in the words on each list:

[θ]			[ð]		
thick	anything	month	the	other	bathe
thousand	something	south	then	either	soothe
third	plaything	north	these	neither	breathe
thorough	bathtub	path	those	another	writhe
theater	toothbrush	bath	there	mother	teethe
thief	catholic	teeth	though	father	scathe

---

[6] Some people produce this sound with the tip of the tongue, but if you are learning the sound for the first time, using the blade will help you avoid other problems.

[7] You will notice that unstressed words with *th* usually have the sound [ð]. Articles, pronouns, and conjunctions spelled *th* plus vowel have [ð]; all others with *th* or *thr* have [θ].

thank	author	beneath	them	bother	tithe
thunder	method	mouth	this	rather	swathe
theory	truthful	cloth	that	leather	
thermal	birthday	earth	thus	farther	
thin	wealthy	faith	their	bathing	
thumb	enthusiastic				
three					
thrill					
threat					
through					
thrive					
thrash					
throat					
thread					
throne					

PROBLEMS TO AVOID

1. Omission of [θ] and [ð] in certain contexts so that *bathtub* [bæθtəb] becomes "batub" [bætəb] and *what's that* [hwʌts ðæt] becomes *what's at* [hwʌts æt].

2. In some instances, substitution of [f] for [θ] and [v] for [ð] so that *bathroom* [bæθrum] becomes "bafroom" [bæfrum] and *mother* [mʌðɚ] becomes "muhver" [mʌvɚ].

☆ **3.** Substitution of [d] for [ð] or [t] for [θ] so that *both* [bouθ] becomes *boat* [bout] and *there* [ðær] becomes *dare* [dær].

☆ **4.** Substitution of [s] for [θ] and [z] for [ð] so that *thumb* [θʌm] becomes *sum* [sʌm] and *that* [ðæt] becomes "zat" [zæt].

☆ **5.** Substitution of [θ] for [ð] and vice versa.

Each problem is analyzed in greater detail. Concentrate on your areas of weakness.

1. Omission of [θ] **and** [ð]   These sounds may be erroneously omitted if preceded or followed by another consonant.

Say each of the following expressions without omitting any sounds.

with feeling	who's there?
miss the bus	get them
what's this?	

Warm-up phrases for practice: I'm the one who asked that, look there, give them this, come then, park the car, like these and like those

[θ] and [ð] may also be left out in final consonant combinations or clusters. Include all sounds in the following words.[8]

---

[8] Although these combinations do not occur frequently, they are excellent exercises for control of the articulators. Take them slowly, *str-e-ng-th-s,* being sure to get every sound in at first. As you start to speed up, pause a beat after the *ng* before adding the last two sounds, blended together, *ths,* thus: *streng-ths.*

deaths   depths
fifths   lengths
widths   clothes

Warm-up phrases for practice: Three-fifths of a dollar, breathed his last, at death's door, the widths and lengths, depths of despair, measured by the hundredths of a point, myths of many faiths

2. **[f] for [θ] and [v] for [ð]**   In certain nonstandard dialects of English, such substitutions are made at the middle or ends of words.
   Say each of these expressions with a clear [θ] or [ð].

toothbrush   smoothed over
both of us   truthful
with me

Warm-up phrases for practice: nothing doing, neither of us, another one, clean bath mat in the bathroom, the fourth time, worth a visit, my wealthy brother, a truthful friend

☆ 3. **[d] for [ð] and [t] for [θ]**   Especially in metropolitan areas in the Northeast one can still hear "deze" and "doze" for *these* and *those*, "tanks" for *thanks*, and the like. Nationwide, nonnative speakers may do the same thing rather consistently throughout their whole vocabulary. The metropolitan American tends to do it most often with the few basic unaccented words that unfortunately recur in practically every sentence uttered. Can you imagine the number of times you say *the* in a minute of talking?

   The important thing for any of you who have *any* kind of difficulty with [θ] and [ð] is to remember that they are *fricatives*. If you make too hard a contact with the tongue against the teeth, you will *stop* the sound, changing the sounds to *plosives*. That is how [ð] comes out [d] and [θ] comes out [t].

   Make sure throughout the following that you keep such a light contact between the teeth and the tongue that you can feel the air continuing to come through the space in between. Imagining that you are cooling off the front of your tongue may help.

   a. [d] *for* [ð]. Remember, it is *this* [ðɪs] and *that* [ðæt], not [dɪs] and [dæt]. Say these words carefully and correctly.

them   over there
the book   whether
together

Contrast the difference in sound and meaning in these word pairs:

there   dare   then   den
those   doze   though   dough
they   day

Warm-up phrases for practice: to the top of the tower, to the end of the line, some of this and some of that, both of them, with them and with their fathers, neither one nor the other, gather together the others, smooth the leather

b. [t] *for* [θ]. Remember, it is *think it through* [θɪŋk ɪt θru], not [tɪŋk ɪt tru]. Say the following words carefully and correctly.

north   mouth
thumb   thread
anything

Contrast the difference in sound and meaning in these word pairs:

theme	team	thought	taught
three	tree	bath	bat
wrath	rat	booth	boot

Warm-up phrases for practice: three thousand dollars' worth, thanks a lot, nothing doing, I think so, both of the authors, faith of the Catholics, a healthy youth, arithmetic method, something worthwhile, Thursday

☆ **4.** [s] **for** [θ] **and** [z] **for** [ð]   Some nonnative speakers make this substitution because, lacking experience with [θ] and [ð], they quite logically substitute fricatives they *do* know: [s] and [z]. Remember that the upper teeth are in contact with the blade of the tongue in the new sounds, whereas the tongue is behind the closed teeth for [s] and [z]. Your ear will also help you tell the difference: [θ] and [ð] are muffled sounds in comparison to [s] and [z], which are whistly and hissing. Exaggerate the sounds at first in the examples that follow.

a. [s] *for* [θ]. *Thank you* is [θæŋk ju], not [sæŋk ju]. Say the following expressions.

thirsty [θɝsti]   sore throat [sɔɚ θroʊt]
my thumb [maɪ θʌm]   thousand [θaʊzənd]
thunder [θʌndɚ]

Contrast the difference in sound and meaning in these word pairs:

thick	sick	mouth	mouse
thing	sing	truth	truce
think	sink	worth	worse

Warm-up phrases for practice: I thought so, a useless theory, a thing of beauty, three thousand dollars, something else, fourth of the month, steady growth, sore tooth, nice things

b. [z] *for* [ð]. *Theirs* is [ðɛɚz], not [zɛɚz]. Say each word carefully and correctly.

mother [mʌðɚ]   weather [wɛðɚ]
another [ənʌðɚ]   rather [ræðɚ]
this [ðɪs]

Contrast the sound and meaning of these word pairs:

breathe	breeze	then	Zen
bathe	bays	writhe	rise
teethe	tease		

Warm-up phrases for practice: their brothers, their fathers, this and that, lies there, take the prize, plays the game, loses the others, another raise, either of them, neither of them

☆ **5. [θ] for [ð] and [ð] for [θ]**   As stated earlier, there are no rules that will be of much use to you in determining through spelling which is which. Practicing the word lists at the beginning of this section and going over the words and phrases under points 3 and 4 should be a big help because the common words have been included and placed in the correct categories, voiceless [θ] and voiced [ð]. The more you use them correctly, the more they will come naturally to you.

ADDING ON FOR PROFICIENCY

1. Repeat each phrase 3 times, building up speed, but never at the expense of accuracy.

    a. thin tin thimbles
    b. death debt
    c. free three thieves
    d. Ruth's roof
    e. both boats
    f. face fate with faith

2. Read the following sentences aloud, monitoring your production of [θ] and [ð].

    a. Ann rather than Dan answered the question about the depth of the earth's surface.
    b. The gauze cloth was lighter than a feather and smoother than anything then known.
    c. They advertise that their brand of anesthetic throat tablets is soothing for a sore throat.
    d. Catherine came with nothing, gave nothing, took nothing, and went away with nothing to show for her time there.
    e. The theme of the twelfth lecture was myths and the half-truths embedded in their fabric.
    f. There are thick growths of trees on the farther side of the mountain because of the warmth of the southern exposure.
    g. The pushcart displayed this sign: "Worth consideration. All lengths of fine leather. All-weather fabric."
    h. On the thirteenth day of the sixth month of this coming year, Matthew may or may not graduate.
    i. "If they cannot do what they are told, they are worthless; if they have to be told what to do, they are worthless too," the old drill sergeant thundered.
    j. With wit it has been said, "Father's Day is just like Mother's Day—only the gift is cheaper."

☆ 3. *For nonnative speakers*   Read these sentences aloud.

    a. The father thought he taught the boys a lot, but they thought not.

b. Do they dare withhold these other grades?

c. Today they gathered up their things and left by the back door.

d. "Sing something." They did. "Thank you," they were told.

e. The pitcher threw a true curve ball, and the player was out.

f. They both bet Beth she would lose the game by a tenth of a point.

g. "What are these Ds doing among these other good grades?"

h. They did not go to the free three-thirty concert.

i. The third Thursday of the month is another payday.

j. The Fourth of July is a thoroughly American holiday.

k. They held a surprise twenty-fifth birthday party for Cathy.

l. There was disappointment that this appointment had been broken still another time.

SUPER EXERCISES

☆ A. *Using [θ] and [ð] in conversational speech*   Verbally describe a scene—your room at home, a supermarket, the college campus, or a scene of your own choosing. The sentence may be a run-on. Do not write it down.

1. How many times can you use *the* in the descriptive sentence? (Six is the minimum; try for ten.)

    Caution: *The* is an article and is unaccented. It receives little stress, but it must be present. *Example:* In the library, the books, the magazines, the newspapers, the scholarly journals, and the reprints are all listed in the reference file by the main desk.

2. In the same sentence, change *the* to *this, that, these,* or *those. Example:* In this library, those books, those magazines, those newspapers, these scholarly journals, and these reprints are listed in that reference file by that main desk.

B. *Mini-challenge exercise*   This exercise is cumulative. If you successfully say sentence 1, repeat it before going on to sentence 2. Repeat 1 and 2 before going on to 3, and so on. However, you are finished the moment you make the slightest mistake on [θ] or [ð]. How far can you get?

1. Brother Ted
2. Brother Ted was fourth in the Smith family.
3. By six months his growth was that of a 13-year-old.
4. On his fifth birthday, guests were thunderstruck at the width of his thighs and the length of his legs.
5. Today Brother Ted is wealthy, earning thousands a week as the "Mammoth Hulk"—and he hasn't even reached his twelfth birthday!

C. *Finish the scene*   Cast two people in the roles of the Young Chef and the Master Chef. Let the class finish the scene.

The Cooking Lesson

SCENE: Kitchen in a well-equipped restaurant.

MASTER CHEF: Ah, so you have paid $300 to learn the secrets of making my mythical Bombe-Torte Cathay.

YOUNG CHEF: That's right, Master Chef. My boss at the Ninth Hole restaurant thought it would add class.

MASTER CHEF: Voilà! That it will—to *that* place. Now listen and watch carefully. I go through this only once. . . .

YOUNG CHEF: Yes, Master Chef.

MASTER CHEF: You take two cups of this and one cup of that. . . . Like this. . . .

YOUNG CHEF: Two cups of this and one cup of that. Got it. But what is the "this" and what is the "that"?

MASTER CHEF: Silence. No repeats. Then I take a pinch of these and a handful of those. . . .

YOUNG CHEF: A pinch of these and a handful of those? *Those?* What are "those"? They look like gravel.

MASTER CHEF: *Silence!* No repeats. Then I beat it like this.

YOUNG CHEF: Beat it like this.

MASTER CHEF: Then I sprinkle on just a bit of that. . . .

YOUNG CHEF: Just a bit of that?

MASTER CHEF: Then I throw the whole thing in the oven like this, and now, voilà! You know how to make Bombe-Torte Cathay

YOUNG CHEF: But Master Chef, I don't know how to make Bombe What's-its-name at all!

[s] and [z]

fonɛtɪk trɪviə

What is Sally's problem?

[səpouz ðæt sæli wɚ tu tɛl əbaut sɛlɪŋ hɚ feiməs siʃɛlz ɪn ðɪs wei: "ai θɛl θiʃɛlð æt ðə θiʃɔɚ." hwʌts rɔŋ?]

Here are some trivia questions:

1. What is the most commonly misarticulated sound in the English language?
2. What is a lisp?
3. How did Castilian Spanish dialect originate?

[s] is the most frequently used and abused phoneme in the English language. The complexity of its production must be matched by a very keen sense of hearing. The term *lisp* is usually misused to refer rather exclusively to the *interdental* (tongue between the teeth) problem that Sally of seashell fame portrays in "Phonetic Trivia." Properly used, it is a broadly generic umbrella term that

encompasses all reasonably consistent distortions or substitutions of the sibilant ("hissing") sounds, and some experts differentiate more than 10 distinct kinds!

Castilian Spanish is the only major dialect of a language with an interdental lisp component. The story may be apocryphal, but this peculiarity of pronunciation is said to have arisen at the time of an early king of Spain who had just such a lisp. Since no one dared to point this out to him—and Heaven forbid that a king be perceived as having something wrong with his speech!—everyone in the court was ordered under threat of dire punishment to adopt such a lisp. The pattern has lasted to this day in the commercial and upper classes of Spain.

Fact or myth, this story has a point: If a whole group of courtiers could learn to lisp, most people can also learn *not* to lisp.

Because problems with these sounds can fall into two basic categories, our discussion will be divided into two parts accordingly.

Part One, for everyone, will consider the proper uses and careless misuses of [s] and [z], exclusive of a lisp. Its format will be the one used for other sounds.

Part Two is a resource section, specifically to help those who do lisp, working under the direction of an instructor or someone trained in speech. Since practice materials are so important in working on this, there will also be supplementary word lists and extra practice materials.

PART ONE: FACTS

Technical description: Both are alveolar (tongue tip to gum ridge) fricatives. [s] is unvoiced and [z] is voiced.

Correct production: The tip of the tongue is retracted slightly from the position for [t] and does *not* touch the gum ridge. It is grooved down the middle with the sides resting against the inner surfaces of the upper back teeth. Air, forced down the groove, hits the cutting edge of the incisors, creating a high-frequency hiss [s] or buzz [z].[9] Make sure that the sound thus produced is unimpeded and sharp but not whistly.

☆ *Spellings:* Usually as each appears or doubled as *ss* or *zz*. There are a few exceptions, however:

1. *c* followed by *e, i,* or *y* is pronounced [s]. *Examples:* celery [sɛləɪ], city [sɪti], cyst [sɪst]. Thus *ce* at the end of a word is always [s], as in *nice* [naɪs].
2. [s] is sometimes spelled *sc* as in *science* [saɪəns] or *sch* as in *schism* [sɪzm].
3. [z] at the ends of many words is spelled *s*. This had to do with assimilation and whether the sound preceding the *s* is voiced, in which case it, too, becomes voiced and is pronounced [z].

IN USE

*S*tudent*s* participating in the *S*pring Dance Fe*s*tival are to be at the *S*tudent *C*enter *S*unday at *s*even.

*Z*eke wa*s* di*zz*y from *z*ig*z*agging la*z*ily to the beat of the ea*s*y mu*s*ic.

---

[9] For readers who need it, a more detailed description of production can be found in Part Two.

Check your pronunciation of [s] and [z] in the words on each list. Listen for a clear, unimpeded hiss on [s] that does not become a whistle and for a strong, clear buzz on [z].

	[s]			[z]	
sing	person	boss	zoo	nozzle	please
sunset	sensitive	base	zinc	design	sneeze
sit	also	dance	zest	desire	raise
circle	baseball	ice	zip	causing	tease
circus	bracelet	less	zany	dozen	has
city	mistake	place	zinnia	noisy	whose
sail	possible	peace	zoology	using	toys
salt	necessary	house	zone	pleasant	calls
sandwich	passage	cross	zither	reason	hers
scissors	December	census		deserve	was
second	listen	glass			fuse
sight	pencil	else			

[s] blends

steam	skip	streak	sweet	speed	spread
stop	skirt	stream	snake	speak	spray
stay	scheme	street	snow	spill	sprint
stick	school	strive	snob	spike	spring
steer	scale	strip	snore	spent	splice
stiff	sky	straight	snarl	spy	splint
still	scarce	stroll	snub	spaniel	splinter

Contrast both sound and meaning in these word pairs:

sip	zip	looser	loser	ice	eyes
Sue	zoo	lacy	lazy	race	raise
sink	zinc	prices	prizes	place	plays

PROBLEMS TO AVOID

Three errors with [s] and [z] stem from careless articulation:

1. Substitution of [ʃtr] for [str] so that *stripe* [straɪp] becomes "shtripe" [ʃtraɪp].
2. Exaggeration of [s].
3. Substitution of [s] for [z], mainly at the end of words so that *his* [hɪz] becomes *hiss* [hɪs].

☆ Foreign students may do any of the above, *but most particularly #3.* Each problem is discussed in greater detail. Concentrate on your area of weakness.

1. [ʃtr] for [str]   The substitution of [ʃtr] for [str] is a perfect example of overassimilation: Anticipating the backward movement of the tongue for [r], a person pulls the tongue back at the beginning of the consonant cluster, thus producing [ʃ] rather than [s].

Slowing articulation to hear a prolonged, clear [s] before the rest of the word is spoken will help.

Pronounce each word slowly and clearly as written:

strict: *ssss-trict*   instruct: *inssss-truct*
strike: *ssss-trike*   destroy: *dessss-troy*
straight: *ssss-traight*   street: *ssss-treet*

Warm-up phrases for practice: withstand stress, strategic withdrawal, straying away, strong string, a strange instructor, show extreme restraint, construction in the streets, a strenuous stroll, stringy pastry, strip off the stripes

2. Exaggeration of [s]   Some people have a recurrent hissing quality throughout their speech. Such a person may well be producing the sound correctly (we are not talking about the whistly, oversibilant [s], which will be treated in Part Two), but they somehow make too much of a good thing, prolonging [s] unnecessarily or pushing too much air through. If this is your problem, reduce your breath pressure and cut the sound short. The exaggerated [s] is very high frequency sound, not at all pleasant to listen to.

Say each word quickly, with a crisp, unexaggerated [s] sound.

sit   answer
save   possible
sick   sister

Warm-up phrases for practice: an essay on democracy, a science series, resistance to saving, assorted sales, historic sites, at cross-purposes, a saucy spinster

3. [s] for [z] at the end of a word   The word *because* is pronounced [bɪkɔz], not [bɪkɔs]. With native speakers the error usually stems from a lack of awareness or simply not making the effort to keep a voiced sound coming through to the end of a word. Doing this is also called *devoicing.*

Nonnative speakers, who have depended on the printed page for a good deal of their familiarity with English, simply don't know that what they see in front of them on the printed page, *s,* is more often than not pronounced [z] when it comes in the middle or at the end of a word.

Here is a rule for both groups to keep in mind: If *s* at the end of a word is preceded by a voiced sound—all vowels are voiced, and the majority of consonants are voiced—the *s* becomes voiced, too, and is therefore pronounced [z]. (This phenomenon is treated in greater depth in Chapter 11.) Thus words ending in *ts, ps, ks, fs,* and *ths* keep the [s] sound because the consonants preceding *s* are unvoiced. Words ending in *ce, us, ous,* or *ss* also stay [s]. Otherwise, most final *s*'s are actually [z]. Contrast these two sentences:

[s]: He hit*s* and kick*s* the ball and skip*s* down the street.
[z]: He run*s*, jog*s*, and crosse*s* the*s*e street*s* with ea*s*e.

Look at the following sentence. Can you tell which are the only two final *s* words that retain [s]?[10] Try it aloud.

---

[10] *socks, belts.*

He chooses his clothes with care, his socks, ties, belts, and shoes, and he does it only in stores that advertise bargains.

Here is another sentence to try:

James has many things on his mind, including exam papers, grades, and fights with his girlfriend.

(Did you figure out that only one final *s* retained [s]?) In phonetics, which gives you the actual sounds, the sentence would be written thus:

[dʒeɪmz hæz mɛni θɪŋz ɑn hɪz maɪnd, ɪnkludɪŋ ɛgzæm peɪpɚz, greɪdz, ænd faɪts wɪθ hɪz gɝlfrɛnd]

Is making such a small distinction in sound only nitpicking? The answer is a resounding no. The final [z], along with all final voiced fricatives, adds a grounding and a carrying power to connected speech. Listen carefully to any good speaker or actor!

Say the following words carefully and correctly with [z].

hers	easy
was	music
has	always

Warm-up phrases for practice: please advise, buys groceries, has his head examined, uses tools easily, was chosen, hides from his friends, is tired of eggs, causes things to happen, loses coins, pays bills, goes as he is (Did you notice that every one of these phrases used [z]?)

ADDING ON FOR PROFICIENCY

1. Repeat the following phrases 3 times, building up speed, but never at the expense of accuracy.

   a. strong songs
   b. nice ice houses
   c. lose loose teeth
   d. expensive kids' kits
   e. the price of prize spaniels
   f. strange, shrill sound

2. Read the following sentences aloud, pronouncing [s] and [z] carefully. Sentences *g* through *l* concentrate on *str* combinations, and sentences *m* through *r* give extra practice with final [s] for [z] substitutions.

   a. It is disturbing to have someone constantly interrupting your concentration while you are studying.
   b. Do not disassemble the Volkswagen until you have studied how to reassemble its parts.
   c. At a garage sale, it is simply impossible to sell certain products.
   d. Some people insist that swimming alone can be dangerous.

e. This recipe calls for a dash of salt, a sprinkle of cinnamon, a teaspoon of baking soda, and a sliver of salmon.

f. Speeding is against the law in this city, in this state, and across the country.

g. Strange structures have been constructed by the art department.

h. The stream named after Timothy Strann is called the Headstrong Strann Stream.

i. The stranger was instructed to either unstrap the strange box or destroy it.

j. There are several string instruments in the orchestra that play strongly—and sometimes strangely!

k. We had to stretch strenuously to peer over the extraordinary structure.

l. Stroll straight down the street and then follow the striped signs to the historic sight.

m. His relatives include sons, daughters, nephews, uncles, both grandmothers, and untold numbers of kissing cousins.

n. The thieves stole necklaces, earrings, gold chains, uncut gems, watches, and other valuables from the store's shelves.

o. If Dorothy Parker said that men rarely make passes at girls who wear glasses, she was in the Dark Ages!

p. "Is she, isn't she, is she, isn't she?" the boy muses as he wonders if his blind date will be as dazzling as she sounds.

q. Specialization increases, and farms that grow potatoes, beans, cucumbers, radishes, and cabbages all in one plot are as rare as the proverbial hen's teeth.

r. Here is what Big Sam ate: two chickens, French fries, three sandwiches, four hot dogs, and countless hamburgers.

☆ 3. *For nonnative speakers*   Say these sentences carefully. Sentences *g* through *r* provide extra practice with final [s] for [z].

a. You have to study to pass your science exam.

b. The instructor presented the class with a seemingly endless assignment.

c. Do not sign your name until you see what you are signing.

d. Ask questions even if they seem silly or simple to you.

e. The school chorus sang several six-part songs.

f. Smoking cigars or cigarettes is forbidden in certain places.

g. Was it easy to come to America?

h. Was the music too loud for your ears?

i. It is always a good idea to speak as much English as you can.

j. It is always easier, however, to speak in your own language.

k. It was his turn to report on the news.

l. It was those last two questions on the exam that I didn't know.

m. These answers were harder than those.

n. These are his, but those are hers.

o. Who has finished reading these papers?

p. His grades are lower than hers because she studies and he does not.

q. The signs on the door read "His" and "Hers."

r. Taxis, trains, buses, and planes are all means of public transportation.

SUPER EXERCISES

☆ 1. *Using* [s] *and* [z] *in conversational speech.* Create a sentence around each of the following words and phrases and say it at a conversational rate. Do not write it down.

a strange experience	instructors
examinations	symbols
sororities	a strong dislike
jobs in industry	a strategic move
school regulations	a wise saying
a museum exhibit	scientific advances
success	suspense movies
superstitions	space program
Star Wars	

2. *Just Incredible! A script for* [s] *and* [z] *in connected speech*   Choose a segment to read aloud.

This is Sally/Sam Strong giving you a sneak preview of some of the out-of-the-ordinary people and places that will be seen in our *Just Incredible!* broadcast this evening. You will meet:

. . . A chimney sweep, whose collection of cinders over the past 16 years has been mixed with cement and sculpted into a realistic life-size statue of the first lady of the United States, complete with inaugural dress.

. . . An Eskimo in Saw Tooth, Alaska, who claims to be 116 years old. The secret of his longevity: wrestling seals, which he does every morning inside a pool carved in the ice of his back yard and which he will demonstrate— *live*— especially for our broadcast audience this evening.

We will also pay a special visit to a tribe of jungle natives never before visited by the press. Sociologists studying their customs have kept their existence a secret, fearful that outside influences would make them self-conscious. They sleep in a standing position, dress from the waist up, and paint stripes on their legs as a sign of status.

Finally, our cameras will take you into the center of a vast salt mine, where salt miners, for centuries, have been carving a larger than life-size nativity scene out of the solid salt walls. You will also see their latest artistic endeavor, a modernized version of Noah, complete with the ark and cages for the animals.

3. *Finish the scene*   Cast two people in the roles of pilot Sam/Sarah Struthers and Copilot Sarge Sipple. After they have played the scene, let the class decide how to finish it.[11]

Space Odyssey

SCENE: Interior of a spaceship in outer space.

---

[11] If you would like to see how the authors finish this scene, turn to the end of Part Two.

PILOT: Steady on, Sarge. Venus on starboard port.

COPILOT: Venus sighted, Boss.

PILOT: Steady and straight on, Sarge. This Super Thrust spaceracer certainly lives up to its advertised claims.

COPILOT: Sixty times the speed of light. Fantastic! Mars sighted, Boss.

PILOT: Steady on, Sarge. There's Saturn, starboard port.

COPILOT: That was Uranus, Boss. Saturn's back of us somewhere. This Super Thrust spaceracer sure burns up the track, eh, Boss?

PILOT: *Burns up the space,* Sarge. Get your metaphors straight—there's no *track* out here. Say, it sort of looks like we're out of our galaxy and into uncharted space. . . .

COPILOT: Super!

PILOT: Uh-oh . . .

COPILOT: Something wrong, Boss?

PILOT: The controls seem to be stuck! Oh, supersonic succotash! They are stuck!

COPILOT: Boss, the thrusters are melting. The seat belts are melting! We're heading straight for the sizzling center of a death star!

PART TWO: LISPS*

Lisps may be due to any number of things, including incorrect placement or configuration of the tongue, incorrect direction of the breath stream, malocclusions, incorrectly spaced teeth, hearing problems, a reverse swallow, the aftermath of braces, or imitation of a faulty model in the language-learning stage.

The critical factor in correcting any of them is ear training. A person has to *hear* what [s] and [z] are meant to sound like, what the erroneous sound sounds like, and the difference between the two. This may take time and patience, and it requires the help of your instructor or someone knowledgeable in speech, as does all the introductory work in correcting a lisp. If the lisp persists, a speech therapist should be consulted.

Although directions in some detail for producing [s] follow, it is stressed that your ear will be your most helpful guide. The articulatory adjustments are complex and exact, but there can be variation in production from person to person, all of whom make perfectly acceptable sounds.

Since it has been our experience that transfer exercises from selected phonetic environments help students the most in learning production of the new acceptable sound whatever the kind of lisp, the larger part of this section will concentrate on these: [t] $\longrightarrow$ [s], [ʃ] $\longrightarrow$ [s], [n] $\longrightarrow$ [s], and [θ] $\longrightarrow$ [s]. It should be determined which of these works best to help the particular student produce [s] correctly with consistency and ease, and efforts should be concentrated there.

Since practice material is so important, additional word lists will be provided at the end of the chapter, along with paragraphs loaded with [s] for more practice.

---

* Sincere appreciation is due Graduate Assistant Cynthia Mills, who developed much of the material in this section in conjunction with her work with lispers in the Montclair State College speech lab.

But as a start, nonsense syllables making combinations with all the vowel sounds are all you will need to work with:

sie-sie-sie,
soh-soh-soh
see-see-see
sah-sah-sah

When you are ready to work with words, start with [s] in the initial position only, then final, then medial; at that point you will consult the back of this section.

Detailed directions for producing [s] *and* [z]

1. Bring your back teeth lightly together. Sometimes at first it helps to get a correct sound by having your front upper and lower teeth artificially in perfect alignment, one on top of the other.
2. Spread your lips, as in a half-smile.
3. Lift the sides of your tongue into firm contact with the inner surfaces of the back teeth. For the correct tactile sensation of the lifted tongue, repeat *tee* many times over.
4. The tongue is grooved along its middle, and air is forced down this narrow trough. If correctly done, a finger tapped against the middle of your front teeth should continually interrupt the sound.
5. The tip of the tongue is close to the gum ridge *but does not touch it.* Think of pronouncing [t], but keep air coming continuously.
6. Direct the airstream along the groove in the tongue in a continuous, uninterrupted hiss for [s] and a voiced buzz for [z].
7. It is usually better to concentrate on [s] at first. [z] will follow along of itself once placement *for your particular structure* for [s] is correct and the sound is correct.
8. If you simply can't seem to get the sound correctly up near the gum ridge, experiment with an alternate placement close to the lower gum ridge.

Some common lisps

1. *Interdental lisp* is also referred to as *frontal lisp* or *central lisp.* This distortion occurs when the tongue is placed too far forward in the mouth. In situations where the tongue is actually protruded between the teeth, [θ] is substituted for [s]. Try to hear a real difference between *sing/thing, sin/thin, sank/thank, sum/thumb, sought/thought.*
2. *Dentalized* [s] usually occurs along with a dentalized [t] and [d]. The person allows the tongue to slip down and hit the back of the teeth, making a kind of spitting, dull sound. Work on correcting [t] and [d] first often improves the tongue position by itself. Such a speaker should concentrate on the fact that [s] is totally unobstructed. *The tip of the tongue hangs free, and air comes over the end continuously.*
3. In a *lateral lisp* the distortion in sound is caused by the airstream's being directed incorrectly over one side of the tongue (unilaterally) or both sides

(bilaterally). This makes for a very mushy sound, and such a speaker must concentrate efforts to feel the sides of the tongue nestling against the upper molars on each side, blocking the air from escaping. Often, but not always, production of [s] is attempted too far back in the mouth, and [θ] ⟶ [s] is a particularly valuable phonetic context to work from. The lateral lisp sometimes extends to sibilants other than [s] and [z], such as [ʃ] as in *ship,* [ʒ] as in *leisure,* [tʃ] as in *child,* and [dʒ] as in *jelly.* If so, simply adapt techniques that helped with [s] and [z] to practice materials and words lists for these sounds.

4. *Strident lisp* can be characterized as a whistly [s] or an oversibilant [s]. This distortion can be caused by too much tension, by grooving the tongue tip too much, or by the passage of the breath stream between the tongue and a hard surface such as bridgework or dentures. [ʃ] ⟶ [s] transfers are often helpful with this.

5. *Occluded lisp* refers to the production of an [s] that has no sibilant quality. This distortion is the result of occluding the airstream in the oral cavity by placing the tongue too far forward or by not allowing for a narrow, grooved passageway for the breath stream to pass between the tongue and the gum ridge.

TRANSFER EXERCISES

Experiment at first with each of the four to see which helps you achieve the desired sound with the most ease and consistency.

A. [t] ⟶ [s]

1. Say the following words *as they are written.*

   eat, eats, catss, eatsss, sss, see
   hit, hits, hitss, hitsss, sss, say
   date, dates, datess, datesss, sss, seem
   meat, meats, meatss, meatsss, sss, sign
   cat, cats, catss, catsss, sss, sing
   treat, treats, treatss, treatsss, sss, sand

2. Say these words as written.

t-sssin	t-sssave	t-ssseven	giftsss-sold
t-sssun	t-sssent	t-sssize	factsss-say
t-sssail	t-ssseen	t-sssself	expectsss-soon

3. Now say these words and sentences.

   a. lasts ⟶ simply: The chocolate lasts ⟶ simply as long as the children do not eat it.
   b. tastes ⟶ steak: Dan tastes ⟶ steak even though he is eating hamburger.
   c. gifts ⟶ sold: The gifts ⟶ sold well.
   d. rejects ⟶ students: The instructor rejects ⟶ students' assignments if they are submitted late.

e. lifts ⟶ seventy: Tony lifts ⟶ seventy-pound weights in each hand.

f. rafts ⟶ sink: Rafts ⟶ sink if they have been punctured.

g. facts ⟶ suggest: The facts ⟶ suggest that someone is lying.

h. expects ⟶ someone: Kurt expects ⟶ someone to answer the phone.

i. interests ⟶ some: Science interests ⟶ some students.

j. acts ⟶ silly: Johnny said Sam acts ⟶ silly all day long.

k. lists ⟶ seem: Lists ⟶ seem to organize my daily schedule of affairs.

l. insists ⟶ Cindy: "I'll make supper!" insists ⟶ Cindy.

m. rents ⟶ saunas: The sign read, "Finns' Furniture Outlet rents ⟶ saunas!"

B. [ʃ] ⟶ [s]

1. Say the following words *as they are written.*

cash, cashs, cashss, cashsss, sss, sun
push, pushs, pushss, pushsss, sss, some
rush, rushs, rushss, rushsss, sss, sink
lash, lashs, lashss, lashsss, sss, sign
flush, flushs, flushss, flushsss, sss, sour
mesh, meshs, meshss, meshsss, sss, supper

2. Say these words as written.

sh-sock	sh-soft	sh-sip	push-SSSam
sh-sat	sh-sand	sh-sell	rush-SSSally
sh-soak	sh-so	sh-soda	cash-sssome

3. Now say these words and sentences.

a. cash ⟶ seems: Cash ⟶ seems so necessary to have.

b. dash ⟶ some: Dash ⟶ some salt on your chicken.

c. fish ⟶ swim: Watch the fish ⟶ swim on their backs.

d. wash ⟶ seven: Mary will wash ⟶ seven coffee cups before dinner.

e. wish ⟶ Sally: Mom said to wish ⟶ Sally a happy birthday.

f. fresh ⟶ smell: The new house has a fresh ⟶ smell.

g. mash ⟶ small: Mash ⟶ small pieces of onion into the gravy.

h. crash ⟶ seemed: The car crash ⟶ seemed to go on forever.

i. flash ⟶ some: Tony, flash ⟶ some light over here.

j. rush ⟶ says: "Don't rush," ⟶ says my father.

k. push ⟶ seven: Push ⟶ seven coins into the slot.

C. [n] ⟶ [s]

1. Say the following words *as they are written,* pronouncing s as [s] rather than [z].

bean, beans, beanss, beansss, sss, stop
man, mans, manss, mansss, sss, sigh

pen, pens, penss, pensss, sss, soup
yawn, yawns, yawnss, yawnsss, sss, seed
plan, plans, planss, plansss, sss, song
teen, teens, teenss, teensss, sss, sofa

2. Say these words as written.

n-sssand	n-sssale	n-sssock	thence-sssir
n-sssir	n-sssuck	n-sssoil	once-sssir
n-ssseal	n-sssigh	n-sssought	hence-sssir

3. Now say these words and sentences:

    a. can ⟶ some: They can ⟶ some applesauce.
    b. Fran ⟶ said: Fran ⟶ said, "Stop being so nice!"
    c. gone ⟶ soon: My sister will be gone ⟶ soon.
    d. one ⟶ sign: Place one ⟶ sign on the side.
    e. canteen ⟶ serves: The canteen ⟶ serves snacks.
    f. women ⟶ sing: Some women ⟶ sing solo roles.
    g. then ⟶ sell: Price the merchandise, then ⟶ sell it.
    h. in ⟶ side: Step in ⟶ side, Sarah.
    i. win ⟶ some: Win ⟶ some, lose some.
    j. ten ⟶ cents: It sold for ten ⟶ cents.

D. [θ] ⟶ [s]

1. Say the following words *as they are written.*

path, paths, pathss, pathsss, sss, sold
tooth, tooths, toothss, toothsss, sss, sap
Beth, Beths, Bethss, Bethsss, sss, said
bath, baths, bathss, bathsss, sss, sight
south, souths, southss, southsss, sss, sign
teeth, teeths, teethss, teethsss, sss, store

2. Say these words as written.

th-sssave	th-sssoft	th-ssseven	both-sssaid
th-sssend	th-sssink	th-sssound	both-sssounds
th-sssock	th-sssold	th-sssays	both-ssseem

3. Now say these words and sentences.

    a. Ruth ⟶ says: Don't do what Ruth ⟶ says.
    b. growth ⟶ spurt: At 16 he experienced a growth ⟶ spurt.
    c. breath ⟶ suffers: They say your breath ⟶ suffers if you smoke.
    d. truth ⟶ seems: Often truth ⟶ seems stranger than fiction.
    e. both ⟶ sorts: I like both ⟶ sorts of rolls.
    f. fourth ⟶ set: He just played his fourth ⟶ set of tennis today.
    g. math ⟶ solves: Math ⟶ solves many everyday financial problems.
    h. faith ⟶ settles: Faith ⟶ settles; man disputes.
    i. wrath ⟶ suffers: He who incurs her wrath ⟶ suffers.
    j. wreath ⟶ sold: The Christmas wreath ⟶ sold for $5.

ADDITIONAL WORD LISTS

Initial position

sea	set	something
side	sound	suggest
sink	scale	situation
soap	science	sample
silver	spout	sauce
socks	service	such
scissors	skin	sometime
soda	source	soft
sofa	sense	second
something	cite	somebody
son	simple	civil
sound	cinnamon	Steven
soup	soon	superb
spoon	south	suppose
summer	size	sunflower
season	seven	surprise
system	several	suburb
September	citizen	sprite
said	super	suffice
sausage	supply	success
save	spread	sandbox
see	sundae	supermarket
serve	sack	Saturday

Final position

boss	infamous	sentence
practice	notice	recess
base	release	produce
dance	stress	influence
business	reference	miss
carrots	documents	voice
dress	strenuous	vice
less	loose	face
course	fearless	generous
horse	lettuce	choice
cross	piece	emphasis
house	police	impulse
glass	force	juice
place	express	once
else	happiness	impress
unless	basis	continuous
tax	experience	embarrass

Medial position

inside	whistle	personal
beside	missing	resources
tricycle	essential	assign
bicycle	conserve	monster
answer	constant	myself
policy	inspire	dresser
bedspread	decide	pencil
glasses	December	cluster
passage	analysis	accent
consider	sister	precede
satisfy	basketball	blossom
falsify	ice cream	concern
resource	personnel	tendency
success	discriminate	facilitate
outside	consonant	penicillin
opposite	discover	hospital

PARAGRAPHS EMPHASIZING [s] AND [z]

Sandy Sanders was a seamstress in a small town called Sunset Valley located outside of Racine, Wisconsin. Sandy was a young woman in her thirties who made a living sewing clothes for the 600-and-some village people who could not afford retail prices. Every Saturday and Sunday, Sandy Sanders and her sister Cindy would stay at home sewing shirts, vests, skirts, sweaters, blouses, socks, and other garments the people of the village had ordered that week. The call for Sandy's services became so great that she soon had to hire extra help to satisfy the customers. After approximately six years, Sandy's small business became a dress-making giant, Sandy Sanders's Supreme Seamstress Establishment, and it was known across the whole country.

Sky Band was a small Indian girl. Sky Band belonged to an Apache tribe consisting of 766 members. She lived in Southwest New Mexico and was the daughter of a medicine man. For a child of 6 she was very smart, and her talents were many. Sky Band was an expert at sand paintings, basketweaving, making tribal costumes, and performing ceremonial dances. She wore a silver bracelet and a squash blossom necklace, given to her by her sister, Crossed Cactus. Sky Band rode a chestnut-colored pony named Sunsill, who wore a brilliantly colored saddle blanket that Sky Band had woven herself. She led a simple life and was considered to be the little princess of her Indian tribe.

Sal Samone is one of the world's finest bicyclists. Sal has won so many races he has lost count, and he is still on a hot streak. Each year Sal packs up his Centurion Le Mans RS racer and heads for Massachusetts, where he competes in the American Bicycle Festival. This year the race will be held on the sixteenth of September starting in Boston and will cover 77 miles of undeveloped seashore along the coastal area south of the city. Sal has one goal in mind—to win this race!

Hester Struthers was an elderly, headstrong woman with stringy silver-gray hair, who thrived on happiness and pleasure found in the simplest things in life. Hester was a strange bird to most people, a straggler, a struggler, a self-sufficient person despite her homelessness. Many citizens referred to Hester as Sister Scavenger. Each day, Hester scoured the streets of Sioux City, her pace extraordinarily slow as she scouted for a bit of this and salvaged a bit of that. Each evening she settled down along the banks of the Sioux River in a "house" she had constructed from slabs of cardboard and discarded boxes. Yesterday, after years of strenuous attempts to survive, Hester retired forever into her shabby, makeshift residence.

One possible ending for "Space Odyssey"   The lights come slowly up as an announcer's voice is heard saying, "That's the conclusion of our 7-D experimental film, *A Space Odyssey*. We hope to see you at Disney World Space Planetarium again soon. Leave your seats in single file, please. No smoking is permitted, and be sure to take your personal belongings."

[ʃ] and [ʒ]

fonɛtɪk trɪvɪɔ

Only one of these lives and breathes. Which?

[ʃɛvrolei, stimʃɪp, waʃɪŋ məʃɪn, kæʃ rɛdʒɪstɚ, gəraʒ, siʃɛlz, trɛʒɚ tʃɛst, ʃugɚ boul]

The sounds [ʃ] and [ʒ] seem relatively easy for most people to produce, and the problem areas are few.

FACTS

Technical description: Both are alveolar fricatives produced with the tongue blade against the back of the gum ridge. The [ʃ] is unvoiced and the [ʒ] is voiced.
Correct production: The lips are slightly rounded, and the tongue is drawn farther back than for [s], and it is less grooved and more flattened. However, as with [s], the sides of the tongue should nestle against the inside of the upper back teeth.
☆ *Spellings:* [ʃ] is spelled *sh* as in *shape, si* as in *pension, ti* as in *nation;* note other rare spellings: *ocean, tissue, conscious, species, Chicago.* [ʒ] occurs only in the middle or at the end of words in English,[12] and spelling rules are of limited help. It can be spelled *z* as in *azure, s* as in *pleasure, si* as in *vision,* and *ge* as in *beige.*

---

[12] A few words beginning with [ʒ] have been taken directly from French.

IN USE

Summer vaca*t*ion fa*sh*ions favor sport *sh*irts, canvas *sh*oes, and wa*sh* and
    wear fabrics.
As u*s*ual, her deci*s*ion occa*s*ioned confu*s*ion.

Check your pronunciation in the words on the following lists.

[s]			[ʒ]	
shut	pressure	fish	casual	garage
shy	fashion	dish	azure	rouge
shark	passion	flesh	confusion	beige
show	wishing	cash	version	corsage
shop	ashamed	flash	persuasion	camouflage
shone	conscience	mesh	Persian	
should	cushion	hash	illusion	
shall	patient	crash	leisure	
shame	washing	tarnish	hosiery	
shed	delicious	wash	collision	
sugar	nation	furnish	usual	
shriek	station	lush	treasure	

PROBLEMS TO AVOID

1. Lateral lisp specific to [ʃ] and [ʒ].
☆ 2. Substitution of [s] for [ʃ] and [z] for [ʒ] so that *shoe* [ʃu] becomes *sue* [su]
    and *collision* [kəlɪʒən] becomes "collizion" [kəlɪzən].

Each problem is analyzed in greater detail. Concentrate on your specific area of
weakness.

1. **Lateral lisp on** [ʃ] **and** [ʒ]   Most people who have such a lateral lisp also
have it on [s] and [z]. Others can make those sounds acceptably but lisp on both
[ʃ] and [ʒ] and [tʃ] and [dʒ]. Correction of [ʃ] and [ʒ] should correct [tʃ] and
[dʒ].
    Ear training is critical. Follow our production suggestions, and use [s] ⟶
[ʃ] transfer exercises, since [s] is already correct.

a. Say these words exactly as written. Then do the same thing with five words
    of your own choosing.

    pass, pass-sh, passsss-shh, shhh, shipwreck
    glass, glass-sh, glasssss-shh, shhh, should

b. Return to the words listed in the left-hand column under [ʃ] in "In Use."
    Read each one aloud, saying [s] before each: *ssss-shut, ssss-shy,* and so on.
c. Do simple [s] ⟶ [ʃ] transfer exercises in sentences, such as these:

dress ⟶ should	keeps ⟶ shouting
Her dress ⟶ should be ironed.	Nan keeps → shouting.

boss ⟶ shut   Matt's ⟶ shoes
My boss ⟶ shut the office door.   Matt's ⟶ shoes are nicely shined.

☆ **2. [s] for [ʃ] and [z] for [ʒ]**   These substitutions are heard occasionally. Work on [ʃ] first; then transfer that same production to its voiced cognate [ʒ].

Two things may help, in addition to ear training. Look in a mirror and contrast the difference in lip position between [ʃ] in *shame* and [s] in *same*. Prolong the initial sounds, and make sure the lips are rounded for [ʃ] and back for [s]. Then feel the difference in tongue position. Make sure that [ʃ] is further back than [s].

Say each word carefully and correctly.

shine   shook
shall   should
shirt

Contrast the difference in sound and meaning in these word pairs:

sack	shack	mess	mesh	class	clash
sore	shore	lease	leash	brass	brash
suit	shoot	mass	mash		

Warm-up phrases for practice: (Use care, as both sounds occur in each phrase.) share some, start to shake, seems shy, shall certainly shop, shouts "stop," fresh seafood, silver dish, washing socks, ashamed to be seen, a passion for soda

ADDING ON FOR PROFICIENCY

1. Repeat the following phrases 3 times, building up speed, but never at the expense of accuracy.

   a. a shy sigh
   b. ocean motion
   c. shaped seashells
   d. rich fish dishes
   e. shear six sheep

2. Read each sentence aloud, monitoring your production of [ʃ] and [ʒ].

   a. "I'm sure I should," said Sheila, when asked if she would share her precious chocolates.
   b. When Shirley shouted, her shrill, harsh voice shook the rafters and made us want to shrink away.
   c. In this shop, the shoes and shirts are shopworn, shoddy, and shamefully out of fashion.
   d. "All the same, it's a shame that this Persian rug was made by machine, not by hand," said the status-conscious shopper while measuring the precious item.
   e. Her delusions of grandeur are quite simply a mirage: She is shabby and a shrew.
   f. It was an unusual decision that surely only added to the confusion of the unfortunate situation.

g. Camouflage is usually meant to trick the vision, he patiently explained to the recruits.

☆ 3. *For nonnative speakers* Say each sentence carefully and correctly. The first five concentrate on [ʃ], the next five on [ʒ].

a. Have you ever had a shore vacation?
b. The student wished the instructor would finish his introduction.
c. Every morning he showers and shaves and then takes a short walk before class.
d. She was part English, Spanish, and Swedish.
e. The invitation to graduation should surely come soon.
f. It's a pleasure to meet you.
g. Is there garage parking on campus?
h. What do you do with your leisure time?
i. There was the usual confusion at registration.
j. The conclusion of the school year is an occasion for a party.

SUPER EXERCISES

☆ A. *Using [ʃ] and [ʒ] in conversation speech* Create a sentence around each of these words and phrases, and say it at a conversational rate.

vacation
the latest fashions
shopping
I wish . . .
machines

the national debt
I should . . .
a favorite dish
elections

B. *Cumulative mini-challenge exercise* How far can you get? Remember, make the slightest error, and you are through.

1. Shirley
  2. Shirley is a survivor.
    3. Shirley searches shops for sale merchandise.
      4. She saves shoelaces, used sacks, and shreds of string.
        5. These things Shirley sells secondhand in her sister's shoe-shine shop.

C. *Book reviews* Choose one of these titles for nonexistent books and make up something about it, the zanier the better. As you give your review of your book in front of the class, be sure to use the title at least three times.

The Joy of Shoes
Shopping the Sahara Desert
The Shredded Banana Mystery
The Passionate Cash Register
The Blonde Shaved Twice
Shearing Turtles for Fun and Profit
How to Shampoo Your Sherpa Guide
Making Trash into Treasures: Shaving-Can Art

[h]

---

fonɛtɪk trɪviə

Where would you *least* like to spend the night?

[ə haʊs, ə hoʊtɛl, jʊɚ oʊn hoʊm, ə haʊsboʊt, ðə hɑspɪtəl, ə həwaɪɪn hʌt]

Look at these four common expressions. How many actually have [h] when you say them aloud?

Oh!
Eh?
Uh-uh.
Ah!

The answer, of course, is none. [h] occurs only at the beginning of syllables, and almost no American speaker has difficulty producing it. Sometimes it may be incorrectly omitted, however, especially by nonnative speakers.

FACTS

Technical description: [h] is a glottal fricative, and it is unvoiced.

Correct production: The vocal folds are brought together just enough to set up a friction sound before the vowel that follows it. No articulatory adjustments are required, although the articulators probably anticipate the position of the following sound. Be sure not to use too much air in its production.

☆ *Spellings:* As is, and *wh* as in *whose.* The letter *h* is silent in such words as *hour, honor, honest,* and *heir.*

IN USE

*H*arriet's Eatery sells *h*am, *h*ash, *h*amburgers, and red-*h*ot chili.

Check your pronunciation of the words on each list:

hand	hid	ahead	rehearse
how	has	behave	perhaps
high	his	behind	somehow
head	hers	inhale	anyhow
who	hold	uphold	overhaul
hit	help	inhabit	high-handed

NOTES ON ASSIMILATION

1. It is acceptable to omit [h] in an unstressed syllable as long as it is not the first word in a sentence. Common acceptable contractions are examples of this: *they'd* for *they had* and *we've* for *we have.* Other examples:

I helped her do it.
He changed his mind.
How could he!

Care must be taken, however, not to omit it in stressed syllables in such words as these:

unhappy	exhale	behind	unholy	withhold
reheal	ahead	behave	mishap	unhurried

2. Although some speakers now say it is acceptable to omit [h] in words with [hju] such as *human* and *huge,* in most parts of the country such an omission is considered nonstandard. Be aware of keeping [h] in words like the following:

humor	Hugh	humanity
humidity	Houston	inhuman
humid	humanize	humiliate

PROBLEMS TO AVOID

☆ About the only error that occurs with this sound is its omission in stressed syllables. Some nonnative speakers may do this because of the nature of their own language system, but in American English such an omission is incorrect. *Head* [hɛd] should not be pronounced *Ed* [ɛd].

Say these words carefully and correctly.

help	heart
happy	house
hurry	

Contrast the difference in sound and meaning in these word pairs.

hold	old	harm	arm
hate	ate	heart	art
his	is	hear	ear

Warm-up phrases for practice: a hard decision, happy times, unheated house, heaven or hell, hold an old passport, his is best, hit it hard, a historic occasion

ADDING ON FOR PROFICIENCY

1. Say the following phrases 3 times, building up speed, but never at the expense of accuracy.

   a. air-drying hair dryer
   b. I'd hide.
   c. Whose ooze is it?
   d. hand and hand
   e. hold old gold

2. Say the following sentences carefully and correctly.

a. How often have we heard the saying "It isn't the heat, it's the humidity"?
b. And how often have we heard, "A house is not a home until there's heart in it"?
c. The Hastings' production of *Hamlet* was too heavy and lacked heart and humanity.
d. Helen hated her huge height, but there was no way she could hide it.
e. Harriet had a habit of holding her hands behind her back.

☆ 3. *For nonnative speakers*   Read each sentence aloud.

a. Henry is happy because he has a letter from home.
b. Half the class hopes to get high grades.
c. How hard is the homework assignment?
d. Helen was in a hurry and did not hang up her hat.
e. Who has taken that history class?
f. He was not hungry, so he ate only half a hamburger.
g. The handsome couple held hands.
h. Hank is a horrible human being!

SUPER EXERCISES

☆ 1. *Using* [h] *in conversational speech*   Create a sentence for each of the following words and phrases, and say it aloud.

home	hospitals
I hate . . .	I have . . .
highway driving	I hope . . .
a hard job	homework
campus housing	a sense of humor

☆ 2. *Finish the scene*   Cast two people as Miss Hunter, the speech teacher, and Harry, the student, and let the class decide how to finish the scene.

The Speech Lesson

SCENE: Classroom.

MISS HUNTER: Harry, if you're going to stay in this country, you must get your "aitches" in!
HARRY: 'Ow right you are, Miss 'Unter.
MISS HUNTER: "*How* right you are, Miss *Hunter*." Now repeat after me: *happy, house, heart.*
HARRY: *Happy, house, 'art.*
MISS HUNTER: *Heart, Harry, heart.*
HARRY: But I go to *art* class after this, not *heart* class, Miss *Hunter*.
MISS HUNTER: (silencing him with a look) Just listen, Harry, and repeat: *hope, hold, ham.*
HARRY: *hope, hold, 'am.*
MISS HUNTER: *Ham, Harry, Ham.*

HARRY: But I just learned to conjugate *I am, you are* . . . , not *I ham, you hare* . . .

MISS HUNTER: 'Arry, I mean *Harry*—now you've got *me* doing it! How can I ever teach you this?

HARRY: I will be happy to try to tell you *how*, Miss *Hunter*. . . .

[tʃ] and [dʒ][13]

fonɛtɪk trɪviə

Which of these games are usually played by only two people?

[brɪdʒ, beɪsbɔl, tʃɛkɚz, tɛnɪs, bæskɪtbɔl, haɪd ænd sik, hɑki, tʃɛs, sɑkɚ, tæg]

Which item would you be unlikely to find in a kitchen?

[dʒus, dʒɛlo, tʃiz, dʒæm, poteɪto tʃɪps, klæm tʃaʊdɚ, læm tʃɑps, hæm sændwɪtʃ, piæno, ɔrɪndʒɪz]

Say the following sentences aloud, exactly as written.

Art lec*sh*ers in colli*tch* are better when accompanied by pic*sh*ers.
Art lec*tu*res in colle*ge* are better when accompanied by pic*tu*res.

Although native speakers do not have much difficulty with the production of [tʃ] and [dʒ], they should beware of careless mistakes. Since these sounds do not occur in several major languages, nonnative speakers may predictably have difficulty with them, compounded by the variety of spellings this cognate pair can masquerade under!

FACTS

Technical description: Both are alveolar fricatives produced with the tongue tip and blade against the gum ridge. [tʃ] is unvoiced and [dʒ] is voiced.

Correct production: The tip and the blade of the tongue are pressed firmly against the gum ridge, with the tongue ready to produce [ʃ]. As the tongue tip drops, a plosive is released as a fricative continuant.

☆ *Spellings:* [tʃ] is spelled *ch* as in *chair* or *tch* as in *match;* rare spellings are *te* in *righteous* and *ti* as in *questions.* [dʒ] at the beginning of a word is either *j* as in *jaw* or *g* as in *giant* or *gesture.* In the middle or at the end it can be *dge* or *ge* as in *judge* or *cage.* Rare spellings include *di* as in *soldier* and *du* as in *gradual.*

IN USE

*C*harles was wat*ch*ing ea*ch* of the *ch*ildren in the kit*ch*en eating *ch*eese sandwi*ch*es.

The *j*et set *j*oked about marria*g*e and enga*g*ed in ma*j*or affairs instead.

---

[13] These sounds are *affricates,* which combine a plosive and a fricative into one sound.

Check your production of [tʃ] and [dʒ] in the words on the following list.

	[tʃ]			[dʒ]	
choose	marching	reach	junior	agent	edge
chin	pitcher	catch	jury	soldier	ledge
chair	hatchet	march	jump	budget	oblige
check	catching	much	giant	larger	rage
chance	peaches	watch	join	major	stage
cherry	enriching	fetch	general	margin	pledge
chicken	riches	wrench	job	region	merge
child	teacher	coach	jog	grudging	sponge
children	matchbox	detach	June	nudging	urge
charge	bachelor	lunch	joke	stranger	orange

Contrast both sound and meaning in these word pairs:

cheer	jeer	lunches	lunges	cinch	singe
chive	jive	batches	badges	perch	purge
chest	jest	searching	surging	rich	ridge

PROBLEMS TO AVOID

Careless articulation among native speakers and unfamiliarity with the sounds among nonnative speakers can cause problems.

1. Substitution of [ʃ] for [tʃ] in certain contexts so that *picture* [pɪktʃɚ] becomes "picshure" [pɪkʃɚ].
2. Devoicing, with substitution of a sound that approximates [tʃ] for [dʒ], particularly at the ends of words so that *edge* [ɛdʒ] becomes *etch* [ɛtʃ].
☆ 3. Various substitutions, detailed in the text.

Each problem is analyzed in greater detail. Concentrate on your area of weakness.

1. **[ʃ] for [tʃ]**   This substitution occurs primarily in the middle of words because of overassimilation.
Be careful to pronounce [tʃ] in these words:

factual   kitchen
actual   exchange
mixture

Warm-up phrases for practice: a permanent fixture, an actual experience, an unattached bachelor, exchange pictures, a factual account, a mischievous etching

2. **Devoicing**   The loss of voice on [dʒ], resulting in a sound like [tʃ], occurs often at the end of a word and sometimes in the middle of a word. The speaker must be made conscious of keeping voice sound coming through to the very end when needed.

As you may recall, final voiced fricatives and the voiced affricate [dʒ] add body and carrying power to speech, so it is not pedantic to suggest that vigilance is important in this area.

Most students think they are producing this sound correctly, but when challenged to exaggerate a final [dʒ] and hold the fricative component for a count of 2, either they just can't do it or it fritters away into a puff of air.

Try prolonging [dʒ] for a count of 2 in each of the following words.

ledge	bridges
cage	larger
knowledge	ledge
courage	merger

Warm-up phrases for practice: speak the language, law of averages, margin for error, college courses, a larger edge, a major change, imaginary stage, bulge from fudge, to pledge revenge

☆   Nonnative speakers who are trying to produce sounds foreign to them may do a number of things. The possibilities are described in points 3 through 7. Determine if any are problems in your particular case.[14]

☆ **3. [tʃ] for [dʒ]**   Nonnative speakers may make this substitution in the beginning of a word, as well as in the middle or at the end as detailed under point 2. (See that section for practice in those positions.) In the initial position, remember that *gin* is pronounced [dʒɪn], not *chin* [tʃɪn].

Say each of these words carefully and correctly.

join	gentle
job	just
jump	generous

Contrast the difference in sound and meaning in these word pairs:

joke	choke	edging	etching	surge	search
jest	chest	ridges	riches	lunge	lunch
Jeep	cheap				

Warm-up phrases for practice: (Be careful, as both sounds occur in each phrase.) change into blue jeans, join the church, a choice gem, watch the Jeep, choose marriage, each jar of jelly, not much of a joke, just the child's way, a general lecture

☆ **4. [ʃ] for [tʃ]**   One sits on a *chair* [tʃɛɚ], not a *share* [ʃɛɚ], while one *watches* [watʃəz], not *washes* TV [waʃəz], hoping to *catch* [kætʃ], not *cash* [kæʃ], a good show.

Pronounce all these with the affricate [tʃ].

---

[14] We refer to these as substitutions, but what is actually happening may be closer to a distortion of the target sound than an actual substitution. For practice purposes, however, the distinction is unimportant.

cheat	catches	each
chin	matches	much
chance	reaching	which
choose	kitchen	such
chop	exchange	couch

Say these with the fricative [ʃ].

shy	dishes	push
show	nation	rush
shop	patient	cash
shout	ocean	fish
shape	machine	dish

Contrast the difference in sound and meaning in these word pairs.

choose	shoes	much	mush
cheap	sheep	witch	wish
cheat	sheet	catch	cash

Warm-up phrases for practice: (Be careful, because both sounds occur in each phrase.) choose new shirts, a shiny kitchen, felt much shame, changed fashions, reach for the salt shaker, a shy teacher, delicious chicken, should I change?, wish for children, ashamed child

☆ 5. [j] **for** [dʒ]   This usually occurs at the beginning of a word, although occasionally it happens medially. *Joke* is pronounced [dʒoʊk], not *yoke* [joʊk].
   Say each word carefully and correctly.

Jack	juice
job	larger
just	

Contrast the difference in sound and meaning in these word pairs:

jet	yet	jeer	year	juice	use
Jew	you	John	yawn	jam	yam

Warm-up phrases for practice: (Both sounds occur in each phrase, so be careful.) yellow jewel, has yet to take a jet, use jelly on toast, a yearly job, jumps in the yard, a journey to Europe, yesterday's genius

☆ 6. [ʒ] **for** [dʒ]   The problem involves simplification of the affricate to its fricative component [ʒ] because the affricate just doesn't exist in the speaker's language. In this case it is important to remember that [dʒ] is a blend of two sounds. The tongue tip goes up to make the stop for [d] and then drops to combine with the fricative [ʒ]. Also, it will be helpful to know that in English the only words that begin with [ʒ] have been taken directly from French, for instance, *genre.* Thus all words that begin with the letter *j* are pronounced [dʒ], as are words beginning with *g* if followed by *i* or *e.*[15]

---

[15] Of course there are exceptions: *get,* for instance, is pronounced with the hard *g* [gɛt].

Pronounce each of the following words with [dʒ]:

giant	jelly	junior	genius
gem	germ	gently	general
jet	jury	jaw	job

In the middle or at the end of a word, either [dʒ] or [ʒ] can occur. However, [ʒ] is heard in relatively few words in English, whereas [dʒ] occurs in *a great many.*

Contrast the difference in sound in the following words:

[ʒ]		[dʒ]	
usual	casual	budget	huge
vision	garage	larger	large
pleasure	rouge	region	edge
occasion	beige	staging	stage

Warm-up phrases for practice: (Use care, because both sounds occur in each phrase.) the usual job, a joyful occasion, the usual urge, a casual gesture, a pleasure to join you, a large treasure, measure the margin

☆ 7. **[ts] for [tʃ] and [dz] for [dʒ]**   These substitutions happen occasionally because the fricative used in the second part of the affricate is the wrong one. *Child* [tʃaɪld] requires [tʃ], not [ts], and *jump* [dʒʌmp] must have [dʒ], not [dz].

Say the words in each column carefully and correctly.

[tʃ]	[dʒ]
chin	joke
matches	major
each	page

Refer to the word list under "In Use" for additional practice.

ADDING ON FOR PROFICIENCY

1. With careful articulation, repeat the phrases that follow, building up speed, but never at the expense of accuracy.

   a. Jim's choice gem
   b. strange arrangements
   c. cheap jungle Jeep
   d. chess championships
   e. pledges marriage
   f. verge of merger

2. Read the following sentences aloud, monitoring your production of [tʃ] and [dʒ]. Sentences *f* through *j* concentrate on clear articulation of final [dʒ].

   a. A factual account of the extraordinary merger is actually Marjorie's responsibility.

    b. Chuck fetches birch logs for the kitchen stove and catches cold in the process.

    c. The picture hanging from the frayed picture wire crashed to the floor and the glass fractured into hundreds of pieces.

    d. He was watchful of the milk mixture on the stove, but the pan was scorched anyway.

    e. The clam chowder, a fixture at the annual beach picnic, had a questionable texture.

    f. Midge edged forward, then plunged through the hedge into the large yard.

    g. George and Marge's marriage was arranged by their parents, and they were obliged to go through with it.

    h. The strange but imaginative stage setting enraged the average theatergoer.

    i. The lawyer nudged the judge and urged him to render his judgment in plain language.

    j. The budget was large, but even so, a huge deficit emerged when the accountant was obliged to open the books.

☆ 3. *For nonnative speakers* Say each sentence carefully and correctly. The first five sentences concentrate on [tʃ], the next five on [dʒ], and the final five on both.

    a. The children had lunch each day at school.

    b. The teacher teaches each child to match colors.

    c. That chicken recipe uses too much ketchup.

    d. Chess matches are not much fun to watch.

    e. Each Sunday, church has started late.

    f. Jim played a strange joke on Jack.

    g. What is in that large orange package?

    h. Just a minute—let me arrange the books.

    i. He started the journey on a jumbo jet.

    j. You can join the club if you pay the general admission.

    k. Midge shared the large chair with Jenny.

    l. Check on each date in June and July.

    m. Charlie liked jelly on his peanut butter sandwich.

    n. Speech and language classes are useful.

    o. He chose shows of general interest.

SUPER EXERCISES

☆ 1. *Using* [tʃ] *and* [dʒ] *in conversational speech* Create a sentence around each of the following words and phrases, and say it at a conversational rate.

jokes	blue jeans
a major problem	speech
jet set	a woman's touch
pictures	magic
choices	children
general rule	Japan
marriage	jobs

2. *Meet Your Match*   Take the role of the announcer or one of the contestants.

ANNOUNCER: It's time to watch *Meet Your Match.* As usual, our specially chosen bachelors and bachelorettes are hidden behind this screen. Each has just a minute to give a personal introduction. Then we will vote for the most eligible bachelor or bachelorette. Drop the screen and *actually meet each one in person!*

BACHELOR #1:   Hi ya! Call me Super Jock or just plain Joe. I'm the most gorgeous hunk of flesh you could ever join up with. My job is driving a charter bus, and I enjoy just about anything to do with beachcombing and jukebox jive. My motto: Why not charter *me,* girls?

BACHELORETTE #1:   Hello. I'm Jennifer. I'm gentle and mature, and my greatest joy in life is reading choice literature. My job is teaching church school, and I enjoy crocheting pot holders and playing checkers. I have no motto. I'm just looking for an enriching platonic exchange with a mature gentleman.

BACHELORETTE #2:   Joy's my name, and that's me, *Joy*—get it? My job's with a travel agency, and do I jet around—get around—get it? Marriage is the farthest thing from my mind, and I enjoy just about everything. My motto: Cool your jets with me, gents—get it?

BACHELOR #2:   Good evening, Jeffrey Jerome is my given name, and I am unattached by choice. My job is a challenging one: I am an expert in jade of the major Chung dynasty, particularly that of the Chin-Jen school. I have no hobbies. Calvin Coolidge is my idol, and I really have no idea why I was chosen to be on this program.

☆ 3. *Finish the scene*   Cast two people as the traffic officer and Jerry, who has just been pulled over for speeding. Have the class decide how to finish the scene.

Just a Minute There!

SCENE: Stopped car. Traffic officer is leaning in the window to talk to a nervous Jerry.

OFFICER: Okay, chum. What's the large rush?

JERRY: No large rush, officer. I was just doing 40.

OFFICER: Just 40 miles an hour, huh? Then how come I clocked you at 70 coming over that bridge?

JERRY: That bridge back there? Why I couldn't have been going that fast on a *bridge,* Officer.

OFFICER: (writing out a ticket) Tell that to the judge, chum. Let me see your driver's license.

JERRY: (feeling nervously through his pockets) Uh, I seem to have just left home without it.

OFFICER: Let me see some other identification, then. Wallet?

JERRY: Not on me. I seem to have just left home without that, too.

OFFICER: Naturally. (looking at him closely) Okay, we'll worry about that later. Let's see your registration.

JERRY: (looking frantically through glove compartment) Gee, Officer . . .

OFFICER: Don't tell me, I know—*you just left home without it!* See this police badge, chum? I just happened to leave home *with* it, and . . .

CHECKPOINT EXERCISES

Fricatives and affricates

1. *Demonstrating carrying power in speech by giving full value to final voiced fricatives and affricates*   Listen for these final sounds as you interpret at least one of the following selections. Record it for playback. *While reading,* mark any final sounds that you devoiced erroneously, and use the recording to check your self-judgment.

   a. Fog everywhere. Fog up the river, where it flows among green meadows: fog down the river, where it rolls defiled among tiers of shipping, and the waterside pollutions of a great—and dirty—city. Fog on the Essex marshes. . . . Fog creeping into the cabooses of collier brigs; fog lying out in the yards, . . . fog drooping on the gunwales of barges and small boats. Fog in the eyes and throats of Greenwich pensioners, wheezing by the fireside of their wards.

      CHARLES DICKENS, *Our Mutual Friend*

   b. Life's a pudding full of plums;
      Care's a canker that benumbs,
      Wherefore waste our elocution
      On impossible solutions?
      Life's a pleasant institution—
      Let us take it as it comes.

      W. S. GILBERT, *The Gondoliers*

   c. No warmth, no cheerfulness, no healthful ease,
      No comfortable feel in any member—
      No shade, no shine, no butterflies, no bees,
      No fruits, no flowers, no leaves, no birds,
         November!

      THOMAS HOOD, "No"

2. *Demonstrating clarity of all fricatives and affricates*   Interpret at least three of the following selections, listening to your production of the fricatives. Record your playback. *While reading,* mark any fricatives that you produced incorrectly, and use the recording to check your self-judgments. Note any errors you still make on the table that follows the selections.

   a. I accept this award with an abiding faith in America and an audacious faith in the future of mankind. I refuse to accept the idea that the "isness" of man's present nature makes him morally incapable of reaching up for the "oughtness" that forever confronts him.

      MARTIN LUTHER KING, JR., when accepting the Nobel Peace Prize

   b. It was interesting, when I dressed before daylight, to peep out of the window, where my candles were reflected in the black panes like two beacons, and, finding all beyond still enshrouded in the indistinctness of last night, to watch how it turned out when the day came on. As the prospect gradually revealed itself . . . I had pleasure in discovering the unknown objects that had been around me in my sleep.

CHARLES DICKENS, *Bleak House*

c. A fox looked at his shadow at sunrise and said,
   "I will have camel for lunch today."
And all morning he went about looking for camels.
But at noon he saw his shadow again—and he said,
   "A mouse will do."

ANONYMOUS

d. Listen . . .
With faint dry sound
Like steps of passing ghosts,
The leaves, frost-crisped, break from the trees
And fall.

ADELAIDE CRAPSEY, "November Night"

e. Those who compare the age in which their lot has fallen with a golden age which exists only in imagination, may talk of degeneracy and decay . . .

LORD MACAULAY, *History of England*

f. As long as you are journeying in the interior of the Desert you have no particular point to make for as your resting place. The endless sands yield nothing but small stunted shrubs; even those fail after the first two or three days, and from that time you pass over broad plains—you pass over newly reared hills—you pass through valleys dug out by the last week's storm, and the hills and valleys are sand, sand, sand, still sand, and only sand, and sand again.

A. W. KINGLAKE, *Eothen*

Substitutions, omissions, distortions, and additions still needing work

[f] and [v] _____

[θ] and [ð] _____

[s] and [z] _____

[ʃ] and [ʒ] _____

[tʃ] and [dʒ] _____

[h] _____

SEMIVOWELS: GLIDES

There are four voiced consonant sounds in English that are neither stopped in their production so that they explode out nor obstructed in such a fashion that friction noise results. They are produced by a slight, continuous gliding movement of the articulators from one position to the next and thus are termed *glides*. They have been described as sounding like vowels in motion, which accounts for the synonymous term *semivowels*. The production of all four assumes the raising of the soft palate so that air does not escape up into the nose. These are the four glides:

[w] as in *win* and [hw] as in *what*   [r] as in *run*
[l] as in *lit*[16]   [j] as in *yet*

[w] and [hw]

fonɛtɪk trɪviə

Which is *not* a city?

[waʃɪŋtən, wɪlmɪŋtən, wɛsthæmptən, wɛst pɑm bitʃ, wɪskɑnsɪn, wɪljəmzbɚg]

Tongue twister: Repeat this line 3 times, dramatically exaggerating the lip movements:

*W*ipe *w*eak *w*obbly *w*indows *w*arily.

[w] and [hw] words have long been favorites with diction coaches because when carefully executed, they become excellent exercises for the lips. Many people, including those with "tight jaws," are slack in their production, and some nonnative speakers make a substitution for them if they are not accustomed to them in their native language.

FACTS

Technical description: Both are bilabial (two-lip) glides. [hw] is unvoiced and [w] is voiced.

Correct production: The lips are in the rounded position to form *oo* as in *boo* with the vocal folds vibrating, and the tongue and lips glide from this position into the position for the vowel that follows. It is the quick widening of the lips that gives the sound its distinctive character. When producing the sound, check that the lips move from puckered to widened.

☆ *Spellings:* as written for both *w* and *wh*. [w] is also spelled *u* as in *queen* and *o* as in *one*. [w] is pronounced only at the beginning of syllables. It is always silent in three instances:

1. At the ends of words, as in *low, few,* and *saw*
2. If *r* follows *w*, as in *write* and *wreck*
3. In these common words: *toward, sword, two, answer*

---

[16] Some phoneticians place this sound in a separate category called "lateral sounds," but since it is the only one that fits into such a category, being made out of the sides of the mouth, and since it has several characteristics in common with the glides, it is more appropriate to include it here.

IN USE

The woman wanted to quit work because she was quite weary.
What, why, where, and when are important aspects of a news story.

Check your pronunciation of the words on each list.

[w]		[hw]	
walk	awake	while	meanwhile
wade	everyone	white	anywhere
wager	anyway	where	nowhere
woman	away	wheel	elsewhere
wide	await	whim	somewhat
wear	unwell	whisper	awhile
wash	anyone	what	
wish	liquid	why	
wing	unwise	which	

NOTES ON ASSIMILATION

Must one still differentiate between unvoiced [hw] and voiced [w], or has assimilation weakened the distinction so that it is no longer important among speakers of Standard American English?

This controversy is unresolved, so the best solution is to go by the standard in the area in which you live.

If the distinction is still important in your area, be sure to use the unvoiced [hw] for words spelled with wh (see word lists for practice).

Contrast the difference in sound and meaning in these word pairs:

where	wear	whale	wail	whine	wine
when	wen	which	witch	whet	wet

Warm-up phrases for practice: what was it, where was it, why will you, where will you, which would, who won't, whether either will, which wish, whirling world

PROBLEMS TO AVOID

1. Slack articulation. Lip movement should be forceful and rapid in these glides; if it is not, articulation will be weak.
☆ 2. Nonnative speakers may substitute [v] for [w] and very occasionally [f] for [hw] so that *west* [wɛst] becomes *vest* [vɛst] and white [hwaɪt] becomes *fight* [faɪt].

Both problems are discussed in greater detail. Concentrate on your area of weakness. Do the exercises for a good general workout for the lips.

1. Slack articulation The sound [w] can be weakened almost beyond recognition if you do not have enough tension in the lips to round them to a small *o* and then rapidly widen them.

To get the feel of the activity in the lips, say each phrase twice, exaggerating the first time, and without exaggeration the second time, but keeping the strong motion.

wash windows well
wide, weird world
one window's walk
willingly wishful
wiggle and wobble

Be particularly careful of this lip activity in words with [w] consonant clusters:

queen	swan	twin
quick	swallow	twig
quite	swim	twinkle
quart	sweep	twist
quiet	swamp	twitch
quit	sweet	twine

Warm-up phrases for practice: a queer sweater, quivering twig, request quiet, swaying swing, twins in tweed, switch dwellings, a swelling choir, sweet liquid

☆ **2. [v] for [w] and [f] for [hw]**   A careful contrast between the production of the two sounds may help. Note that [w] starts from a rounded lip position, whereas [v] requires actual contact between the lower lip and the upper front teeth. Contrast and exaggerate just the first sound in *was* and *very*.
Say each word carefully and correctly.

will	want
was	week
were	why

Contrast the difference in sound and meaning in these word pairs:

went	vent	wary	vary	while	file
wet	vet	wine	vine	white	fight

Warm-up phrases for practice: (Use care, because both sounds occur in each.) was very slow, have wondered, every week, wanted a vacation, very much wiser, obviously worse, valuable words, weak vowel sounds

ADDING ON FOR PROFICIENCY

1. Read these sentences aloud carefully and correctly.

   a. World War II was the war that was meant to end all wars.
   b. If I want what I want when I want it, why must I always wait?
   c. The weather was worse than ever, with the wind blowing wildly.
   d. Picture windows are wide, but the view through them is not always the wonderful picture it is meant to be.
   e. Once a week, William and Wilma went windsurfing on Lake Winnipeg.

f. It was wet and the wind whistled through the trees and worried the glass in the windows.

g. The wooden sign wobbled wildly over the bar: William had had too much whisky.

h. Broadway, the Great White Way, is where people go to watch plays—and each other.

☆ 2. *For nonnative speakers*   Say these sentences. Sentences *a* through *e* feature [w] and [hw]; the remainder contrast [w] and [v].

a. Which one of your courses is your worst one?
b. When and where were you born?
c. What is the word for *welcome* in your language?
d. Which women in world history do you wish to emulate?
e. Will you want to stay in this country when you finish college?
f. Which words would you like to review?
g. William said he felt very well.
h. Was your visit to the viewing deck worthwhile?
i. Why weren't we invited to that wonderful party?
j. Why does every word have to be so heavy with overtones?
k. Some students work very hard and still worry about their grade-point average.
l. We were advised to water the plants very well just once every week.

SUPER EXERCISES

☆ 1. *Using* [w] *and* [hw] *in conversation speech*   Create a sentence for each of the following words and phrases and say it aloud.

the weather	I want . . .
I wish . . .	I will . . .
A person is wise if . . .	the way to win
William Shakespeare	the world
the end of the week	walking
college requirements	welcome

2. *A Something's Wrong Story*   Read the story. Then discuss all the errors in it.

William was 12. He had never been to the Natural History Museum before, and he was wildly excited. "I wish we didn't have to go, Mama! Why can't we go right away?" His mother assured him they would go as soon as the baby-sitter came to watch the older brothers and sisters.

They walked downtown on public transportation, and once at the museum went straight to the Dinosaur Room. The gigantic plaster brontosaurus filled William with wonder. He requested a quarter from his mother to buy food to feed it, and she gave it to him willingly. The Human Growth Room was next, and they agreed that the skeleton of a women as a baby next to the skeleton of the same woman as a grown-up was a wonderful way to show the process of aging. They admired the live great whale hanging in the hallway, and as they left, William bought an iguana for his wife, who by this time was getting worn-out and whiny. They went home by water taxi, their pockets overflowing with fine white sand.

☆ 3. *Finish the scene* Cast two people as the clerk at the men's watch counter and the customer. Let the class decide how to finish the scene.

So That's *What He Wanted!*

SCENE: A department store jewelry counter.

CLERK: Would you like to see some watches, sir?
CUSTOMER: I certainly would.
CLERK: Which price range were you thinking of?
CUSTOMER: I wasn't. Just show me what you've got.
CLERK: Well, these watches are very nice. They're self-winding.
CUSTOMER: (looks) Not what I want.
CLERK: What about these digital watches?
CUSTOMER: (looks) Not what I want.
CLERK: Hmm. These watches are the Wafer-Thins, our most expensive line.
CUSTOMER: (looks carefully) Not what . . .
CLERK: Don't tell me, sir, I know. *Not what you want.* Perhaps, you'd like the other end of our line?—the, uh, "more affordable" ones, the old wind-up tick-tock?
CUSTOMER: No. These won't do either.
CLERK: (a bit huffily). Perhaps if you'd tell me what you *do* want, sir. (notices customer has already started to move away, busies himself replacing watches on shelves, and realizes two Wafer-Thins are missing) *Sir! Wait a minute, sir!* . . .

AN EXTRA ACTION
WORKOUT SOUND

[r]

fonɛtɪk trɪviə

Only one of these people did *not* live in the White House. Which one?

[ranəld reigən, fræŋklɪn rouzəvɛlt, hɚbɚt huvɚ, wʊdro wɪlsən, martɪn luθɚ kɪŋ, rɪtʃɚd nɪksən]

[r] appears in many forms and guises:

See these lines heah?
Any pwoblems with them?

They're not vurry difficult.
Get the idear?

Not only is [r] subject to all sorts of articulation errors, substitutions, omissions, distortions, and additions, but the nonnative speaker with his own form of [r] can shake his head and wonder if he is ever going to learn this strange American speech! To compound matters, [r] exists as both a consonant and a vowel. It is a consonant when it initiates a syllable, as in *run* or *around,* or when it is part of a consonant cluster, as in *tree.* At the end of a word it is always considered a vowel, and it appears as a vowel in the middle of some words, such as *bird.* Since these vowel forms are considered in the vowel chapter and their errors analyzed there, this discussion will concentrate on the consonant form.

FACTS

Technical description: [r] is a palatal glide, produced with the tongue behind the
    gum ridge, and it is voiced.
Correct production: There are two ways to produce [r].

1. Bring the tip of the tongue close to the gum ridge and then curl it back slightly.
2. Lower the tip slightly and raise the whole lightly tensed central part of the tongue toward, but not touching, the hard palate. This is an *alternate* placement called *central* [r].

    Whether you use the first or the second, the placements are simply where the sound *starts,* as your tongue immediately glides to the position for the following vowel.

☆ *Spellings:* As written, doubled, or *wr* as in *write.*

IN USE

*R*alph *r*eadily ag*r*eed to ca*rr*y the *r*ed banner a*r*ound the pa*r*ade g*r*ounds.

Check your pronunciation of [r] in the words on each list.

rich	rat	cry	great	narrow	career
read	ray	cream	gray	around	erode
ripe	rain	crayon	grasp	carry	uproot
rate	rink	crowd	green	squirrel	direct
rug	row	crash	grass	marry	aroma
wreck	revenge	creep	grade	moral	enrage
write	reverse	crest	group	bury	arise
round	rubber	crime	ground	oral	unreal
rice	wrought	crawl	gravy	correct	area
rage	rave			arrange	arrest
red	raise			bureau	career
rough	racket			erase	erupt
region	wrap			fairy	macaroni

rule	wrong			tomorrow	arrow
repeat	ride			hurry	disrupt
pray	bring	friend	three	tree	dry
praise	brought	fry	thrill	trash	drop
practice	breeze	freeze	thrift	try	drink
proud	bright	free	throw	trip	drip
prove	break	frame	thrash	trunk	dream
profit	broad	front	thread	true	drape
pretty	brush	frail	threat	transit	draft
print	brief	fresh	throat	train	draw
press	brass			trouble	dread

PROBLEMS TO AVOID

1. Retroflex [r], which involves producing [r] too far back in the mouth.

2. Weakened [r], either substituting [w] for [r] so that *run* [rʌn] becomes *won* [wʌn]; or, far more common, distorting it to something between [w] and [r].

3. Intrusive [r], which involves adding [r] in certain contexts where it does not belong so that *law* [lɔ] becomes *lore* [lɔr].

☆ **4.** Nonnative speakers may transfer their native-language [r], including trills, taps, and other variations to English, thus distorting the sound.

☆ **5.** Native speakers of Oriental languages will tend to substitute [l] for [r] so that *rim* [rɪm] becomes *limb* [lɪm]

Each problem is analyzed in greater detail. Concentrate on your area of weakness.

1. Retroflex [r]   Midwesterners are particularly prone to what is called a *retroflex* [r], producing [r] too far back in the mouth. It is important to correct this because it colors the vowels around the [r], giving them a "dark" sound and contributing to an overall throaty quality to one's speech.

One of the leading early voice specialists, Vera Sickels, herself the possessor of a magnificent voice, talks of the beauty of [r] and suggests a very pointed image to help produce such a sound: "The *underside* of the tip [of the tongue] is placed *near enough* to the teeth ridge so that air in passing over produces a slight murmuring sound . . . . its beauty depends on its being made very far forward in the mouth."[17]

a. Usually, the person with a back placement is actually curling the tongue way back toward the tonsils. Using the words *read* and *red,* find your customary tongue placement. Then, prolonging the initial sound, try Sickels's placement, and try to stabilize her placement.

b. Practice on words like the following. Remember, it is *very,* not "vurry."

American	terrible
where	marry
library	

---

[17] *First Principles of Speech Training* (New York: D. Appleton and Co., 1928), p. 296.

c. Now move back to the word lists, trying to maintain this forward placement. (Reviewing suggestions for clearing the throaty voice in the chapter on resonation may be in order if the retroflex [r] is quite severe.)

Warm-up phrases for practice: a very red rose, read where Ray tells you, sharing rags and riches, run right there, a real American writer, buried really deep, charity-drive receipt

2. Weakened [r]   This category ranges all the way from outright substitution of [w] for [r] to a distortion somewhere between [w] and [r]. Among children the substitution is quite common, but among adults the problem is primarily the distortion; the speaker is said to have a "weak" [r].

Several things may help:

a. Ear training is critical. Get a good model of a strong [r] and keep comparing it with your production.
b. It is important to focus on *tongue* action, not *lip* action. [r] is *totally* a product of tongue movement. Most people with this problem are letting the lip action of the easier glide sound [w] cover the weakness of the production of the harder glide, [r].

   Look in a mirror and say the words *read, right, red. The lips should be back out of the way,* not puckering in at all. If you can't keep them back, actually hold them back with your forefingers so you get the *feel* of the tongue doing all the work to produce [r].
c. Production with the tongue curled back is generally preferable to the alternative central tongue placement.
d. Can you say the vowel [ɝ] in words like *her* and *sir?* If so, isolate the [ɝ] and transfer from this each time to words beginning with [r]: er ⟶ red, er ⟶ read, er ⟶ right, and so on. Refer to word lists, practicing first [r] in initial position, then in the medial position. Concentrate finally on the [r] blend lists, because it is on these sounds that the weakness most often occurs.
e. Here is a helpful tip about the production of the blends: Have your tongue in the position to make the [r] before you ever form the consonant in front. This will prevent any accidental vowel sound between the first two consonants. Start with *pride, crayon, bring;* then practice on the [r] blend words listed toward the beginning of this section.

Warm-up phrases for practice: pruning roses, a gravelly road, ground round, drum roll, rapid transit, ripe fruit, fried rice, drip-dry curtains, bring around, broken record, fresh raspberries

3. Intrusive [r]   The addition of [r] where it does not belong is especially prevalent in the Eastern United States. It occurs when a word ends in a vowel, most often when the next word begins with a vowel. Do you get the *idear* about this?

Say each word carefully and correctly.

soda   potato
America   area
sofa

Warm-up phrases for practice: saw a bargain, the idea of it, raw eggs, comma in the wrong place, draw a lucky number, soda and Danish, tomato and lettuce, Asia and Africa

☆ **4. Distorting [r] by substituting a foreign form**   As already stated, [r] worldwide comes in many different guises, and there is even a difference between the vowel *er* in American [ɝ] and British English [ɜ]! Because your native language is different from American English, you may trill your [r], tap it, or do any number of other legitimate things with it—legitimate for your language, that is. The pattern is deeply engrained. Thus it is best to think of the American [r] as a totally new sound—not necessarily better or more beautiful, but new.

Choose an American model to copy. Review the two ways of producing the sound at the beginning of this section, and keep working at it as you further refine your ear, which is what will help you most. As you are able to produce an acceptable new American sound, practice with the word lists and other materials in this chapter.

☆ **5. [l] for [r] (and vice versa)**   If you spoke an Oriental language before learning English, you will have a great deal of difficulty hearing a difference between [l] and [r]. These are *separate* phonemes in English, but to you they will sound like allophones of the same sound.

Thus ear training is again critical. Also, you will need to build a very strong awareness of the different tongue placements and differences in tongue tension required to produce the two sounds. Basically, [l] is made with the tip of the tongue *touching the gum ridge,* whereas [r] is made with the tongue *not* touching but curled back behind the ridge. Contrast *lake* (touching) with *rake* (not touching).

It is easier to start with [l], which has a definite point of articulation, and become thoroughly familiar with that before attempting the more difficult [r]. Suggestions for overcoming this problem will therefore be found in the section on [l].

ADDING ON FOR PROFICIENCY

1. Say the following phrases 3 times, building up speed, but not at the expense of accuracy.

   a. bury very carefully
   b. ribbon wound round
   c. flaking fried rice
   d. rapid transit trouble
   e. rip-roaring riot
   f. cheerful earful

2. Say the following sentences carefully and correctly. Sentences *f* through *j* concentrate on [r] blends.

   a. Ralph hired a car from Rent-a-Wreck rather than one from Hertz.

b. The restaurant ran out of orange juice, and the oranges on hand weren't ripe enough for processing.

c. Many errors in writing were corrected by the remedial reading instructor.

d. He rented the royal suite at the luxury hotel for the first day; after that he could barely afford a room.

e. The proud parents were enraged by the rude behavior of their former darlings.

f. The brother of the bride did not approve of the rather prudish groom, although he was prissy himself.

g. The crowd gathered into an angry group on the grass to protest the crew's clumsy rowing.

h. Frozen fruit is not as good as fruit freshly picked from the orchard— especially when it's free.

i. He had a dreadful dream about a train crashing through a drawbridge at full throttle.

j. Although the playwright was praised by the press, his words were practically unknown beyond a fringe of avid fans.

☆ 3. *For nonnative speakers*   Keep a strong American [r] as you read the following sentences aloud.

a. The team ran around the arena to warm up.
b. The rooms in the dorm are rather small.
c. The radio was really too loud.
d. Are you ready to read tomorrow's assignment?
e. The restaurant was right off campus on the corner.
f. Ray was told to report to the registrar.
g. Rose had three wrong answers.
h. It is not hard to read Russian—if you are Russian!
i. Rita and Randy returned to Rome on Thursday.
j. The opera was really rather boring and long.

SUPER EXERCISES

☆ 1. *Using* [r] *in conversational speech*   Make up a sentence for each of the following words and phrases and say it aloud.

a good restaurant	dreams
pride	term papers
reading	art
New York	winter
freedom	research
friends	

2. *Just Incredible!*   Choose one segment of the script to read aloud.

And so, ladies and gentlemen, on tonight's *Just Incredible!* show we will visit . . .

. . . Someone who claims man's best friend is his camel. Roco, as the dromedary is familiarly known, lives in a riverside apartment with his proud owner, Ralph Rugby. They dwell in a ground floor apartment because residents complained about a camel in the elevator. Ralph will lead Roco through some of his tricks—rolling over and playing dead, pulling a baby carriage with his teeth, and wriggling his humps to the rhythm of the rhumba.

. . . A man who has spent a lifetime inventing shoes that won't wear out. Martin Reese's secret process has resulted in a whole fashion line of wrought-iron shoes in a selection of lacy patterns. The line, called Eternal Footwear, will be shown for the first time ever on our broadcast tonight. Mr. Reese says the shoes are practical and comfortable, and the only problem may be hot pavements.

We will also make a special trip to a restaurant in Richmond that specializes in kangaroo meat. It is evidently marinated first for three weeks in Concord grape juice, and the owners will share the complete recipe on the air for us tonight. Mama and Papa Rivoli say it really keeps the diners hopping.

3. *Finish the scene*   Cast two people as Rose, the radio call-in listener, and Dr. Redd, famed radio psychologist.

What Is the Problem?

SCENE: The call-in voice and the voice of the radio psychologist.

DR. REDD: Hello, you're on the air.
ROSE: Doctor, oh, I can't believe I finally got through to you! My name is Rose, and I've got such a problem!
DR. REDD: And what is your problem, Rose?
ROSE: It's my son, Roy. Oh, doctor, he's brilliant, you wouldn't believe how brilliant . . .
DR. REDD: That doesn't seem to be much of a problem, Rose.
ROSE: But he talks back to me. He's rude to me. And recently—you won't believe this—he even hit me!
DR. REDD: Rose, that is a problem. Have you sought professional advice?
ROSE: I've had him to three psychiatrists and a psychotherapist already.
DR. REDD: And what did they say the problem was?
ROSE: They refused to treat him, doctor; every one of them refused. And my husband refuses to help.
DR. REDD: You *do* have a terrible problem, Rose. No wonder you're concerned. Let's start with the striking incident. When he hit you? What did he strike you with?
ROSE: His Kermit the Frog doll—right on top of my head.
DR. REDD: Uh, Rose, how old is Roy?
ROSE: Two years old, doctor. And the psychiatrist just laughed and said to forget it. Oh, doctor, I'm a good mother, and someone's got to help me with my problem . . .

[1]
_____

fonɛtɪk trɪviə

Whatever happened to Mary's lamb?

[mæri hæd ə lɪtl̩ læm
ɪts flis wʌz hwaɪt æz snoʊ
bʌt ɪt gru ʌp ænd dʒɔɪnd ə flɑk
kɔz ʃip aə̩t pɛts ju noʊ

Say these sentences below exactly as written:

1. The jackpot has *aw*ready reached *aw*most a mi*ji*on in *code* cash.
2. The jackpot has a*l*ready reached a*l*most a mi*ll*ion in co*l*d cash.

[l], the only lateral sound in English, requires a good deal of tongue-tip activity. Lacking this, many speakers fall into careless articulation of it.

FACTS

Technical description: [l] is a lateral alveolar sound produced with the tongue tip against the forward gum ridge. It is voiced. It is classified with the glides.

Correct production: The tip of the tongue makes a firm contact with the upper gum ridge while the blade of the tongue simultaneously lowers slightly to allow the vocalized air to escape over its sides. Be sure that the tip, not the blade, makes the contact and that the sound is not dentalized by allowing the tip to touch the teeth except before [θ] or [ð], as in *wealth.*

☆ *Spellings:* as is or doubled as in *follow.* In a number of words with *l* before a consonant, it is silent. *Examples:* wou*l*d, ha*l*f, shou*l*d, cou*l*d, ta*l*k, ca*l*m, cha*l*k, sta*l*k, sa*l*mon.

IN USE

Sa*ll*y rea*ll*y *l*iked Pau*l*, but Pau*l* was a*l*ready in *l*ove with B*l*anche.

Say the words on each list.

like	elevate	roll
love	election	fail
learn	sailor	jail
lose	salad	fall
lace	elope	fell
late	fellow	tile
let	follow	seal
low	swallow	real
lake	palace	rule
lean	mellow	hall
lack	elated	pal
lost	hallow	bowl

[l] blends

please	blue	sleep	flower	clay	glad
place	black	slow	fleece	claim	glaze
plate	blaze	slum	flame	clothes	glint

plank	blush	slipper	flip	clear	glitter
platter	blame	slam	flow	clean	glib
plump	blister	slate	floor	clip	glut

ADDITIONAL FACTS ABOUT [l]

1. There are two forms of the [l]. *Clear* [l] occurs at the beginning of a syllable before a vowel, as in *let* or *below,* or as a part of a consonant cluster, as in *play. Dark* [l] occurs at the end of a syllable or words, as in *fall. Both are articulated in the front of the mouth* as described, but they differ in the position of the *back* of the tongue. On clear [l] the back of the tongue is *low* in the mouth, and on dark [l] it rises *up* toward the soft palate. Contrast the difference in *let* and *call.*

2. *Syllabic* [l̩] (notice the dot under the symbol to indicate this form) comes at the end of a word if *t, d, n, s,* or *z* precedes it. [l̩] thus forms a syllable without needing a vowel before it. Thus *little* is pronounced [lɪtl̩], not [lɪtəl]. Say these words: *meddle* [mɛdl̩], *tunnel* [tʌnl̩], *thistle* [θɪsl̩], *nozzle* [nɑzl̩].

PROBLEMS TO AVOID

Although some people may dentalize [l] or confuse the dark and clear forms of it, there are three major problems:

1. Omission or distortion due to slack articulation so that *cold* [koʊld] sounds something like *code* [koʊd].
2. Substitution of a sound resembling [w] for [l] so that *let* [lɛt] sounds something like *wet* [wɛt].
☆ 3. Substitution of [r] for [l] so that *law* [lɔ] sounds like *raw* [rɔ].

Each problem is analyzed in greater detail. Concentrate on your area of weakness.

1. Omission or distortion due to slack articulation

a. When *l* is followed by another consonant, the tendency is to omit it, as in [twɛv] for *twelve,* or to substitute [ə], as in [mɪək] for *milk.* In some instance it is distorted to something like a partial dark [l] sound in which only the back of the tongue rises, with no front gum-ridge placement, making it sound like [jə]; thus *billion* [bɪljən] becomes [bɪjən].

Say each word carefully and correctly.

gold	civilian
self	already
William	

b. [l] can also be omitted from the ends of words. *Football* is [fʊtbɔl], not [fʊtbɔ].

Say each word, pronouncing final [l] clearly.

| all | call |
| well | fall |

The critical thing to realize is that wherever [l] comes in a word, there must be a firm tongue-tip contact with the gum ridge.

Practice raising the tongue on every [l] sound in the following phrases:

all little lollipops
a lively, lilting lullaby
twelve awful film clips
William told Wilma hello

Warm-up phrases for practice: all were welcome, spill our milk, all right to help, almost a million, a little too tall, settle it all, feel cold, a metal railroad car, all ready to dial

2. A sound resembling [w] **for** [l]   Quite a number of young children have difficulty with [l], typically substituting the glide [w] or [j]. If they *like* you, they either "wike" you or "yike" you. By adulthood, however, this pattern is seldom heard, but some people still make a distortion of the sound, halfway between [l] and [w]. It is particularly noticeable on the *pl* and *bl* blends, as in *plate* and *black.*

The important thing to remember here is that [l] is entirely a product of tongue activity. The lips should be back out of the way, not puckering in as they do for [w]. Look in the mirror and check your lip movements on words beginning with [l], such as *love, like,* and *leave* (see the word lists toward the beginning of this section). Then practice the [l] blend words in the same list in the same way. On these, it will help to have your tongue already up to produce [l] before you say the consonant that precedes it. Listen for a clear, strong sound.

Warm-up phrases for practice: let me play, black and blue, plenty of leeway, a clever plan, plant flowers, glance over the plot, please don't lay blame, slippery black eels, a plausible slip

☆ **3.** [r] **for** [l] **and vice versa**   Speakers of Oriental languages with this problem will do best to start to clarify the confusion among the sounds by learning to produce a good strong [l] before tackling [r]. Review the correct production suggestions at the beginning of this section, watching in a mirror with the jaw dropped to see the tongue lifting to a *firm contact* with the gum ridge. Here are additional [l] words to practice on:

lame	cooling	cool
lick	ceiling	sale
light	alive	pill
load	college	will
loose	allow	full
lot	falling	ball

Contrast the feel of the firm contact of the tongue tip with the gum ridge on [l] with production of [r]. For this sound, the tongue is pulled back *behind* and *not touching* the gum ridge while the center of the tongue tenses. An American model for ear training in hearing the difference is important. You will probably wish to review the comments on correct [r] production and the word lists and exercises in that section.

Finally, contrast the difference in tongue position, sound, and meaning in the following pairs:

limb	rim	alive	arrive	fall	far
light	right	belong	be wrong	tall	tar
lead	read	elect	erect	peel	peer
blue	brew	play	pray	fly	fry
bloom	broom	cloud	crowd	bleed	breed
flame	frame	blink	brink		

Here are some words that contain both sounds and will be a real challenge to pronounce:

terrible	calendar	letter
sailor	already	library
pearls	relief	relish

Warm-up phrases for practice: a red light, like to read, love to write, a terrible lunch, a lonely ride, a ready laugh, a little room, a large wreck, look around, a ripe lemon

ADDING ON FOR PROFICIENCY

1. Say the following phrases 3 times, building up speed, but not at the expense of accuracy.

   a. lemon liniment
   b. yellow lilies
   c. colder older milk
   d. clanging jangling bells
   e. pleasantly plausible plan

2. Say the following sentences carefully and correctly.

   a. William did not like being a total failure.
   b. The cold spell lingered all week long.
   c. The older child was unfortunately a little wild.
   d. The metal bolts on the boat floor had come loose.
   e. The audition sign read: "Call for tall men only."
   f. Literally millions and millions of flowers grow all over southerly hillsides.
   g. Lily mailed her last application to college a little too late.
   h. Lou failed in all kinds of valuable ploys to become a millionaire.
   i. Baseball, football, basketball, and golf are all popular sports on television.
   j. All public schools will be closed on national holidays.

☆ 3. *For nonnative speakers*   Read these sentences aloud. Sentences *a* through *f* concentrate on [l]; sentences *g* through *l*, contrast [l] and [r].

   a. Helen liked all her classes in college.
   b. Leo longs for mail from home.

c. Is it likely that you will all fail at least one exam?
d. They all laughed a lot at the television show *I Love Lucy.*
e. Football is always played on a large playing field.
f. Lily liked the light taste of lemon or lime in her tea.
g. A child should learn very early to follow the rules.
h. July fourth is a legal holiday all over America.
i. Children usually learn to read in the first grade.
j. Oriental rugs last a long time.
k. Ross listened to a violin solo on the radio.
l. The Statue of Liberty is a real national landmark.

SUPER EXERCISES

☆ 1. *Using* [l] *in conversation speech*   Create a sentence for each of the following words and phrases and say it at a conversational rate.

something valuable	living room
I like . . .	"Live and let live"
mail	liberty
Los Angeles	elevators
elections	I love . . .
college classes	Abraham Lincoln

2. *A Something's Wrong Story*   After reading the story, discuss all the errors you can find.

Lila was getting dressed for her blind date with Alan. They had gone together since high school, and tonight they were going to his formal sorority ball. Lila got into her long silk gown and carefully unzipped it all the way to the floor. She put curlers in her hair and brushed it until it shone. Then she put on her makeup, using the special new lipstick that matched her blue eyes. She was ready! She stepped out of the ball gown, took the elevator across to the other side of the dorm, and crossed her legs for good luck as she walked to the door to greet Alan. Everyone commented on what a lovely couple they made. "And you know," said someone, "you not only make a terrific pair, but you really look almost like sisters."

3. *Finish the scene*   Cast two people as the credit department clerk and the lady who has come to return a lamp. Have the class decide how to finish the scene.

Lemons I Have Known

SCENE: Department store credit counter.

LADY: I'd like to return this lamp.
CLERK: Certainly. Sales slip, please?
LADY: I lost it. But I bought it here last month, and I'd like my money back.
CLERK: Why are you returning the lamp?
LADY: I just don't like it, that's all.

CLERK: Let me see the lamp, please. (holds it) But lady, look, the wiring's all loose.

LADY: That's not my fault. You sold me a lemon.

CLERK: And the lamp base is cracked!

LADY: That's not my fault either. That lamp's a real lemon. (raising her voice) Look, I'd like my money back, and *I will not leave this place until I get it!*

CLERK: Lady, you're accusing us of selling a lemon and you don't even have the sales slip?

LADY: (beginning to shout) I'll call the manager. I'll complain to the president!

CLERK: (trying to calm her) Hold it, hold it. I'll see what I can do. (looks carefully at the lamp again) Uh-oh. Look there. That's not even our store label on this lamp! . . .

[j]

fonɛtɪk trɪviə

Which of these traits would you prefer *not* to have?

[ə sɛns əv hjumɚ, bjuti, mjuzɪkəl əbɪlɪti, ə hjudʒ weɪstlaɪn, ə tʌtʃ əv dʒinjəs, ə juθfəl aʊtlʊk]

Almost no one has difficulty producing [j], although some speakers may carelessly omit it or add it, and certain nonnative speakers substitute [dʒ] in its place.

FACTS

Technical description: [j] is a palatal glide that is voiced.

Correct production: With the tip of the tongue behind the lower front teeth, the front of the tongue is raised up toward the hard palate, much as if it were producing the vowel [i] as in *see* [si]. The tongue glides quickly from there to the position of the vowel that follows, however. The lips are usually in the position of the vowel that follows also.

☆ *Spellings:* [j] only occurs before a vowel and thus never falls at the end of a word. At the beginning of a word it is spelled *y* as in *year* and *u* as part of the diphthong [ju] in words like *unite*. When it starts a later syllable in a word, its spellings may vary, but it is most often *i* as in *union*.

IN USE

*Y*esterday, as *u*sual, we revie*w*ed the money we had *u*sed this *y*ear that was be*y*ond our budget.

Say the words on each list.

young	huge	amuse
you	humor	senior

your	humility	junior
yours	hue	genius
yellow	humidity	million
youth	Hugh	beauty
yoke	humid	cupid
yen	Houston	cube
yearn	human	fuel
yet	humane	onion
yearly		familiar
yield		commune

☆ SOME NOTES ABOUT [j]

Nonnative speakers sometimes ask, "How do I know when to say [u] and when to add [j] to make it [ju]?" Most Americans "just know" because they are familiar with the language, and this familiarity will come with experience. However, for those of you who feel more comfortable with rules, we can state these:

1. Generally, if the spelling is *oo,* as in *soon, too,* or *mood,* this represents the simple vowel [u].
2. The spelling *eu, ew,* or *u* at the beginning of a word is pronounced [ju], as in *Europe, few,* and *union.*
3. Usually after *h, p, b, m, k,* or *v* the spelling *u, eu, ew, ue,* or *iew* is pronounced [ju], as in *humor* [hjumɚ], *pure* [pjuɚ], *music* [mjuzɪk], *fuel* [fjuəl], and *view* [vju].

Note the correct pronunciation of each word as you say it.

[u]	[ju]	[u]	[ju]
food	fuel	cool	cue
moon	mule	poor	pew
hoot	hue	booze	abuse

4. If *t, d,* or *n* precedes the spellings given in point 3, the speaker has the option of using either [u] or [ju]. The latter is used mostly in formal speaking styles. Such a speaker might say [nju jɔɚk] for *New York* [nu jɔɚk]. Let you ear be your guide to usage in your area.

Here are some words that can be pronounced with either [u] or [ju]:

duplex	news	attitude
duly	nude	Tuesday

PROBLEMS TO AVOID

1. Some speakers may carelessly omit it in certain contexts, so that *opinion* [opɪnjən] becomes "opinuhn" [opɪnən].
2. Others may add an intrusive [j] before a vowel so that *I am* [aɪ æm] becomes *I yam* [aɪ jæm].

☆ **3.** Certain nonnative speakers substitute [dʒ] for [j] so that *job* [dʒɑb] becomes "yob" [jɑb].

Each problem is analyzed in greater detail. Concentrate on your area of weakness. Awareness is the key to conquering problems with [j].

1. Omission of [j]   If [j] occurs right after [l] or [n], some speakers may tend to omit it.[18]
Say each of these words carefully, being sure to include [j].

companion	onion
regulation	junior
billion	rebellion

Warm-up phrases for practice: senior citizens, the Dominion of Canada, a strong opinion, battalion of soldiers, music pavilion, Daniel Boone, take communion, a yapping spaniel

2. Addition of intrusive [j]   If a syllable ends in either [i] as in *see* or [ɪ] in the diphthong [aɪ] as in *buy,* [ɔɪ] as in *toy,* or [eɪ] as in *play,* and the next word begins with a vowel, careless articulation will allow the tongue to glide from the one to the other, rather than making a separation between. Thus *see any* becomes "see yany" and *my ankle* becomes "my yankle."

Say each phrase without intrusive [j].

we are	be angry
may own	my opinion
see it	

Warm-up phrases for practice: be above it, why are we?, play alone, I am here, lie outside, my attitude, sigh aloud, toy airplane, joy of cooking

☆ **3. [dʒ] for** [j]   Some nonnative speakers may say [dʒɛs] for *yes* [jɛs] or [dʒʌŋ] for *young* [jʌŋ].
One of the things that will help most is to *feel* how very differently these two sounds are produced as you *listen* for the difference in sound. [dʒ] starts with the firm contact of the tip of the tongue against the gum ridge, whereas [j] never makes any tongue contact as the blade rises toward, but *does not touch,* the palate.
Contrast the difference in tongue contact, sound, and meaning in these word pairs:

jet	yet	Jell-O	yellow
jot	yacht	joke	yoke
jarred	yard	jam	yam

Read the word lists under "In Use" for further practice.
Warm-up phrases for practice: (Use care, because both sounds occur in each

---

[18] In this phonetic context, however, the more common omission is the [l].

phrase.) his usual jokes, journey to Europe, yield gently, a young marriage, not just yet, do a yard job, his junior year, just yesterday, a Jewish youth

ADDING ON FOR PROFICIENCY

1. Say the following sentences carefully and correctly.

   a. Do you appreciate the joy of pure music?
   b. On your diet, you may eat the egg whites, but not the yellow yolks.
   c. "In my opinion," Daniel said, "Yale University has one of the most beautiful campuses in the United States."
   d. William is young, opinionated, and devoid of humor.
   e. Their civilian companions were familiar with army regulations.
   f. A few of the juniors and seniors refused to use the usual student parking.

☆ 2. *For nonnative speakers* Read these sentences aloud. The first six concentrate on [j]; the remainder contrast [j] and [dʒ].

   a. The school year has not yet ended.
   b. Do you appreciate being told you are too young?
   c. What do you use to cure your usual winter colds?
   d. Some navy uniforms are really beautiful.
   e. Use pure water when you make ice cubes.
   f. The professor said, "Leave your books and your notes in your cubicles."
   g. When did New York join the Union?
   h. She has yet to join the jet set.
   i. Do you review your notes just before you take a general exam?
   j. The class held its usual reunion in June.
   k. In future years, you will have a full-time job of your own choosing.
   l. By your junior year you must choose a major.

SUPER EXERCISES

☆ 1. *Using* [j] *in conversational speech* Create a sentence for each of the following words and phrases and say it at a conversational rate.

   "Yes" means . . .   You should . . .
   a European vacation   United States
   I used to . . .   future plans
   New York City   music
   museums   beauty

2. *Commercial* Read the following aloud at the rate at which it would be presented on radio or television.

   Young Always!

   Women, they say mirrors don't lie, but do you wish yours sometimes did?
   Are you losing your youth?
   Have the years abused your face?
   Has Cupid abandoned you forever?

Cheer up! You are not beyond help! Young Always, a unique beauty cream formula, originally used by the Three Muses and discovered in a European museum tomb site, will come to your rescue!

Young Always is guaranteed to take three years off your face for every month's use, so use it sparingly after the first year. Be the first in your geriatric center to be refused a drink at a bar!

Ask for Young Always, your secret formula to a new you!

CHECKPOINT EXERCISES

Glides

Demonstrating control of the glides   Listen to your production of the glide sounds as you interpret at least two of the following selections. Record them for playback. Mark any glides that you produce incorrectly *while you are reading,* and use the recording to check your self-judgments. Note any errors you still make on the table that follows the selections.

Brighter than the blossom
   On the rose's bough
Sits the wizened orange,
   Bitter berry now.

   EDNA ST. VINCENT MILLAY

I recently read that the preamble to the Declaration of Independence contains 300 words. The Ten Commandments has 297. The Gettysburg Address comes in at 267, while the Lord's Prayer has less than 100.

However, a recent report from the Federal Government on the pricing of cabbages allegedly contains 26,911 words. I will confine my remarks to something between the Lord's Prayer and the pricing of cabbages.

   CHARLES L. GOULD

Ploffskin, Pluffskin, Pelican jee!
We think no birds as happy as we!
Plumpskin, Ploshkin, Pelican jill!
We think so then, and we thought so still.

   EDWARD LEAR

On, on, on, over the countless miles of angry space roll the long heaving billows. . . . Pursuit and flight, and mad return of wave on wave, and savage struggle, ending in a spouting wave of foam that whitens the black night. . . . On, on, on they roll, and darker grows the night, and louder howls the wind, and more clamorous and fierce become the million voices in the sea, when the wild cry goes forth upon the storm, "A ship!"

   CHARLES DICKENS, *Martin Chuzzlewit*

I lingered round them, under that benign sky: watched the moths fluttering among the heath and harebells; listened to the soft wind breathing through the grass; and wondered how anyone could ever imagine unquiet slumbers for the sleepers in that quiet earth.

   EMILY BRONTË, *Wuthering Heights*

Substitutions, additions, distortions, and omissions still needing work:

[w] and [hw] _____

[r] _____

[l] _____

[j] _____

THE NASALS

Only three sounds in English are produced by purposely directing air through the nose: [m], [n], and [ŋ]. The soft palate is lowered and the oral cavity is blocked off—at the lips for [m], the gum ridge for [n], and the soft palate for [ŋ]. The point of blockage of the oral cavity for use as a resonator determines the unique characteristics of each sound. It is particularly important for nonnative speakers to learn these three exact points of articulation; otherwise they may erroneously nasalize the vowels preceding *m, n,* and *ng* and omit the consonants entirely.

The nasal sounds, when correctly produced, are particularly pleasing and add carrying power and depth to a person's speech. Good speakers make sure they give each nasal sound full value wherever it occurs in a word, and if it comes at the end of a syllable, they may sustain it just slightly longer than the other sounds to give a musical quality to their speech.

We are not talking about being overly theatrical! However, try reading these sentences as written—first with a slight elongation of each of the nasals and the second time without.

1. The grummm-bling of the thunnn-der was becominnng more insistennn-t.
2. The grumbling of the thunder was becoming more insistent.

Which had better resonance?

SUGGESTION FOR ALL THE NASALS

Since all three nasals should be given their full value wherever they occur in a word, and people carelessly tend to cut them too short, everyone should study the listings of common overassimilations and do some of the Proficiency Exercises and Super Exercises for [m], [n], and [ŋ]. Concentrate on careful articulation and resonant sound.

[m]
_____

fonɛtɪk trɪviə

All these characters are legendary, but only one actually lived. Which?

[mɪki maʊs, mʌðɚ gus, supɚmæn, mɪni maʊs, mærɪlɪn mənroʊ, lɪtl̩ mɪs mʌfɪt]

Read these sentences exactly as written.

1. He clai*n*ed, "I'*n* never wrong about so*n*ething like that."
2. He clai*m*ed: "I'*m* never wrong about so*m*ething like that."

Unless a person has a nasal obstruction of some sort, [m] is universally an easy sound and among the first any child learns. However, if carelessly articulated, it can be cut too short, lose its identity, or be replaced by another nasal sound.

FACTS

Technical description: [m] is a bilabial nasal that is voiced.
Correct production: With the soft palate lowered and the air blocked from exiting through the oral cavity at the two lips, the vibrating air is forced up through the nasal passages, creating a resonant humming sound. Be sure that the lips are *lightly* but *firmly* brought together.
☆ *Spellings:* As is, or doubled as in *summer.* It is sometimes preceded or followed by a silent letter, as in *phlegm, limb, balm,* or *condemn.*

IN USE

*M*ary was beco*m*ing cal*m*er now that the su*mm*er *m*onths were co*m*ing and the school ter*m* was al*m*ost over.

Make sure you have a light but firm lip closure on the words on each list.

man	empty	seem
moon	remark	room
meek	permit	gleam
mean	simple	aim
me	complain	same
meal	terminal	blame
month	human	dream
middle	omit	climb
milk	remedy	form
mist	humor	alarm
mail	cement	slam
made	remove	column
mend	almost	autumn
map	umbrella	stem
most	combine	comb
my	complete	plum
make	cream	hum

NOTES ON ASSIMILATION

Most of the problems with [m] have to do with overassimilation, moving its point of articulation to that of the consonant following. This may be easier, but it is considered nonstandard. Awareness is the key.

1. **[n] for** [m]   If a consonant that is produced in the vicinity of the gum ridge, such as *t, d, l, n,* or *s,* follows [m], [n], also made at the gum ridge, is substituted, as in "I'n talking" for *I'm talking.*

Take care that you make a firm and complete lip closure for [m] on words or phrases like the following:

[mt]	[md]		[ml]
timetable	same day	claimed	seem lazy
seem tired	I'm doing	screamed	firm losses
prime time	some dinners	exclaimed	chrome lamps

[mn]	[ms]	[mθ]	[mʃ]
some nights	themselves	something	I'm sharing
I'm not	I'm sorry	bomb threat	some sugar
home number	clumsy	I'm thirsty	come shopping

2. **[ŋ] for [m]**   If [m] is followed by [k] or [g], both of which are made with the back of the tongue against the velum, there is a natural tendency to produce the velar nasal [ŋ] instead. The phrase *I'm cooking* should not be "I'ng cooking" [aɪŋ kʊkɪŋ].

Listen for clear [m] in phrases like these:

I'm going	home cooking	same cover	let him go
I'm giving	room cleaning	seem crazy	blame Karen

3. **[m] distortion**   If [f] or [v] follows [m], the latter may be made with the lower lip against the upper teeth rather than with both lips, resulting in a distorted nasal sound. Be sure there is complete closure of the lips on [m] in words and phrases like these:

comfortable	come first	warm fire	camphor
I'm feeling	climb fast	some votes	numb feet
I'm finding	room full	come forth	I'm fascinated

PROBLEMS TO AVOID

There are only two fairly consistent errors with [m]:

1. Substitution of something resembling [b] for [m] so that *more* [mɔr] sounds like *bore* [bɔr].

☆ **2.** Omission of [m], with nasalization of the vowel that precedes it instead.

Each problem is analyzed in greater detail. Concentrate on your area of weakness.

1. **[b] for [m]**   If the vibrating air is not or cannot be directed through the nose with enough force to provide adequate nasal resonance, the orally produced sound [b], made at the same point of articulation, will be approximated instead. Thus *meet* sounds rather like *beet* and *my* seems closer to *by*. If the problem is not temporary, due to a cold or an allergy, such substitutions are really a *denasality* problem. Refer to the discussion of correcting for denasality in Chapter 6.

☆ **2. Omission of [m] and nasalization of the vowel preceding it**   Some languages feature nasalized vowels, but not English! When a vowel or a diphthong is followed by [m] as in *sometime,* the [m] has *no effect* on the vowel. Thus *sometime* is [sʌmtaɪm], not [sʌtãɪ], and *impossible* is [ɪmpɑsɪbl̩], not [ĩpɑsɪbl̩].

Listen for unnasalized vowels and clear [m] in the following words and phrases.

I'm going	aimed to	company	important	seems so
I'm happy	someone	sometime	employ	same time

Say the words listed in the second and third columns under "In Use," carefully monitoring your production of each.

Warm-up phrases for practice: combing her hair, coming home, climbing stairs, blaming himself, aim to do it themselves, a number of things, remember the time, room for them

ADDING ON FOR PROFICIENCY

1. Try to achieve a very resonant tone on the following phrases. Exaggerate each italicized *m* the first time through, holding for a count of 2. The second time repeat normally, with just the slightest prolongation on each [m].

   a. a pri*m*e exa*m*ple
   b. an e*m*pty ho*m*e
   c. a me*m*orable drea*m*
   d. cli*m*bed from the botto*m*
   e. reme*m*bered autu*m*ns
   f. drea*m*s of an e*m*pire

2. Make sure every [m] is given its full value in the following sentences.

   a. Mae's home was a simple one, but it was becomingly decorated and had a welcoming atmosphere.
   b. Many small museums make much of seemingly musty-looking, un-memorable material.
   c. Mighty Man Mountain was the name of a wrestler with enormously powerful arms and a massive chest.
   d. My aim is to be both slim and trim, but achieving that is by no means simple!
   e. The teammates grumbled as they stumbled and tumbled in the mud of the swamped stadium.
   f. The more Mark remembered of the night before, the more Mark became ashamed.
   g. "You must remember me," the man prompted the unsmiling woman. "You complimented me on my sense of humor when we met last month."
   h. Making mistakes is human, and to make the mistake of claiming to make no mistakes is immature.
   i. "Perform a miracle of miracles?" the magician responded. "Simple. I'm going to make a monkey that you can't see become a camel that you can."
   j. The committee members were mindlessly bored as the mayor monoto-

nously rambled on about improvements in the maintenance of municipal machinery.

☆ 3. *For nonnative speakers*   Say each sentence, monitoring for clear [m]. Do not nasalize any vowel that precedes [m].

a. "I'm going home," Pam informed some of her friends.
b. The alarm went off, but there was no bomb.
c. The dorm room was empty.
d. They were jumping and climbing in the gym.
e. Autumn comes after summer.
f. Sometimes, simple problems take time to solve.
g. The math assignment seems impossible.
h. A comedy team is on the list of coming attractions.
i. He will do something nice for his roommate some other time.

SUPER EXERCISES

☆ 1. *Using* [m] *in conversational speech*   Make up a sentence for each of the following words and phrases and say it aloud at a conversational rate.

family	My home . . .
names	My room . . .
December	a sense of humor
dreams	women
Many movies . . .	games

2. *Finish the scene*   Cast two people as Maurie and his wife Marie and have them read this dialogue. The class must decide how it should end.

Communication

SCENE: Dinner table. Maurie is reading the sports pages of a newspaper while Marie is trying to have a conversation over dessert.

MARIE: Maurie?
MAURIE: Mmm?
MARIE: Maurie, remember what today is?
MAURIE: Mmm?
MARIE: Come *on*. Do you?
MAURIE: Mm-*mm*.
MARIE: *Talk to me*. Remember what today is?
MAURIE: Mmm?
MARIE: Monday, May 6th. Must I remind you?
MAURIE: Mm-*mm*.
MARIE: Remember what day we were married?
MAURIE: Mmmmm . . .
MARIE: (imitating him, but petulantly) *Mmmmmmmm?* That's all I hear, *mmmmmmmmm*.
MAURIE: (looks up from paper) Marie, whatever is the matter with you?

Why are you making that ridiculous sound? If you have something to say to me, *say* it. . . .

[n]

fonɛtɪk trɪvɪə

Which one of these is a *verb?*

[nɛsəsɛri, naɪt, neɪʃən, noʊbḷ, nɔti, noʊ, hʌni.
hɪnt: ɪf ju hæv lɝnd sʌmθɪŋ, ju _____ ɪt.

Say the following sentences exactly as written.

1. We i*ng*quired if we should u*m*pack the sa*m*wiches.
2. We i*n*quired if we should u*n*pack the sa*n*dwiches.

Like [m], [n] tends to lose its identity in careless articulation or take on the articulatory position of the sound that follows it. This should be avoided, as [n] is another sound that adds resonance to speech and should be given full value.

FACTS

Technical description: [n] is a tongue-tip alveolar ridge nasal that is voiced.
Correct production: With the velum lowered and the jaw slightly dropped, the tongue tip is in contact with the gum ridge, and the vibrating air is resonated in the area behind the lifted tongue and in the nose. Make sure that the tongue does not slip down to contact the teeth, thus dentalizing the sound.
☆ *Spellings:* As is, or doubled as in *funny.* Also *gn* as in *gnaw, kn* as in *kn*it, and *pn* as in *pn*eumonia.
Syllabic note: Final [n] can form a syllable without a vowel between it and the consonant that precedes it. After *t, d, s,* and *z* there is usually no break, and [n] becomes syllabic. Examples: satin [sætṇ], sudden [sʌdṇ], listen [lɪsṇ], reason [rizṇ].

IN USE

Because of i*n*flation, pe*nn*y ca*n*dy ca*nn*ot be bought for eve*n* a *n*ickel.

Say the words on each list, being sure to give [n] full value.

knee	intend	soon
nose	income	can
nice	inner	plan
never	money	run
night	many	win
news	any	done
know	inquire	fine
knew	answer	line

number	unfair	sign
knife	unfasten	brown
needle	candy	gone
necessary	dinner	begin
nation	fence	ten
name	vanish	then
now	kindly	turn
neighbor	standing	seen

NOTES ON ASSIMILATION

[n] is an easy sound to produce, but like [m], it is prone to nonstandard assimilations in carelessly articulated speech. Because it is easier to produce a nasal sound at the point of articulation of the sound that follows, one should check careful articulation of it. The tongue tip should be firmly in contact with the gum ridge in all the sample words or phrases that follow.

1. *Substitution of* [m] *for* [n] *if followed by* [p] *or* [b]. It is *unbelievable,* not *umbelievable.* Listen for clear [n] in these words and phrases.

unbuckle	unbend	government	It can be . . .
earn money	inbred	unprofessional	He can pay . . .
unpaid	inmate	unpredictable	When buying . . .

2. *Substitution of* [ŋ] *for* [n] *if followed by* [k] *or* [g]. It is *income,* not *ing-come.* Avoid this when saying the following words.

concrete	incorrect	enclose	uncomfortable	inconceivable
increase	incomplete	include	inclined	inconclusive

3. *Distortion of* [n]. If [f] or [v] follows [n], a nasal sound may be attempted using the position of these consonants (upper teeth against lower lip). Keep [n] clear when you say these words.

involve	confess	convince	unfriendly	invest	confuse
inflate	confide	invent	unfortunate	unfair	unfasten

If [s], [ʃ], [j], or [r] follows [n], the nasal sound may be attempted with the blade of the tongue rather than the tip. Listen for clear [n] in the following words.

insect	mention	insurance	incident	onion	unreliable
conscious	sunshine	consider	construct	union	unrelated

PROBLEMS TO AVOID

There are only two fairly consistent errors with the [n]:

1. Substitution of something resembling [d] for [n] so that *knock* [nɑk] sounds like *dock* [dɑk].

☆ **2.** Omission of [n], with nasalization of the vowel that precedes it instead.

Each problem is analyzed in greater detail. Concentrate on your area of weakness.

1. [d] **for** [n]   If the vibrating air is not or cannot be directed through the nose with enough force to provide adequate nasal resonance, the orally produced sound [d], made at the same point of articulation, will be approximated instead. Thus *need* sounds like *deed* and *nose* like *doze*. If the problem is not a temporary one due to a cold or an allergy, such substitutions are really a *denasality* problem. Refer to the discussion of correcting for denasality in Chapter 6.

☆ **2. Omission of** [n] **and nasalization of the vowel preceding it**   This is a fairly common tendency among some nonnative speakers when [n] is preceded by a vowel. Remember that English has no nasalized vowels. The word *invite* is pronounced [ɪnvaɪt], not [ĩvaɪt].

Listen for a clear oral vowel followed by a clear [n] in the following words.

telephone	unreal	unfriendly	unfair	bonfire	can be
untold	onion	insane	invent	branch	can go

Now monitor your articulation of medial and final [n] in the words listed under "In Use."

Warm-up phrases for practice: can't go, when ready, won't do it, his own things, plan again, around nine, in the end, done then, open in on

ADDING ON FOR PROFICIENCY

1. In the following phrases, without sounding overly theatrical, capitalize on the beauty of final [n] in a syllable by holding each one very slightly longer then the rest of the sounds.

   a. inte*n*d to cha*n*ge ha*n*ds
   b. begi*n* to da*n*ce agai*n*
   c. needs huma*n* co*n*tact soo*n*
   d. a lo*n*ely moo*n*lit night
   e. gentleme*n*, take o*n*e step dow*n*
   f. a fi*n*e, golde*n* mor*n*ing

2. Give every [n] its full value in the following sentences.

   a. Every night, the grandmother insisted on dining by candlelight at seven like a grand lady.
   b. In a barn dance, the participants spin around the room in a never-ending marathon.
   c. For lunch, Nan served ground sirloin with onions, plain noodles, and green beans with almonds.
   d. Norm phoned his friend to find out when the French paper was to be handed in to the instructor.
   e. In case of any new nasal infection, Nat was to go to the infirmary for treatment between nine and noon.
   f. "Never say 'never,' say 'probably not in the near conceivable future,'" Ann's thesis adviser instructed.
   g. Nina was the name of the friendly 19-year-old lion who mainly napped in the sun in front of her cage.

h. Aunt Nancy's niece and nephew were known far and near as nuisances and neighborhood menaces.

i. The accident was not merely a fender bender; neither the new Honda nor the nine-year-old Pinto would ever burn up the highways again.

j. Ogden Nash wrote the funny and ingenious line "Candy is dandy, but liquor is quicker."

☆ 3. *For nonnative speakers*   Read these sentences aloud, articulating [n] clearly. Do not nasalize the vowel that precedes [n].

a. "Don't burn your bridges behind you" is a well-known guideline for living.

b. Norman was instructed about the change in plans.

c. *In* and *on* have different meanings in English.

d. "In eleven minutes the test must be finished," the instructor announced.

e. The student center is connected to the science building.

f. Manny was absent from class again and again.

g. He was involved in the beginning and the ending of the student unrest.

h. Eleven and seven add up to eighteen.

i. When does the winter vacation begin?

j. The quotation "In the beginning was the Word" can be found in the New Testament of the Christian Bible.

SUPER EXERCISES

☆ 1. *Using* [n] *in conversation speech*   Make up sentences for each of the words and phrases below and say them aloud.

entrance examinations	I plan . . .
airplane flights	I want . . .
the month of June	Disneyland
candy	France
dancing	men

2. *Role-plays*   Let several sets of students take the roles in the following situations.

Noodles, Anyone?

CAST: 1 boss; 1 waiter/waitress; 3 customers who come in one by one

SITUATION: The boss of Nan's Luncheonette has just announced that the waiter/waitress will be fired unless he/she really starts pushing the daily specials. Today's special is *Nan's "sirloin of tuna and noodles."* "Stand up there and sell!" exhorts the boss.

Customer 1 has just awoken and wants pancakes.

Customer 2 has an ulcer and wants something bland.

Customer 3 is fantasizing about a thick pastrami sandwich.

RESOLUTION: Up to each individual customer. The waiter/waitress should try to repeat the special's name three times in each sales pitch.

Knock Knock

CAST: 1 door-to-door encyclopedia sales representative; 3 potential customers

SITUATION: The sales rep is dependent on the commissions from *Warner's Ninth Encyclopedia of All Known Knowledge* to pay college tuition bills. He/she knocks on three doors in turn.
Behind the first door is a harried housewife with three small children.
Behind the second door is a hard-of-hearing grandfather.
Behind the third door is a teenager who doesn't want to miss a soap opera.

RESOLUTION: Up to each potential customer. The sales rep should try to repeat the product name at least three times to each.

I'm the Perfect Candidate

CAST: 1 interviewer for Noonan's Sign Painters; 3 interviewees

SITUATION: There is a job opening in Noonan's public relations department.

Interviewee 1 is Norman/Norma Boone, who has just completed a communications major in college but has no experience.

Interviewee 2 is Ned/Natalie Bryan, who has worked in the accounting department at Noonan's for 20 years and wants to be promoted from within but has no experience in p.r.

Interviewee 3 is Nick/Naomi Sands, who is a very glib talker and lies about public relations experience with other firms; his/her only experience is selling pans at flea markets.

RESOLUTION: Up to the interviewer. Among questions asked of candidates, these should be included:

1. Why do you want to work at Noonan's?
2. What do you know about Noonan's?
3. What do you personally have to offer Noonan's?

[ŋ]

_____

fonɛtık trɪviə

Which takes physical effort?

[rʌnɪŋ, dʒʌmpɪŋ, slipɪŋ, ɛksɚˑsaɪzɪŋ, boulɪŋ, ridɪŋ, skɪpɪŋ, rɛstɪŋ]

_____

Say the following sentences exactly as written.

1. I'm thinki*n'* at le*n*th that I'm usi*n'* all my stre*n*th sitti*n'* idly by.
2. I'm thinki*ng* at le*ng*th that I'm usi*ng* all my stre*ng*th sitti*ng* idly by.

[ŋ] is a sound that masquerades all too often in the guise of another sound, [n]. It occurs only in the middle or at the end of words in English, and when given full value, it adds beauty and carrying power to speech.

FACTS

Technical description: [ŋ] is a velar nasal that is voiced.

Correct production: Vibrating air is prevented from entering the oral cavity by the firm contact of the back of the tongue with the lowered velum. The air is resonated in the nasal cavities.

☆ *Spellings:* ng as in *ring*, n as in *ink*, and *ngue* as in to*ngue.*

Assimilation note: In root words such as *ink*, spelled with an *n* but pronounced with [ŋ], assimilation has become the rule: When an *n* is followed by [k], the easier transference of the [n] back to the velar nasal is accepted pronunciation. *Examples:* bank [bæŋk], think [θɪŋk]. However, if the *n* is in a prefix followed by [k], as in *income,* such assimilation is *not* acceptable.

IN USE

A spri*ng* garden requires constant planti*ng,* sowi*ng,* weedi*ng,* and mulchi*ng.*

Be aware of your production of [ŋ] in the words in each column.

swing	swinging	trying	link
ring	ringing	carrying	think
long	longing	staying	thank
rang	gonging	doing	drink
gong	wronging	trading	bank
strong	clanging	sitting	bunk
wrong	banging	standing	wink
evening	clinging	running	flunk
young	singing	pointing	pink
sing	bringing	seeing	rank
song	springing	agreeing	trunk
string	stringing	looking	junk

PROBLEMS TO AVOID

1. Substitution of [n] for [ŋ] so that *going* [goʊɪŋ] becomes "goin" [goʊɪn].
2. Substitution of something like [g] for [ŋ] so that *long* [lɔŋ] sounds something like *log* [lɔg].
3. Addition of an extra [k] for [g] after [ŋ] when not indicated so that *Long Island* [lɔŋ aɪlənd] sounds something like "Long Guyland" [lɔŋ gaɪlənd].

☆ 4. Omission of [ŋ], with nasalization of the vowel preceding it instead.

Each problem is analyzed in greater detail. Concentrate on your area of weakness.

1. [n] for [ŋ]   Many people refer to this substitution error (*doin'* for *doing*) as "dropping the *g,*" but this is not the case. Although the *spelling* of the phoneme [ŋ] uses two letters, *n* and *g,* it is a single nasal sound made by blocking the oral cavity through contact of the back of the tongue with the velum. Note this as you say *sing* and *thing.* Thus, when someone says *doin',* a different sound—the nasal sound made by blocking the oral cavity with the tongue at the gum ridge—is substituted.

This substitution does not occur in root words like *wing* or *sing* because such a substitution would alter meanings (to *win* and *sin*). Rather it occurs in the suffix ending *-ing,* which abounds in English expressions and in which meaning is not affected (*coming* or *comin'* signals the same thing).

This is a perfect example of overassimilation. Many more English sounds are made at the gum ridge than at the velum, so it is easier to move the nasal sound up to the point of articulation of the majority.

In very informal conversational settings, a speaker's "What's doin'?" or "Be seein' you" may give a sense of belonging to the group, but these same expressions, in a more formal setting, may call attention to the speaker and may draw the label "slack" or "careless." It is important to be in control of this for any given occasion, and several suggestions to this end follow.

a. Develop a clear sense of the difference in the points of articulation *and* sound between [n] and [ŋ] by contrasting word pairs such as these:

pan	pang	fan	fang	ban	bang
win	wing	thin	thing	gone	gong

b. Use negative practice. Contrast the same differences in articulatory position and sound in the wrong and right pronunciations of words:

speakin'	speaking	hearin'	hearing	passin'	passing
nothin'	nothing	readin'	reading	writin'	writing

c. The substitution error tends to occur in rapid connected speech. Practice on individual words may result in perfect production of [ŋ], but as soon as the speaker gets caught up in conversation, the easier pattern of *doin'* and *comin'* slips back in. To heighten awareness, each of the practice words below has been written incorrectly. Correct each word; then use the correct form in a short sentence you make up spontaneously. For example, *writin'.* You will correct it to *writing* and say something like "I don't have time to do much writing."

comin'	passin'	tryin'	eatin'	walkin'	playin'
goin'	leavin'	tellin'	thinkin'	askin'	findin'

2. [g] for [ŋ]   If *thing* sounds like *thig* and *spring* like *sprig* and you do not have a head cold or an allergy, you have the symptoms of *denasality,* and you are referred to the suggestions for improvement in Chapter 6.

3. Addition of [g] or [k] to [ŋ]   Pronouncing the [g] in *Long Island* is known as the [ŋ] *click.* People who speak with the [ŋ] click add [g] if the sound following is voiced and [k] if it is unvoiced. This is acceptable in certain foreign languages, and immigrants who spoke these languages applied the same technique to English. Other speakers may add the click in a mistaken attempt at being precise.

Keep in mind that in most cases in English, the spelling *ng* requires pure [ŋ], with no additions. This is the case in all words that end in *ng,* whether they are root words or ones to which an *-ing* suffix has been added. Here are a few examples:

| sting | gang | bang | trying | flying | drinking |
| strong | bring | string | riding | typing | washing |

It is also true in all root words to which *any* suffix is added.[19] Here are some examples:

| hanger | singer | kingly | springing | thronging |
| hanging | singing | clinging | ringing | belonging |

However, there are some few instances in English in which it is correct to add [g] or [k] after [ŋ], and a simple rule will help you identify most of these, all of which are in words of more than one syllable: If the second part of the word after the [ŋ] is removed and the root word remaining has no meaning, the sound is added.[20] For instance, *linger* has the added sound because the root word left, after the *-er* was removed, *ling,* has no meaning. *English* is another example, for *Eng* is meaningless by itself. Notice how this rule applies to the following words:

| jangle | anguish | jungle | jingle | distinguish |
| mingle | language | finger | extinguish | tingle |

Test yourself. In the following sentence, only one word requires the addition of [g]. Which? Say the sentence aloud.

> Coming into the room one fine spring morning, Joe's anger knew no bounds when he saw two men climbing out his window carrying his valuables.

(anger)

Here's a tip to help you avoid the addition error. Do not drop the back of the tongue until *after* the voiced sound has stopped. For instance, say *sing* slowly, and do not drop the back of the tongue until a count of 1 after phonation has stopped. This will build awareness. Apply the same self-monitoring as you add the *-ing* suffix to the following words:

| hang | bring | throng | prolong | sting |
| wing | ring | belong | sing | spring |

Warm-up phrases for practice: (Be careful, because there is an even stronger temptation to add the extra sound if a vowel comes right after [ŋ].) hanging around, going a long way, wrong again, a thing of beauty, string of beads, strong arms, gang of thugs, ring around the collar, spring ahead

☆ **4. Omission of [ŋ] and nasalization of the preceding vowel** In all [ŋ] words, be sure to have a firm contact between the back of the tongue and the velum, and

---

[19] Exceptions are the comparative forms of *young, strong,* and *long.*
[20] Exception: *gingham.*

make sure the vowel preceding [ŋ] is not nasalized. *Along* is pronounced [əlɔŋ], not [əlɔ̃].

Go back and practice all the words listed under "In Use" the same way.

Warm-up phrases for practice: bring it over, lending an ear, spring fever, king for a day, a long way, the wrong way, clang of the gong, string along, sing again

ADDING ON FOR PROFICIENCY

1. Sustain [ŋ] slightly longer than the other sounds for resonant effect as you say these phrases.

   a. singing a song
   b. yearning for the spring
   c. winding along the river
   d. long, long ago
   e. waging a raging battle
   f. the ringing and clanging of the bells

2. Read these sentences aloud, giving each [ŋ] full value, without ever substituting [n] for [ŋ] or adding the [ŋ] click.

   a. The length of the race track was sapping the strength of the runners, who were used to doing the 100-yard dash.
   b. Rather than staying at the party, becoming bored, and eating and drinking too much, Ralph was smart to leave.
   c. The mother was beginning the story: "Long, long ago, in a kingdom by a gleaming, glistening sea . . ."
   d. Long Island has clamming, fishing, windsurfing, sunbathing, yachting, bi-kini watching—and lengthy traffic jams!
   e. Amanda took forever getting ready—combing her hair, doing her nails, painting her eyebrows, powdering her nose, and generally admiring herself in the looking glass.
   f. No fighting, no biting, no hitting, no tickling, and no talking out of turn were the rules at the baby-sitting clinic.
   g. Nat was busying himself to keep from studying—rearranging his desk, restacking books, sharpening pencils, and doing anything that would avoid his having to look at the open English text.
   h. The police car's siren was whining and wailing, its red light was flashing, and Joe was worrying that he was going to be stopped along the roadside.
   i. Fred found that owning a long-haired mongrel was a tiring, never-ending chore of walking, feeding, brushing, and cleaning up messes.

   ☆ 3. *For nonnative speakers*   Say each sentence correctly, with clear [ŋ] and no nasalized vowels.

   a. Spring on campus brings out sun-seeking students.
   b. Drinking in college buildings is not permitted.
   c. In English, "I'll give you a ring" means "I'll be phoning you sometime soon."

    d. With summer coming, airline bookings to Europe are increasing.

    e. Is anything better than something, and is something better than nothing?

    f. Learning five new English words a day is a way of gaining a larger vocabulary.

    g. Thanksgiving is the day for eating too much, feeling too full, and liking it.

    h. After finishing college, are you going back to Hong Kong?

SUPER EXERCISES

1. *Using basic words with clear* -ing *endings*   Even if the sentence is long, how many of the following words can you put into one adding *-ing* to each? They need not be in order. Here is a possible start: "As I was coming home, feeling rotten and wishing . . ."

come	go	do	see	think	feel
feel	be	look	stay	find	wish

2. *Using* [ŋ] *in connected speech*   Let various pairs of students read the following dialogue, having decided among themselves what the particular situation is. Four suggestions are made at the end of the script; they may use these or ones of their own devising.

Nonsense Script

A: Why aren't you talking to me?
B: There's nothing to say.
A: Nothing?
B: Nothing.
A: What are you doing?
B: Nothing.
A: You must be doing something?
B: Not a thing.
A: You ought to be doing *something.*
B: I'm going to do something—later.

Situations

    a. A worried mother to her teenager in his room

    b. Two lovers talking on the phone

    c. Anxious father-to-be who has caught his wife's doctor in the hospital corridor

    d. Two high officials whose embezzlement scheme is about to come to light

CHECKPOINT EXERCISES

Nasals

Demonstrating pleasing resonance on the nasals   Listen to your production of the nasals as you interpret at least two of the following selections. Record for playback. *As you read,* mark any nasals that you did not give full value or that you produced incorrectly, and use the recording to check your self-judgments. Note any errors you still make on the table that follows the selections.

1. Five miles meandering with a mazy motion
       Through wood and dale the sacred river ran
   Then reached the caverns measureless to man
       And sank in tumult to a lifeless ocean.

   SAMUEL TAYLOR COLERIDGE, "Kubla Khan"

2. There was a rustling that seemed like a bustling
   Of merry crowds justling at pitching and hustling;
   Small feet were pattering, wooden shoes clattering,
   Little hands clapping and little tongues chattering,
   And, like fowls in a farm-yard where barley is scattering,
   Out came the children running.

   ROBERT BROWNING, "The Pied Piper of Hamelin"

3. Somebody must take a chance. The monkeys who did became men, and the monkeys who didn't are still jumping around in trees making faces at the monkeys who did.

   LINCOLN STEFFENS

4. Four ducks on a pond,
   A grass bank beyond,
   A blue sky of spring,
   White clouds on the wing;
   What a little thing
   To remember for years—
   To remember with tears.

   WILLIAM ALLINGHAM, "Four Ducks on a Pond"

5. Girls of fifteen are always laughing. They laugh when Mr. Binney helps himself to salt instead of sugar. They almost die of laughing when Old Mrs. Tomkins sits down upon the cat. But they are crying the moment after. They have no fixed abode from which they see that there is something eternally laughable in human nature, some quality in men and women that forever excites our satire. They do not know that Lady Greville who snubs, and poor Maria who is snubbed, are permanent features of every ballroom. But Jane Austen knew it from her birth upwards.

   VIRGINIA WOLF, *Jane Austen*

Substitutions, additions, distortions, and omissions still needing work

[m] _____

[n] _____

[ŋ] _____

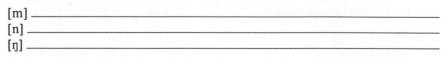

11

A GUIDE
FOR THE FOREIGN SPEAKER
OF AMERICAN ENGLISH

A great multitude, which no man could number,
of all nations, and kindreds, and people, and
tongues . . .

THE REVELATION OF ST. JOHN THE DIVINE,
The New Testament

Challenge exercise   Translate the following sentences.

1. Keep your shirt on.
2. Go to the head of the class.
3. He bit off more than he could chew.
4. She had to eat her words.
5. They see eye to eye on that.
6. Keep an eye on her.
7. Don't put all your eggs in one basket.
8. Take that with a grain of salt.
9. His bark is worse than his bite.
10. It's over his head.

You thought you were really beginning to learn English and we threw you a curve ball like this. "To throw a curve ball" is an idiom meaning that someone did something unfair; and indeed we did, because all ten expressions are also idioms. According to the *American Heritage Dictionary of the English Language,* an idiom is defined as "A speech form that is peculiar to itself within the usage of a given language."

The foreign speaker of American English, as the foreign speaker living in any country, needs to seek out the idioms of any land in order to "speak like a native." Idioms abound in any culture and enhance the meanings that lie below the surface, giving a subtlety to expressions, which permits the foreign speaker to gain increased control of the language.

Therefore, in case you didn't understand the idioms in the Challenge Exercise, here are their definitions.

1. Don't be in such a hurry.
2. You gave the correct answer.
3. He took on too many tasks.
4. She had to apologize.
5. They agree.
6. Watch out for her. (Her actions may be positive or destructive).
7. Have more than one option when making a decision.
8. Don't place too much importance on it.
9. He sounds more threatening than he actually is.
10. It's too difficult for him to understand.

How many idioms can you add to this list to help you speak like a native-born American? Several nonnative students of our acquaintance have found listening to TV commercials a very good way to learn American English. Commercials are generally full of idioms, and students can copy down any they don't understand for later explanation by an American friend. Also, commercials use a lot of repetition, and the language is intentionally simple.

The main focus of this chapter is on the speech sounds that present difficulties to specific nationalities and cross-referencing to the exercises elsewhere in the book that will be helpful in learning standard American English pronunciation. However, if you really want to sound more like a native-born American, you must consider more than articulation. As mentioned, idiomatic expressions are one factor, and there are several others that can only be touched on in this basic text. Mention here, though, may at least make you more aware of some of the avenues to pursue, should you be so inclined.

STRESS

Stress is used to describe the relative loudness, duration, and accent used when uttering the vowel or diphthong in a syllable. In American English and also in British English, the characteristic of "unstressing" is heard in the spoken language, which means that certain syllables receive the force, duration, or accent, while other syllables are uttered with less prominence. This vocalization of *stressing* and *unstressing* is apparent in words containing more than one syllable, giving normal value, or primary stress, to the accented syllable and weakening the vowels in the unstressed syllables.

To acquire a believable American accent, it is important to understand that only vowels in the stressed syllable will be pronounced with normal value, while in the unstressed syllables vowels are weakened to a neutral sound like [ə] or [ɪ] regardless of spelling. The unstressed syllables are also reduced in force and time spent pronouncing them. For example, let us use underlining for designating the changes in the primary and secondary stress—two lines for primary stress, one line for secondary stress—in the following words in order to illustrate our point. Notice also the changes in vowel sounds as well as changes in stress from one to more syllables.

One syllable	More than one syllable
up [ʌp]	upon [əpán]
on [ɑn]	undo [əndú]
til [tɪl]	until [əntíl]
be [bi]	beneath [bəníθ]
leave [liv]	believe [bəlív]
pact [pækt]	impact [ímpækt]
sell [sɛl]	seldom [sɛ́ldəm]
base [beɪs]	basis [béɪsɪs]
ten [tɛn]	tender [tɛ́ndɚ]
fan [fæn]	phantom [fǽntəm]

In words of more than two syllables, in English, one syllable receives the primary stress in accent and length and the other syllables receive the weaker stress. Here are some examples:

communicate [kəmjúnɪket]
arithmetic [əríθmətɪk]
scientific [saɪəntífɪk]
literature [lítɚətʃuɚ]
conclusive [kənklúsɪv]
medecine [médəsɪn]
liberty [líbɚti]
immediate [ɪmídiəl]
announcement [ənáʊnsmənt]
television [télətvɪʒən]

Changes in vowel stress also reflect parts of speech. The following sentences show the changes that occur when a word is used as both noun and adjective or verb.

1. His conduct [kándəkt] was very good.
   A guest will conduct [kəndʌ́kt] the orchestra.

2. John won the contest [kántɛst].
   The mayor will not contest [kəntɛ́st] the election returns.

3. The permit [pɝ́mɪt] will permit [pɚmít] us to enter the amusement park for a month.

4. He is making a record [rékɚd] of his singing voice.
   Do not record [rɪkɔ́rd] while there is noise in the studio.

5. They will survey [sɚveí] the property.
   No one will leave while the survey [sɝ́ve] is being made.

6. I do not object [əbdʒɛ́kt] to working if I know my work will be of some use. What object [ábdʒɪkt] is there in studying this?

7. The increase [ínkris] in my salary will be of no use if expenses also increase [ɪnkrís].

8. They will present [prəzɛ́nt] their present [prɛ́zənt] to the teacher at the end of the last class.

9. Mathematics is my best subject [sʌ́bdʒɪkt].
   We subject [səbdʒɛ́kt] our students to a great deal of homework.

10. The manufacturer wishes to perfect [pɚfɛ́kt] the merchandise in order to make his product perfect [pɝ́fəkt].

INTONATION

Intonation refers to the musical notes or pitch changes that are heard when any language is spoken. These intonation patterns and rhythm, meaning the rate and flow, are unique to each communication system. By this we mean that if you could only hear the melody and rhythm of a particular language, without hearing the words, you would probably be able to identify it because of these features. In addition, within the larger, recognizable intonation pattern, alterations in intonation within a phrase can change the meaning of a sentence, at least in English. That is because emphasis, pitch, and rhythm affect meaning. In the simplest instance, a rising inflection at the end of an English sentence implies a question, a falling inflection expresses finality, and a circumflex inflection (rising and falling) suggests uncertainty or sarcasm.

For example, take the following sentence. The arrows indicate a rising or falling inflection.

I really like her.	(I do).
I really like her.	(I'm not sure if I do.)
I really like her.	(Despite what I say, I don't).
That's a nice car.	(It is).
That's a nice car.	(I'm not sure it is.)
That's a nice car.	(You call that heap of junk a car?)

Generally in English, a command ends with a falling inflection, for example:

Leave that alone!

Also, if a question starts with *who, what, where, when, why, how,* or *whom,* the inflection tends to fall downward, for example:

How are you going to do that?

Practice correct intonation by saying these sentences.

(declarative)	I'd like some coffee.
(doubtful)	I did well on my test?
(circumflex)	How much does that cost?
(command)	Hand me my term paper!
(question)	When can I expect my grade?

Good speech is easily understood. A different melody pattern will probably not interfere with communication, and even these rules of intonation vary with circumstances. It is very difficult to explain to the foreign speaker of American English a system of intonation changes without an auditory reference because there are no scientific ways of describing those changes accurately in a text, as we can phonetic changes, using the symbols of the International Phonetic Alphabet (IPA). To become aware of how American English intonation and rhythm differs from your native language, it is best to find a live speech model and copy that model's intonation pattern.

PRONOUNCING THE ENDINGS OF AMERICAN WORDS

Before we analyze the differences in sounds between foreign languages and American English, let us review certain pronunciation rules of English that will be helpful regardless of your native tongue.

Final -ed: [t], [d], or [ɪd]?

1. If the verb to which the -ed is added ends in a *t* or *d*, pronounce the extra syllable:

want + -ed = [wɑntɪd]
hand + -ed = [hændɪd]

Say these words with the extra syllable [ɪd]:

attended	interested
affected	decided
intended	melted
needed	folded
excited	planted

2. If the verb to which the -ed is added ends in an unvoiced sound (a sound like *ssss* that is produced only with air), -ed stays unvoiced as well, becoming [t].

These are the unvoiced sounds that the verb can end in:

[s]: pass + -ed = [pæst]
[k]: pack + -ed = [pækt]
[p]: pipe + -ed = [paɪpt]
[ʃ]: wash + -ed = [wɑʃt]
[tʃ]: watch + -ed = [wɑtʃt]

Say these words with final [t].

crossed	kicked	hopped
placed	backed	ripped
missed	picked	topped
tossed	soaked	roped
kissed	liked	escaped
washed	hatched	
clashed	fetched	
rushed	reached	
pushed	matched	
crashed	latched	

3. All others become [d]:

roar + -ed = [rɔɚd]
bore + -ed = [bɔɚd]
pull + -ed = [pʊld]
clear + -ed = [kliɚd]
view + -ed = [vjud]

Say these with final [d]:

dawdled	crawled	saved
marveled	brawled	braved
handled	sprawled	craved
assembled	furled	loved
revealed	toiled	convened

Final *s:* [s] or [z]?

English spelling is very confusing. When we want to indicate a plural form, we add *s;* we do the same to form the third-person singular of a verb; and we add *'s* to show possession—yet most of the time the *s* that is added is not pronounced as an *s* at all but as a *z!*

As usual, in English, there are exceptions to any rule you learn, but the following guidelines *usually* work since [s] is the phoneme that occurs most frequently in English. If you can get its final pronunciation right, you will be several steps along to sounding more American. There is an additional advantage: The [z] that *s* usually has at the ends of words adds more carrying power to your speech. Here is the general rule:

If the preceding sound is unvoiced (just air), *s* is pronounced as [s]. If the preceding sound is voiced, *s* is pronounced [z].

1. All vowel sounds are voiced. Thus *s* following a vowel sound, as occurs in most simple everyday words, is pronounced [z]:

is	has	his
as	these	easy
was	those	nose
because	blows	choose

2. In English, if the pronunciation at the end of a word is to remain [s], it is usually written with a *ce, ss, us,* or *ous:*

ice	pass	plus
nice	toss	us
niece	glass	thus
piece	press	gracious
fleece	bless	cautious

3. The letter *s* added to three unvoiced endings of root words—*k, p,* and *t*—is pronounced [s]:

kick + s = [kɪks]
hop + s = [hɑps]
hat + s = [hæts]

licks	stops	belts
pecks	ropes	lets
locks	maps	fits
clocks	slaps	hits
blinks	clips	knits

4. If a root word ends in *s, ce, sh, ch,* or *ge,* the *s* ending is pronounced [ɪz]:

pass + (e)s = passes [pæsɪz]
ice + (e)s = ices [aɪsɪz]
push + (e)s = pushes [pʊʃɪz]
catch + (e)s = catches [kætʃɪz]
page + (e)s = pages [peɪdʒɪz]

glasses	vices	rushes	batches	rages
glosses	sacrifices	gushes	matches	gauges
mosses	slices	blushes	watches	mirages
bosses	devices	flushes	clutches	garages
flosses	entices	hushes	lurches	barges

5. In almost every other case, a final *s* is pronounced [z]. This makes up the majority of words to which the suffix *s* is added.

bed + s = [bɛdz]
leg + s = [lɛgz]
bell + s = [bɛlz]
bear + s = [bærz]
roam + s = [roʊmz]
win + s = [wɪnz]
crib + s = [krɪbz]
song + s = [sɔŋz]

heads	pegs	pills	wears	foams	loans	cubs	sings
feeds	begs	wills	cares	domes	teens	clubs	wings
leads	plugs	falls	pears	sums	fans	bulbs	pangs
seeds	tags	mills	tears	teams	tons	globes	hangs
deeds	lags	tells	blares	seams	bins	tubs	clings

IF YOU LEARNED ENGLISH IN AFRICA

If you have come to America from Africa, south of the Sahara, even though you may have spoken English in your home country, you will find that English pronunciation can vary greatly from spoken Standard American. Here are some target sounds for you to be aware of.

Sound	Sample Word	Incorrect	Correct	Exercises (page)
ɪ/i	east	[ɪst]	[ist]	144
i/ɪ	inch	[intʃ]	[ɪntʃ]	147
e/eɪ	face	[fes] (pure vowel)	[feɪs] (diphthong)	151
ɑ/æ	have	[hɑv]	[hæv]	158
ɑ/ɚ	mother	[mʌdɑ]	[mʌðɚ]	184
o/ɑ	bother	[bodɑ]	[bɑðɚ]	162*
ɛ/ɝ	early	[ɛli]	[ɝli] (tongue retracts)	184
d/ð	then	[dɛn]	[ðɛn]	230
t/θ	three	[tri]	[θri]	231
s/z	is	[is]	[ɪz]	237
−t	about	[əbaʊ]	[əbaʊt]	208
−d	joined	[dʒɔɪn]	[dʒɔɪnd]	208

Note: The slash (/) indicates the substitution of the first sound for the second. The minus sign (−) indicates the omission of a sound where it should be pronounced.

IF YOUR FIRST LANGUAGE IS ARABIC

If you have come to America from any of the Arabic speaking countries, here are some target sounds for you to be aware of:

Sound	Sample Word	Incorrect	Correct	Exercises (page)
ɛr/ɝ	turn	[tɛrn]	[tɝn]	184
oʊ/aʊ	town	[toʊn]	[taʊn]	191*
b/p	pray	[breɪ]	[preɪ]	203
z/ð	then	[zɛn]	[ðɛn]	231
f/v	visit	[fɪzɪt]	[vɪzɪt]	224
t/d	lend	[lɛnt]	[lɛnd]	208
−t	sight	[saɪ]	[saɪt]	208

* Here and throughtout * refers you to the correct production of the sound, since no specific exercise is included.

Note: [r] in Arabic is pronounced as a tongue-tip tap or lightly trilled. American palatal *r* is produced with the tongue retracted to approximately the center of the palate. θ and ð may also be substituted for [t] and [d].

IF YOUR FIRST LANGUAGE IS CHINESE

If you have come to America from China, Cambodia, Laos, or Vietnam, here are some target sounds for you to be aware of.

Sound	Sample Word	Incorrect	Correct	Exercises (page)
i/ɪ	fix	[fiks]	[fɪks]	147
ɔ̃/ɔ	Hong Kong	[hɔ̃kɔ̃]	[hɔŋkɔŋ]	297
r=l	lily	[riri]	[lɪli]	277
l=r	rest	[lɛst]	[rɛst]	272
ts/tʃ	China	[tsaɪnə]	[tʃaɪnə]	259
dz/dʒ	enjoy	[ɛndzɔɪ]	[ɛndʒɔɪ]	259
d, z/ð	this	[dis] [zis]	[ðɪs]	230
s/θ	thin	[sin]	[θɪn]	231
s/z	is	[is]	[ɪz]	237

Note: Because in Chinese words end in a vowel sound, and are monosyllabic, the Chinese speaker of English tends to omit final consonants. Be on your guard for this.

Sample Word	Incorrect	Correct
boat	[bo]	[boʊt]
side	[saɪ]	[saɪd]
nights	[naɪ]	[naɪts]
time	[taɪ]	[taɪm]
ten	[tɛ]	[tɛn]

The slash (/) indicates the substitution of the first sound for the second. The tilde (˜) indicates nasality on the vowel instead of pure vowel plus nasal consonant. The equal sign (=) indicates nondifferentiation of two sounds in English that are not distinguished as two sounds in the native language.

IF YOUR FIRST LANGUAGE IS FRENCH

If you have come to America from France or a French-speaking country like Belgium, Switzerland, Algeria, Morocco, Canada, or Haiti, here are some target sounds for you to be aware of.

Sound	Sample Word	Incorrect	Correct	Exercises (page)
ɪ/i	even	[ɪvən]	[ivən]	144
i/ɪ	it	[it]	[ɪt]	147
œ/ɛ	met	[mœt]	[mɛt]	154*
e/eɪ	day	[de] (pure vowel)	[deɪ] (diphthong)	151
o/oʊ	low	[lo] (pure vowel)	[loʊ] (diphthong)	170
ɛ̃/æ	can	[kɛ̃] (*n* omitted)	[kæn] (*n* pronounced)	292
y/u	to	[ty] (lips tightly rounded)	[tu] (lips less rounded)	175*
z/ð	that	[zæt]	[ðæt]	231
s/θ	thin	[sɪn]	[θɪn]	231
ʀ/r	rouge	[ʀuʒ]	[ruʒ]	272
ʃ/tʃ	church	[ʃœʀʃ]	[tʃɝtʃ]	257
ʒ/dʒ	just	[ʒœst]	[dʒʌst]	258
—h	how	[aʊ]	[haʊ]	253

Note:

[p], [t], and [k] are more aspirate in English and have a stronger explosion than in French.

[t], [d], and [n] do not use the dental placement of French (tongue touching inside upper front teeth) but elevate the tongue tip to the gum ridge *above* the inside of the upper teeth.

[h] is sometimes added in front of words beginning with a vowel by some French speakers so that *angry* becomes [hæŋri].

[œ] is the French round-lipped equivalent of [ɛ], for which, in English, the lips must be spread instead of rounded.

[ɛ̃] is the French nasalized equivalent of [æ], for which, in English, emission of air must be restricted to the mouth.

[ʀ] is the French uvular trilled *r* produced in the back of the throat; American palatal *r* is produced with the tongue retracted to approximately the center of the palate. (In some French-speaking countries, *r* is pronounced as a tongue-tip trill.)

[y] is a sound with more lip rounding than is used in English.

The slash (/) indicates the substitution of the first sound for the second. The minus sign (−) indicates the omission of a sound where it should be pronounced.

IF YOUR FIRST LANGUAGE IS GERMAN

If you have come to America from Germany, the German part of Switzerland, or any other German-speaking country, here are some target sounds for you to be aware of.

Sound	Sample Word	Incorrect	Correct	Exercises (page)
e/eɪ	ache	[ek] (pure vowel)	[eɪk] (diphthong)	151
o/oʊ	open	[opən] (pure vowel)	[oʊpən] (diphthong)	170
ɜ/ɝ	world	[vɜlt] (no *r* color)	[wɝld] (*r* color)	184
ə/ɚ	center	[sɛntə] (no *r* color)	[sɛntɚ] (*r* color)	184
ɛ/æ	and	[ɛnt]	[ænd]	158
v/w	west	[vɛst]	[wɛst]	266
f/v	five	[faɪf]	[faɪv]	224
d, z/ð	the	[də] or [zə]	[ðə]	230
t, s/θ	through	[tru] or [sru]	[θru]	231
tʃ/dʒ	stage	[stetʃ]	[steɪdʒ]	257
s/z	is	[ɪs]	[ɪz]	237
z/s	so	[zo]	[soʊ]	236*
t/d	said	[sɛt]	[sɛd]	207*
ʀ, ř/r	try	[tʀaɪ] or [třaɪ]	[třaɪ]	272

The slash (/) indicates substitution of the first sound for the second. [ʀ] is the German uvular trilled *r* produced in the back of the throat and [ř] is a tongue-tip trill; American palatal *r* is produced with the tongue retracted to approximately the center of the palate.

IF YOUR FIRST LANGUAGE IS GREEK

If you have come to America from Greece, here are some target sounds for you to be aware of:

Sound	Sample Word	Incorrect	Correct	Exercises (page)
ɪ/i	Greek	[grɪk]	[grik]	144
i/ɪ	miss	[mis]	[mɪs]	147
ɑ/ʌ	much	[mɑtʃ]	[mʌtʃ]	181
ɛr/ɝ	learn	[lɛrn]	[lɝn]	184
s/z	pains	[peɪns]	[peɪnz]	237

Note: the [h] sound in Greek is a much more constricted sound—a lingua-uvular fricative. In English, the sound of h is a freer, breathier sound originating solely from the glottis in the larynx, without any throat constriction. [r] in Greek is pronounced as a tongue-tip tap or lightly trilled. American palatal *r* is produced with the tongue retracted to approximately the center of the palate.

Also, some speakers may have difficulty with [ŋ, ʃ, ʒ, tʃ, dʒ] and diphthongs.

IF YOU LEARNED ENGLISH IN INDIA

If you have come to America from India or Pakistan, here are some target sounds for you to be aware of:

Sound	Sample Word	Incorrect	Correct	Exercises (page)
i/ɪ	in	[in]	[ɪn]	147
e/eɪ	play	[ple] (pure vowel)	[pleɪ] (diphthong)	151
o/oʊ	own	[on] (pure vowel)	[oʊn] (diphthong)	170
u/ʊ	good	[gud]	[gʊd]	173
ɑ, ʌ/ɝ	earth	[ɑt]	[ɝθ]	184
d/ð	then	[dɛn]	[ðɛn]	230
t/θ	thing	[tiŋ]	[θɪŋ]	231
v/w	way	[ve]	[weɪ]	266
+ᵏ	going	[goɪŋᵏ] ("[ŋ] click")	[goʊɪŋ]	296
ř/r	train	[třen]	[treɪn]	272
d/t	time	[dɑɪm]	[tɑɪm]	211

Note that [k], [p], and [t] in Indian languages are unaspirated and tend to sound like [g], [b], and [d], whereas American [k], [p], and [t] sound more explosive. The overall rate needs to be slower in English, and vowel sounds need to be elongated.

The slash (/) indicates substitution of the first sound for the second. The plus sign (+) indicates the addition of a sound. [ř] is a tongue-tip trilled *r;* the American *r* is a palatal sound produced with the tongue retracted to approximately the center of the palate.

IF YOUR FIRST LANGUAGE IS ITALIAN

If you have come to America from Italy or any other Italian-speaking area, here are some target sounds for you to be aware of.

Sound	Sample Word	Incorrect	Correct	Exercises (page)
i/ɪ	big	[big]	[bɪg]	147
ɪ/i	seat	[sɪt]	[sit]	144
u/ʊ	foot	[fut]	[fʊt]	173
ʊ/u	shoe	[ʃʊ]	[ʃu]	176
ɛř/ɝ	church	[tʃɛřtʃ]	[tʃɝtʃ]	184
ɛř/ɚ	sister	[sistɛř]	[sistɚ]	184

Sound	Sample Word	Incorrect	Correct	Exercises (page)
ɛ/eɪ	take	[tɛk]	[teɪk]	151
o/oʊ	phone	[fon] (pure vowel)	[foʊn] (diphthong)	170
uɑ/w	one	[uɑn]	[wʌn]	264*
op, ɑp/ʌp	up	[op] [ɑp]	[ʌp]	181
d/ð	these	[dɪz]	[ðɪz]	230
t/θ	thing	[tiŋ]	[θɪŋ]	231
z/s	base	[bez]	[beɪs]	236*
řr/r	read	[řɪd]	[rid]	272
−h	who	[ʊ]	[hu]	253

Note: Most Italian words end in a vowel sound, so there is a tendency for the Italian speaker learning English to add the vowel sound [ə] to the ends of words ending in consonants. Do not add vowel sounds after consonant endings.

Note that in English [t], [d], and [n] do not use dental placement of Italian (tongue touching the inside upper front teeth), but are produced by elevating the tongue tip to the gum ridge above the inside upper teeth.

The slash (/) indicates substitution of the first sound for the second. The minus sign (−) indicates the omission of a sound that must be pronounced. [ř] in Italian is a tongue-tip trilled or flapped *r*, whereas the American *r* is a palatal sound produced with the tongue retracted to approximately the center of the palate.

IF YOUR FIRST LANGUAGE IS JAPANESE

If you have come to America from Japan, here are some target sounds for you to be aware of.

Sound	Sample Word	Incorrect	Correct	Exercises (page)
ɑ/æ	man	[mɑn]	[mæn]	158
ɑ/ʌ, ə	cup	[kɑp]	[kʌp]	181
ɑ/ɝ	her	[hɑ]	[hɝ]	184
ɑ/ɚ	banker	[bɑŋkɑ]	[bæŋkɚ]	184
i/ɪ	in	[in]	[ɪn]	147
s/ʃ	she	[si]	[ʃi]	250
ʃ/s	sing	[ʃiŋ]	[sɪŋ]	236*
ts/t	tune	[tsun]	[tun]	207*
b/v	very	[bɛli]	[vɛri]	225

Sound	Sample Word	Incorrect	Correct	Exercises (page)
r=l	lady	[redi]	[leɪdi]	277
l=r	read	[lid]	[rid]	272
z/ð	father	[fɑzɑ]	[fɑðɚ]	231
s/θ	theme	[sim]	[θim]	231

Note: In Japanese, a consonant sound is always followed by a vowel. The Japanese speaker of English thus has a tendency to add an extra vowel sound, usually [u] or [ə], after a word ending in a consonant. Guard against this tendency.

Sample Word	Incorrect	Correct
big	[bigu]	[bɪg]
then	[zɛnə]	[ðɛn]
came	[kemə]	[keɪm]
size	[ʃaɪzu]	[ʃaɪz]
and	[andə]	[ænd]

The slash (/) indicates substitution of the first sound for the second. The equal sign (=) indicates nondifferentiation of two sounds in English that are not distinguished as two separate sounds in the native language.

IF YOUR FIRST LANGUAGE IS POLISH

If you came to America from Poland, here are some target sounds for you to be aware of.

Sound	Sample Word	Incorrect	Correct	Exercises (page)
ɪ/i	people	[pɪpəl]	[pipəl]	144
v/w	with	[vɪt]	[wɪθ]	266
d/ð	that	[dat]	[ðæt]	230
t/θ	thief	[tɪf]	[θif]	231
t/d	Poland	[polɛnt]	[poulənd]	207*
řr/r	crease	[křis]	[kris]	272
ɛř/ɝ	first	[fɛřst]	[fɝst]	184
ɛř/ɚ	spender	[spɛndɛř]	[spɛndɚ]	184
+ᵏ	wedding	[vɛdɪŋᵏ] ("[ng] click")	[wɛdɪŋ]	296

The slash (/) indicates the substitution of the first sound for the second. The plus sign (+) indicates the addition of a sound. [r] in Polish is either a tongue-tip trill or a flapped *r*, whereas American *r* is a palatal sound produced with the tongue retracted to approximately the center of the palate.

IF YOUR FIRST LANGUAGE IS RUSSIAN

If you have come to America from the Soviet Union, here are some target sounds for you to be aware of.

Sound	Sample Word	Incorrect	Correct	Exercises (page)
i/ɪ	ship	[ʃip]	[ʃɪp]	147
ɪ/i	sheep	[ʃɪp]	[ʃip]	144
ɔ/o	toast	[tɔst]	[toust]	168*
ɑ, ɔ/ʌ, ə	butter	[batɛř]	[bʌtɚ]	181
ɔř/ɝ	work	[vɔřk]	[wɝk]	184
ɛř/ɚ	mother	[madɛř]	[mʌðɚ]	184
ř/r	rent	[řɛnt]	[rɛnt]	272
z, d/ð	this	[zɪs] [dɪs]	[ðɪs]	230
s, t/θ	thought	[sɔt] [tɔt]	[θɔt]	231
v/w	wife	[vaɪf]	[waɪf]	266
ɫ/v	alive	[alaɪf]	[əlaɪv]	224
nj/n	money	[mɔnjɪ]	[mʌni]	290*
x/h	how	[xaʊ]	[haʊ]	252*
+ᵏ	singing	[sɪŋgiŋᵏ] ("[ng] click")	[sɪŋɪŋ]	296

Note: Many consonants in Russian are palatalized and need to be placed more forward for English pronunciation.

[t], [d], and [n] do not use the dental placement of Russian (tongue touching the inside upper front teeth) but are produced in English by elevating the tongue tip to the gum ridge above the inside upper teeth.

[b], [d], [g], [dʒ], and [ʒ] tend to become unvoiced and sound like [p], [t], [k], [tʃ], and [ʃ], so be aware of adding voice to these sounds, especially at the ends of words.

The slash (/) indicates the substitution of the first sound for the second. The plus sign (+) indicates the addition of a sound. [ř] in Russian is either a tongue-tip trill or palatalization at the end of a syllable, whereas American *r* is a palatal sound produced with the tongue retracted to approximately the center of the palate. [x] is a voiceless guttural sound that does not occur in English.

IF YOUR FIRST LANGUAGE IS SPANISH

If you have come to America from Spain, South or Central America, Mexico, Cuba, Puerto Rico, or any other Spanish-speaking area, here are some target sounds for you to be aware of.

Sound	Sample Word	Incorrect	Correct	Exercises (page)
i/ɪ	if	[if]	[ɪf]	147
ɪ/i	sleep	[slɪp]	[slip]	144
e/eɪ	say	[se] (pure vowel)	[seɪ] (diphthong)	151
o/oʊ	go	[go] (pure vowel)	[goʊ] (diphthong)	170
o, ɑ/ʌ, ə	love	[lov]	[lʌv]	181
ɛř/ɝ	earth	[ɛřt]	[ɝθ]	184
ɛř/ɚ	flavor	[flevɛř]	[fleɪvɚ]	184
+ɛ	street	[ɛstrɪt]	[strit]	236*
d/ð	they	[de]	[ðeɪ]	230
t/θ	thick	[tik]	[θɪk]	231
b/v	very	[beři]	[vɛri]	225
ř/r	read	[řɪd]	[rid]	272
dʒ/j**	you	[dʒu]	[ju]	282
tʃ/ʃ**	shoe	[tʃu]	[ʃu]	248*
ʃ/tʃ**	chip	[ʃɪp]	[tʃɪp]	257
s/z	always	[ɔlwes]	[ɔlweɪz]	237
ŋ/n	ten	[tɛŋ]	[tɛn]	290*

Note: [p], [t], and [k] are aspirated in English, which makes them sound more explosive than in Spanish, where these sounds are unaspirated, tending to sound more like English [b], [d], and [g], respectively. Note also that [t], [d], and [n] do not use the dental placement of Spanish (tongue touching the inside upper front teeth) but are produced in English by elevating the tongue tip to the gum ridge above the inside upper teeth.

The slash (/) indicates substitution of the first sound for the second. The plus sign (+) indicates the addition of a sound. [ř] is the tongue-tip trilled *r* of Spanish, whereas American *r* is a palatal *r* produced with the tongue retracted.

** Typical of speakers of certain dialects only.

PHONETIC PRACTICE

ADAGES TO DECIPHER

1. [ə stɪtʃ ɪn taɪm seɪvz naɪn]
2. [pipl̩ hu lɪv ɪn glæs haʊzɪz ʃʊdn̩t θroʊ stoʊnz]
3. [pɛni waɪz ænd paʊnd fulɪʃ]
4. [ə bɝd ɪn ðə hænd ɪz wɝθ tu ɪn ðə bʊʃ]
5. [ə wɝd tu ðə waɪz ɪz səfɪʃənt]
6. [laɪtnɪŋ nɛvɚ straɪks twaɪs]
7. [doʊnt baɪ ə pɪg ɪn ə poʊk]
8. [bɝdz əv ə fɛðɚ flɑk tugɛðɚ]
9. [nɛvɚ lʊk ə gɪft hɔɚs ɪn ðə maʊθ]
10. [bɪwɛɚ əv griks bærɪŋ gɪfts]
11. [ju kænt meɪk ə sɪlk pɝs aʊt əv ə saʊz iɚ]
12. [doʊnt meɪk ə maʊntɪn aʊt əv ə moʊlhɪl]
13. [doʊnt bit ə dɛd hɔɚs]
14. [an apəl ə deɪ kips ðə dɑktɚ əweɪ]
15. [ə pɛni seɪvd ɪz ə pɛni ɝnd]
16. [ɔl ðat glɪtɚz ɪz nɑt goʊld]
17. [nɛvɚ seɪ nɛvɚ]
18. [stɪl wɔtɚz rʌn dip]
19. [ə ful and hɪz mʌni aɚ sun paɚtɪd]
20. [doʊnt kaʊnt juɚ tʃɪkənz bɪfɔɚ ðeɪ hætʃ]
21. [doʊnt pʊt ɔl juɚ ɛgz ɪn wʌn bæskɪt]
22. [ɛvri klaʊd hæz ə sɪlvɚ laɪnɪŋ]
23. [hwɛɚ ðɛɚz ə wɪl ðɛɚz ə weɪ]
24. [tʃærɪti bɪgɪnz at hoʊm]
25. [du əntu ʌðɚz az ju wʊd hæv ʌðɚz du əntu ju]
26. [ðə tʌŋ ɔlwez siks ði eɪkɪŋ tuθ]
27. [ɪntu ɛvri laɪf ə lɪtl̩ reɪn mʌst fɔl]
28. [ə roʊlɪŋ stoʊn gæðɚz noʊ mɔs]
29. [hoʊm ɪz hwɛɚ ðə hɑrt ɪz]
30. [ði æpl̩ nɛvɚ fɔlz far frʌm ðə tri]

CLICHÉS TO DECIPHER

1. [ə tʃɪp ɔf ðɪ oʊld blɑk]
2. [wæɚ jʊɚ hɑrt ɑn jʊɚ sliv]
3. [hæv ə naɪs deɪ]
4. [lʊk laɪk ə mɪljən dɑlɚz]
5. [kjut az ə bʌtn̩]
6. [fɔl hɛd oʊvɚ hilz ɪn lʌv]
7. [daɪ læfɪŋ]
8. [smɑrt az ə hwɪp]
9. [slaɪ az ə fɑks]
10. [bɪzi az ə bi]
11. [fæt az ə pɪg]
12. [sloʊ az məlæsɪz]
13. [θɪk az θivz]
14. [flæt az ə pænkeɪk]
15. [θɪn az ə reɪl]
16. [mæd az ə hætɚ]
17. [hwaɪt az ə ʃit]
18. [prɪti az ə pɪktʃɚ]
19. [sɔft az ə beɪbiz bɑtəm]
20. [fɔl laɪk ə tʌn əv brɪks]
21. [az ʃɑrp az ə tæk]
22. [az blæk az mɪdnaɪt]
23. [fist ɔɚ fæmɪn]
24. [slip laɪk ə lɑg]
25. [ə skwæɚ pɛg ɪn ə raʊnd hoʊl]
26. [kreɪzi az ə lun]
27. [pɝlz bɪfɔr swaɪn]
28. [slɪpɚi az ən il]
29. [ə hɔɚs əv ə dɪfrənt kʌlɚ]
30. [bjuti ɪz oʊnli skɪn dip]

SCRAMBLED TITLES

The words in each title are out of order. How many can you figure out?

Books and plays

1. [əv ræθ greɪps ðə]
2. [tu əv sɪtiz ə teɪl]
3. [mɛn əv ænd maɪs]
4. [wʊlf əv huz vɚdʒɪnjə əfreɪd]
5. [baʊnti ɑn mjutɪni ðə]
6. [wɪzɚd ðə əv az]
7. [raɪ ðə ðə ɪn kætʃ]
8. [wɛl wɛl ɔlz ɛndz ðæt]

9. [deɪz læst ðə pɑmpeɪ əv]
10. [sizɚ dʒuliəs]
11. [gætsbi greɪt ðə]
12. [pʌnɪʃmənt kraɪm ænd]
13. [wʌndɚlænd ɪn ælɪsɪz ədvɛntʃɚz]
14. [wɪmɪn lɪtl̩]
15. [pis wɔɚ ænd]
16. [lʌvɚ tʃætɚliz leɪdi]
17. [haɪts wʌðɚɪŋ]
18. [houmz əv ədvɛntʃɚz ðə ʃɝlɑk]
19. [wɛdɪŋ ə əv mɛmbɚ ðə]
20. [froum iθən]
21. [prɛdʒədɪs praɪd ænd]
22. [twɪst ɑlɪvɚ]
23. [pɔpɚ prɪns ðə ðə ænd]
24. [ɔlso raɪzɪz sʌn ðə]
25. [dɪk moubi]

Songs and rhymes

1. [ouvɚ reɪnbo ðə]
2. [maɪs blaɪnd θri]
3. [stɑr ju hwɛn əpɑn wɪʃ ə]
4. [bjutɪfəl əmɛrɪkə ðə]
5. [əweɪ æŋkɚz]
6. [mjuzɪk ðə əv saʊnd]
7. [rudɑlf rɛd nouzd ðə reɪndɪɚ]
8. [lɪtl̩ hæd mɛri ə læm]
9. [dudl̩ dændi jæŋki]
10. [spæŋgl̩d stɑr bænɚ ðə]
11. [klaʊnz ðə ɪn sɛnd]
12. [wɝld ðə ɪn əraʊnd deɪz eɪti]
13. [hwaɪt krɪsməs]
14. [rouzɪz ʌp kʌmɪŋ ɛvriθɪŋz]
15. [wizl̩ gouz ðə pɑp]

GLOSSARY

abdominal breathing   see *diaphragmatic breathing*

abduction   the opening or pulling away of the vocal folds to enable breathing

adduction   the coming together of the vocal folds in order to produce phonation

affricates   consonant sounds created by the stopping of the breath stream and its subsequent release as a fricative, recognized as one phoneme [tʃ, dʒ]

alveolar   produced with the tip of the tongue against the alveolar ridge, as [t, d, s, z, l, n]

alveolar ridge   the bumpy gum ridge above the teeth at the beginning of the hard palate

amplitude of sound   volume or loudness

articulation   the shaping of sound into speech, primarily within the oral cavity

arytenoid cartilages   pyramid-shaped small cartilages attaching to the inner muscles of the larynx at the back

assimilation nasality   a whiny voice quality on vowel sounds preceding or following [m], [n], or [ŋ]

back vowels   vowels articulated with the tongue positioned in the back of the mouth: [u, ʊ, o, ɔ, ɑ]

bilabial   articulated with both lips, as [p, b, m, hw, w]

breath support   control of the exhaled air used for speech

breathy   describing a voice quality resulting from too little tension of the vocal folds, allowing an excess of air to escape

central breathing   see *diaphragmatic breathing*

central vowels   vowels articulated with the tongue positioned in the center of the mouth: [ɝ, ɚ, ʌ, ə]

cerebellum   the small part of the brain that coordinates movement and balance

choppy   characterized by inappropriate pauses in an individual's speaking rate

cilia   hairlike nerve endings of the auditory nerve

clavicles   the collarbones

clavicular breathing   breathing with the upper chest in order to elongate the chest cavity for increased air supply

cochlea   the inner ear

cognates   two phonemes produced in the same manner, with the same placement of the articulators, differentiated by the fact that voice is added to one but not the other

consonants   stopped or hindered sounds

cricoid cartilage   the signet ring–shaped cartilage that forms the structural base in the larynx

cricothyroid muscles   muscles of the vocal folds, capable of being tensed or loosened in order to alter pitch

denasality   a quality fault caused by too little air directed through the nose on [m], [n], and [ŋ]

diaphragm   the large tent-shaped muscle that separates the chest cavity from the abdominal cavity

diaphragmatic breathing   controlled action of the abdominal muscles in breathing used for speech; also called *abdominal, central,* or *medial breathing*

diphthong   a pair of vowels that begin with the resonating characteristics of the first vowel sound and glide toward the resonating characteristics of the second vowel sound

duration   rate of utterances

fading   having too little air to sustain a strong tone through a phrase or sentence

frequency   rate of vibrations of sound, which determines perceived speech

fricatives   consonant sounds produced by narrowing the outgoing breath stream: [f, v, θ, ð, s, z, ʃ, ʒ, h]

front vowels   vowels articulated with the tongue positioned in the front of the mouth: [i, ɪ, e, ɛ, æ]

fundamental frequency   basic vibration occurring when sound is generated

glides   consonant sounds produced while the articulators are in motion, gliding toward the vowel sound that follows: [hw, w, r, j]

glottal attack   a blowing apart with a clicking sound of the vocal folds at the onset of phonation, noticeable on words beginning with a vowel

glottal fry   an unpleasant quality sounding like popping or frying of the voice

glottal stop   an abrupt break in phonation, symbolized [ʔ], usually in place of the [t] sound

glottis   the space between the vocal folds

gluteal muscles   fleshy muscles at the back of the hips

hard palate   the roof of the mouth

harsh   descriptive of a strained voice quality caused by too much muscle constriction in the throat and neck

hoarse   descriptive of a raspy, strained voice quality caused by inflammation or improper vocal habits

husky   descriptive of a breathy, strained voice quality similar to hoarseness but less harsh

incus   one of the small bones in the middle ear

inflection   the melody pattern of the voice used to underline and shade meanings

intercostal muscles   muscles attached to the ribs

labiodental   produced with the lips and teeth, as [f, v]

larynx   the organ at the top of the windpipe (trachea) where the vocal folds are housed and sound is produced

lateral consonant   the consonant *l*, produced by the outgoing breath stream being emitted at the sides of the tongue

lateral cricoarytenoid muscles   muscles in the larynx that adduct the vocal folds

levatores costarum   muscles that help move the ribs outward and upward

linguadental   produced with the tongue between the teeth, as [θ, ð]

malleus   one of the small bones in the middle ear

mandible   the lower jaw

medial breathing   see *diaphragmatic breathing*

medulla   a small inner brain that monitors the vital processes

modal pitch   the pitch range a person uses most often

nasal cavity   the interior of the nose

nasality   a whining voice quality caused by air escaping into the nose on sounds other than [m], [n], and [ŋ]

nasals   consonant sounds produced by the outgoing breath stream exiting the nose: [m, n, ŋ]

nonphonemic diphthongs   diphthongs from which the second vowel can be removed without altering the meaning

optimum pitch   the pitch level of maximum efficiency for speech

oral cavity   the mouth

oval window   membrane that separates the middle ear from the inner ear

overtones   covibrations set up along with a fundamental frequency producing a complex tone of frequencies; also called *partials*

palatal   produced with the tongue at or near the hard palate, as [ʃ, ʒ, tʃ, dʒ, r, j]

partials   see *overtones*

pharynx   the throat cavity between the esophagus and the nasal cavity

phonation   the creation of sound as the vocal folds are drawn together

phoneme   the most basic unit of recognizable speech sound in a language system

phonemic nasality   a whiny quality that results from letting air escape through the nose on certain vowel sounds

pitch   sound resulting from the frequency of vibration of a vibrating body, resulting in perceived changes

plosives   consonant sounds produced by stopping and then releasing the breath stream: [p, b, t, d, k, g]

pons   small inner brain that monitors the vital processes

posterior cricoarytenoid muscles   muscles in the larynx that abduct the vocal folds

quality   tone or timbre of a sound; the selective amplification of overtones by a resonator

resonance   the power of selective reinforcement, giving another sonorous body (resonator) the ability to amplify sound and alter quality

respiration   the air supply needed to breathe and provide power for speech

scalenes   muscles that help lift the upper ribs and the whole rib cage

soft palate   see *velum*

sound waves   alterations in air pressure moving in all directions from the vibrating source

stapes   one of the small bones in the middle ear

strident   descriptive of a piercing, harsh voice quality

thin   descriptive of a voice quality characterized by a high-pitched, childlike sound

thorax   the chest, containing the ribs, lungs, and muscles

throaty   descriptive of a cavernous, hollow, voice quality

thyroarytenoid muscles   muscles in the vocal folds themselves

thyroid cartilage   the large shield-shaped cartilage of the larynx

trachea   the main air tube, a series of cartilaginous rings above the lungs, commonly called the windpipe

velum   a movable fold of strong muscle at the rear of the hard palate; also called *soft palate*

vocal folds   two folds of elastic connective tissue capable of being set into vibration, thereby creating sound; also called *vocal bands* or *vocal cords*

volume   loudness or softness of sound, depending on the amplitude of the sound waves

vowels   shaped sounds that are the product of resonance

BIBLIOGRAPHY

Anderson, Virgil, *Training the Speaking Voice* (New York: Oxford University Press, 1942).

Asimov, Isaac, *The Human Brain* (Boston: Houghton Mifflin, 1963).

Avery, Elizabeth, Jane Dorsey, and Vera Sickels, *First Principles of Speech Training* (Englewood Cliffs, N.J.: Prentice-Hall, 1928).

Bartlett, John, *Bartlett's Familiar Quotations,* 14th ed. (Boston: Little Brown & Co., 1968).

Bianchi, Doris, Balin, Wayne Bond, Gerald Kandel, and Ann Seidler, *Easily Understood* (Wayne, N.J.: Avery Publishing, 1981).

Bloodstein, Oliver, *Speech Pathology:* An Introduction (Boston: Houghton Mifflin, 1979).

Blunt, Jerry, *Stage Dialects* (New York: Harper & Row, 1967, 1980).

Borden, Gloria J., and Katherine Harris, *Speech Science Primer* (Baltimore: Williams & Wilkins, 1980).

Bronstein, Arthur, *The Pronunciation of American English* (Englewood Cliffs, N.J.: Prentice-Hall, 1960).

Burke, Kenneth, *Language as Symbolic Action: Essays on Life, Literature, and Method* (Berkeley: University of California Press, 1966).

Chreist, Fred M., *Foreign Accent* (Englewood Cliffs, N.J.: Prentice-Hall, 1964).

Colson, Greta, *Speech Practice* (London: Museum Press, 1967).

Eisenson, Jon, *Voice and Diction,* 5th ed. (New York: Macmillan, 1985).

Espy, Willard, *Words at Play* (New York: Clarkson N. Potter, 1975).

Fisher, Hilda, *Improving Voice and Articulation* (Boston: Houghton Mifflin, 1975).

Floyd, James, *Listening: A Practical Approach* (Glen View, Il.: Scott Foresman, 1982).

Hibbert, George, and Richard A. Norman, *Guide to Speech Training* (New York: Roland Press, 1964).

Kantner, Claude E., and Robert West, *Phonetics* (New York: Harper & Row, 1960).

Kenyon, John Samuel, *American Pronunciation* (Ann Arbor, Mich.: George Wahr Publishing, 1982).

King, Robert G., and Eleanor Di Michael, *Articulation and Voice: Improving Oral Communication* (New York: Macmillan, 1978).

Lado, Robert, and Charles C. Fries, *English Pronunciation: Exercises in Sound Segments, Intonation, and Rhythm* (Ann Arbor: University of Michigan Press, 1954.)

Langaker, Ronald, *Fundamentals of Linguistic Analysis* (Orlando, Fla.: Harcourt Brace Jovanovich, 1972).

Lowry, Sara, and Gertrude Johnson, *Interpretative Reading* (Englewood Cliffs, N.J.: Prentice-Hall, 1942).

Mayer, Lyle V., *Voice and Diction,* 7th ed. (Dubuque, Iowa: Brown, 1985).

Modisett, Noah F., and James G. Luter, Jr., *Speaking Clearly* (Minneapolis: Burgess, 1979).

Newcombe, P. Judson, *Voice and Diction* (Raleigh, N.C.: Contemporary Publishing Co., 1986).

Prochnow, Herbert V., and Herbert V. Prochnow, Jr., *The Public Speaker's Treasure Chest* (New York: Harper & Row, 1942).

Sampson, Geoffrey, *Making Sense* (New York: Oxford University Press, 1980).

Sapir, Edward, *Language* (Orlando, Fla.: Harcourt Brace Jovanovich, 1921).

Sarnoff, Dorothy, *Speech Can Change Your Life* (New York: Dell, 1970).

Sarnoff, Dorothy, *Make the Most of Your Best* (New York: Holt Rinehart Winston, 1970).

Smith, Frank, and George A. Miller, *The Genesis of Language: A Psychoanalytic Approach* (Cambridge, Mass.: M.I.T. Press, 1966).

Trager, George L., *Language and Languages* (New York: Intext, 1972).

Van Riper, Charles, *Speech Correction,* 5th ed. (Englewood Cliffs, N.J.: Prentice-Hall, 1972).

Van Riper, Charles, and Dorothy Smith, *An Introduction to General American Phonetics,* 3d ed. (New York: Harper & Row, 1979).

Voice Print Identification Manual (Sommerville, N.J.: Voice Identification, Inc., 1969).

Weiss, Curtis, Harold Lillywhite, and Mary E. Gordon, *Clinical Management of Articulation Disorders* (St. Louis: Mosby, 1980).

Wise, Claude Merton, *Applied Phonetics* (Englewood Cliffs, N.J.: Prentice-Hall, 1957).

INDEX